Risk, Resilience, and Cybersecurity in Complex Systems and Public Sectors

Darrell Norman Burrell
https://orcid.org/0000-0002-4675-9544
Marymount University, USA

IGI Global
Scientific Publishing
Publishing Tomorrow's Research Today

Vice President of Editorial Melissa Wagner
Director of Acquisitions Mikaela Felty
Director of Book Development Jocelynn Hessler
Production Manager Mike Brehm
Cover Design Jose Rosado

Published in the United States of America by
IGI Global Scientific Publishing
701 East Chocolate Avenue
Hershey, PA, 17033, USA
Tel: 717-533-8845 | Fax: 717-533-7115
Website: https://www.igi-global.com E-mail: cust@igi-global.com

Library of Congress Cataloging-in-Publication Data

LCCN: 2026017853 (CIP Data Pending)
ISBN13: 9798260010211
Isbn13Softcover: 9798260010228
EISBN13: 9798260010235
British Cataloguing in Publication Data
A Cataloguing in Publication record for this book is available from the British Library.

Table of Contents

Detailed Table of Contents

This study examines the pivotal, yet frequently overlooked, concept of risk velocity, the speed at which risk repercussions unfold after an initial trigger. It highlights how existing risk management, focused mainly on probability and impact, is inadequate for handling rapidly escalating events, as seen in crises like the COVID-19 pandemic, the CrowdStrike–Microsoft outage, the Change Healthcare ransomware attack, and the Aflac data breach. These incidents reveal how swift-moving threats can outpace traditional response mechanisms, causing severe operational and reputational harm. In today's fast-evolving threat landscape, technologies such as AI, AGI, ML, deep learning, and autonomous response act as risk multipliers and critical mitigation tools. AI-driven threats accelerate incident velocity but, conversely, enable faster detection and automated response. Building on models like Time-to-Impact Analysis and Agility and Resilience Theory, this chapter advocates for incorporating risk velocity alongside probability and impact, with velocity-aware matrices and AI-enhanced simulations.

This paper examines how information systems improvements could have mitigated operational disruptions in the aviation industry during the 2025 U.S. government shutdown. Using a socio-technical systems (STS) framework, it analyzes the synergy between technology, governance, and human factors within the U.S. aviation industry. Findings indicate that aviation resilience depends on integrating cloud-based infrastructure, AI-assisted decision systems, robust cybersecurity frameworks, and human factors in the entire lifecycle of technical design decisions. The study proposes a four-layer mitigation strategy encompassing infrastructure resilience, digital coordination, cybersecurity hardening, and human factors integration. Results highlight that organizational agility is achieved through aligning technical innovation with institutional adaptability, ensuring continuity during fiscal or staffing crises. The paper concludes with actionable recommendations for technologists and

on technical controls rather than human behavior. This case study examines insider threats through the integrated lenses of criminal psychology and organizational psychology, emphasizing how organizational culture, employee motivation, moral disengagement, and perceived injustice contribute to counterproductive work behaviors. Using a management consulting intervention framework, the study synthesizes interdisciplinary literature to identify behavioral, cultural, and technological drivers of insider misconduct, including malicious, negligent, and opportunistic actions. The analysis highlights the limitations of conventional detection mechanisms and underscores the necessity of psychologically informed strategies that integrate AI-driven behavioral analytics, ethical leadership, training, and cultural transformation.

This study analyzes software supply chain attacks in financial cybersecurity using a qualitative literature review and case studies. It integrates cybersecurity, supply chain, and financial risk concepts to address sector-specific gaps in taxonomy and mitigation. Findings show attackers exploit trust in software distribution: 61% of malicious packages use typosquatting and 56% activate at install time, with average dwell times of 209 days and 49% employing obfuscation (Ohm et al., 2020). Interconnected financial and cyber-physical systems heighten systemic risk (Yeboah-Ofori & Islam, 2019). While neural networks outperform alternative classifiers, detection still struggles with obfuscation and conditional execution (Li, 2024). The study concludes that perimeter-centric defenses are insufficient and calls for integrated controls—vendor assurance, provenance verification, advanced detection, and incident response, aligned with regulatory requirements (Alshammari & Singh, 2025).

industry standards like NIST, HIPAA, GDPR, CISA, ISO/IEC 27001, peer-reviewed journals and articles, authors from medical journals and related sources. The research used qualitative evidence synthesis, that is, findings from other credible researchers. Robust cybersecurity and cooperation between healthcare, tech, and regulators are vital to secure medical devices, protect patients and ensure reliable care.

The partnerships between companies bring operational improvements and innovation but they create major cybersecurity threats. With the advent of technologies like Internet-of-Things (IoT) and Internet of Medical Things (IoMT), healthcare organizations need third-party vendors to access essential services which include cloud storage, electronic health records and embedded devices. Organizations move their operations to outside vendors lose their ability to control vendor security which makes them vulnerable to supply chain attacks and regulatory violations The combination of complex vendor networks with insufficient subcontractor operation monitoring creates security risks which threaten patient data privacy while causing financial damage and damaging organizational reputation. The evaluation examines Risk Management Theory which evaluates common attack vectors; Change Management Theory which examines regulatory challenges, and Risk Resilience Theory which examines ways to limit the attack surface on healthcare IT infrastructure.

This article examines cybersecurity breaches in healthcare through an organizational psychology and leadership performance lens, arguing that human factors and cultural dynamics are central drivers of cyber risk. Using an action research–based management consulting framework, the study integrates incident analysis, policy and training reviews, and interviews with cybersecurity professionals and healthcare employees to diagnose misalignment between technology, workflows, and leadership behavior. The research applies organizational culture, human factors, and change management theories to identify how cognitive load, normalization of deviance, psychological safety, and leadership signaling shape cybersecurity outcomes. A set of leadership performance indicators is proposed to operationalize accountability for human-error risk reduction, learning, and resilience. Findings demonstrate that cybersecurity effectiveness improves when leadership designs error-tolerant systems, embeds security into clinical workflows, and institutionalizes effective organizational culture practices.

Human trafficking remains a data-deficient and rapidly evolving global crisis. While technology such as AI and geospatial analytics hold promise for detection and prevention, anti-trafficking efforts are limited by fragmented data, inconsistent reporting, and weak collaboration. This chapter introduces the Platform of Freedom, a conceptual framework that integrates data and technology, collaboration, and policy to cultivate organizational and national agility in the anti-trafficking context. Grounded in Socio-Technical Systems Theory, Actor-Network Theory, and Critical Data Studies, the model reframes anti-trafficking work as a socio-technical challenge requiring ethical governance, interoperability, and adaptive data ecosystems. It argues that technology alone cannot disrupt trafficking without coordinated networks that enable secure information exchange. The Platform of Freedom offers a guide for transforming fragmented systems into cohesive, ethically governed infrastructures that strengthen prevention, protection, and policy innovation in the fight against human trafficking.

This study found that applying technological innovation can influence the behavior of construction professionals and enhance organizational safety. The Bureau of Labor Statistics (BLS) report on construction safety issues revealed that falls, slips, and trips caused 35.3 percent of construction and extraction worker deaths in 2020 (BLS, 2020). This study argues that the construction industry can enhance safety by aligning its practices with the concerns of employees and supervisors. This

Preface

The accelerating complexity of modern systems, spanning public institutions, critical infrastructure, financial networks, and healthcare ecosystems, has fundamentally reshaped how we must understand and manage risk. No longer confined to static probabilities and predictable impacts, today's threat landscape is dynamic, interconnected, and often amplified by digital technologies. In this environment, resilience is not merely a defensive posture; it is an organizational capability rooted in foresight, adaptability, and the integration of human, technological, and institutional intelligence.

Risk, Resilience, and Cybersecurity in Complex Systems and Public Sectors brings together a diverse and interdisciplinary set of perspectives that collectively address one of the most urgent challenges of our time: how to design, govern, and sustain systems that can withstand, and evolve through, disruption. The chapters in this volume move beyond conventional cybersecurity discourse to examine the behavioral, organizational, and socio-technical dimensions of risk. They emphasize that resilience is not achieved through technology alone, but through the alignment of culture, leadership, policy, and innovation.

CHAPTER OVERVIEW

This volume begins by redefining how we conceptualize risk itself. Chapter 1 introduces the critical concept of risk velocity, arguing that the speed at which risks materialize is as important as their likelihood and impact. Through contemporary case examples and theoretical models, the chapter demonstrates how rapidly evolving threats, often accelerated by artificial intelligence, demand new analytical tools, including velocity-aware risk matrices and AI-enhanced simulations.

Building on this foundation, Chapter 2 explores resilience in the context of national infrastructure, using the 2025 U.S. government shutdown as a case study in aviation systems. The authors present a socio-technical framework that highlights the interplay between digital infrastructure, governance, cybersecurity, and human factors, offering a layered strategy for maintaining operational continuity during systemic disruptions.

Chapter 3 shifts attention to the public sector more broadly, examining the barriers to digital transformation in government agencies. It reveals how entrenched bureaucracy, fragmented systems, and security vulnerabilities impede modernization efforts, while offering structured pathways, grounded in change management and digital maturity models, for achieving secure, citizen-centered reform.

The human dimension of cybersecurity risk is brought sharply into focus in Chapter 4, which investigates insider threats through the lenses of organizational and criminal psychology. The chapter underscores how cultural dynamics, perceived injustice, and behavioral factors contribute to cybersecurity vulnerabilities, advocating for psychologically informed strategies that complement technical controls.

Expanding the discussion to financial systems, Chapter 5 analyzes the growing threat of software supply chain attacks. It demonstrates how attackers exploit trust within digital ecosystems and calls for a shift from perimeter-based defenses to integrated approaches that include vendor assurance, provenance verification, and advanced detection mechanisms.

Chapter 6 continues this focus on human-centered risk within the banking sector, presenting a case study that reveals how employee behavior and organizational culture can serve as primary drivers of cybersecurity incidents. The chapter emphasizes the importance of cultivating a culture of accountability and awareness, supported by behavioral analytics and strategic interventions.

Healthcare systems, as highly complex and high-stakes environments, are the focus of several chapters in this volume. Chapter 7 examines vulnerabilities in connected medical devices, highlighting how weaknesses in authentication, encryption, and patch management can compromise patient safety. The authors call for stronger collaboration among healthcare providers, technologists, and regulators to secure these critical systems.

Complementing this analysis, Chapter 8 addresses the risks associated with third-party vendors in healthcare cybersecurity. As organizations increasingly rely on external partners, the chapter illustrates how supply chain dependencies introduce new vulnerabilities, necessitating robust governance, monitoring, and risk mitigation strategies.

In Chapter 9, the focus returns to organizational psychology, exploring how leadership behavior, cultural norms, and cognitive dynamics influence cybersecurity outcomes in healthcare settings. The chapter proposes performance indicators that link leadership accountability to resilience, emphasizing the importance of embedding security into everyday workflows and organizational practices.

Broadening the scope to global humanitarian challenges, Chapter 10 introduces the Platform of Freedom, a conceptual framework for combating human trafficking through data agility and technological collaboration. The chapter highlights the limitations of fragmented data systems and argues for integrated, ethically governed infrastructures that enable coordinated action across sectors and borders.

Workplace safety and technological innovation intersect in Chapter 11, which examines how artificial intelligence, virtual reality, and augmented reality can transform safety practices in the construction industry. By aligning technological tools with human behavior and organizational priorities, the chapter demonstrates how preventable injuries can be significantly reduced.

Finally, Chapter 12 addresses one of the most persistent public health challenges: alcohol-impaired driving. The authors explore how AI-enabled systems, ranging from predictive analytics to real-time monitoring, can enhance prevention and enforcement efforts while maintaining ethical safeguards related to privacy, equity, and accountability.

Taken together, these chapters offer a comprehensive and forward-looking exploration of risk and resilience in complex systems. They challenge us to rethink traditional assumptions, to embrace interdisciplinary approaches, and to recognize that the future of cybersecurity lies not only in technological advancement, but in the thoughtful integration of human insight, organizational design, and ethical governance.

It is our hope that this volume will serve as both a scholarly resource and a practical guide for researchers, practitioners, policymakers, and leaders navigating the evolving landscape of risk and resilience. In an era defined by uncertainty and rapid change, the ability to anticipate, adapt, and respond is not optional, it is essential.

Darrell Burrell
Marymount University, USA

Chapter 1
Risk Velocity:
The Third Dimension of Assessing Risk

Laura Ann Jones
http://orcid.org/0000-0002-0299-370X
Capitol Technology University, USA

ABSTRACT

This study examines the pivotal, yet frequently overlooked, concept of risk velocity, the speed at which risk repercussions unfold after an initial trigger. It highlights how existing risk management, focused mainly on probability and impact, is inadequate for handling rapidly escalating events, as seen in crises like the COVID-19 pandemic, the CrowdStrike–Microsoft outage, the Change Healthcare ransomware attack, and the Aflac data breach. These incidents reveal how swift-moving threats can outpace traditional response mechanisms, causing severe operational and reputational harm. In today's fast-evolving threat landscape, technologies such as AI, AGI, ML, deep learning, and autonomous response act as risk multipliers and critical mitigation tools. AI-driven threats accelerate incident velocity but, conversely, enable faster detection and automated response. Building on models like Time-to-Impact Analysis and Agility and Resilience Theory, this chapter advocates for incorporating risk velocity alongside probability and impact, with velocity-aware matrices and AI-enhanced simulations.

INTRODUCTION

The Department of Homeland Security's (DHS) 2025 Homeland Threat Assessment (HTA) indicates that the danger environment is anticipated to remain high in the forthcoming year; thus, assessing risk is imperative (U.S. Department

DOI: 10.4018/979-8-2600-1021-1.ch001

of Homeland Security, 2025). Rapid technological innovation, shifting global dynamics, and increasingly complex systems, facilitates an imperative for precise and adaptive risk evaluation has intensified with artificial intelligence (AI), artificial general intelligence (AGI), deep learning, machine learning (ML) models, and autonomous response systems now serving as both a catalyst for risk evolution and a foundational pillar in the defense against emerging threats (Chen et al., 2021; (Naim, 2022; Ravichandran et al., 2022).

Risk assessment lies at the heart of contemporary strategy (Mizrak, 2024), enabling leaders to chart the unseen terrain of uncertainty and make informed decisions that protect their stakeholders and resources (Holomozenko & Stasiuk, 2024). This chapter investigates how the centuries-old quest to quantify risk has been transformed by AI-powered analytics, which deliver real-time, context-aware insights and fundamentally alter both the speed and sophistication of modern risk assessment methodologies (Landoll, 2021). As the prevalence of emerging technology expands at an unprecedented pace, organizations and societies find themselves negotiating a transformed risk landscape. The amalgamation of AI, AGI, deep learning architectures, and ML models has not only accelerated operational capabilities but also introduced novel and increasingly insidious cybersecurity threats (Naim, 2022; Ravichandran et al., 2022). In an ecosystem marked by rapid change and intricate interdependencies, precision and adaptability in risk evaluation have become paramount. Naim (2022) posits that AI and its variants now operate dually, as both a catalyst driving new forms of cyber risk and as a foundational element in the defense against these evolving dangers.

The proliferation of AI-powered cyberattacks has ushered in an era of exceptionally adaptive threats (Naim, 2022). Advanced malware, leveraged by sophisticated AI algorithms, exhibits the capacity for real-time code morphing and behavioral evolution, effectively rendering traditional signature-based detection obsolete. Polymorphic malware learns from defensive responses (Gazzan et al., 2025), assimilates environmental cues, and autonomously alters its footprint, evading detection, persisting within networks, and deepening the potential for covert exploitation (Belea, 2023). Meanwhile, the emergence of deepfakes has introduced a potent tool for deception and social engineering (Mustak et al., 2023). Enabled by generative adversarial networks and powerful deep learning models, deepfakes produce hyper-realistic synthetic media that convincingly mimic real individuals (Mustak et al., 2023). These digital forgeries have been deployed to perpetrate financial fraud, manipulate public opinion, and undermine trust in authentic communications, posing challenges to the integrity of everything from personal correspondence to national elections.

AI-facilitated phishing further exemplifies the rising sophistication of adversarial tactics. Generative AI models craft phishing communications that are contextually aware, linguistically impeccable, and tailored to individual targets (). These messages, designed to outmaneuver conventional detection filters, dramatically increase the success rate of credential theft, business email compromise, and broader social engineering campaigns (Rawat et al., 2024). Yet, AI's impact is symbiotic, fortifying the cyber-defensive apparatus with unparalleled speed and efficacy (Rawat et al., 2024).

Machine learning-powered systems tirelessly process vast amounts of telemetry data, identifying intricate patterns of both legitimate and anomalous activity (Kinyua & Awuah, 2021). Through continuous monitoring, these technologies detect emergent threats and subtle deviations in behavior, enabling defenders to identify and neutralize attacks at their incipient stages (Ebute, 2024). Automated response systems (Kinyua & Awuah, 2021), often built on top of reinforcement learning methodologies, empower security infrastructures to contain breaches, isolate infected nodes, and remediate incidents, all with minimal human intervention. This orchestration not only reduces the dwell time of malicious actors but also permits defenders to prioritize strategic and complex challenges over routine tasks.

Moreover, the cyclical interplay between offensive and defensive AI systems has catalyzed a relentless arms race. As adversaries refine their generative and adaptive capabilities, defenders must reciprocate with equally innovative, self-learning security paradigms. The imperative is clear: organizations must anchor their risk management strategies in the continuous evolution of AI (Ravichandran et al., 2022), cultivating robust technological, ethical, and procedural frameworks that can confront the next wave of digital threats. In this context, AI transcends its traditional role as a mere tool (Naim, 2022); it is both the architect of novel vulnerabilities and the bulwark against them. Safeguarding the digital commons in an era of autonomous, intelligent, and adaptive threats demands vigilance, collaboration, and an unwavering commitment to innovation at the intersection of technology (Chen et al., 2021) and trust.

While early risk thinking was influenced by chance, as evident in ancient games and folklore (Sève & Wolfe, 2024), the systematic quantification of uncertainty did not fully emerge until the mathematical revolutions of the Renaissance and Enlightenment. The correspondence between Blaise Pascal and Pierre de Fermat in the mid-17th century was instrumental in establishing probability theory as a rigorous analytical toolkit and initiating a paradigmatic shift in the knowledge and management of risk (Mathieu & Miermont, 2023; Pascal, 2024). Such mathematical foundations enabled subsequent generations to differentiate risk from mere speculation and superstition. The institutionalization of probabilistic principles occurred in tandem with the evolution of commercial, insurance, and actuarial practices (Aldemir, 2024; Hu et al., 2022; Salo et al., 2022). By the eighteenth century, mortality tables and actuarial computations, exemplified by Edmond Halley's foundational work, provided empirical benchmarks for evaluating life and property risk, solidifying probability and anticipated consequences as core tenets of the field (Connor, 2024; Guillen, 2022). Modern business environments have adapted these principles, employing the probability-impact (Acebes et al., 2024), to prioritize threats and structure their responses. This matrix, now ubiquitous in project and enterprise risk management, visualizes each risk along two axes: likelihood and potential severity, thus informing resource allocation and strategic planning (Iqbal, 2023).

Recent years have witnessed a growing recognition that risks no longer manifest as isolated, predictable events. The digital age, interconnectivity, and increasingly volatile environments have accelerated the speed at which emergent threats materialize. In response, scholars and practitioners are advancing the concept of risk velocity—the speed at which the effects of a risk are expected to be realized—as a crucial, often overlooked, dimension in contemporary assessments (Ramamoorti et al., 2017; Ramamoorti et al., 2019). *Risk velocity* denotes the rate at which an object moves in a specific direction. In risk management, risk velocity represents the speed at which a risk can impact an organization (Ramamoorti et al., 2019). The velocity of risk can be evaluated by a qualitative analysis (i.e., high versus low) as a component of risk assessment. This study argues that incorporating velocity into assessment methodologies provides a more nuanced and actionable understanding of organizational vulnerability.

Identifying risk velocity as the third dimension of risk assessment significantly improves organizational structures by providing leaders with the means to address the increasingly unpredictable threat environment of today. Organizations encountering disruptions that arise within hours or minutes may no longer depend exclusively on probability and impact for effective risk prioritization or mitigation. The incorporation of technical insights, such as AI-driven analytics, machine learning-based detection, and autonomous response systems, facilitates real-time awareness and swift action across various risks, including cyber threats and reputational crises. Integrating velocity-sensitive scoring models, simulations, and adaptive playbooks into risk management frameworks enables businesses to be more agile, resilient, and proactive, thereby protecting assets and maintaining operations in the face of rapidly evolving threats.

This chapter elucidates the historical evolution, theoretical frameworks, and methodological debates that underscore risk assessment. It situates contemporary challenges within this text, demonstrating how ancient intuitions, mathematical rigor, and digital-era urgency converge to inform present practice by expanding the focus from the foundational probability-impact matrix (Iqbal, 2023) to embrace the triad of likelihood, impact, and velocity. The study aims to deliver a model relevant for dynamic and demanding risk environments. The exploration that follows is organized in the following sequence: Contextual Background, Review of Theoretical Foundations, Methodological Innovations in Risk Assessment, and Research Gaps and Future Directions.

Contextual Background

The origins of risk assessment are deeply intertwined with humanity's ancient rituals and the early desire to predict and manage chance (Niall, 2023). Before the advent of formal probability, risk was conceived broadly through frameworks of fate and divination, as evidenced in the games of chance found in Mesopotamian and Roman societies. These practices provided a primitive lens for understanding uncertainty, and their prevalence across cultures highlights an enduring anxiety toward the unpredictable (Risk Sciences International, 2020). With the onset of the scientific revolution, thinkers like Cardano and Galileo introduced probabilistic reasoning to the study of games (Aldemir, 2024; Hu et al., 2022; Salo, et al., 2022), marking a critical intellectual transition from superstition to calculation (Leung, n.d.). By formalizing the concepts of expectation and fairness within gaming and contracts, early mathematicians enabled risk to be understood apart from divine or arbitrary forces (Sève & Wolfe, 2024).

The seminal correspondence between Pascal and Fermat addressed not only gambling dilemmas but also fundamental questions around the fair division of stakes, giving rise to core probability concepts such as expected value and combinatorial analysis (Mathieu & Miermont, 2023). Their insights were rapidly disseminated and adopted across Europe, influencing the structuring of marine and life insurance contracts. By the late seventeenth century, these probabilistic methods were codified for use in calculating annuities and forecasting collective risk (Aldemir, 2024; Hu et al; Salo et al., 2022), thus embedding scientific uncertainty into commerce and finance.

As actuarial science matured in the eighteenth and nineteenth centuries, it leveraged increasingly reliable data to refine risk pricing and build the complex insurance markets we know today (Connor, 2024). The establishment of mortality tables by Halley exemplified this new empirical rigor, permitting actuaries to estimate life expectancies with far greater accuracy (Guillen, 2022). During the twentieth century, foundational distinctions between risk and uncertainty further elevated the discipline. Frank Knight's articulation of quantifiable risk versus unquantifiable uncertainty, along with later advances in Bayesian inference (Bylund, 2021), provided organizations with sophisticated frameworks to guide decision-making (Dawson et al., 2024) in volatile environments (Bylund, 2021).

The probability-impact matrix, first formalized in the mid-20th century, has become a staple of risk assessment (Iqbal, 2023) across various sectors, including construction, aviation, nuclear energy, and finance. The matrix's enduring popularity stems from its intuitive visualization and ability to guide prioritization amid complexity (Iqbal, 2023). Contemporary literature, however, increasingly argues that risk velocity, the measure of how rapidly threats translate into operational or financial effects, demands equal consideration. As organizations navigate a landscape marked by cyber threats, regulatory flux, and global supply chain vulnerabilities, a timely response is paramount. Failure to account for risk velocity can undermine even the most meticulously crafted mitigation strategies, resulting in delays, miscommunication, or missed opportunities for intervention (Ramamoorti et al., 2017; Ramamoorti et al., 2019).

Current scholarship thus identifies a pressing need for augmented models of risk assessment, which integrate traditional metrics (Hubbard & Seiersen, 2023) with dynamic, temporal dimensions. This study is situated at the nexus of historical continuity and methodological innovation. By critically appraising the trajectory and current state of risk assessment theory and practice, the ensuing analysis offers a consolidation of foundational knowledge (Dodla & Jones, 2023) and a springboard for future frameworks apt for a rapidly evolving risk landscape.

PROBLEM STATEMENT

While enterprise risk management methodologies have advanced considerably, traditional frameworks still predominantly emphasize the use of probability and magnitude to assess threats (Lam, 2017), often overlooking the critical dimension of risk velocity (Ramamoorti et al., 2019), specifically, the rapidity with which a risk event can propagate and exert disruptive influence throughout the organization. This gap significantly undermines the ability to make timely and effective decisions in today's fast-paced digital and interconnected context (Holomozenko & Stasiuk, 2024). The 2024 IBM Cost of a Data Breach Report, published by IBM and the Ponemon Institute, revealed that the average global cost of a data breach in cybersecurity rose to $4.88 million in 2024, with average recovery times now exceeding seven months due to sluggish responses to rapidly evolving threats.

Moreover, resultant reputational crises trigger adverse repercussions such as share price declines twice as steep as in the pre-digital era, indicative of the accelerated damage high-velocity events inflict. As a result of the accelerated pace of change, 59% of global executives now identify high-velocity risks as their primary concern, surpassing traditional issues such as compliance and credit (Protiviti & North Carolina State University, 2025). Without the explicit incorporation and appraisal of risk velocity into assessment frameworks (Ramamoorti et al., 2019), organizations continue to assess risk using a two-dimensional model, resulting in limited insights and delayed or missed opportunities to assess risk more accurately (Baloglu & Cakali, 2022).

RESEARCH METHOD AND DESIGN

This study employs a qualitative, multiple-case study approach grounded in the systematic analysis of secondary data and archival organizational documentation (Halkias et al., 2022; Miri & Macke, 2022). The objective is to explore how established organizations adapt risk assessment frameworks to incorporate risk velocity across select sectors. The research centers on publicly available documents, internal policy manuals, crisis reports, industry whitepapers, and relevant datasets obtained from institutional repositories and publicly accessible regulatory filings (Benson & Arksey, 2021; Venters et al., 2021).

Data collection for this research revolved around the aggregation and examination of organizational case studies reported in professional literature, government and industry reports, corporate disclosures, and reputable news sources. The inclusion criteria required that documents and archival records pertain to risk events occurring after 2020, with sufficient detail to contextualize the presence or absence of velocity considerations in risk assessment (Venters et al., 2021; Low et al., 2022). In addition, technological and sector-specific databases were utilized to identify trends and benchmark practices across targeted industries (Benson & Arksey, 2021).

Observational insights were derived through the review of publicly broadcast risk management meetings, webinars, and conference proceedings, ensuring that all information was in the public domain and independent of direct researcher involvement (Benson & Arksey, 2021). Purposeful sampling was applied to the identification and selection of case organizations and risk events. Rather than recruiting participants, the study focused on a curated set of high-profile enterprises publicly recognized for innovative or challenged risk management practices in the context of high-velocity and low-velocity risk occurrences. The criteria for inclusion were industry relevance, the presence of detailed public documentation on risk episodes, and explicit referencing of risk assessment or velocity considerations. This approach is supported by qualitative guidance on robust non-participant case study research (Venters et al., 2021).

The research procedures began with a comprehensive literature search and archival data collection (Fisher et al., 2024). All relevant documents were systematically collated into a central digital repository. Documents were then coded using a pre-established rubric focused on themes of risk identification, risk prioritization, assessment frameworks, velocity metrics, and mitigation strategies. Thematic analysis proceeded in three phases: (1) open coding for salient concepts related to risk velocity, probability, and impact; (2) comparison across cases and industries to identify patterns and divergence; (3) synthesis of findings into best practices and observed challenges (Venters et al., 2021).

Analysis was supported by qualitative data analysis software, such as NVivo, to organize and code textual data. Document management employed secure cloud-based storage in line with academic best practices (Venters et al., 2021). The coding rubric and thematic development template were based on established standards within qualitative content analysis and organizational studies (Low et al., 2022). Several strategies were employed to enhance the validity and reliability of this archival qualitative design. Triangulation was achieved by cross-referencing findings from multiple document types and sectors. The systematic coding of documents using explicit, replicable rubrics ensured consistency, while the exclusion of non-public data or unverifiable sources protected credibility. Analytical documentation and clear audit trails were maintained to document research decisions and the evolution of themes, supporting transparency and replicability (Venters et al., 2021).

The research design employed an embedded, multi-case study framework (Halkias et al., 2022; Miri & Macke, 2022), allowing for in-depth exploration of diverse organizational approaches to risk velocity without relying on human subject research. Each case was examined holistically, drawing from diverse archival and documentary evidence to elucidate internal logic, contextual pressures, and strategic adaptations. Cross-case synthesis facilitated the extraction of generalizable themes and the development of actionable recommendations. This methodological stance enabled theoretical advancement and provided insight into risk management practice, grounded in rigorously curated secondary data (Low et al., 2022; Venters et al., 2021).

Assumptions, Limitations, And Delimitations

This section clarifies the foundational conditions and boundaries that shape the inquiry into risk velocity as a critical dimension in risk assessment. By explicitly outlining the assumptions, acknowledging the limitations, and defining the delimitations of the research design (Berenson, 2023), the chapter establishes the contours within which findings should be interpreted. Articulating these elements is essential not only for methodological transparency but also for supporting scholarly dialogue and evaluation of the study's broader applicability (Berenson, 2023). The explicit recognition of underlying premises and boundaries provides a framework for contextualizing results and for guiding future research directions (Berenson, 2023) in the evolving field of risk management.

Assumptions

Several underlying assumptions inform the design and execution of the analysis presented in this chapter. First, it is presumed that the documentary and archival materials reviewed, including industry case studies, reports, and regulatory filings, accurately depict organizational risk practices (Crotty & Daniel, 2022) and reliably reflect the phenomena under investigation. This trust in the factual veracity and completeness of published accounts is critical, since secondary sources form the empirical foundation of the study in the absence of direct access to organizational environments (Benson & Arksey, 2021).

It is further assumed that the concept of risk velocity, although variably operationalized across industries, possesses intrinsic value as an analytical lens for examining organizational adaptability, resource deployment, and risk mitigation efficacy (Ramamoorti et al., 2017; Ramamoorti et al., 2019). While sector-specific differences abound, it is conceived that these fields encounter analogous challenges regarding the temporal dynamics of risk and will therefore yield meaningful comparative insights (Venters et al., 2021). The study further assumes that organizations are increasingly subject to high-velocity risk events, influenced by digital transformation, global interconnectivity, and evolving threat vectors, which together amplify the significance of velocity as a risk assessment criterion.

The analytical process rests on the presumption that thematic analysis, supported by established qualitative tools such as NVivo, can reliably identify and synthesize patterns from heterogeneous archival sources (Dhakal, 2022). The study adopts the view that robust coding frameworks and systematic document review ensure the emergence of valid and credible themes regarding risk velocity practices (Low et al., 2022). Even with cross-sectoral variability in reporting, it is assumed that methodological rigor in document analysis will compensate for variations in depth and breadth of secondary source material.

Limitations

While this chapter aims to provide a comprehensive exploration of risk velocity within organizational risk management, several limitations necessarily affect the scope and generalizability of its findings. The exclusive reliance on secondary data and document analysis, rather than primary data collection or direct observation, presents inherent limitations. Specifically, the analysis is bound by the breadth, depth, and accuracy of available documents, which may not capture the full range of behind-the-scenes deliberations, informal protocols, or emergent practices within organizations (Low et al., 2022). Secondary sources might exhibit reporting bias, selective emphasis, or unintentional omission, thereby shaping the narrative in ways that elude direct verification (Benson & Arksey, 2021).

Furthermore, the variable granularity across published accounts and industry reports can result in inconsistent detail regarding the operationalization and measurement of risk velocity. Some cases may emphasize formal policy adaptations

(Couretas, 2022), while others foreground strategic narratives, making cross-case comparison complex and potentially incomplete. The study cannot control for the heterogeneity of terminologies and frameworks employed by organizations when describing risk velocity or the decision to prioritize velocity in risk assessment (Venters et al., 2021).

Another limitation concerns temporal and sectoral relevance. Organizations that publicly disclose detailed risk management practices may differ systematically from those of lower-profile firms, particularly in terms of resource availability, regulatory scrutiny, or market visibility. As such, the chapter's insights may disproportionately reflect the practices of large, well-documented organizations rather than offering a comprehensive view (Benson & Arksey, 2021). Moreover, the fast-evolving nature of risk typologies, emerging technologies, and global trends means that conclusions drawn from documents published since 2020 may require further update to capture new dynamics.

Lastly, although employing rigorous thematic analysis, interpretive bias remains a possibility, coding and synthesis of qualitative data necessarily involve subjective judgment, and the derivation of themes may be influenced by the researcher's orientation and prior knowledge (Mwita, 2022). While thematic validity is pursued through systematic coding, complete objectivity can never be entirely assured in qualitative research, particularly when working with secondary data (Low et al., 2022).

Delimitations

The chapter's analysis is purposefully delimited in several respects to maintain methodological coherence and analytic focus. First, the research primarily confines its investigation to organizational risk assessment practices from 2020 onward, with a deliberate emphasis on the most current dynamics shaped by digital (Burrell, 2023) and post-pandemic volatility. However, scholarly work before 2020 is referenced for its relevance and seminal purposes. This temporal scope is designed to ensure relevance and resonance with the evolving risk landscape.

Secondly, the scope includes various occurrences affected by high-velocity risk events. Examining these cases enables in-depth thematic synthesis, but it inherently limits the generalizability of conclusions to sectors with distinctly different risk profiles (Venters et al., 2021). The organizations selected for case analysis are those with publicly available documentation that meet explicit inclusion criteria, excluding entities that lack sufficient detail or transparency in their disclosures. The interpretive findings are positioned as exploratory and illustrative rather than statistically generalizable or predictive. By focusing exclusively on codified policy documents, crisis reports, and industry whitepapers, the chapter intentionally delimits analysis to that which is verifiable and reproducible by future scholars with access to the public domain (Benson & Arksey, 2021).

Finally, thematic emphasis is placed squarely on the integration and operationalization of risk velocity as a dimension in risk assessment, rather than on comprehensive cataloguing of all risk management approaches or a comparison of non-velocity frameworks. The exploration is thus sharply tailored to contribute new knowledge regarding the application and utility of risk velocity, with broader risk management issues treated only insofar as they inform this central inquiry.

LITERATURE REVIEW

Navigating the contemporary landscape of risk management requires a critical reassessment of inherited frameworks, as organizations confront increasingly volatile, complex, and interconnected operational environments. Whereas traditional paradigms have privileged quantitative clarity through the measurement of likelihood and consequence (Hardy & Saunders, 2022), emerging literature compels a more nuanced analysis that accounts for temporal dynamics, methodological innovation, and context-sensitive vulnerabilities (Baloglu & Cakali, 2022). This review synthesizes seminal themes and critical debates within the field, foregrounding the theoretical, practical, and methodological advancements that are shaping the evolution of risk assessment in the digital era (Przetacznik, 2022). Three primary themes emerged from the literature review: Classical Risk Analysis, Contemporary Evolutions, and Understudied Risk Dynamics. The literature overwhelmingly situates the probability-impact matrix as the analytical backbone of risk management. The next explored is the traditional use of probability and impact to frame risk.

Traditional Risk Analysis: Probability and Impact

From industrial safety to financial actuarial science, the classical risk matrix enables organizations to assess and prioritize threats by estimating the likelihood of occurrence and evaluating the severity of consequences (Iqbal, 2023). The prevalent adoption of standards such as Enterprise Risk Management (ERM) and the International Organization for Standardization (ISO) 31000:2018 – Risk Management – Guidelines has entrenched this bi-dimensional paradigm, making it not only a technical tool but also a regulatory imperative (Salihu & Dervishi, 2024). Committee of Sponsoring Organizations of the Treadway Commission's (COSO) Enterprise Risk Management (ERM) - Integrated Framework (2024), for example, frames the identification, assessment, and monitoring of risks around quantifying the possible occurrence and impact upon organizational objectives (Committee of

Sponsoring Organizations of the Treadway Commission, 2024; Salihu & Dervishi, 2024; Olaniyi & Omubo, 2023; Yuni et al., 2024).

Globally recognized frameworks, such as ISO 31000 and COSO ERM, emphasize the importance of cultural, legislative, and ethical factors in incorporating risk velocity into organizational risk management. ISO 31000 identifies risk culture as fundamental to effective risk management, emphasizing that a strong risk culture fosters informed decision-making, collective accountability, and ethical, sustainable results in addressing swiftly evolving risks. COSO's ERM framework emphasizes governance, culture, and ethical values, highlighting that effective risk response is contingent upon prioritizing leadership integrity and transparent communication across the firm (Salihu & Dervishi, 2024; Olaniyi & Omubo, 2023; Yuni et al., 2024). These frameworks promote the integration of risk velocity with a comprehensive perspective on culture and regulatory compliance, ensuring that swift risk escalation is balanced with accountability, equity, and adherence to cultural norms.

Although formalized in codes and frameworks, this approach has not been without critique. Scholars emphasize that the matrix format, while intuitive, can induce cognitive biases and a false sense of quantification (Lam, 2017) when underlying probabilities are uncertain or data is sparse. Additionally, actuarial models, while mathematically sophisticated, often rely on steady-state assumptions that may be discordant with modern hyperdynamic operational contexts (). Still, the probability-impact schema remains globally normative, not merely for compliance but due to its communicability and the comparative ease it provides in aligning stakeholder priorities (Jones, 2021). Recent research on risk visualization suggests that two-dimensional mapping is easily understood by non-technical executives, thereby favoring its continued predominance.

Subsequent studies have begun questioning the adequacy of the classical model (Anderson, 2024), particularly in the context of digital transformation and multi-dimensional risks. The consensus remains that, while probability and impact are fundamental, an exclusive focus on these elements risks underestimating rapid-onset risks, complex system interactions, and the evolving nature of threats, especially in cyber-physical environments (Capenter & Wyman, 2022). While the maintainers of risk management frameworks have ensured a level of operational consistency through the entrenched probability-impact model, recent literature makes clear that this approach, as codified through COSO ERM and ISO 31000:2018, exhibits significant methodological limitations in the face of emergent threats.

The prevalence of cognitive biases in risk matrix interpretation, as identified by Cox (2008), demonstrates an inherent vulnerability to subjective misjudgment, even as frameworks attempt to standardize assessment criteria. Similarly, Power's (2022) critique of actuarial inertia underscores the risks associated with relying on historical data in rapidly evolving technological contexts. These insights suggest that, although the classical model endures for its simplicity (Anderson, 2024) and communicative strength, its one-size-fits-all precision is increasingly illusory. Nuanced and context-adaptive enhancements are imperative, especially considering risks characterized by high uncertainty and rapid unfolding (Baloglu & Cakali, 2022). The hyper-evolving risk landscape demands the use of risk velocity.

Contemporary Evolution in Introducing Risk Velocity and Dynamic Assessment

The intensification of organizational complexity, particularly in digitalized and interconnected operational landscapes, has prompted scholars to advocate for the explicit inclusion of risk velocity in assessment. *Risk velocity*, defined as the speed with which the effects of a risk event are manifested, represents a third axis of awareness that challenges the static results yielded by traditional models (Anderson, 2024; Landsittel et al., 2024; Ramamoorti et al., 2019). The growing discourse around risk velocity emerges from experiences in cybersecurity, crisis management, and supply chain disruptions, where organizations have observed that the temporal characteristics of a risk can be material (Hardjomidjojo et al., 2022).

Notably, while ISO 31000:2018 urges a holistic and contextual appreciation of risks, its explicit omission of velocity as a distinct evaluation factor has drawn scholarly attention. Authors such as Hamir and Sum (2021) and Makajić-Nikolić (2023) illustrate that risk velocity remains an under-addressed dimension, often subsumed within broader impact discussions but insufficiently operationalized in practice. Where velocity is recognized, it is typically embedded in risk scenario simulations or is an afterthought in post-mortem analyses, rather than a proactive input into strategic risk prioritization (Landsittel et al., 2024). Recent empirical studies increasingly call for the integration of risk velocity into enterprise risk management architectures (Baloglu & Cakali, 2022; Ramamoorti et al., 2019), arguing that organizations in sectors such as finance, healthcare, and technology face risks where the window between identification and materialization has drastically narrowed. These works underscore that effective agility now depends upon risk comprehension, not only the potential severity of adverse effects, but also how fast adverse effects can unfold (Baloglu & Cakali, 2022).

The literature's emerging consensus on the necessity of including risk velocity signals marks an advance and a complication in risk assessment methodologies. While the tri-dimensional framework promises improved responsiveness, significant gaps persist regarding the operationalization of velocity measures. The lack of standardized metrics and process integration, as noted by Hamir and Sum (2021), means that risk velocity frequently remains an ad hoc consideration rather than a core analytic criterion (Ramamoorti et al., 2019). Moreover, the abundant focus on scenario planning reveals that many practitioners still regard velocity as situational (Baloglu & Cakali, 2022), rather than structural, complicating efforts to institutionalize its assessment. Notably, the divergence between theoretical endorsement and practical adoption suggests that further empirical research is warranted regarding metric formulation, stakeholder training, and embedding velocity into digital risk management (Ivanov & Dolgui, 2022; Makajić-Nikolić, 2023). The call for velocity-sensitive frameworks is compelling, yet methodological clarity lags behind rhetorical enthusiasm. Next explored are security controls, methodological advances, and research gaps.

Security Controls, Methodological Advances, and Research Gaps

The field of risk management has also seen significant developments in security controls and assessment methodologies (Przetacznik, 2022), exemplified by the growing popularity of the MITRE ATT&CK Framework (Möller, 2023) and the 2024 National Institute of Standards and Technology Cybersecurity Framework (NIST CSF). These controls are meticulously designed to counter emergent digital risks by promoting structured, iterative risk management processes, including the implementation of technical, procedural, and managerial safeguards (National Institute of Standards and Technology, 2024). Nonetheless, evidence suggests that despite the adoption of advanced modeling techniques, including quantitative risk analytics, Monte Carlo simulations, and scenario forecasting, organizations still predominantly rely on the dual axes of likelihood and impact (Hardy & Saunders, 2022; Iqbal, 2023).

A review of recent methodological literature highlights persistent limitations: quantitative models often falter due to incomplete data or a lack of real-time threat intelligence (Anderson, 2024; Wolniak, 2023), and qualitative approaches risk subjective bias or oversimplification, especially when assessing complex cyber threats. Regional biases and sector-specific blind spots are prevalent, as research tends to cluster in industries or geographies with high regulatory scrutiny, while neglecting less regulated but highly vulnerable sectors, such as digital supply chains (Ivanov & Dolgui, 2022;). Furthermore, advances such as quantum cryptography or AI-enhanced intrusion detection remain insufficiently explored (Ravichandran et al., 2022), pointing to a clear gap in forward-looking risk assessment research (Capenter & Wyman, 2022). This methodological overview thus reveals an evolving landscape, energized by the introduction of new frameworks and analytical tools, but also fragmented by ongoing challenges in reliability, comprehensiveness, and operational flexibility.

Calls for mixed methods approaches, dynamic risk assessments (Aldemir, 2024; Hu et al., 2022), and longitudinal studies of post-breach recovery are now widespread, emphasizing the need for methodological diversity in future research. The evidence reviewed illustrates that the proliferation of security controls and analytic innovations has yet to supplant the enduring reliance on probability and impact for risk comparisons. While frameworks like the NIST CSF offer blueprint-level guidance, their implementation is often hindered by resource constraints and disparities in organizational maturity (National Institute of Standards and Technology, 2024).

Quantitative models promise rigor (Hardy & Saunders, 2022), but they stumble with data scarcity and difficulties in translating stochastic representations into actionable intelligence. Qualitative and scenario-based approaches continue to offer richness (Grojek et al., 2024; Iqbal, 2023; Truong et al., 2021) but are vulnerable to inconsistency and bias, particularly in cross-sectoral applications. Meanwhile, emerging risk domains such as quantum threats or AI-driven attacks are currently under-theorized, reflecting a scholarly and practical lag between technological innovation and robust risk methodologies (Burton, 2024). Thus, moving forward, a concerted research agenda is needed that not only enhances methodological rigor but also broadens the contextual and technological horizons of risk management.

Increasing Acknowledgment of Risk Complexity and Leveraging Risk Velocity

Organizations now face a swiftly changing environment influenced by digital transformation, hyper-connectivity, and heightened volatility (Burrell, 2023). Incidents such as cyberattacks, social media crises, pandemics (Pujawan & Bah, 2022), and cascading supply failures (Ivanov & Dolgui, 2022) illustrate that risks are characterized not only by their probability and impact but also by the rapidity of their emergence (Baloglu & Cakali, 2022). This emerging knowledge has revealed significant deficiencies in traditional risk assessment, which frequently undervalues or neglects the temporal aspect, risk velocity, in its fundamental calculations. Although likelihood and impact provide necessary insights into risk scale and prioritization, contemporary risk management increasingly necessitates models that acknowledge the rapid propagation of disruption, its potential to surpass controls, and its effect on organizational value (Acebes et al., 2024; Anderson, 2024).

Cultural, Regulatory, and Ethical Dimensions

As organizations elevate risk velocity from a technical measure to an operational necessity, they must acknowledge that its practical implementation is influenced by entrenched cultural beliefs, regulatory requirements, and shifting ethical standards.

The speed at which risks manifest and intensify is determined not only by technology or analytics but also by the extent to which a culture promotes risk escalation, the rigor of regulatory mandates on reporting and response times, and the degree to which leaders assess the societal ramifications of swift decisions. Effectively addressing risk velocity requires a comprehensive approach that integrates novel assessment methods with the distinct cultural attitudes, regulatory requirements, and ethical expectations inherent to each organization's specific context.

Cultural Considerations

Organizational culture influences the identification, escalation, and management of fast hazards. Cultures that prioritize transparency, education, and empowerment facilitate more rapid and truthful risk identification and mitigation. Conversely, societies that penalize error reporting or promote concealment experience delayed knowledge and greater consequences when immediate risks arise. Implementing velocity-centric risk models necessitates intentional change management. Organizations should initiate the revision of risk assessment procedures to require the evaluation of velocity in conjunction with likelihood and impact. Cross-functional training, scenario-based exercises, and the incorporation of velocity measures into dashboards and reporting formats most facilitate this modification. Regular communication regarding the significance of velocity assessments, along with prominent executive endorsement, helps overcome cultural inertia. Continuous evaluation and post-event analyses guarantee that insights from rapid occurrences are systematically recorded and that opposition to new procedures is constructively managed.

Regulatory Consequences

Regulators are increasingly stressing the importance of prompt response protocols and reporting systems, particularly in finance, manufacturing, and critical infrastructure sectors.

A growing imperative exists to incorporate velocity measurements into enterprise risk management frameworks and disaster recovery plans, ensuring that organizations adhere to minimum response and reporting durations during incidents.

Exploration of Ethical Implications

The incorporation of risk velocity, primarily when driven by AI and automated decision-making, presents significant ethical implications. The automation of risk escalation may diminish human oversight, leading to apprehensions over responsibility, bias, and the clarity of decision-making processes during emergencies. Ethical stewardship necessitates transparency in the generation of velocity-driven alerts, meticulous governance of privileged access during swift responses, and the fair distribution of resources, ensuring that urgent interventions do not unintentionally neglect slow-emerging yet equally significant risks. Organizations must reconcile efficiency with equity, implementing safeguards to avoid velocity-driven models from intensifying bias or worsening vulnerabilities among under-resourced populations. The use of risk velocity provides a risk dimension that supports organizational stewardship and accountable decision-making.

Risk Velocity as a Predictive Missing Force Multiplier

While the emphasis on probability and impact has rooted risk management in a solid mathematical tradition, contemporary risk environments have exposed significant shortcomings in this classic framework. In an age defined by rapid technological change, interconnected systems, and unprecedented event propagation, the timing with which risks unfold has become as critical as their likelihood or severity. This growing complexity has revealed a crucial gap: the need for risk assessment methods that not only quantify probabilities and outcomes but also account for the temporal dynamics that can dramatically amplify or mitigate organizational consequences (Baloglu & Cakali, 2022). Recognizing this, scholars and practitioners have called for the integration of additional dimensions, most notably, the concept of risk velocity, into modern risk management practices (Tarasenko & Steinmeier, 2024). *Risk velocity* denotes the rapidity with which the consequences of a risk manifest after activation (Ramamoorti et al., 2019). This focus on the speed of risk illustrates the rapidity with which a risk can affect an organization following its emergence (Ramamoorti et al., 2017; Ramamoorti et al., 2019), varying from virtually immediate occurrences (such as cyberattacks) to those that evolve over weeks, months, or even years (such as regulatory changes) (Baloglu & Cakali, 2022).

Risk velocity has become a crucial aspect of contemporary risk management, supplementing the traditional emphasis on probability and impact (Hillson, 2023; Ramamoorti et al., 2019). A more pervasive use of techniques to distinguish the speed of risk is required (Ramamoorti et al., 2019). Risk velocity fundamentally denotes the rapidity with which the repercussions of a risk event materialize following its activation, encompassing the immediacy and urgency of its effect on an organization (Mann, 2024; Ramamoorti et al., 2019).

Furthermore, Hillson (2023) defines clockspeed in risk management as a concept that differentiates the timing and quality of information available for decision-making under uncertainty. Risk clockspeed refers to the velocity at which pertinent risk information is accessible relative to the timeframe for executing an acceptable risk response. A higher clockspeed necessitates swift decision-making, frequently with incomplete information, demanding prompt and perhaps instinctive responses (Hillson, 2023). A reduced clockspeed provides more time between the acquisition of high-quality information and the moment a response is required, facilitating thoughtful and reasonable decision-making. Hillson (2023) highlights this differentiation in an analysis of clockspeed versus velocity, arguing that understanding the clockspeed of a risk enables businesses to tailor their decision-making strategy, ensuring they respond with appropriate speed to changing circumstances (Hillson, 2023).

Rapidly emerging risks, including cyberattacks, supply chain disruptions, or viral social media disasters, can manifest within minutes or hours, providing decision-makers with minimal or no advance notice for planning or response (Baloglu & Cakali, 2022; Jones, 2021; Parkin, 2021). Low-velocity risks, such as regulatory modifications or demographic transformations, typically develop slowly over months or years, providing ample opportunity for study, stakeholder involvement, and response. Identifying these distinctions is essential, as the opportunity to address high-velocity threats may be minimal, necessitating the development of effective early warning systems, crisis management protocols, and flexible tactics. In comparison, a high-velocity risk can lead to disruption within minutes or hours (e.g., cyberattacks or social media crises). In contrast, a low-velocity risk may take months or years to manifest material repercussions (Parkin, 2021) (e.g., regulatory changes or demographic shifts). Probability (the likelihood of an event occurring) or impact (the extent of its effect), risk velocity pertains explicitly to the rapidity with which the risk materializes and begins to influence an organization (Ramamoorti et al., 2019).

Integrating risk velocity into enterprise risk management necessitates a calculated, hybrid strategy that harmonizes quantitative and qualitative evaluations to provide a more holistic understanding of organizational risks. Initiate with a quantitative scoring rubric that allocates numerical values to the anticipated time-to-impact (for instance, a 1–5 scale where 1 represents months/years and 5 signifies minutes/hours), which can be integrated with scores for probability and impact in a formula such as Risk Score = Likelihood × Impact × Velocity. Notably, several pertinent factors should be understood to enhance the integration of risk velocity into organizational risk frameworks:

Time to Impact. This refers to the interval between the initiation of a triggering event and the manifestation of its complete effects (Baloglu & Cakali, 2022; Parkin, 2021). Risk velocity and time to impact are intrinsically linked (Ramamoorti et al., 2017; Ramamoorti et al., 2019); elevated velocity corresponds to a shorter time to impact, necessitating prompt responses.

Escalation Speed. Denotes the rapidity with which a risk amplifies upon activation, potentially beyond controls or resources (Parkin, 2021). Although akin to velocity, escalation speed highlights the advancement or intensification of danger rather than its initial emergence.

Time to Detect. This quantifies the speed at which an organization recognizes a risk event after it has occurred. While not equivalent to risk velocity, reduced detection times are essential for the effective management of high-velocity threats.

Method for Measuring Risk Velocity. Risk velocity can be assessed using qualitative and quantitative metrics.

Qualitative Risks. Qualitatively, risks are classified descriptively, for example:

Extremely Rapid (minutes to hours)
Expeditious (hours to days)
Moderate (duration of days to weeks)
Gradual (weeks to months)
Extremely Protracted (months to years)

Quantitative Risks. Quantitatively, an applied quantitative method for measuring risk velocity begins with defining measurable scales for how fast a risk can manifest and impact operations:

Step 1: Assign a Timeframe-Based Scale.

Quantitatively rate risk velocity based on the time from risk event initiation to organizational impact:

1 = Months to Years
2 = Weeks to Months
3 = Days to Weeks
4 = Hours to Days
5 = Minutes to Hours

Step 2: Integrate Velocity into Risk Scoring.

Common formulas include:

Risk Score = (Likelihood + Velocity) × Impact
Risk Score= (Likelihood × Impact) + Velocity

For example, if Likelihood = 5 (critical), Impact = 5 (severe), and Velocity = 3 (days to weeks), then examples are: (5 + 3) × 5 = 40, or (5 × 5) +3 = 28, or (4 × 4) +3 =19.

Likelihood and impact scores are inherent to the organization's risk framework and may differ depending on the organization's perspective of risk. Velocity is associated with specific timeframes, typically delineated in hours, days, weeks, or months (e.g., "impacts will manifest within 4 hours"), or assigned number scores to aid in ranking and prioritization.

Step 3: Use Data and Scenario Analysis.

Strengthen the scale with real case timelines (e.g., average time for a known cyber risk to propagate in similar organizations). Complement with performing scenario analysis and simulations to assess evolving risks.

Advanced quantitative approaches may also be employed. Utilize velocity-adjusted probability distribution functions to assess time-dependent losses using stochastic modeling in Key Risk Indicators, dashboards, and monitoring systems. Additionally, organizations can modify risk registers, heat maps, and bell curves to illustrate and prioritize risks across three dimensions: probability, consequence, and speed, using color gradients or overlays to signify urgency. By evaluating risk velocity in conjunction with probability and impact, companies may more effectively prioritize actions (Ramamoorti et al., 2019), allocate resources, and execute superior mitigation measures for rapidly evolving and gradually emerging threats (Acebes et al., 2024; Ramamoorti et al., 2019).

Acceleration of Risk Velocity through Transformative Models

The rise of AI has heightened the necessity for clear differentiation of machine-generated data or language, requiring explicit disclosure to maintain trust and avoid the unintentional blending of human and AI contributions (Naim, 2022; Nobles & Burrell, 2024). It is equally imperative to recognize and address hidden biases in AI analyses (Weng & Wu, 2024), requiring both developers and users to rigorously validate, annotate, and accurately attribute all content, ensuring that the origin, methodology, and clarity of research findings are beyond criticism. AI currently functions as a double-edged sword in cybersecurity, equipping both attackers and defenders with unparalleled capabilities (Naim, 2022). AI empowers thieves to create highly persuasive phishing schemes and deepfake impersonations. These programs generate emails, texts, and synthetic audio or video that closely resemble authentic humans, enabling attackers to mislead victims on a large scale while circumventing conventional detection techniques (Weng & Wu, 2024). Deepfakes are employed in advanced impersonation tactics (Gambin et al., 2024), occasionally replicating the voices or appearances of CEOs to facilitate fraudulent transactions or distort public opinion.

Conversely, defenders utilize generative AI to enhance security frameworks via automated intrusion detection and immediate threat mitigation (Weng & Wu, 2024).

AI-driven systems rapidly discern anomalous behaviors and emerging attack patterns within networks, executing swift countermeasures, such as isolating systems or obstructing hostile traffic, frequently before human intervention (Nobles & Burrell, 2024). Automated reactions driven by AI not only expedite threat neutralization but also consistently adjust to emerging techniques, rendering them essential in today's rapidly changing threat environment (Weng & Wu, 2024). The interaction between offensive and defensive AI illustrates how artificial intelligence has transformed the power dynamics in cybersecurity, instigating a continuous arms race between malicious actors and security experts.

Concurrently, the evolution of AI and real-time data systems has not only accelerated the pace of decision-making (Naim, 2022; Ravichandran et al., 2022) but also increased the speed at which threats can emerge and spread through digital networks. Instantaneous information dissemination, cyber vulnerabilities, and automated processes (Kinyua & Awuah, 2021) enhance the propagation of risk and stakeholders' reactions. In this new reality, conventional risk models, centered solely on static, periodic estimates of likelihood and impact, fall short of capturing the dynamic, time-sensitive nature of many modern threats.

To adapt to these accelerated conditions, integrating risk velocity into assessment frameworks has become essential for organizations seeking to prioritize urgent risks (Mann, 2024), deploy mitigation strategies more effectively, and build real-time resilience (Stachowiak & Pawłyszyn, 2021; Wolniak, 2023). High-velocity risks, such as cybersecurity breaches or reputational crises driven by viral social media (Jones, 2021; Louisot, 2024; Ryzhakova et al., 2024), demand immediate action, whereas slower-moving risks, like regulatory shifts, require sustained strategic planning. A three-dimensional risk model, incorporating probability, impact, and velocity, enables organizations to allocate resources better, streamline crisis response protocols, and protect stakeholder value in a world defined by rapid change and disruption (Hillson, 2024). The post-pandemic landscape and the transformative impact of AI underscore that evaluating how quickly risks unfold is now just as critical as assessing their likelihood or severity of consequences (Naim, 2022).

Even in a hyper-evolving cybersecurity and technical landscape, the majority of traditional risk assessment models and prominent governance, risk, and compliance (GRC) systems continue to focus on static, periodic evaluations of probability and consequence (Adisuria & Jayadi, 2023; Awasthi, 2025). This dual-dimensional approach, however fundamental, is becoming insufficient for accurately representing the dynamic, time-sensitive nature of contemporary threats. *Risk velocity*, the rate at which a risk manifests following its trigger, is frequently excluded from integrated risk assessment modules, dashboards, and decision-support processes (Ramamoorti et al., 2019). Consequently, even advanced digital GRC systems may not notify decision-makers and risk owners of the urgency presented by rapidly evolving threats (Mann, 2024), leading to delayed responses and inadequate mitigation measures.

Recent industry evaluations underscore this disparity. The Institute of Risk Management (IRM) emphasizes that risk velocity is one of the most underutilized risk elements (Baloglu & Cakali, 2022) in GRC advancements, despite its significant practical value in Mizrak (2024 and continuity planning (Mizrak, 2024). Furthermore, a 2024 Enterprise Risk Management technology study reveals that fewer than one-third of significant GRC and risk management platforms provide integrated functionality for evaluating or visualizing risk velocity as a standard metric. The predominant majority persist in organizing risk registers and heat maps solely based on probability and impact. However, risk leaders are increasingly advocating for solutions that consider real-time escalation and dissemination (Burrell, 2023; Burton et al., 2023; Wolniak, 2023).

CONCEPTUAL FRAMEWORKS AND RISK MODELS

The integration of risk velocity into contemporary risk assessment models has marked a significant evolution in the discipline (Przetacznik, 2022), expanding the traditional focus on probability and impact to reflect the time-sensitive nature of emerging threats. Several conceptual frameworks and risk models now explicitly account for velocity, transforming qualitative evaluations and quantitative metrics (Hubbard & Seiersen, 2023). Discussed next are models related to risk velocity.

Three-Dimensional Risk Assessment Model. Historically, most risk assessments have employed a two-dimensional approach, evaluating risks based on their likelihood (the probability of occurrence) and their impact (the severity of consequences) (*Likelihood x Impact*). While this approach has provided a foundational basis for risk prioritization, it often fails to capture the urgency associated with rapidly materializing risks (Mann, 2024). The three-dimensional risk assessment model addresses this gap by introducing velocity as a critical third axis. In this conceptualization, velocity refers to the speed at which a risk can impact an organization once triggered. By incorporating velocity, risk heat maps transition from static, two-dimensional matrices to more dynamic representations that allow organizations to distinguish not only what risks are most likely and severe, but also which require the fastest response. Quantitatively, some frameworks express the risk score as *(Likelihood + Velocity) x Impact = Risk Score*, providing a formal mechanism for integrating urgency into risk prioritization (Hardy & Saunders, 2022). As a result, high-velocity risks can be flagged for immediate attention (Parkin, 2021), even when their standalone likelihood or impact might otherwise seem moderate.

Risk Response Urgency Matrix. *The Risk Response Urgency Matrix* (RRUM) further advances the integration of velocity within organizational risk frameworks. Unlike traditional approaches that may treat all risk responses as requiring the same level of reactivity, the RRUM plots risks across three axes: impact, likelihood, and required speed of response. By explicitly incorporating urgency (Baloglu, 2021; Mann, 2024) or velocity, this matrix helps guide real-time decision-making (Wolniak, 2023) and dynamic resource allocation. Escalation protocols are established based on velocity tiers, such as immediate, short-term, or long-term, enabling the organization to tailor its responses to the speed at which threats may unfold. This framework is beneficial for prioritizing high-velocity events, ensuring that escalation and mitigation actions are pre-planned and proportionate to the time-sensitive nature of particular threats.

Agility and Resilience Theory. At its foundation, the *Agility and Resilience Theory* posits that organizational survival and sustained performance depend on the dual interplay of agility, the capacity to sense, interpret, and respond rapidly to unexpected threats, and resilience (Goraya et al., 2024; RosmarlindaRosli & Almuallimi, 2024), the structural and cultural ability to absorb shocks, recover, and adapt post-incident. In cybersecurity, where threats like zero-day attacks emerge and evolve with startling speed (Prakash, 2025), the velocity of risk can quickly outpace defensive protocols designed for a more static threat landscape. Agility is manifested in an organization's preparedness to pivot in the face of novel attack vectors. which involves adopting real-time detection technologies, orchestrating rapid cross-functional responses, and maintaining adaptive governance frameworks. This nimble orientation enables security teams to preempt or, at the very least, contain threats before they escalate into widespread compromise.

Resilience, complementing agility, transcends reactive recovery by embedding learning mechanisms and adaptive improvement cycles throughout the organization. When an unforeseen breach strikes an enterprise, its ability to bounce back is not simply a measure of technical recovery but also cultural elasticity, resource allocation, and mission continuity. Embedding resilience requires a systematic commitment (Stachowiak & Pawłyszyn, 2021) to scenario-based planning, rapid communications, and the institutionalization of lessons learned so that each crisis strengthens the collective immune system. A clear understanding of risk velocity, how rapidly a threat can escalate, propagate, and inflict harm, shapes the prioritization of investments and the configuration of layered defenses. Conversely, organizations that lack clarity about the speed of evolving threats are more likely to be caught off guard by disruptive incidents. By internalizing risk velocity into the decision-making process, companies can refine their vigilance (Ramamoorti et al., 2017; Ramamoorti et al., 2019), ensuring that internal auditors assist organizations in prioritizing risks and developing resilience plans (Ramamoorti et al., 2019). Resilience is then not an afterthought but an emergent property of a culture that plans for rapid changes and adapts fluidly. In an era when cyberattacks can escalate from compromise to crisis in minutes, organizational agility and resilience fuel a continuous cycle of anticipation, adaptation, and advancement, sustaining trust and ensuring the viability of critical digital functions amidst perpetual uncertainty.

Integrated Quantitative Models. Quantitative models have also adapted to accommodate the dimension of velocity. In practice, risk velocity is integrated with loss distribution techniques to estimate the time-dependent nature of potential impacts, especially relevant in operational risk environments and within the financial sector. These models utilize probability distribution functions (Acebes et al., 2024) that are adjusted for velocity, enabling more granular evaluations of how quickly risks can escalate into losses. Applications of such models span risk registers, scenario planning, and the use of velocity-informed key risk indicators (KRIs) within dashboards and similar monitoring systems. By quantifying velocity through probabilistic and non-quantitative data, organizations can make informed, evidence-based decisions about which risks require urgent mitigation versus those that are suitable for longer-term strategic planning (Aldemir, 2024).

Theoretical models underpinning these frameworks offer valuable insight into the rationale for integrating velocity into risk assessment. Dynamic Risk Theory posits that risks should be viewed as evolving phenomena, with velocity serving as a mediator of the speed of consequences (Aldemir, 2024). According to this theory, rapidly moving risks necessitate agile and adaptive controls rather than rigid, static plans. The Agility and Resilience Theory further supports this perspective by emphasizing an organization's capacity for rapid response and the development of resilience (Stachowiak & Pawlyszyn, 2021), which are enhanced by explicit attention to risk velocity (Acebes et al., 2024). Additionally, Time-to-Impact Analysis is employed within some models to forecast escalation speed and inform disaster recovery and business continuity planning, using time-to-event and escalation analyses to plan for immediate and slow-emerging threats.

Integration into Risk Heat Maps, Risk Matrices, and Bell Curves. Organizations should first define and audit risk velocity as a discrete attribute, indicating the speed at which risk events may occur (Ramamoorti et al., 2019). This attribute should then be integrated into risk heat maps, risk matrices, and bell curves (Lam, 2017), alongside probability and effect. In heat maps and matrices, incorporate a distinct velocity dimension, which can be illustrated using color gradients (Kummer & Mendling, 2021), three-dimensional axes, or layered overlays to emphasize dangers that possess not only high probability or impact (Acebes et al., 2024) but also necessitate swift intervention. For instance, each risk can be charted according to its probability and consequence; thereafter, it can be enhanced or highlighted based on its velocity classification (e.g., employing icons or color coding for high, medium, or low velocity).

When utilizing bell curves or probability distributions for scenario analysis, modify the standard deviation or form parameters to indicate the rapidity of risk escalation, distinguishing between swiftly developing threats and those with gradual implications. Lam (2017) posits that not all risks are dispersed symmetrically; any organizational risk may instead be depicted as a bell curve, with the horizontal axis representing a spectrum of potential outcomes and the vertical axis indicating the likelihood of each occurrence (Lam, 2017). The complete curve collectively represents the overall risk profile, aiding decision-makers in comprehending both the probability and consequences of deviations from anticipated performance.

Certain risks, such as market or interest rate risk, exhibit bell curves with symmetrical probabilities for both the upside and downside, whereas others, like operational or credit risk, are typically asymmetric, presenting substantial negative potential and limited upside. Comprehending the form and asymmetry of the risk bell curve is crucial for adjusting suitable mitigation strategies and for recognizing the rapidity with which risk velocity can alter outcomes beyond anticipations (Lam, 2017). Integrating risk velocity into these tools enables decision-makers to discern not just the most severe or probable hazards but also those requiring the swiftest intervention, thus facilitating more efficient and agile risk prioritization and resource allocation (Holomozenko & Stasiuk, 2024).

Challenges, Limitations, and Pitfalls of Embedding Risk Velocity

Integrating risk velocity into enterprise risk management presents several significant issues (Acebes et al., 2024; Ramamoorti et al., 2019). Initially, objectively evaluating velocity, particularly for intricate or nascent risks, proves challenging, as numerous such threats lack historical benchmarks or clear metrics for assessing the speed at which their consequences may materialize (Hubbard & Seiersen, 2023). This uncertainty may lead to inconsistent or subjective assessments (Baloglu & Cakali, 2022), thereby compromising the credibility of prioritization within the risk portfolio. Moreover, the impetus to incorporate velocity as a tertiary component in evaluations must be weighed against the potential for excessively complicating risk frameworks. Enhancing analytical granularity can provide deeper insights (Belea, 2023), but excessive complexity may diminish the utility and clarity of risk management solutions, rendering results less actionable and accessible to decision-makers.

Organizations frequently encounter significant opposition to change, especially when transitioning from long-standing, two-dimensional evaluations to more dynamic frameworks. Integrating risk velocity necessitates revisions to policies, tools, and workflows, as well as a comprehensive cultural shift that promotes risk accountability, immediate responsiveness, and interdisciplinary collaboration. Surmounting these obstacles necessitates unwavering endorsement, specialized training, and continuous involvement to foster confidence in the significance and applicability of advancing organizational resilience (Burrell, 2023; Burrell, 2018; Burton, 2024; Burton et al., 2023).

Measurement and Data Limitations. A significant challenge is the objective assessment of velocity, particularly for new or complex risks that lack established historical standards or defined measurements. In contrast to likelihood and effect, which are typically based on documented actuarial data or loss records, risk velocity often depends on qualitative evaluations or scenario analyses, rendering outcomes vulnerable to subjectivity and variability within firms. This engenders the risk of inconsistent priority and resource misallocation.

Increased Model Complexity. Incorporating velocity as an extra analytical variable may complicate risk frameworks, introducing additional layers of calculation or evaluation that hinder clarity and usability. This complexity threatens to alienate decision-makers seeking actionable information and may diminish the overall utility of risk models if the integration lacks comprehensive training and user-friendly tools.

Organizational and Cultural Resistance. Transitioning from traditional two-dimensional (probability and impact) models to three-dimensional (adding velocity) approaches requires enterprises to rework their rules, protocols, data gathering techniques, and escalation procedures. Such moves typically encounter opposition, particularly in institutions accustomed to old systems or with cultures that are slow to adopt rapid change, transparency, or proactive risk mitigation.

Methodological and Terminological Inconsistencies. Currently, there is an absence of uniformity regarding the definition, measurement, and operationalization of risk velocity across various sectors. Diverse businesses and industries may utilize varying terminologies and methodologies for assessing velocity, which hinders benchmarking, cross-case comparison, and the widespread implementation of best practices.

Overemphasis and Dilution Risks. When velocity is prioritized excessively over likelihood and impact, businesses may distort their risk prioritizing and neglect slow-moving yet significantly consequential issues. Conversely, neglecting the distinct characteristics of velocity, particularly in relation to the development of digital risks, may result in mitigation solutions failing to keep pace with the acceleration of risk.

Technical Pitfalls with Automation and AI Integration. Automation and AI Integration

Incorporating velocity into AI-driven or automated risk management systems can lead to unforeseen repercussions, such as concealed algorithmic biases or excessive reliance on automated escalation, thereby undermining nuanced human judgment in critical situations. The dual function of AI as both an enhancer and reducer of risk velocity complicates the situation, highlighting the necessity for meticulous validation of data sources and interpretative frameworks.

By recognizing and undertaking these challenges, including measurement ambiguity, heightened complexity, organizational inertia, insufficient methodological clarity, the potential for misaligned priorities, and technical dependence, organizations can more efficiently incorporate velocity as a vital element within dynamic, resilient risk management frameworks across industries. The following are case studies of risk velocity and its impact on organizations that suffered significant risk exposure.

In-depth Case Studies Across Industries - Risk Velocity Impacts

To illustrate the practical consequences of inconsistent risk velocity oversight, four case studies across different industries are examined. The case studies pertain to the impacts of the COVID-19 Pandemic (2019-2025), CrowdStrike-Microsoft outage (2024), Change Healthcare (UnitedHealth Group) ransomware attack (2024), and the Aflac data breach (2025).

Case Study 1: COVID-19 Pandemic: The Speed of Global Disruption

Overview of the Event

In late 2019, news of a novel virus gave most worldwide organizations merely weeks to prepare for the enforcement of lockdowns and significant disruptions (AlAli, 2020; Klein, 2025; Meyer et al., 2022). By March 2020, enterprises experienced abrupt supply chain failures, facility shutdowns, and decreased demand (Ozdemir et al., 2022; Pujawan & Bah, 2022). Cross-border logistics and access to essential labor and commodities were immediately disrupted (Meyer et al., 2022). Many organizations failed to activate mitigation plans until mandated by governmental closures, leading to prolonged operational disruptions and exacerbated losses. The COVID-19 pandemic served as an unprecedented global stress test (AlAli, 2020; Klein, 2025; Meyer et al., 2022; Ozdemir et al., 2022; Pujawan & Bah, 2022), starkly illuminating the limitations of conventional risk management frameworks and underscoring the importance of understanding risk velocity.

Unlike traditional hazards that unfold within anticipated timelines (Carpenter & Wyman, 2022; McLennan, 2022), the pandemic unleashed cascading disruptions that spread with remarkable swiftness, transcending sectoral and geographic boundaries (AlAli, 2020; Klein, 2025; Meyer et al., 2022; Ozdemir et al., 2022; Pujawan & Bah, 2022). Lockdown mandates, supply chain failures, and market volatility materialized with little lead time (McLennan, 2022; van Hoek, 2021), demonstrating that the interval between risk identification and operational impact can be drastically compressed under extraordinary circumstances.

Velocity Assessment

- High-Speed Impact. The operational and financial impacts became evident within days to weeks. Even globally established, well-resourced companies were compelled to respond nearly instantaneously to successive disruptions (Klein, 2025).

Risk Assessment and Failed Risk Velocity Implementation

- Missed Early Signals. Although an authentic possibility, pandemic warnings often led many risk registers to categorize pandemics as low-probability, slow-emerging risks, resulting in a lack of preparedness for fast-moving disruptions.
- Static Plans. Over-reliance on rigid, linear mitigation frameworks inhibited organizations from rapidly reallocating resources and experimenting with temporary, trial-and-error solutions.
- Insufficient Scenario Planning. The lack of integrated, velocity-sensitive scenario analysis left businesses unable to pivot swiftly, thereby prolonging recovery times (Meyer & Miermont, 2023).

Organizational Impact

- Immediate and profound financial losses due to sunk costs and lost revenue.
- Supply chain reconfigurations and shifts to regional sourcing models.
- Accelerated digital transformation (e.g., remote work, e-commerce adoption) (Burrell, 2023).

Lessons Learned and Recommendations

- Crisis Task Forces. Empowering cross-functional teams for immediate, authoritative action is vital (Mizrak, 2024).

- Iterative Adaptation. Learning-based approaches and quick fixes help organizations keep pace with evolving crises (Burrell, 2023; Burrell, 2018; Burton, 2024; Burton et al., 2023).
- Digitalization and Transparency. Investing in digital infrastructure and dashboards enhances analysis (Wolniak, 2023) and responsiveness to high-velocity threats.
- Preparedness from Experience. Institutional learning and scenario planning can dramatically reduce future response lags (Truong et al., 2021; Yakovchenko et al., 2023.

The increasing complexity, interconnectivity, and unpredictability of organizational environments, exacerbated by the global impact of COVID-19 (AlAli, 2020; Ozdemir et al., 2022; Pujawan & Bah, 2022) and rapid technological advancements such as AI, AGI, deep learning, ML models, and autonomous response systems, have intensified the need to assess risk velocity as a core component of modern risk management (Chen et al., 2021; Ravichandran et al., 2022; Tarasenko & Steinmeier, 2024). The COVID-19 pandemic highlighted how quickly disruptions can spread across global supply chains (Klein, 2025; Pujawan & Bah, 2022), workforce operations, and financial markets, transforming what were once considered low-probability risks into rapidly unfolding crises (AlAli, 2020). Public health directives, policy shifts, and social responses were disseminated in real-time, compelling organizations to adapt their strategies, sometimes within hours, rather than relying on review cycles that historically measured risk in weeks or quarters (AlAli, 2020; Meyer et al., 2022).

Further compounding these challenges, the digitization of business operations and the ubiquity of remote work rapidly intensified cyber threats and the velocity with which vulnerabilities could be exploited (Deloitte, 2021; PwC, 2022). Fragilities once seen as distant hypotheticals, such as global shortages of critical goods or widespread system failures, became immediate operational realities. As a result, risk velocity emerged not as an optional analytic refinement but as an indispensable criterion for timely intervention, resource allocation, and organizational resilience in the face of profound systemic distress (Ivanov & Dolgui, 2021; Renn et al., 2022; Roach, 2021). The pandemic, by condensing timelines and amplifying uncertainty, accelerated the discourse and practice of dynamic, velocity-sensitive risk management.

Case Study 2: CrowdStrike-Microsoft Outage: The Speed of Widespread Business Disruption

Overview of the Events

On July 19, 2024, CrowdStrike, a leading cybersecurity firm, deployed a faulty update for its Falcon Sensor software, triggering catastrophic crashes on Microsoft

Windows systems globally (Alsowaigh, 2025; George, 2024; Ogundipe & Aweto, 2024; Sowby et al., 2025). The flaw resulted in nearly 8.5 million devices experiencing the infamous "Blue Screen of Death" (BSOD) (Venkata, 2025). Industries, ranging from airlines and hospitals to banking, retail, and government services, were paralyzed, with widespread interruptions to emergency services, stock markets, and supply chains. Financial damages are estimated to exceed $10 billion, and the outage is regarded as the most significant IT incident in history (Alsowaigh, 2025; George, 2024; Sowby et al., 2025).

The disruption did not originate from a cyberattack, but rather from a routine software update meant to improve security defenses (Alsowaigh, 2025; Sowby et al., 2025). This faulty update was pushed out universally, including to critical infrastructures, due to failures in regression testing and version validation. The error at the kernel level of Windows rendered affected systems unable to restart, immediately halting operations across the globe. Though not a traditional attack, the incident compressed the "attack chain" by removing expected segmentation and privilege controls. The routine update was pushed with insufficient staggered rollout or version checks, sending the flaw directly into production environments, including the most sensitive sectors, without isolation (Alsowaigh, 2025; Sowby et al., 2025).

Velocity Assessment

- Speed of Escalation. The outage unfolded at unprecedented speed: minutes after the update, millions of computers worldwide crashed simultaneously (Alsowaigh, 2025; Sowby et al., 2025). The velocity of disruption far outpaced standard monitoring and contingency protocols, with thousands of organizations affected before the cause was fully identified.
- Detection: CrowdStrike and Microsoft immediately identified that the incident was not a cyberattack, but a technical error within a specific update ("Channel File 291") (Alsowaigh, 2025). The companies responded within hours, publishing fixes and manual recovery steps. However, complete remediation required hands-on intervention to restore millions of affected endpoints, resulting in lingering disruptions and slow recovery for many organizations (Alsowaigh, 2025; Sowby et al., 2025).
- Response Lag. Despite quick recognition of the issue, recovery lagged significantly behind escalation. Endpoints needed manual intervention and reboots; critical services experienced delays for several days, exposing gaps in automated rollback capabilities and emergency patch deployment.

Risk Assessment and Failed Risk Velocity Implementation

- Regression Testing Failures. Missing compatibility checks failed to catch errors between old and new data formats.
- No Staggered Rollout. The update was globally deployed, leaving no time for early detection or quarantine of the flaw.
- Inadequate Version Control. Absence of version fields in configuration files prevented quick identification of compatibility issues.
- Privileged Access Risks. Falcon's kernel-level installation amplified the impact of software faults.
- Weak Emergency Protocols. Organizations lacked automated, scalable mechanisms for mass rollback and endpoint recovery, resulting in prolonged outages.

Organizational Impact

- Worldwide Service Disruptions. Airlines, hospitals, banks, manufacturers, and critical infrastructure suffered outages, canceling flights, delaying care, and interrupting financial markets.
- Multi-Billion Dollar Losses. The financial cost of the outage and subsequent lawsuits will impact CrowdStrike and its clients for years (Alsowaigh, 2025; Sowby et al., 2025).
- Reputational Harm. Questions arose regarding CrowdStrike's software quality controls and Microsoft's reliance on third-party providers for Azure services.
- Lasting Scrutiny. The outage prompted global reviews of business continuity and IT dependency, forcing boards and regulators to examine crisis response plans more closely (Alsowaigh, 2025; Sowby et al., 2025).

Lessons Learned and Recommendations

- Software Risk Velocity is as Dangerous as Malicious Activity. Well-intended updates can trigger catastrophic effects at speeds comparable to those of large-scale cyberattacks.
- Continuous Controls Monitoring. Real-time, automated controls and rollback mechanisms are essential for software updates and security updates.
- Staggered Rollouts and Version Checks. Critical updates should be tested and deployed in stages, with robust versioning and compatibility validation.
- Third-Party Risk Consideration. Dependency on external security providers introduces systemic vulnerabilities, requiring vigilant oversight of update processes and emergency recovery capability (Jones, 2021; Pujawan & Bah, 2022).

- Transparency and Incident Response. Swift, transparent communication and cross-industry cooperation minimized panic and enabled targeted recovery, while also highlighting the fragility of global digital infrastructure.

Case Study 3: Change Healthcare (UnitedHealth Group): The Speed of Ransomware and Reputation Risk

Overview of the Events

On February 21, 2024, Change Healthcare, one of the most significant medical claims processing networks in the United States and a subsidiary of UnitedHealth Group, suffered a ransomware attack (Kanter et al., 2024; Neprash et al., 2024; Streck & Meyer, 2025) by the group ALPHV Black Cat (Kanter et al., 2024). The breach rapidly halted critical transaction processing across its nationwide systems, resulting in widespread disruptions to prescription fulfillment, provider payments, and insurance claims. The American Hospital Association described the incident as the most impactful cyberattack in U.S. healthcare history (Streck & Meyer, 2025). Financial repercussions surpassed $2.8 billion, with additional billions allocated to support affected providers (Kanter et al., 2024; Streck & Meyer, 2025). Beyond immediate costs, the attack caused lasting reputational damage as clients, patients, and partners questioned Change Healthcare's ability to safeguard sensitive information and ensure business continuity (Kanter et al., 2024; Streck & Meyer, 2025). The attackers' use of trusted third-party credentials effectively bypassed perimeter controls, compressing the attack chain and accelerating the breach (Neprash et al., 2024). Insufficient risk segmentation and dynamic access restrictions on privileged vendor accounts enabled the rapid spread of malware and data theft. In some cases, sensitive records were exfiltrated for potentially millions of individuals, including patients, providers, and business partners. Exposed data included names, addresses, billing details, medical information, and insurance identifiers, raising significant risks of identity theft and medical fraud (Kanter et al., 2024; Streck & Meyer, 2025).

Velocity Assessment

- Speed of Escalation. Attack progression was swift: after compromising external credentials, attackers rapidly established persistence, traversed Change Healthcare's extensive network, and deployed ransomware within days. The velocity and scale of the attack overwhelmed routine monitoring and response protocols.
- Detection. Despite existing cybersecurity measures, the breach was detected after core systems had already been encrypted, and service outages had already occurred. Attackers were able to camouflage malicious actions amidst

legitimate network traffic. The delayed detection meant response actions, including account disabling, password resets, and network lockdowns, were executed after substantial damage had occurred.

- Response Lag. Due to the lag in threat detection and escalation, attackers were able to accomplish targeted objectives before Change Healthcare could intervene. Vendor-related risk feeds and behavioral anomaly alerts did not trigger immediate action, highlighting the significant gap between incident velocity and the company's incident response timeline.

Risk Assessment and Failed Risk Velocity Implementation

Key risk management failures contributing to the scale and velocity of the breach included:

- Reactive escalation protocols. Change Healthcare's response procedures were activated after the breach reached an advanced stage, proving inadequate against the event's explosive speed.
- Insufficient adaptive risk measures. Reliance on traditional, periodic vendor risk assessments did not account for dynamic, high-velocity threat scenarios or support real-time credential revocation for compromised accounts.

Organizational Impact

- Sensitive health and financial data for millions, spanning patients, providers, and insurers, was exposed, heightening the risk of identity theft and healthcare fraud (Kanter et al., 2024; Streck & Meyer, 2025).
- Change Healthcare and UnitedHealth Group faced regulatory investigations, lawsuits, and extensive remediation costs.
- Hundreds of thousands of physician practices, hospitals, and pharmacies using Change Healthcare's services were unable to file claims or receive payments (Kanter et al., 2024). Due to the prolonged paralysis and cumbersome transition to alternate procedures, some facilities were incapacitated in providing treatment and were confronted with financial insolvency. Trust among partners and clients eroded, resulting in reputational damage, which can affect competitive standing and business relationships for years to come (Jones, 2021; Kanter et al., 2024; Streck & Meyer, 2025).

Lessons Learned and Recommendations

- Real-time threat escalation demands and detection. Exploitation of third-party credentials can enable near-instantaneous attack progression. Organizations must deploy adaptive, automated monitoring and response that considers risk velocity, not just risk likelihood and impact.

- Delays amplify losses. Delays in detection, particularly of high-privilege or vendor-originated threats, significantly increase the magnitude of breaches. Real-time behavioral analytics and access controls are essential for containing incidents before they cascade (Wolniak, 2023).
- The emergence of AI has brought about a significant transformation in the realm of Cyber Security, specifically in the crucial domains of Identity Management and Account Takeover (ATO) prevention (Tsaliki, 2024). Organizations should employ modern, AI-driven solutions to expedite detection and response to cyber incidents.
- Trust pathways are high-risk routes. Access continues to pose significant cyber risks. Risk velocity modeling, continuous monitoring, and rapid containment protocols for third-party accounts must become standard practices in modern healthcare cybersecurity (Burrell, 2023).

Case Study 4: Aflac (2025): A Rapid Response and Reputation Risk

Overview of Events

On June 12, 2025, Aflac, one of the largest U.S. supplemental insurance providers, filed a disclosure with the U.S. Securities and Exchange Commission (SEC) (Alder, 2025; Halock, 2025; Rabb, 2025). Aflac detected suspicious activity within its internal network and announced that it had suffered a cyberattack resulting in data theft (Alder, 2025; Halock, 2025; Rabb, 2025). This swift discovery triggered immediate incident response, containing the intrusion within hours and preventing operational disruption. While ransomware was not deployed (Alder, 2025; Rabb, 2025), the scope and sensitivity of the compromised data placed affected individuals at risk of identity theft, privacy violations, and further phishing attacks. Aflac engaged third-party cybersecurity experts, notified regulators, and offered up to two years of complimentary credit and identity monitoring for impacted parties and Medical Shield coverage (Halock, 2025). The breach generated legal scrutiny (Rabb, 2025), engendering financial and reputational risk. The Aflac data breach highlighted the increasing threat of social engineering attacks targeting the insurance sector. The breach emphasized the need for continuous security awareness, strong identity verification protocols, and real-time detection capabilities to reduce both the speed of risk and potential reputational damage. Alder (2025) warned that insurance providers must remain vigilant against cyberattacks.

Velocity Assessment

- Speed of Escalation. Attackers executed a rapid intrusion after successfully leveraging social engineering tactics, including impersonating trusted Aflac employees, to gain initial access. Once inside, the adversaries moved swiftly to identify and exfiltrate valuable personal and health-related data from Aflac's internal network. Immediate detection and containment by Aflac's security team curtailed further progression (Alder, 2025; Halock, 2025).
- Detection. Aflac's existing cybersecurity controls enabled quick recognition of suspicious activity within the internal network. The breach was identified before attackers could deploy further tools (such as ransomware) to disrupt business operations (Alder, 2025). However, the use of advanced social engineering and impersonation allowed the threat actors to bypass initial identity verification protocols, blending malicious behavior with legitimate user activity and enabling the rapid exfiltration of data before containment.

Response. In contrast to incidents where detection delays amplify operational damage, Aflac's incident response team acted within hours, successfully containing the breach and preventing operational outages (Adler, 2025). However, the incident resulted in customers expressing their legal concerns (Rabb, 2025).

Risk Assessment and Failed Risk Velocity Implementation

- Incomplete adaptive controls. Pre-incident risk measures did not provide adaptive, real-time identity verification or continuous multi-factor authentication capable of challenging dynamic, high-velocity threats like Scattered Spider's attack. However, Aflac responded quickly to the attack once it was discovered and minimized further harm, such as a ransomware attack.
- Customers' legal concerns. The intrusion posed a high-risk velocity for individuals whose data was exposed, denoted by their expressed concern over Aflac's pre-incident protections (Rabb, 2025).

Organizational Impact

- Aflac faced immediate regulatory scrutiny and legal exposure, with state and federal authorities notified. The organization also committed to providing affected individuals complimentary credit and identity monitoring services and Medical Shield coverage for 24 months following the data breach (Halock, 2025).
- Customer trust was eroded due to the nature of the stolen data, which amplified reputational harm and raised concerns among business partners and pol-

icyholders about Aflac's ability to protect confidential information, as noted in the legal aftermath involving Aflac customers (Rabb, 2025).

Lessons Learned and Recommendations

- Real-time escalation and adaptive risk measures are crucial. As social engineering attacks accelerate and compromise timelines become shorter, insurance providers must employ continuous behavioral analytics, dynamic access controls, and real-time incident escalation to identify and contain threats before data can be exfiltrated.
- Every minute matters. Even rapid detection and response may not prevent substantial losses. Organizations must emphasize both prevention (resistant identity verification, social engineering training) and detection (Burton, 2024; Chen et al., 2021) to reduce breach velocity.
- Trust pathways need constant monitoring. Employee, partner, and agent credentials are prime targets for high-velocity attacks. Insurers must model risk velocity for these access points, deploy granular monitoring for unusual activity, and establish rapid credential revocation protocols to ensure high-risk accounts can be quickly isolated without operational disruption.

The four cases related to the velocity of risk are examined: the COVID-19 Pandemic, the CrowdStrike-Microsoft outage, the Change Healthcare (UnitedHealth Group) ransomware attack, and the Aflac data breach. Each of these crises highlights how the swift onset of threats can undermine even resilient organizations when the velocity of risk presents challenges. Notably, this study does not suggest that all exploits can be avoided by applying a three-dimensional approach to risk management. For example, in 2025, Microsoft suffered a zero-day exploit due to an unforeseen vulnerability (Prakash, 2025).

A lack of real-time detection-to-rapid-response processes and real-time digital sentiment analysis can preclude opportunities (Wolniak, 2023) for prompt, measured communication, converting a singular incident into a billion-dollar brand catastrophe almost instantaneously. Collectively, these case studies illustrate that without a specific focus on risk velocity, even the most thorough risk management systems may be inadequate, rendering firms incapable of keeping pace with the rapid evolution of risks and substantially increasing the potential for damage (Przetacznik, 2022). Table 1 presents a summary of the case study on risk velocity and societal and organizational resilience.

Table 1. Case Study Summary of Risk Velocity on Societal and Organizational

Case Study	Assessed Risk Velocity	Mitigation Timing	Effectiveness Drivers Needs
COVID-19 Pandemic (AlAli, 2020; Klein, 2025; Ozdemir et al., 2022; Pujawan & Bah, 2022)	High	Real-time monitoring; instant response	Pre-set triggers, coordinated global response
CrowdStrike-Microsoft Outage (Alsowaigh, 2025; George, 2025; Ogundipe & Aweto, 2024; Sowby et al., 2025)	High	Immediate escalation, public response	24/7 monitoring, crisis communication, social listening
Change Healthcare (UnitedHealth Group (Kanter et al., 2024; Neprash et al., 2024; Streck & Meyer, 2025)	Low	Weeks to months for planning	Early alerts, cross-functional coordination
Aflac Data Breach (Alder, 2025; Rabb, 2025)	Variable	Hours to days	Contingency plans, rapid, real-time supplier assessment and notification

Note: The source for Table 1 is the author of this chapter.

Each of the four case studies, from the prolonged global disruptions of the COVID-19 pandemic to the acute cyber incidents involving CrowdStrike-Microsoft, Change Healthcare, and Aflac, underscores that high-velocity risks, whether triggered by health crises, technological failures, or targeted cyberattacks, require mitigation strategies that match the immediacy and scale of the threat. These incidents underscore the need to integrate enhanced risk velocity into assessment frameworks, ensuring that risk identification is closely linked to rapid detection, precise escalation, and swift response execution. Conversely, these incidents demonstrated the unforgiving tempo of cybersecurity threats, where minutes, not days, define the difference between containment and crisis. In a hyper-connected operating environment, where disruptions propagate instantly across systems, supply chains, and stakeholder networks, aligning robust preventive controls with the tempo of emerging risks is essential for safeguarding operational resilience, financial stability, and institutional trust in an era defined by rapid, unpredictable change.

RESULTS AND RECOMMENDATIONS

In modern risk management (Awasthi, 2025; Tarasenko & Steinmeier, 2024), the concept of risk velocity has become a crucial aspect for assessing organizational hazards. Distinguishing between high-velocity and low-velocity risks is vital for effective risk prioritization, resource allocation, and the development of mitigation strategies. Most businesses encounter a portfolio of high- and low-velocity risks, necessitating the customization of mitigation strategies based on the expected pace of risk manifestation. Neglecting to consider risk velocity may lead to significant delays for rapidly evolving dangers or complacency regarding gradually intensifying threats (Baloglu & Cakali, 2022). Consequently, incorporating velocity into risk assessments improves the timing and efficacy of mitigation strategies, ensuring that resources and responses correspond with the unique requirements dictated by the nature of the risk. The capacity to identify and strategically prepare for diverse risk velocities (Roach, 2021) is therefore fundamental to effective and adaptive risk management in contemporary times.

Recognizing and strategically anticipating the implications of risk timing across pre-incident, intra-incident, and post-incident phases is indispensable for robust organizational resilience (Sari et al., 2023; Stachowiak & Pawłyszyn, 2021). Deliberate foresight into the time-based dimensions of risk allows leaders to architect tailored interventions that address vulnerabilities, ensure agile mobilization and containment during unfolding events, and enable informed recovery and adaptation in the aftermath (Sari et al., 2023). Outlined below are high-level, phase-specific actions designed to equip organizations with the proactive measures necessary to confront and manage risk with precision and agility at every stage of the threat lifecycle.

Before an Event.

Perform Scenario Planning. Develop a plan to address potential risks that could impact organizational objectives. Conduct "what-if" analyses to anticipate likely scenarios (Iqbal, 2023). Expand such exercises by employing diverse risk velocity scenarios, ranging from gradually emerging threats to those that intensify in minutes or hours, to evaluate the agility and robustness of current protocols. Additionally, for high-velocity risks, assign dedicated internal resources to scenario modeling, enabling the real-time evaluation of cascading impacts and rapid resource mobilization. Facilitate timely stakeholder engagement through targeted communication drills (Grojek et al., 2024; Truong et al., 2021), ensuring that critical decision-makers are consistently informed and ready to authorize urgent interventions. Formulate multi-tiered mitigation solutions that include not only immediate technical countermeasures (Harris et al., 2024) but also the proactive adaptation of organizational workflows, periodic review and modification of response policies, and ongoing investment in automated detection and response platforms. By establishing an infrastructure that supports continuous scenario-based learning (Iqbal, 2023) and rapid escalation for fast-moving risks, organizations foster resilience, adaptability, and sustained readiness in the face of increasingly dynamic threat environments (Jones, 2021, 2024; Sari et al., 2023).

Execute Pre-approved, Rapid-Response Playbooks. Develop and implement well-rehearsed, step-by-step mitigation efforts tailored to the specific incident (Yakovchenko et al., 2023). Formulate specialized mitigation playbooks for high-velocity risks, including cyberattacks or reputational threats, that feature pre-approved actions requiring no further deliberation during crises (Stevens et al., 2022; Yakovchenko et al., 2023). Incorporate decision and communication models into risk management, utilizing automated systems or process triggers (Dawson et al., 2024). To address the unique demands of risk velocity, embed explicit time thresholds and escalation pathways within the playbooks to ensure that responses remain agile and immediate, precluding delays that could amplify organizational exposure or operational disruption (Stevens et al., 2022; Yakovchenko et al., 2023).

Conduct Drills. Before an incident, conduct debriefs based on simulated scenarios to reinforce learning and improve protocols (Grojek et al., 2024; Truong et al., 2021). Ensuring relevant cross-functional teams practice implementing plans within constrained timescales (Agner, 2021; Sari et al., 2023). These exercises should actively challenge participants to operate under realistic stressors and abbreviated timelines, enhancing their capacity for swift coordination and decisive action during genuine emergencies (Grojek et al., 2024; Truong et al., 2021). By cultivating interdepartmental familiarity with time-sensitive protocols through repeated rehearsal, organizations foster a culture of readiness and collective accountability (Efunniyi et al., 2024) that significantly elevates overall incident response effectiveness (Agner, 2021; Grojek et al., 2024; Sari et al., 2023; Truong et al., 2021).

Implement Regular AI-based Training. Proactively conduct ongoing AI-based training to ensure teams are prepared for various scenarios. Implement continuous training programs that inform personnel at all tiers about the significance of risk velocity and the designated processes for swift reaction (Burrell, 2018; Burton, 2024). Implement awareness campaigns to enhance recognition of velocity-based key risk indicators, escalation triggers, and procedural modifications (Ansari et al., 2022). Consistent training ensures that teams remain alert, grasp their responsibilities (Burrell, 2018; Burton, 2024; Jones, 2024), and can respond decisively in fast-paced scenarios, thereby minimizing the chances of delays or confusion during an actual event (Burrell, 2018; Nobles & Burrell, 2024).

Monitor Systems. Establish real-time or near-real-time systems to detect emerging threats (Ebute, 2024; Wolniak, 2023). To mitigate high-velocity risks and slow-emerging risks, firms must implement continuous tools (Ebute, 2024), such as AI-driven threat identification, social media analysis, or supply chain analytics, that deliver immediate alerts upon the activation of key risk indicators (KRIs). The importance of risk velocity lies in its ability to rapidly escalate organizational exposure, requiring the prompt detection and escalation of threats to prevent their amplification or spread across critical infrastructures.

At Risk Trigger.

Execute Notification and Escalation Protocols. Be prepared for the notification of an occurrence and activate predefined communication and action plans as soon as a risk indicator crosses critical thresholds (Grojek et al., 2024). Formulate and document standardized escalation procedures that are triggered automatically or promptly upon the breach of a high-velocity risk threshold. This encompasses specifying the individuals to be notified, the actions authorized without executive authorization, and the systems implicated in the response.

Plan Activation. Initiate preestablished response protocols to address the situation effectively. Note any required deviations from the plan (Grojek et al., 2024). Carefully consider the velocity at which risks materialize and escalate, so that rapid threats trigger immediate escalation steps while slower-moving threats allow for more controlled responses (Ramamoorti et al., 2019). As risk velocity increases, ensure that contingency measures and escalation paths are dynamically adapted to prevent response lag and secondary impacts (Ramamoorti et al., 2019). Promptly record any deviations necessitated by the pace or unpredictability of unfolding events, allowing for post-incident evaluation and optimization of response frameworks for future high-velocity scenarios.

Deploy Automated Safeguards. Implement automatic controls or interventions (such as system shutdowns or alerts) in case of rapidly developing events. Where high-risk velocity is evident, leverage automated mechanisms to ensure immediate engagement of containment measures, minimizing the time between threat detection and remediation. Deploy autonomous system-driven responses (Kinyua & Awuah, 2021) to prevent escalation and limit adverse impacts in scenarios where manual intervention might be too slow (Chen et al., 2021). Autonomous response systems integrating generative AI, AGI, deep learning, and machine learning models not only foster rapid containment but also enable real-time monitoring and adaptive risk management, allowing critical systems to remain resilient amid swiftly unfolding threats.

After Response (and partially during).

Conduct After Action Reviews. Acquire feedback from stakeholders (Paul, 2021). Through structured debriefings and methodical analysis of incident responses or major security events, organizations can extract critical insights into response efficacy and areas of vulnerability (Paul, 2021). Systematically integrating lessons learned from reviews into revised policies and training programs not only rectifies identified weaknesses but also fortifies the organization's preparedness for future contingencies (Burrell, 2018; Burton, 2024; Burton et al., 2023).

Capture Updates. Understand what happened, note changes in risk evaluation, and adjust the risk management framework based on the event's outcomes (Salihu & Dervishi, 2024). Update the risk register, governance documents, including communications plans, and safeguards. For the risk register, record risk velocity as a parameter. Categorize hazards using a rating system (Salihu & Dervishi, 2024), such as high, medium, or low velocity, and synchronize mitigation deadlines and responsibilities accordingly. Implementing these practical measures allows firms to synchronize response actions with the pace of risk emergence, maintaining agility against rapidly evolving threats while optimizing resource allocation for increasingly complex challenges. Furthermore, implementing these practical steps can provide benefits for the organization. Update policy and guidance documents, communication plans, and technical controls (Salihu & Dervishi, 2024).

Perform Drills and Simulations. After action, run debriefs or simulations to reinforce learning and improve protocols (Truong et al., 2021). Regularly conduct simulations or tabletop exercises that particularly evaluate response times for high-velocity events (Agner, 2021; Sari et al., 2023). These exercises should be designed to stress-test both automated and manual controls by simulating rapidly evolving threat scenarios, ensuring that incident response teams are adept at recognizing and adapting to abrupt surges in risk (Grojek et al., 2024; Truong et al., 2021). Through realistic and time-compressed drills and cross-functional collaboration, organizations can identify procedural blockages, measure time-to-containment metrics, and assess the efficacy of escalation protocols under pressured conditions (Truong et al, 2021). Integrating these findings into continuous improvement cycles fosters an environment where teams remain vigilant and capable of rapidly mitigating high-velocity incidents, ultimately enhancing their resilience to swift and unpredictable threats.

Incorporate Continuous Enhancements. Continuously update the ability to respond to risks effectively by identifying opportunities for betterment. This process necessitates the systematic evaluation of existing protocols, incorporating emerging threat intelligence and technological advancements to drive adaptive change. In particular, attention must be paid to the velocity at which risks emerge and escalate (Ramamoorti et al., 2017; Ramamoorti et al., 2019). Rapidly evolving threats demand accelerated review cycles and prompt remedial action to prevent escalation. Organizations should establish agile mechanisms for rapidly reassessing and integrating new controls that directly address fast-moving or time-sensitive risks (Awasthi, 2025; Mizrak, 2024). This ensures that response capabilities evolve in tandem with threat dynamics (Chen et al., 2021; Louisot, 2024; Mizrak, 2024). By fostering an organizational culture committed to iterative refinement and proactive vigilance, leaders can ensure sustained resilience and optimal alignment with the evolving cybersecurity landscape, efficiently managing the pace and scope of emerging cyber threats (Jones, 2021).

This high-level set of activities helps organizations become more resilient to both rapidly emerging and slowly evolving risks, supporting ongoing improvement. Figure 1 illustrates the Risk Response Phases-to-Action Timeline, which outlines high-level activities for pre-, during-, and post-event actions, emphasizing the interconnectedness of steps throughout a risk event's lifecycle.

Figure 1. Risk Response Phases-to-Actions Timeline

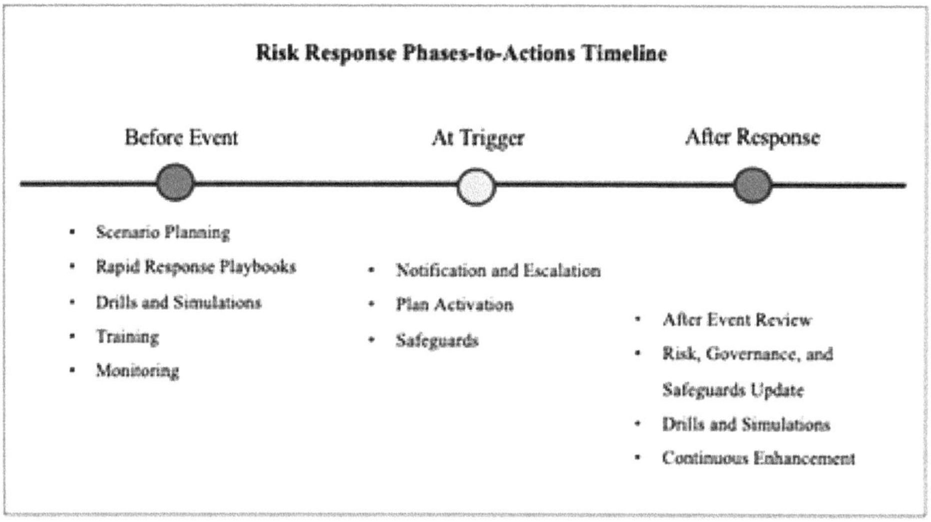

Note. The source for this figure is the author of this chapter.

CONCLUSION

Although significant advancements have been made in enterprise risk management, most conventional methodologies continue to emphasize the probability and consequences of risks (Baloglu & Cakali, 2022), while overlooking the rapidity with which a danger can propagate and destabilize an organization. This oversight renders companies susceptible to delayed and inadequate responses (Baloglu & Cakali, 2022), as evidenced by substantial financial losses, extended project delays, escalating costs resulting from cybersecurity incidents, and heightened reputational damage, leading most executives to prioritize fast-moving risks as their primary concern. Businesses must be vigilant with their security controls, be it human-centered

(Nobles & Burrell, 2024), technical, managerial, or administrative, as organizations can be left with zero days to prepare or defend (Prakash, 2025). To protect against zero-day attacks, companies must adopt a proactive, layered defense strategy that anticipates unknown vulnerabilities rather than relying solely on known exploits (Prakash, 2025). This includes deploying advanced threat detection technologies, such as behavioral analytics and AI-driven anomaly monitoring, that can identify suspicious activity indicative of zero-day exploitation before widespread damage occurs. Additionally, technical controls should be tended with regularity to ensure their effectiveness.

For example, patch management programs should be rigorous and nimble, with the capability to prioritize and implement emergency updates as soon as new information surfaces. Network segmentation, strict access controls, and the principle of least privilege help minimize lateral movement in the event of a compromise (Ebute, 2024). Continuous security awareness training for employees further reduces their susceptibility to social engineering techniques, which are often used in conjunction with zero-day exploits (Prakash, 2025). Finally, establishing robust, regularly tested incident response plans ensures that detection, containment, and mitigation actions can be executed at pace, thereby limiting the fallout from even the most rapidly evolving threats (Grojek et al., 2024; Truong et al., 2021). By integrating these adaptive and anticipatory controls, organizations strengthen their defenses against the unpredictable and rapidly evolving landscape of zero-day attacks (Prakash, 2025). Maintaining a focus on security controls coupled with the high-level activities of the Risk Response Phases-to-Action Timeline can reduce the risk of exploits.

Collectively, these approaches related to risk velocity signify a paradigm shift in organizational risk management (Parkin, 2021). The recognition that the temporal dimension, how quickly a risk can impact the organization, is as critical as probability and impact has inspired more nuanced, responsive, and resilient risk strategies (Baloglu & Cakali, 2022; Hillson, 2023). By integrating risk velocity into assessment protocols and theoretical models, organizations are better equipped to anticipate, prioritize, and manage the full spectrum of contemporary threats (Baloglu & Cakali, 2022; Hillson, 2023). Moving forward, research should abandon static, two-dimensional frameworks in favor of dynamic, context-adaptive models that incorporate velocity, complex system interactions, and emerging technological threats. Methodological pluralism, melding quantitative robustness with qualitative depth, should guide future inquiry (Benson & Arksey, 2021; Crotty & Daniel, 2022; Low et al., 2022; Miri & Macke, 2022). Furthermore, the next generation of risk assessment frameworks must address systemic vulnerabilities (George, 2024; Renn et al., 2022), regional disparities, and under-theorized threat landscapes. The path forward is thus one of critical expansion, methodological innovation, and a relentless pursuit of practical relevance guided by empirical evidence and real-time contextual awareness.

To adapt to these accelerated conditions, incorporating risk velocity into risk assessment and utilizing generative AI, deep learning, and machine learning models in GRC platforms is crucial for prioritizing imminent threats (Adisuria & Jayadi, 2023; Awasthi, 2025), implementing mitigation techniques in real-time, and enhancing organizational resilience (Wolniak, 2023). Integrating risk velocity into risk intelligence will help advance three-dimensional risk models (Roach, 2021). High-velocity risks, such as cyber catastrophes or reputational crises exacerbated by viral social media, necessitate prompt escalation (Jones, 2021; Louisot, 2024; Ryzhakova et al., 2024), but slower-moving challenges, such as regulatory developments, require ongoing strategic planning.

A three-dimensional risk model that integrates likelihood, impact, and velocity (Ravichandran, 2021) allows firms to allocate resources effectively, enhance crisis response, and safeguard stakeholder value in an environment characterized by constant change and disruption. The insights from the post-pandemic period (Klein, 2025) and the transformative impact of AI highlight that recognizing the rapid emergence of risk is now equally crucial as assessing the probability or severity of those risks (Naim, 2022).

Recommendations for Technology Implementation to Cultivate Organizational Agility

Invest in adaptive, modular Enterprise Risk Management (ERM) and Governance, Risk, and Compliance (GRC) platforms that inherently incorporate risk velocity indicators, including probability and effect, allowing organizations to visualize and prioritize the speed and magnitude of emerging threats. In addition, integrate AI-based detection and automatic response systems into these platforms to reduce latency between risk identification and mitigation, thus enhancing real-time resilience against rapid threats. Organizations should implement ongoing technological training initiatives for their workforce, emphasizing scenario-based learning, velocity-aware escalation procedures, and role-specific duties under time constraints. This approach equips teams to respond swiftly and efficiently to emerging and evolving risks. Additionally, advocate for the implementation of digital simulations, drills, and tabletop exercises that assess the organization's responsiveness to high-velocity crises, thereby fostering continuous improvement of both automatic and manual controls.

Revising Policies, Risk Assessment Instruments, and Governance Frameworks

Recognizing risk velocity as a crucial element in risk assessment significantly enhances mitigation and response strategies by ensuring organizations consider not only the probability and impact of adverse events but also the speed at which those events may influence operations, reputation, or financial stability (Jones, 2021; Louisot, 2024; Ryzhakova et al., 2024). Organizations must revise their current rules and tools to mandate the evaluation of risk velocity during the risk identification, analysis, and mitigation planning processes. Amend risk assessment procedures to require the reporting of velocity for each risk and to set minimum requirements for monitoring and escalation deadlines.

To address organizational resistance, leaders must integrate velocity requirements into risk policies, offer interdisciplinary training, and implement scenario-based drills that highlight the rationale and operational significance of velocity-aware practices, bolstered by ongoing communication from senior management to promote cultural assimilation. In terms of ethics and governance, it is essential to align swift automated actions with robust oversight mechanisms, including pre-approved thresholds for automated responses, transparent audit trails, and periodic evaluations by governance entities to ensure fairness, reduce algorithmic bias, and maintain human judgment for decisions with substantial stakeholder implications.

Revise risk assessment instruments, such as risk matrices and scoring rubrics, to include a third axis or scoring column for velocity (Baloglu & Cakali, 2022) and ensure that software platforms and dashboards can integrate this supplementary data. Governance frameworks must be modified to incorporate speed as a criterion for escalation and resource distribution; for instance, high-velocity threats should automatically convene response teams (Grojek et al., 2024) or activate established authority to circumvent regular approval processes (Mizrak, 2024). Conduct policy audits and provide training to governance entities on the importance and implementation of risk velocity, ensuring that all oversight bodies comprehend their responsibilities in rapid-response situations (National Institute of Standards and Technology, 2024).

Actionable Activities for Advancing Risk Velocity

To effectively integrate risk velocity into risk frameworks, enterprises must include risk velocity as a common attribute in their risk registers, heat maps, and assessment frameworks (Baloglu & Cakali, 2022). This process begins with the establishment of explicit, organization-specific criteria for classifying risk velocity (e.g., immediate, quick, moderate, slow) and associating these classifications with customized reaction expectations. Incorporate velocity ratings directly into ERM dashboards and reporting templates to emphasize which risks necessitate immediate attention. Engage cross-functional teams in scenario planning exercises (Grojek et al., 2024) that consider the probability, impact, and velocity of emerging risks. Consistently assess actual incident timelines about risk velocity ratings to verify and refine criteria. Incorporating risk velocity into risk prioritization and reporting, underscored by the use of autonomous platforms, enables businesses to empower decision-makers to respond promptly and decisively to swiftly evolving risks (Baloglu & Cakali, 2022).

In contrast to conventional models that may assess two risks similarly based on probability and consequence (Acebes et al., 2024), an awareness of risk velocity allows organizations to differentiate between threats that could manifest within hours and those that develop over months or years, thereby facilitating customized interventions and resource distribution for each scenario. Rapidly escalating risks, such as a viral social media event or a significant cyberattack (Jones, 2021), can evolve into comprehensive crises before traditional escalation pathways or deliberative governance mechanisms can commence, highlighting the imperative for automated controls, pre-approved response protocols, and practiced drills to be established in advance (Grojek et al., 2024; Truong et al., 2021).

To enhance agility and resilience against rapid risks, businesses must prioritize empowering teams to make prompt, decentralized decisions (Goraya et al., 2024) once velocity thresholds are reached. Develop and rehearse rapid-response playbooks that clearly delineate explicit responsibilities, escalation protocols, and the authority to act autonomously (Chen et al., 2021), without requiring protracted approvals (Stevens et al., 2022; Yakovchenko et al., 2023). Invest in continuous training and immersive scenario-based exercises that replicate high-velocity risk situations, enhancing team cohesion and situational awareness. Promote a culture that values accountability (Efunniyi et al., 2024) by analyzing near-misses and significant occurrences through post-event assessments and promptly incorporating the insights gained into protocols and procedures (Burton et al., 2023; Jones, 2021). Utilize digital instruments to automate preliminary alert notifications, interdepartmental communication, and crisis management coordination. By institutionalizing these practices, businesses may swiftly reallocate resources, resume operations, and modify strategies, ensuring that resilience is not only a theoretical objective but a tangible capability in real-world, time-sensitive situations. Successfully navigating the current volatile risk environment requires more than simply assessing the probability and potential consequences of negative occurrences (Mizrak, 2024; Möller, 2023).

Organizations must consider the rate at which risks develop, a factor that can significantly impact the timing, efficacy, and coordination of mitigation strategies (Jones, 2021, 2024; Louisot, 2024). In light of rapid digital disruptions, supply chain disturbances, and reputational issues, it is crucial to comprehend the nature of existing risks and their potential for swift realization to ensure robust and proactive risk management (Jones, 2021; Louisot, 2024; Ozdemir et al., 2022; Ryzhakova et al., 2024). This section examines the pivotal importance of risk velocity in formulating mitigation methods, emphasizing that the rate at which threats intensify should directly impact the design, implementation, and continuous improvement of risk response systems.

High-velocity risks are defined by their rapid emergence and quick escalation, frequently providing organizations with limited opportunity to respond before substantial consequences occur. These dangers commonly require prompt notice and action due to their capacity to undermine operations, reputation, or safety swiftly (Jones, 2021). A cybersecurity problem can rapidly grow, compromising critical information and undermining stakeholder trust before traditional crisis management strategies can be implemented entirely (Ebute, 2024; Klein, 2025). The brief interval between the risk trigger and its consequences necessitates that risk managers depend on real-time monitoring systems (Parkin, 2021; Wolniak, 2023), automated controls, and established escalation mechanisms to guarantee timely and effective mitigation. High-velocity risks underscore the importance of operational agility, technological readiness, and the ability to make prompt, decisive decisions under time constraints (Parkin, 2021).

Conversely, low-velocity risks are characterized by impacts that unfold gradually, frequently over weeks, months, or even years (Parkin, 2021). Risks such as legislative changes, demographic shifts, and the slow decline of brand reputation provide firms additional time to identify, assess, and formulate thorough reaction strategies (Jones, 2021; Louisot, 2024; Ryzhakova et al., 2024). The gradual emergence of these threats facilitates a more intentional and collaborative approach to risk reduction, allowing for comprehensive scenario planning, stakeholder involvement, and systemic modification of company strategies. Regulatory changes rarely have an immediate impact, allowing firms to evaluate compliance obligations, seek legal counsel, and adjust operational processes methodically. While the need to respond is diminished, the long-term consequences of low-velocity hazards can be significant, altering competitive landscapes or jeopardizing organizational viability if neglected. The incorporation of risk velocity as a third dimension of risk assessment is not only essential but also a strategic imperative (Baloglu & Cakali, 2022).

FUTURE RESEARCH DIRECTIONS

This study presents practical guidelines for incorporating risk velocity into risk assessment systems. This encompasses strategic planning, comprehensive data monitoring systems, the implementation of autonomous response systems (Chen et al., 2021), and ongoing training to ensure sustained awareness and effectiveness (Burton, 2024; Burton et al, 2023). The research advocates for a measured approach to integrating risk velocity, ensuring that the advantages of risk management are leveraged without compromising the core process of assessing and prioritizing risk.

Future research should formulate and evaluate quantitative models that explicitly incorporate risk velocity into current risk assessment frameworks. This may entail the development of AI-enhanced risk matrices or improved heat maps that incorporate velocity as a fundamental variable alongside likelihood and impact. The duration of risk is another component that needs to be integrated (Baloglu & Cakali, 2022). Simulation studies utilizing historical and hypothetical risk incidents can assess the usefulness of incorporating velocity, evaluating enhancements in risk prioritizing, resource allocation, and loss mitigation. Assessing the quantitative integration of risk velocity will determine whether firms that consider risk velocity achieve significantly faster and more efficient responses to rapidly evolving risks, thereby confirming the role of risk velocity in mitigating losses and enhancing overall risk management outcomes.

Researchers should conduct comparative case studies across various highly regulated industries to investigate how firms currently interpret, operationalize, and benefit from risk velocity in assessment processes. This should encompass comprehensive interviews with risk professionals, examination of incident reports, and benchmarking against industry standards to identify exemplary practices and obstacles to implementation. This research will uncover sector-specific challenges and successes, illustrating where risk velocity yields the most substantial improvements in reactive capability and strategic resilience. Results will guide the customization of assessment instruments to align with industry requirements and facilitate the broader implementation of risk velocity and meaningful methodologies. This equilibrium is essential for optimizing the beneficial effects of incorporating risk velocity as a fundamental component of risk assessment (Baloglu & Cakali, 2022).

Lastly, it is recommended that researchers conduct longitudinal studies to examine the impact of standardizing and integrating risk velocity and duration into GRC systems. Researchers should track changes in the precision of the risk register, incident response durations, the extent of losses, and organizational learning. This investigation can help validate the enduring importance of risk velocity in fostering more adaptive and resilient companies and elucidate how an ongoing focus on risk velocity can perpetuate enhancements in risk culture and readiness beyond the initial implementation.

REFERENCES

Acebes, F., González-Varona, J. M., López-Paredes, A., & Pajares, J. (2024). Beyond probability-impact matrices in project risk management: A quantitative methodology for risk prioritisation. *Humanities & Social Sciences Communications*, *11*(1), 1–13. DOI: 10.1057/s41599-024-03180-5

Adisuria, K. F., & Jayadi, R. (2023). Analysis Of The Implementation GRC Information System in Supporting Performance Optimization. [JOISM]. *Journal of Information System Management*, *4*(2), 97–106. DOI: 10.24076/joism.2023v4i2.975

Adler, S. (2025, June). Aflac Latest Insurer to Suffer Cyberattack and Data Breach. The HIPAA Journal. https://www.hipaajournal.com/aflac-data-breach/

Agner, J. (2021). Tabletop exercises. In *a guide to healthcare facility dress rehearsal simulation planning: simplifying the complex* (pp. 55-62). Emerald Publishing Limited. DOI: 10.1108/978-1-80117-554-820211006

AlAli, M. S. (2020). Risk velocity and financial markets performance: measuring the early effect of COVID-19 pandemic on major stock markets performance. *International Journal of Economics and Financial Research, 10.*

Aldemir, T. (2024). Dynamic probabilistic risk assessment (PRA): Theory, tools, and applications for uncertainty quantification. In *Risk-Informed Methods and Applications in Nuclear and Energy Engineering* (pp. 43-54). Academic Press.

Alsowaigh, R. E. (2025). CrowdStrike Causes Global Microsoft Outage: A Case Study. *Journal of Information Security and Cybercrimes Research*, *8*(1), 63–76. DOI: 10.26735/QHDD4798

Anderson, E. J. (2024). *Business risk management: models and analysis*. John Wiley & Sons.

Ansari, M. F., Sharma, P. K., & Dash, B. (2022). Prevention of phishing attacks using AI-based Cybersecurity Awareness Training. *Prevention*, *3*(6), 61–72. DOI: 10.47893/IJSSAN.2022.1221

Awasthi, A. (2025). GRC automation in manufacturing modernizing compliance and risk management. *International Journal of Computer Engineering and Technology*, *16*(1), 10–34218.

Baloglu, G., & Cakali, K. R. (2022). Missing Aspects of the Risk: Speed and Duration. *Journal of Economics Finance and Accounting*, *9*(1), 12–21. DOI: 10.17261/Pressacademia.2022.1541

Belea, A. R. (2023, May). Methods for detecting malware using static, dynamic and hybrid analysis. *In Proceedings of the International Conference on Cybersecurity and Cybercrime-2023*, (pp. 258-*265). Asociatia Romana pentru Asigurarea Securitatii Informatiei.*

Benson, A., & Arksey, H. (2021). Qualitative research using secondary data: A systematic review. *BMC Medical Research Methodology*, *21*(1), 29. PMID: 33568059

Berenson, C. (2023). Identifying a tradition of inquiry: Articulating research assumptions. In *SoTL in Action* (pp. 42–52). Routledge. DOI: 10.4324/9781003447047-7

Burrell, D. N. (2018). An Exploration of the Critical Need for Formal Training in Leadership for Cybersecurity and Technology Management Professionals. *International Journal of Hyperconnectivity and the Internet of Things*, *2*(1), 52–67. DOI: 10.4018/IJHIoT.2018010105

Burrell, D. N. (2023). *Transformational interventions for business, technology, and healthcare*. IGI Global. DOI: 10.4018/979-8-3693-1634-4

Burton, S. L. (2024). Advancements in AI-Driven Education: Transforming Learning and Training with Intelligent Technologies. *World Journal of Business Research*, *4*(1), 9.

Burton, S. L., Burrell, D. N., Nobles, C., & Jones, L. A. (2023). Exploring the nexus of cybersecurity leadership, human factors, emotional intelligence, innovative work behavior, and critical leadership traits. *Scientific Bulletin-Nicolae Balcescu Land Forces Academy*, *28*(2), 162–175. DOI: 10.2478/bsaft-2023-0016

Bylund, P. L. (2021). Introduction to the special issue on the centenary of Frank H. Knight's risk, uncertainty, and profit. *Journal of Institutional Economics*, *17*(6), 877–881. DOI: 10.1017/S1744137421000564

Carpenter, G., & Wyman, O. (2022). Realizing New Possibilities. 2022 Annual Report. Marsh & McLennan. https://www.marshmclennan.com/assets/v2/investors/2022/MarshMcLennan 2022AnnualReport.pdf

Chen, H., Wen, Y., Zhu, M., Huang, Y., Xiao, C., Wei, T., & Hahn, A. (2021). From automation system to autonomous system: An architecture perspective. *Journal of Marine Science and Engineering*, *9*(6), 645. DOI: 10.3390/jmse9060645

Committee of Sponsoring Organizations of the Treadway Commission (COSO). (2004). *Enterprise risk management—Integrated framework: Executive summary.* COSO. https://www.coso.org

Connor, H. (2024). John Graunt FRS (1620-74): The founding father of human demography, epidemiology and vital statistics. *Journal of Medical Biography*, *32*(1), 57–69. DOI: 10.1177/09677720221079826 PMID: 35167377

Couretas, J. M. (2022). Cyber Policy, Doctrine, and Tactics, Techniques, and Procedures (TTPs). In *An Introduction to Cyber Analysis and Targeting* (pp. 13–36). Springer International Publishing. DOI: 10.1007/978-3-030-88559-5_2

Crotty, J., & Daniel, E. (2022). Cyber threat: its origins and consequence and the use of qualitative and quantitative methods in cyber risk assessment. *Applied Computing and Informatics*, (ahead-of-print).

Dawson, C., Julku, H., Pihlajamäki, M., Kaakinen, J. K., Schooler, J. W., & Simola, J. (2024). Evidence-based scientific thinking and decision-making in everyday life. *Cognitive Research: Principles and Implications*, *9*(1), 50. DOI: 10.1186/s41235-024-00578-2 PMID: 39110276

Dhakal, K. (2022). NVivo. *Journal of the Medical Library Association: JMLA*, *110*(2), 270. DOI: 10.5195/jmla.2022.1271 PMID: 35440911

Dodla, T. R., & Jones, L. A. (2023). Mitigating knowledge management internal and external risk factors: A literature review of best practices. *Scientific Bulletin-Nicolae Balcescu Land Forces Academy*, *28*(1), 44–54. DOI: 10.2478/bsaft-2023-0005

Ebute, M. (2024). CONTINUOUS MONITORING AND ASSESSMENT MECHANISMS IN CYBERSECURITY: BEST PRACTICES FOR SUSTAINED PROTECTION OF CRITICAL ASSETS. *Available at SSRN* 4912624. DOI: 10.2139/ssrn.4912624

Efunniyi, C. P., Abhulimen, A. O., Obiki-Osafiele, A. N., Osundare, O. S., Agu, E. E., & Adeniran, I. A.Christianah Pelumi EfunniyiAngela Omozele AbhulimenAnwuli Nkemchor Obiki-OsafieleOlajide Soji OsundareEdith Ebele AguIbrahim Adedeji Adeniran. (2024). Strengthening corporate governance and financial compliance: Enhancing accountability and transparency. *Finance & Accounting Research Journal*, *6*(8), 1597–1616. DOI: 10.51594/farj.v6i8.1509

Fisher, G. G., Chaffee, D. S., & Petery, G. A. (2024). Research using archival data. In *Advanced research methods for applied psychology* (pp. 87–98). Routledge. DOI: 10.4324/9781003362715-9

Gambín, Á. F., Yazidi, A., Vasilakos, A., Haugerud, H., & Djenouri, Y. (2024). Deepfakes: Current and future trends. *Artificial Intelligence Review*, *57*(3), 64. DOI: 10.1007/s10462-023-10679-x

Gazzan, M., Alobaywi, B., Almutairi, M., & Sheldon, F. T. (2025). A Deep Learning Framework for Enhanced Detection of Polymorphic Ransomware. *Future Internet, 17*(7), 311. DOI: 10.3390/fi17070311

George, A. S. (2024). When trust fails: Examining systemic risk in the digital economy from the 2024 crowdstrike outage. *Partners Universal Multidisciplinary Research Journal, 1*(2), 134–152.

Goraya, M. A. S., Yaqub, M. Z., Khan, M. A., Akram, M. S., & Alofaysan, H. (2024). Transforming performance: How agility, response, resilience and support shape success in digital strategies. *Information Technology & People.*

Grojek, A. E., Sikos, L. F., Holmes, D. J., & Guidetti, O. (2024). Incident response drills on cyber ranges. *Psybersecurity: Human Factors of Cyber Defence*, 202.

Guillen, D. (2022). A Simpler Annuity. *undergraduate research journal volume 16*, 102.

Halkias, D., Neubert, M., Thurman, P. W., & Harkiolakis, N. (2022). *The multiple case study design: Methodology and application for management education.* Routledge. DOI: 10.4324/9781003244936

Halock (2025). Aflac Breach Shows Value Of Rapid Response. https://www.halock.com/aflac-breach-shows-value-of-rapid-response/

Hamir, H., & Sum, R. M. (2021). An analysis of risk management processes and comparison with ISO31000: 2018. *Asian Journal of Research in Business and Management, 3*(4), 16–30.

Hardjomidjojo, H., Pranata, C., & Baigorria, G. (2022, July). Rapid assessment model on risk management based on ISO 31000: 2018. [). IOP Publishing.]. *IOP Conference Series. Earth and Environmental Science, 1063*(1), 012043. DOI: 10.1088/1755-1315/1063/1/012043

Hardy, M. R., & Saunders, D. (2022). *Quantitative enterprise risk management.* Cambridge University Press. DOI: 10.1017/9781009089470

Harris, E., Harris, J., & Beall, M. (2024). Defense in depth: An action plan to increase the safety and security of advanced AI. *Gladstone AI, available upon request at* https://www. gladstone. ai/action-plan

Hillson, D. (Ed.). (2023). *The Risk Management Handbook: A practical guide to managing the multiple dimensions of risk.* Kogan Page Publishers.

Holomozenko, V., & Stasiuk, Y. (2024). Risk in management decisions of the modern organization and methods of management of this risk. *Challenges and Issues of Modern Science, 2*, 377–381.

Hu, Y., Parhizkar, T., & Mosleh, A. (2022). Guided simulation for dynamic probabilistic risk assessment of complex systems: Concept, method, and application. *Reliability Engineering & System Safety, 217*, 108047. DOI: 10.1016/j.ress.2021.108047

Hubbard, D. W., & Seiersen, R. (2023). *How to measure anything in cybersecurity risk*. John Wiley & Sons. DOI: 10.1002/9781119892335

IBM and the Ponemon Institute. (2024). Cost of a data breach 2024: Financial Industry. https://www.ibm.com/think/insights/cost-of-a-data-breach-2024-financial-industry

International Organization for Standardization. (2018). *ISO 31000:2018 risk management — Guidelines*. https://www.iso.org/standard/65694.html

Iqbal, M. (2023, January). Probability and Impact Matrix: PMP/CAPM. Monte Carlo Simulation Tool. *Mudassir Iqbal*. https://mudassiriqbal.net/probability-and-impact-matrix/

Ivanov, D., & Dolgui, A. (2022). Stress testing supply chains and creating viable ecosystems. *Operations Management Research : Advancing Practice Through Research, 15*(1), 475–486. DOI: 10.1007/s12063-021-00194-z

Jones, L. A. (2021). A content analysis review of literature to create a useable framework for reputation risk management. Handbook of Research on Multidisciplinary Perspectives on Managerial and Leadership Psychology, 91-133. DOI: 10.4018/978-1-7998-3811-1.ch006

Jones, L. A. (2024). *Cybersecurity Leadership: Traversing The Interminable Prospective For Cyber Risk Transmogrification*. https://www.researchgate.net/publication/394356399_cybersecurity_ leadership_ traversing_the_interminable_prospective_for_cyber_risk_transmogrification

Kanter, G. P., Rekowski, J. R., & Kannarkat, J. T. (2024, September). Lessons from the Change Healthcare ransomware attack. []. American Medical Association.]. *JAMA Health Forum, 5*(9), e242764–e242764. DOI: 10.1001/jamahealthforum.2024.2764 PMID: 39302668

Kinyua, J., & Awuah, L. (2021). AI/ML in Security Orchestration, Automation and Response: Future Research Directions. *Intelligent Automation & Soft Computing, 28*(2), 527–545. DOI: 10.32604/iasc.2021.016240

Klein, M. (2025). NOT OFF-LIMITS: AN EMPIRICAL STUDY OF COVID-19 CYBERSECURITY.

Kummer, T. F., & Mendling, J. (2021). The effect of risk representation using colors and symbols in business process models on operational risk management performance. *Journal of the Association for Information Systems, 22*(3), 649–694. DOI: 10.17705/1jais.00676

Lam, J. (2017). *Implementing Risk Management: From Methods to Application.* Wiley. DOI: 10.1002/9781118922415

Landoll, D. (2021). *The security risk assessment handbook: A complete guide for performing security risk assessments.* CRC press. DOI: 10.1201/9781003090441

Leung, M. (n.d.). The beginning of probability and statistics. University of Texas at El Paso, Department of Mathematical Sciences. https://www.math.utep.edu/faculty/mleung/probabilityandstatistics/beg.html

Louisot, J. P. (2024). Managing Risk to Reputation. In *Enterprise Risk Management in Today's World: A Current and Futuristic View of the Complexity, Resilience, Responsibility and Tools in ERM, Part B* (pp. 105-115). Emerald Publishing Limited. DOI: 10.1108/978-1-83608-392-420241009

Low, J., Mansfield, K. E., & Chaturvedi, N. (2022). Secondary analysis of qualitative data. *BMJ (Clinical Research Ed.), 376*, e068270.

Makajić-Nikolić, D. (2023). ISO 31000: Risk Management Guidelines. In *Encyclopedia of Sustainable Management* (pp. 2078–2080). Springer International Publishing. DOI: 10.1007/978-3-031-25984-5_314

Mann, Z. A. (2024, July). Urgency in cybersecurity risk management: toward a solid theory. In *2024 IEEE 37th Computer Security Foundations Symposium (CSF)* (pp. 651-664). IEEE. DOI: 10.1109/CSF61375.2024.00051

Mathieu, P., & Miermont, G. (2023). Blaise Pascal et Pierre de Fermat, géomètres du hasard. *Courrier Blaise Pascal, 45*, 53–89. DOI: 10.4000/cbp.1058

McLennan, M. (2022). The global risks report 2022 17th edition. Coligny, Switzerland: World Economic Forum.

Meyer, B. H., Prescott, B., & Sheng, X. S. (2022). The impact of the COVID-19 pandemic on business expectations. *International Journal of Forecasting, 38*(2), 529–544. DOI: 10.1016/j.ijforecast.2021.02.009 PMID: 35185229

Miri, D. H., & Macke, J. (2022). Gamification, motivation, and engagement at work: A qualitative multiple case study. *European Business Review*, *34*(2), 263–276. DOI: 10.1108/EBR-04-2020-0106

Mizrak, K. C. (2024). Crisis management and risk mitigation: Strategies for effective response and resilience. *Trends, challenges, and practices in contemporary strategic management*, 254-278.

Möller, D. P. (2023). NIST cybersecurity framework and MITRE cybersecurity criteria. In *Guide to Cybersecurity in Digital Transformation: Trends, Methods, Technologies, Applications and Best Practices* (pp. 231–271). Springer Nature Switzerland. DOI: 10.1007/978-3-031-26845-8_5

Mustak, M., Salminen, J., Mäntymäki, M., Rahman, A., & Dwivedi, Y. K. (2023). Deepfakes: Deceptions, mitigations, and opportunities. *Journal of Business Research*, *154*, 113368. DOI: 10.1016/j.jbusres.2022.113368

Mwita, K. M. (2022). Strengths and weaknesses of qualitative research in social science studies. *International Journal of Research in Business and Social Science*, *11*(6), 618–625. DOI: 10.20525/ijrbs.v11i6.1920

Naim, A. (2022). Role of artificial intelligence in business risk management. *American Journal of Business Management, Economics, and Banking*, *1*, 55–66.

National Institute of Standards and Technology. (2024). *Cybersecurity framework version 2.0*. U.S. Department of Commerce. https://www.nist.gov/cyberframework

Neprash, H. T., Dameff, C., & Tully, J. (2024). Cybersecurity lessons from the Change Healthcare attack. *JAMA Internal Medicine*, *184*(11), 1283–1284. DOI: 10.1001/jamainternmed.2024.3162 PMID: 39250110

Niall, K. K. (2023). The Theory of Games of Chance. In *Johannes von Kries: Principles of the Probability Calculus: A Logical Investigation* (pp. 31–46). Springer International Publishing. DOI: 10.1007/978-3-031-36506-5_3

Nobles, C., & Burrell, D. (2024). Exploring the variability of human factors definitions in cybersecurity literature.

Ogundipe, O., & Aweto, T. (2024). The shaky foundation of global technology: A case study of the 2024 CrowdStrike outage. *International Journal of Multidisciplinary Research and Growth Evaluation*, *5*(5), 106–108.

Olaniyi, O. O., & Omubo, D. S. (2023). The importance of COSO framework compliance in information technology auditing and enterprise resource management. *International Journal of Innovative Research and Development*, *12*(4).

Ozdemir, D., Sharma, M., Dhir, A., & Daim, T. (2022). Supply chain resilience during the COVID-19 pandemic. *Technology in Society*, *68*, 101847. DOI: 10.1016/j.techsoc.2021.101847 PMID: 35075312

Parkin, R. (2021). What has time to do with risk? A preliminary communication. *New Zealand Journal of Employment Relations*, *46*(2), 26–30. DOI: 10.24135/nzjer.v46i2.61

Pascal, B. (2024). *Blaise Pascal Thoughts*. Lebooks Editora.

Paul, M. (2021). After-Action Reviews.

Prakash, D. S. (2025). Zero-day Vulnerabilities: An In-depth Analysis.

Protiviti & North Carolina State University. (2025). *Executive perspectives on top risks for 2025 and 2034: Key issues being discussed in the boardroom and C-suite*. Protiviti. https://www.protiviti.com/sites/default/files/2025-02/nc-state-protiviti-2025-top-risks-survey-global.pdf

Przetacznik, S. (2022). The evolution of risk management. *Zeszyty Naukowe Małopolskiej Wyższej Szkoły Ekonomicznej w Tarnowie*, *53*(1-2), 95–107.

Pujawan, I. N., & Bah, A. U. (2022, January). Supply chains under COVID-19 disruptions: Literature review and research agenda. In *Supply chain forum* [). Taylor & Francis.]. *International Journal (Toronto, Ont.)*, *23*(1), 81–95.

Rabb, W. (2025, June). Aflac Hit With Class Action Over Data Breach. Insurance Journal. https://www.insurancejournal.com/news/national/2025/06/25/829012.htm

Ramamoorti, S., Baskin, D. L.Jr, Epstein, B. J., & Wanserski, J. (2017). Managing risk at the speed of change: A new risk vocabulary and a call to the profession. *The CPA Journal*, *87*(6), 6–9.

Ramamoorti, S., Wanserski, J. H., & Stover, R. (2019). The velocity of risk. *Internal Auditor, 76*(2).

Ravichandran, P., Machireddy, J. R., & Rachakatla, S. K. (2022). AI-Enhanced data analytics for real-time business intelligence: Applications and challenges. *Journal of AI in Healthcare and Medicine*, *2*(2), 168–195.

Rawat, U. Abhishek, Singh, H., & Ur Rehman, A. (2024). Cybersecurity Challenges and Risks in AGI Development and Deployment. In *Artificial General Intelligence (AGI) Security: Smart Applications and Sustainable Technologies* (pp. 291-314). Singapore: Springer Nature Singapore.

Renn, O., Laubichler, M., Lucas, K., Kröger, W., Schanze, J., Scholz, R. W., & Schweizer, P. J. (2022). Systemic risks from different perspectives. *Risk Analysis*, *42*(9), 1902–1920. DOI: 10.1111/risa.13657 PMID: 33331037

Roach, L. (2021, May 11). Embedding speed and agility into strategy execution. *Harvard Business Review*. https://hbr.org/sponsored/2021/05/embedding-speed-and-agility-into-strategy-execution

RosmarlindaRosl & Almuallimi. (2024). A Theoretical Framework Examining The Impact Of Strategic Agility And Strategic Resilience On Organizational Performance, *Educational Administration. Theory into Practice*, *30*(6), 1835–1845. DOI: 10.53555/kuey.v30i6.5596

Ryzhakova, G., Reznik, N., Lazebnyk, V., Ivanova, T., Fedorov, V., & Omelianenko, M. (2024, November). Reputation Management in the Age of Information Transparency. In *International Conference on Business and Technology* (pp. 167-177). Cham: Springer Nature Switzerland.

Salihu, A., & Dervishi, R. (2024, October). Evaluating the Impact of Risk Management Frameworks on IT Audits: A Comparative Analysis of COSO, COBIT, ISO/IEC 27001, and NIST CSF. In *2024 International Conference on Electrical, Communication and Computer Engineering (ICECCE)* (pp. 1-8). IEEE. DOI: 10.1109/ICECCE63537.2024.10823548

Salo, A., Tosoni, E., Roponen, J., & Bunn, D. W. (2022). Using cross-impact analysis for probabilistic risk assessment. *Futures & Foresight Science*, *4*(2), e2103. DOI: 10.1002/ffo2.103

Sari, I. P., Khairani, L., & Ginting, R. (2023). Enhancing Disaster Resilience: Evaluating the Implementation of an Early Warning System through Table Top Exercises. *PERSPEKTIF*, *12*(4), 1253–1260. DOI: 10.31289/perspektif.v12i4.10341

Sève, B., & Wolfe, C. (2024). Playing with Chance. *Figures of Chance I: Chance in Literature and the Arts (16th–21st Centuries).*

Sowby, R. B., Sela, L., & Salomons, E. (2025). Water System Cybersecurity after the Microsoft–CrowdStrike Disruption of July 2024. *Journal of Water Resources Planning and Management*, *151*(3), 02525001. DOI: 10.1061/JWRMD5.WRENG-6828

Stachowiak, A., & Pawłyszyn, I. (2021). From Fragility through Agility to Resilience: The Role of Sustainable Improvement in Increasing Organizational Maturity. *Sustainability (Basel)*, *13*(9), 4991. DOI: 10.3390/su13094991

Stevens, R., Votipka, D., Dykstra, J., Tomlinson, F., Quartararo, E., Ahern, C., & Mazurek, M. L. (2022, April). How ready is your ready? assessing the usability of incident response playbook frameworks. In *Proceedings of the 2022 CHI Conference on Human Factors in Computing Systems* (pp. 1-18). DOI: 10.1145/3491102.3517559

Streck, P., & Meyer, M. H. (2025). Ransomware strikes a large healthcare provider. *Journal of Information Technology Case and Application Research, 27*(1), 28–58. DOI: 10.1080/15228053.2025.2477361

Tarasenko, M. Y., Steinmeier, S. K. M., & Zelezinskii, A. L. (2024). MODERN RISK MANAGEMENT TECHNIQUES. *Экономический вектор, 4* (39), 113-120.

Thornton, D. (2018). Developing a theory of dynamic risk. In *Dynamic Risk Factors* (pp. 137–149). Routledge.

Truong, Q., Zalog, R., & Chang, B. (2021). Scalable Detection and Drill-down of Cybersecurity Events.

Tsaliki, K. C. Revolutionizing Identity Management with AI: Enhancing Cyber Security and Preventing ATO. *International Research Journal of Modernization in Engineering Technology and Science, 6.*

U.S. Department of Homeland Security. (2025). *Homeland Threat Assessment.* Office of Intelligence and Analysis. Washington, DC: DHS.

van Hoek, R. (2021). Exploring progress with supply chain risk management during the first year of the COVID-19 pandemic. *Logistics (Basel), 5*(4), 70. DOI: 10.3390/logistics5040070

Venkata, B. (2025). Unraveling the 2024 CrowdStrike Incident: How a Security Patch Led to Global System Failure and Blue Screen of Death.

Venters, W., Whitley, E. A., & Cornford, T. (2021). The view from the cloud: Organizational design for cloud computing. *Information Systems Journal, 31*(3), 343–371.

Weng, Y., & Wu, J. (2024). Leveraging artificial intelligence to enhance data security and combat cyber attacks. *Journal of Artificial Intelligence General science (JAIGS) ISSN: 3006-4023, 5*(1), 392-399.

Wolniak, R. (2023). *Functioning of real-time analytics in business.* Zeszyty Naukowe. Organizacja i Zarządzanie/Politechnika Śląska. DOI: 10.29119/1641-3466.2023.172.40

Yakovchenko, V., Rogal, S. S., Goodrich, D. E., Lamorte, C., Neely, B., Merante, M., Gibson, S., Scott, D., McCurdy, H., Nobbe, A., Morgan, T. R., & Chinman, M. J. (2023). Getting to implementation: Adaptation of an implementation playbook. *Frontiers in Public Health, 10*, 980958. DOI: 10.3389/fpubh.2022.980958 PMID: 36684876

Yuni, S., Yuniati, A., & Umbing, G. B. (2024). A COSO ERM integrated framework evaluation of it governance risk management. *Journal of Interest: Economics, Business, and Accounting Review, 1*(1), 38–42.

KEY TERMS AND DEFINITIONS

Dynamic Risk Theory: The theory recognizes that dangers are ever-changing and developing, in contrast to static risk assessment. It emphasizes the importance of ongoing risk monitoring and reevaluation to adapt to new circumstances and challenges. This method is essential in dynamic settings where conditions might change quickly, necessitating a responsive and adaptable approach to risk management.

Governance, Risk, and Compliance (GRC): GRC is a systematic practice employed by organizations to ensure the reliable attainment of objectives, manage uncertainty, and uphold integrity through governance, risk, and compliance capabilities.

Integrated Quantitative Model: Different quantitative models or datasets are combined in an Integrated Quantitative Model (IQM) to produce a more thorough and accurate analysis than would be possible with just one model, thereby improving decision-making by utilizing the advantages of multiple methodologies and frequently incorporating qualitative insights.

Resilience: A company's ability to foresee, plan for, respond to, and adjust to unforeseen occurrences, disturbances, and crises while sustaining its essential operations and attaining enduring success. It involves sustaining business operations and returning to normal operations after a business disruption.

Risk Response: The steps taken to mitigate risks that have been identified, whether they are positive or negative. Selecting suitable tactics to either reduce, avoid, transfer, or accept risks is a crucial stage in managing potential adverse effects.

Risk Velocity: Refers to the speed at which an organization experiences the effects of a risk; a crucial component of risk management, particularly in today's rapidly evolving business world.

Scenario-based Assessment and Analysis: In cybersecurity and risk management, scenario-based assessment and analysis is a systematic method that simulates actual attack scenarios to assess an organization's capacity to detect, prevent, and respond to specific threats. This approach aims to go beyond broad theoretical risk models by concentrating on how real-world occurrences could transpire, allowing for customized testing of organizational controls, procedures, and personnel.

Three-Dimensional Risk Assessment Model: A framework for assessing risk that leverages three different aspects of risk assessment: probability, impact, and velocity, giving it more depth and context than conventional two-dimensional models that typically concentrate on impact and likelihood.

Time-to-Impact Analysis: The goal of risk management's Time-to-Impact (TTI) analysis is to understand how long it will take for a risk to materialize and have a substantial impact on an organization's objectives or operations. Understanding the seriousness and urgency of possible threats is an essential first step in developing more efficient mitigation and response plans.

Two-dimensional Risk Assessment Model: A risk assessment framework that typically concentrates on impact and likelihood.

Chapter 2
Grounded Resilience:
Lessons in Aviation Information Systems From the 2025 U.S. Government Shutdown

Annamaria Szakonyi
http://orcid.org/0000-0002-1958-2042
Embry-Riddle Aeronautical University, USA

ABSTRACT

This paper examines how information systems improvements could have mitigated operational disruptions in the aviation industry during the 2025 U.S. government shutdown. Using a socio-technical systems (STS) framework, it analyzes the synergy between technology, governance, and human factors within the U.S. aviation industry. Findings indicate that aviation resilience depends on integrating cloud-based infrastructure, AI-assisted decision systems, robust cybersecurity frameworks, and human factors in the entire lifecycle of technical design decisions. The study proposes a four-layer mitigation strategy encompassing infrastructure resilience, digital coordination, cybersecurity hardening, and human factors integration. Results highlight that organizational agility is achieved through aligning technical innovation with institutional adaptability, ensuring continuity during fiscal or staffing crises. The paper concludes with actionable recommendations for technologists and policymakers to strengthen aviation system resilience and safeguard operational continuity during crises.

DOI: 10.4018/979-8-2600-1021-1.ch002

INTRODUCTION

The 2025 U.S. government shutdown exposed deep systemic vulnerabilities in the nation's aviation infrastructure, revealing how political instability can cascade into technological fragility. The event disrupted critical operations across the Federal Aviation Administration (FAA), causing over 2,700 flight delays in a single weekend and halting progress on the agency's $12.5 billion modernization initiative (FAA, 2025; Yamat, 2025). The economic consequences of repeated shutdowns are staggering: the 2018–2019 event alone cost an estimated $11 billion in lost output, while the 2013 shutdown reduced GDP growth by $20 billion (Targeted News Service, 2025). Productivity losses, quantified as more than 56,000 years of lost federal work time, illustrate how governance instability directly erodes public service capacity and national infrastructure resilience (Targeted News Service, 2025).

Although the 2025 shutdown occurred within a U.S. political context, the vulnerabilities it exposed mirror challenges faced by aviation authorities worldwide, highlighting the international relevance of resilient information systems and harmonized digital governance (Cook et al., 2023; Gu et al., 2024). Similar disruptions in Europe, Asia, and Australia have demonstrated that operational continuity increasingly depends on globally interoperable digital architectures and shared standards for automation, cybersecurity, and crisis communication (Eurocontrol, 2023; International Civil Aviation Organization [ICAO], n.d.).

Despite extensive scholarship on aviation resilience, crisis impacts, and modernization challenges, current research offers limited analysis of which specific information system architectures and digital coordination mechanisms could have mitigated operational failures during a government shutdown. Prior studies emphasize staffing shortages, economic losses, and delays in modernization (Cook et al., 2023; Gu et al., 2024), but comparatively few examine how cloud redundancy, data-link technologies in digital communication, AI-assisted decision support, or harmonized cybersecurity frameworks perform under the unique constraints of governance disruptions (Alhalabi et al., 2025; Welsh & Benkhelifa, 2020). Likewise, much of the existing literature treats infrastructure, governance, and human factors as independent domains rather than interdependent socio-technical components (Baxter & Sommerville, 2011), leaving a gap in holistic system-level guidance for aviation continuity during political or fiscal instability.

This study addresses these gaps by evaluating how modernized information systems (including cloud-based redundancy strategies, automated data-link communication, AI-enabled decision-support tools, and cyber-resilient architectures) could have reduced the operational and safety impacts observed during the 2025 shutdown. Grounded in socio-technical systems (STS) theory, the paper analyzes how technological tools, organizational processes, and workforce dynamics interact to shape resilience under crisis conditions, extending longstanding STS insights about joint system optimization (Bostrom & Heinen, 1977; Trist & Bamforth, 1951). By synthesizing technological, organizational, and human-factor evidence into a layered IS mitigation framework, the study contributes a system-level perspective that advances both scholarly understanding and practical governance strategies for enhancing aviation resilience (Westin et al., 2020; Welsh & Benkhelifa, 2020).

In summary, this paper examines how the 2025 government shutdown magnified existing limitations within the aviation environment, and how various information system improvements could have mitigated operational disruptions during the shutdown. Through the lens of socio-technical systems (STS) theory, this paper explores the interdependencies between technology, human performance, and institutional structures that determine aviation resilience. By examining how system design, governance structures, and human performance intersect, the study provides actionable insights into building a layered information systems strategy that supports operational continuity, safety, and adaptability. It highlights current risks related to aging technology, centralized funding dependencies, and insufficient system interoperability, and how various IS improvements can sustain continuity under crisis conditions. This work illustrates that strengthening information infrastructure is not only a technical goal but a national governance imperative for resilient aviation in the digital age.

PROBLEM STATEMENT

The 2025 U.S. government shutdown exposed critical weaknesses in the U.S. aviation infrastructure, where funding interruptions and staffing shortages led to widespread operational disruptions, including postponed safety checks, halted modernization projects, excessive overtime requirements straining an already understaffed workforce, and widespread travel delays in both commercial and general aviation (FAA, 2025; Targeted News Service, 2025; Yamat, 2025). These events demonstrate how political and fiscal instability can quickly erode the safety and reliability of national airspace operations.

Research consistently shows that aviation systems are particularly vulnerable when funding instability intersects with aging technical infrastructure, limited automation, and fragmented information flows. International analyses demonstrate that staffing shortages, delays in maintenance, and halted modernization efforts disproportionately affect safety-critical systems when information architectures rely on centralized, non-redundant services (EUROCONTROL, 2023; ICAO, n.d.). Shutdowns and similar governance disruptions amplify these risks by interrupting long-term modernization programs, reducing system monitoring, and constraining routine safety processes such as inspections, certification renewals, and training cycles (Cook et al., 2023). These findings reinforce that the U.S. shutdown did not simply expose operational strain but revealed deeper socio-technical misalignments between aviation information systems, governance structures, and human performance requirements.

Yet, an important question emerges: *What specific information system improvements could have mitigated operational disruptions in the aviation industry during the 2025 government shutdown?* Despite the shutdown's immediate operational and economic toll, it also revealed opportunities to strengthen aviation resilience through improved data integration, automation, cybersecurity, and system interoperability (Abeyratne, 2020; Brooker, 2008; Darr et al., 2008; Eleimat & Őszi, 2025; Florido-Benítez, 2024; Olaganathan, 2024; Smith & Baumann, 2020). Without resilient, modular, and automated information systems capable of sustaining continuity during fiscal or technical crises, the national airspace system remains susceptible to systemic failure.

While prior research has evaluated shutdown-related operational disruptions, little attention has been paid to the question of which specific information system improvements (such as cloud redundancy, automated digital communication systems, cross-agency data integration tools, or cyber-resilience architectures) could have mitigated these failures. Studies highlight the importance of interoperable data environments, predictive automation, and resilient communication layers for sustaining continuity during crisis events (Welsh & Benkhelifa, 2020; Westin et al., 2020), yet few analyses apply these insights directly to the context of political or fiscal disruptions. This gap underscores the need for a socio-technical examination of how modern information systems could prevent shutdown-induced vulnerabilities from cascading into large-scale aviation failures.

This study examines what specific information system improvements could have mitigated these disruptions and how future modernization efforts can enhance operational agility, cybersecurity, and organizational resilience across the aviation sector. It explores information systems related possibilities to determine how modernized information systems could sustain continuity and safeguard aviation safety during future governance disruptions.

SIGNIFICANCE

The demand for air travel has expanded dramatically, with air traffic increasing by more than 86% over the past twenty years (Cokorilo, 2020; Eleimat & Őszi, 2025, p. 169). Yet, the 2025 U.S. government shutdown demonstrated how political disruptions can quickly cascade into operational breakdowns within the U.S. aviation industry. Flight delays, halted modernization projects, and reduced staffing revealed the fragility of aviation systems that depend on centralized budgets and legacy infrastructure. By examining these failures through the lens of information systems design and governance, this study provides insights into how digital modernization could mitigate similar impacts in the future.

The significance of this issue extends beyond the immediate consequences of the 2025 shutdown because aviation systems worldwide face increasing pressure from rising traffic demand, aging technical infrastructure, cyber threats, and limited workforce capacity. Global aviation authorities emphasize that resilient, interoperable information systems are now essential components of safe and efficient airspace management, particularly under conditions of operational stress or administrative disruption (EUROCONTROL, 2023; ICAO, n.d.).

Research on aviation crises shows that when governance instability intersects with outdated or non-redundant technologies, disruptions can propagate quickly across the socio-technical system, affecting everything from frontline controller workload to national economic performance (Cook et al., 2023; Gu et al., 2024). Thus, understanding how information systems contribute to operational continuity is a critical component of modern aviation resilience.

If the vulnerabilities revealed during the shutdown are left unaddressed, the aviation sector risks recurring interruptions to safety oversight, degraded system performance, escalating human-factor risks, and widening gaps in modernization timelines. Persistent reliance on legacy, centralized IT systems makes air traffic operations particularly susceptible to single-point failures during funding disruptions, cybersecurity events, or staffing shortages (Welsh & Benkhelifa, 2020). Without stronger digital redundancy, automation-enhanced coordination, and integrated data-sharing architectures, shutdown-induced operational strain may increasingly result in long-term capacity reductions, diminished safety margins, and public loss of trust in national aviation governance (ICAO, 2022; Gu et al., 2024).

This project is significant because it addresses a critical gap in understanding how information systems can sustain aviation operations during governance and funding crises. By examining how modern information systems, such as cloud-based infrastructures, AI-assisted decision tools, and interoperable data networks, can mitigate the operational impacts of funding disruptions, this study contributes to the advancement of resilient aviation governance.

The findings have implications beyond the 2025 shutdown, offering insights into how aviation authorities, technologists, public administrators and policymakers can future-proof critical infrastructure sectors against political, economic, and cyber disruptions. Ultimately, this study highlights that modernized, resilient information systems are not merely technical upgrades but strategic safeguards, vital to maintaining public trust, operational continuity, and the stability of the global aviation ecosystem.

METHODOLOGY

This study is a qualitative, interpretive commentary designed to critically analyze current events through the lens of established organizational and information systems theories. It synthesizes scholarly literature, policy documents, and recent news reporting to explore the intersection of technology, governance, and organizational agility in the Federal Aviation Administration.

This study follows a qualitative interpretive synthesis approach, which is well suited for integrating heterogeneous sources (such as academic studies, policy documents, technical standards, and crisis reports) into a unified analytical narrative. Interpretive synthesis is commonly used in information systems and organizational research to identify patterns across diverse evidence and to understand how socio-technical dynamics shape complex phenomena (Dixon-Woods et al., 2006; Walsham, 1995). This analytical strategy allowed the study not only to summarize existing aviation research but to examine underlying mechanisms linking governance instability, technical infrastructure, and human performance within air traffic operations.

The study employed an AI-assisted semantic literature search to identify research relevant to information system improvements that could mitigate operational disruptions in air traffic control (ATC) environments. Using the Elicit academic search engine (which indexes over 138 million papers from Semantic Scholar and OpenAlex), we queried, "What specific information system improvements could have mitigated operational disruptions in air traffic control systems during the 2025 government shutdown?"

To complement this process and ensure broader coverage, a manual Google Scholar search was also conducted using combinations of keywords such as government shutdown, aviation, flight control, and information systems. This dual approach enhanced the comprehensiveness and robustness of the literature identification process. Additional articles were also identified through citation tracking of the papers retrieved in both searches. Collected materials also included policy and technical documents, contemporary news and industry reports documenting the 2025 government shutdown and its impacts.

Each article was screened against a structured set of inclusion criteria to ensure relevance to both air traffic control and information systems research. Studies were included if they focused on ATC operations, aviation information systems, digital infrastructure, automation, or decision-support technologies within the context of operational continuity, disruption management, or crisis response.

Following screening, a large language model was used to assist with structured data extraction from the selected studies. Extracted data included information about the type of information system studied, the identified vulnerabilities, proposed technological or procedural improvements, and mechanisms by which these improvements could mitigate operational disruptions. Contextual factors influencing implementation, such as regulatory frameworks, organizational readiness, and technical dependencies, were also reviewed. The final dataset consisted of studies that collectively offered insights into lessons relevant to maintaining aviation operations through information systems during crisis events such as the 2025 government shutdown.

The analysis proceeded through iterative coding cycles in which conceptual categories were developed around four central domains: infrastructure resilience, digital coordination mechanisms, cybersecurity vulnerabilities, and human-system interactions. This method aligns with established qualitative coding practices used in information systems research, where themes are developed iteratively to reveal socio-technical relationships rather than isolate variables (Miles et al., 2014). These categories informed the construction of the layered information systems mitigation framework presented in the results section.

This paper adopts a socio-technical systems (STS) lens to guide its analytical perspective on aviation information systems and their role during the 2025 government shutdown. STS was selected because it provides a holistic understanding of the mutual shaping of technology and organizational behavior (Bostrom & Heinen, 1977; Cherns, 1976; Trist & Bamforth, 1951). Alternative frameworks, such as dynamic capabilities or institutional theory, were considered but STS offers a clearer pathway to understanding interdependence and adaptation within complex government information infrastructures.

The selection of a socio-technical systems framework reflects the methodological need to examine aviation resilience across interdependent technical, human, and organizational dimensions. STS-based analyses are widely used in studies of safety-critical industries because they highlight how disruptions often emerge from misalignments between people, technologies, and institutional structures (Baxter & Sommerville, 2011). Applying STS enabled this study to interpret the 2025 shutdown not as a technical failure alone, but as an event shaped by governance processes, workforce dynamics, and the limitations of legacy information systems.

As an information technology professional with experience in systems integration and governance, the author's perspective is further informed by practitioner insights into the challenges of aligning technical innovation with bureaucratic structures. This experiential standpoint enriches the interpretive analysis while acknowledging potential biases that come with professional proximity to the subject matter. As the analysis was conducted by a researcher with professional experience in information systems and technology governance, reflexivity was incorporated into the methodological process. Prior assumptions about digital modernization were examined and checked against empirical evidence. Reflexive practice is central to interpretive qualitative research and helps ensure that the findings emerge from the data rather than from the researcher's prior beliefs (Walsham, 2006).

LITERATURE REVIEW

The 2025 Government Shutdown

The October 2025 U.S. government shutdown revealed deep, systemic weaknesses in the nation's aviation infrastructure; most notably in staffing capacity, operational continuity, and technology modernization; demonstrating how fragile the aviation ecosystem becomes when political instability interrupts essential federal functions (Yamat, 2025). The shutdown caused significant flight delays and disruptions, extended security wait times, postponed safety checks, and the critical staffing shortage forced air traffic controllers to work without pay (FAA, 2025; Yamat, 2025; Targeted News Service, 2025).

The government shutdown resulted in severe and far-reaching impacts on aviation safety, operations, and the broader economy, compromising both workforce stability and public safety (Targeted News Service, 2025). Funding disruptions undermine aviation safety by delaying safety inspections and equipment maintenance, halting training programs, and forcing essential personnel to work without pay. These conditions heighten stress, fatigue, and financial hardship among aviation professionals (Jin et al., 2024; Targeted News Service, 2025). The Federal Aviation Administration (FAA) has already been operating with fewer than 11,000 fully certified controllers, which is far below recommended staffing levels, resulting in deeper stress and fatigue of operators (Targeted News Service, 2025).

On November 6, 2025, the U.S. Department of Transportation (DOT) and the Federal Aviation Administration introduced a temporary plan to reduce flights by up to 10% at 40 of the nation's busiest airports to maintain safety and manage stress on the air traffic system during and after the government shutdown (FAA, 2025). Airlines were required to provide full refunds for canceled flights but were not required to reimburse travelers for secondary costs such as lodging or meals. The policy applied only to domestic flights at the 40 listed airports, including ATL, LAX, ORD, and SFO, while international flights remained unaffected (FAA, 2025).

These immediate operational challenges were compounded by the suspension of a $12.5 billion FAA modernization initiative intended to replace outdated systems, halting progress on long-overdue technological upgrades (Yamat, 2025). Technological stagnation further magnifies these risks: the freeze on modernization projects delays implementation of advanced safety systems that could otherwise mitigate human workload and reduce systemic vulnerabilities (Yamat, 2025).

Together, these insights reveal how federal shutdowns weaken the aviation system's resilience (Targeted News Service, 2025). Underinvestment in personnel and infrastructure can magnify negative effects (Targeted News Service, 2025). Mandatory unpaid labor erodes morale and retention, while delayed maintenance and training degrade the FAA's ability to uphold consistent safety standards (Targeted News Service, 2025). The systemic risks compound over time: even short shutdowns can produce lasting operational gaps, forcing remaining staff into unsustainable overtime cycles (Targeted News Service, 2025).

The 2025 incident highlights the urgent need for modernization of air traffic operations. These observations point to a central conclusion: protecting aviation safety requires technical upgrades to prevent the long-lasting impact of similar situations. Sustainable aviation safety and national infrastructure resilience requires accelerated technology upgrades for critical systems that ensure continuity of public safety (Yamat, 2025). Similar "shock events" (such as economic downturn, pandemics, terrorist incidents, and natural disasters) disrupt airport operations and reshape strategic management practices (Gu et al., 2024). These events, however, create not only recurring operational vulnerabilities but also opportunities to redefine resilience as a dynamic and adaptive capability rather than a static crisis management and recovery process (Gu et al., 2024).

Taken together, it is evident that shutdown-induced disruptions expose latent fragilities created by staffing shortages, deferred maintenance, and stalled modernization initiatives (Cook et al., 2023; Gu et al., 2024). Although the specific operational manifestations differ across events, the underlying vulnerabilities consistently stem from interdependencies between governance processes, technical infrastructure, and workforce capacity. Scholars note that while shutdowns may appear temporary, their cascading effects accumulate within the aviation system, degrading resilience over time (Dave, 2025). Yet, despite this consensus, few studies evaluate how information system architectures themselves (such as data integration tools or redundant digital communication platforms) could mitigate these failures. This gap sets the stage for examining aviation disruptions through a socio-technical systems lens.

FAA's Technology Modernization

Air Traffic Management (ATM) systems play a critical role in ensuring the safe and efficient coordination of aircraft within the airspace. The recent shutdown is just one example of the roadblocks facing the Next Generation Air Transportation System (NextGen) program, the ongoing attempt of the United States to modernize its air traffic control (ATC) infrastructure (Brooker, 2008; Darr et al., 2008; Dave,

2025; Eleimat & Őszi, 2025). Modernization programs such as NextGen seek to transform ATM through advanced technologies, including Automatic Dependent Surveillance–Broadcast (ADS-B), 4D trajectory management, and System-Wide Information Management (SWIM) (Eleimat & Őszi, 2025, pp. 173–174). These innovations can enhance efficiency, capacity, and performance.

Despite its technological promise, structural and institutional barriers continue to limit the effectiveness of this initiative (Dave, 2025). Modernization is not merely a technical upgrade, but a complex organizational transformation that demands governance reform, long-term investment, and workforce adaptation to ensure aviation safety and equity (Dave, 2025). Prior modernization efforts, such as the Advanced Automation System in the 1980s and 1990s, collapsed under technical failures and budget overruns (the original $2.5 billion estimate gradually increased to $30+ billion, with a timeline delayed with over a decade), serving as a cautionary tale for federal technology programs (Dave, 2025, p. 5).

Conceived as a multi-decade initiative spanning from 2012 to 2025, NextGen seeks to fundamentally transform air traffic management by integrating advanced surveillance, communication, digital data exchange, and meteorological technologies to enhance efficiency, capacity, and safety (Brooker, 2008; Darr et al., 2008; Eleimat & Őszi, 2025). NextGen is the successor to the radar- and voice-based ATC systems that have guided U.S. aviation since the mid-20th century (Dave, 2025). These legacy systems now exhibit inefficiencies, capacity limits, and emerging safety vulnerabilities (Dave, 2025). NextGen seeks to replace these with satellite-based navigation, digital communications, and automation, yet nearly twenty years after its inception, deployment remains inconsistent (Brooker, 2008; Darr et al., 2008; Dave, 2025; Eleimat & Őszi, 2025). Unstable funding, just like budget gaps caused by the 2025 shutdown, is a key limiter for this deployment (Dave, 2025).

Across the modernization literature, scholars agree that NextGen promises substantial gains in capacity, automation, and system-wide efficiency (Brooker, 2008; Eleimat & Őszi, 2025). However, persistent funding instability, procurement delays, and institutional inertia continue to constrain progress, creating long-term exposure points in the national airspace system (Dave, 2025). These tensions highlight that modernization is not merely a technical challenge but a systemic governance problem in which outdated information systems amplify the effects of administrative disruption. Importantly, prior work rarely examines how information system redesign might preserve continuity during short-term shutdowns or funding gaps. This omission highlights the need for a more integrated, resilience-based IS framework.

Theoretical Framework of Socio-Technical Systems

Originating from the pioneering work of Eric Trist, Ken Bamforth and Fred Emery in the 1950s, STS theory argues that organizational effectiveness arises from the joint optimization of social and technical subsystems (Bostrom & Heinen, 1977; Cherns, 1976; Trist & Bamforth, 1951). Within this framework, technological infrastructures, human actors, and institutional processes are viewed as interdependent components of a larger adaptive system (Bostrom & Heinen, 1977; Cooper & Foster, 1971; Kaminski, 2022; Mumford, 2006; Pasmore et al., 2019). By applying this perspective, the study interprets the digital aviation environment not merely as a collection of tools or databases but as a complex socio-organizational ecosystem shaped by policy, culture, and human decision-making.

The STS approach is particularly useful for this commentary because it supports a holistic, integrative analysis of the interdependencies exposed during the 2025 government shutdown. The methodology employs critical synthesis (drawing on scholarly literature, government reports, and aviation technology documents) interpreted through the STS framework to explore how technical fragility, organizational rigidity, and interagency coordination failures jointly affect operational resilience (Baxter & Sommerville, 2011). This interpretive method aligns with the goals of this paper by using established theory to reflect on patterns, surface systemic insights, and propose actionable frameworks for future practice in information system governance and crisis management.

Through the STS lens, the analysis focuses on the dynamic relationship between technological systems (such as aviation IT infrastructure, cybersecurity platforms, and predictive systems) and social systems (specifically related to workforce management, budgetary constraints, and communication networks). This theoretical grounding helps explain how disruptions emerge not solely from technical faults but from misalignments between human and technical subsystems. Consequently, this methodology supports the paper's broader argument: cultivating organizational agility within the FAA and similar public institutions requires redesigning both technological architectures and the social systems that govern them, thereby ensuring adaptive capacity and resilience in the face of political, fiscal, or technical crises (Cherns, 1987; Davis et al., 2014).

Literature Summary

In summary, the literature on aviation resilience highlights how technical infrastructure, institutional constraints, human performance, and cybersecurity collectively shape safety and operational continuity in modern airspace systems. Scholars emphasize that disruptions (whether caused by political shocks, funding instability, labor shortages, or technological failures) expose the interdependence of these socio-technical components (Cook et al., 2023; Gu et al., 2024). Prior research on air traffic management modernization demonstrates the promise of digital architectures and automation, but also underscores persistent limitations tied to legacy systems and uneven governance structures (Brooker, 2008; Dave, 2025). At the same time, work in human factors, cyber-resilience, and digital communication technologies reveals opportunities to strengthen continuity through targeted information systems design. This review synthesized these areas of scholarship to establish the context for analyzing how specific information system improvements could mitigate shutdown-induced aviation disruptions.

RESULTS AND RECOMMENDATIONS

Infrastructure in the Age of IoT and Cloud

The aviation industry's migration toward cloud-based infrastructures marks a significant shift in how operational data and digital services are managed. Airlines increasingly depend on cloud computing to scale services, improve operational flexibility, and achieve cost efficiencies, while airports utilize big data analytics and the Internet of Things (IoT) to optimize passenger flow, resource allocation, and cross-agency coordination (Abeyratne, 2020; Eleimat & Őszi, 2025). These technologies collectively enable real-time analytics, automated alerts, and data-driven planning, reinforcing predictive management and enhancing the overall passenger experience (Abeyratne, 2020). The integration of big data through cloud technologies into operational workflows allows for dynamic forecasting, enabling aviation stakeholders to make proactive decisions on maintenance, scheduling, and infrastructure development (Abeyratne, 2020).

Approximately 28% of airports now qualify as Smart, integrating IoT enabled technologies, real-time data exchange, and interconnected digital networks to improve operational efficiency and passenger experience (Eleimat & Őszi, 2025, p. 176). IoT serves as the hub of the smart airport ecosystem, embedding sensors and networked devices across terminals, maintenance facilities, and aircraft systems (Abeyratne, 2020). These devices enable predictive maintenance, real-time baggage tracking, passenger movement analytics, and environmental control (Abeyratne, 2020). When paired with AI, IoT technologies facilitate automated navigation, beacon-based passenger guidance, and infrastructure monitoring, turning airports into responsive, data-driven environments (Abeyratne, 2020).

The shutdown of 2025, which temporarily halted FAA's air traffic modernization program, exposed how dependent aviation infrastructure remains on centralized funding and aging technical architectures. This interruption highlights the urgency of advancing toward redundant, cloud-based, and modular information systems capable of sustaining operations even when traditional budget cycles or administrative processes are disrupted. As the aviation industry increasingly integrates IoT networks, big data analytics, and AI-enabled decision platforms, system design must evolve beyond efficiency to embed cyber-physical resilience, ensuring that critical communication, navigation, and surveillance systems remain operational during fiscal or technical crises (Abeyratne, 2020; Eleimat & Őszi, 2025).

Legacy dependencies, particularly on aging radar and communication networks, compound risk when modernization efforts pause, leaving essential airspace functions vulnerable to maintenance backlogs and cybersecurity exposures. A sustainable digital transformation strategy therefore requires distributed architectures, automated fault recovery, and federated data management frameworks that maintain service continuity across both human and technological layers. In the new age of aviation, infrastructure resilience is no longer just a technical goal, it is a governance imperative that links fiscal stability, technological adaptability, and public safety.

Overall, the results suggest that cloud-based services, big data analytics, and IoT-enabled smart airport ecosystems can substantially enhance operational resilience by distributing workloads and reducing dependence on legacy systems (Welsh & Benkhelifa, 2020; EUROCONTROL, 2023). However, these benefits materialize only when governance structures reliably sustain modernization schedules, cybersecurity protocols, and interagency data standards; conditions that are disrupted during shutdowns. International initiatives such as SESAR highlight that distributed digital architectures are most effective when paired with strong, stable cross-jurisdictional oversight (Brooker, 2008). The 2025 shutdown illustrates that fragmented data environments and legacy dependencies remain critical vulnerabilities in the U.S. system. These findings support the need for more modular, interoperable infrastructure within the layered mitigation framework proposed in this study.

Blockchain

Blockchain is an emerging candidate in aviation's digital transformation, with its core strength lying in the creation of transparent, tamper-resistant data ecosystems (Abeyratne, 2020). Blockchain technology can be applied as a means to strengthen transparency, traceability, and security across various aviation operations, including passenger data management, ticketing, cargo tracking, and aircraft registration (Eleimat & Őszi, 2025). The technology is currently being piloted across several operational domains.

Blockchain strengthens digital identity and ticketing systems, enabling immutable and auditable records that strengthen both data integrity and security (Abeyratne,

2020). In airport logistics and cargo operations, distributed ledgers help mitigate fraud, cut paperwork, and enhance coordination across global supply chains (Abeyratne, 2020). Smart contracts automate flight bookings, settlements, and service agreements, reducing administrative friction and increasing transactional trust among airlines, airports, and service providers (Abeyratne, 2020). By providing an immutable and verifiable record of transactions, blockchain has the potential to reduce dependence on intermediaries and streamline regulatory oversight.

Blockchain's immutability, however, can become a liability, as erroneous entries cannot be amended, and the absence of a standardized global regulatory framework leaves unresolved questions about governance, accountability, and interoperability (Abeyratne, 2020). As aviation systems evolve toward greater digital interdependence, blockchain's long-term value will depend not only on its technical robustness but also on the industry's ability to develop unified regulatory frameworks, ethical standards, and interoperable architectures that transform innovation into sustainable, resilient infrastructure.

Overall, while blockchain offers potential benefits for traceability, identity management, and maintenance integrity, current aviation applications remain experimental and fragmented (Abeyratne, 2020). Regulatory uncertainty, interoperability limitations, and the immutability of erroneous entries constrain near-term adoption, especially during crisis scenarios requiring rapid updates or cross-agency coordination. Unlike cloud or data-link technologies, blockchain does not yet provide mature, scalable resilience capabilities for shutdown conditions. As such, it should be considered an adjunct, not a foundational, component of an aviation resilience strategy.

Automation and AI-Assisted Operations

Artificial intelligence (AI) has become a transformative force in aviation, reshaping how airlines, airports, and regulators manage operations, safety, and the passenger experience. Within the air transport ecosystem, AI applications extend beyond automation to encompass predictive, analytical, and decision-support roles that enhance both efficiency and risk management (Abeyratne, 2020). NextGen operational enhancements emphasize the adoption of advanced automation capabilities and decision-support tools designed to improve air traffic efficiency and predictability (Smith & Baumann, 2020)

Predictive analytics and simulation modeling tools can effectively sustain on-time performance even under conditions of rising air traffic demand (Agbolosu-Amison & Mondoloni, 2012; Olaganathan, 2024). Real-time exchange of aircraft scheduling information between FAA controllers and airline operations centers improves the accuracy of predicted arrival times, strengthens strategic fleet arrival planning, and supports more informed divert/no-divert decisions. These types of AI-driven scheduling and decision-support systems can temporarily reduce dependence on human controllers during critical shortages.

Machine learning (ML) methods can not only enhance predictive accuracy but also reveal underlying risk patterns that can inform proactive safety management and regulatory decision-making (Odetayo & Haruna, 2024). AI can be leveraged for predictive maintenance by identifying equipment anomalies before failure occurs, and can improve the prediction of accident severity in commercial aviation (Abeyratne, 2020; Odetayo & Haruna, 2024). These machine learning models can detect early signs of safety risk before human fatigue or understaffing causes incidents. Shifting the focus from reactive analysis toward predictive oversight, regulators and airlines can identify potential high-risk scenarios, enabling more efficient allocation of inspection and training resources (Odetayo & Haruna, 2024). Furthermore, robotic inspections, blockchain-secured maintenance records, and additive manufacturing (3D printing) can support automation and reduce human workloads to strengthen aviation safety (Olaganathan, 2024). Similar intelligent automations can help maintain essential administrative processes even when staffing is disrupted.

In addition, machine learning and deep learning systems are increasingly integrated into airport security screening, where they automate threat detection and support risk-based passenger and baggage assessments. AI can enable biometric identification technologies that streamline check-in, security screening, boarding, and customs processes, creating a seamless end-to-end passenger experience (Abeyratne, 2020). These systems improve accuracy and speed while reducing reliance on manual interpretation, thereby strengthening overall security protocols (Abeyratne, 2020). Blockchain further complements these systems by storing biometric credentials in decentralized digital identities, reducing the likelihood of data breaches and misuse (Abeyratne, 2020). This convergence of biometrics, blockchain, and AI represents a new era of privacy-aware automation that can streamline passenger and worker experience by integrating their identity into their workflows and processes as they interact with aviation systems (Abeyratne, 2020).

It is important to note, however, that these systems should serve only as decision-support tools, and human expertise should remain indispensable for interpreting these model outputs (Odetayo & Haruna, 2024). Technology must come parallel with investments in human factors training and organizational learning to avoid new risks to materialize (Olaganathan, 2024). When implemented strategically, these technologies can augment human judgement, reducing the potential negative impacts of the existing limits on the aviation system. Integration of AI-based automation and predictive tools into existing systems could create a data-driven, anticipatory system, where insights derived from machine learning complement expert analysis to prevent incidents before they occur (Odetayo & Haruna, 2024). Furthermore, combining datasets across regions and regulatory systems can enhance model robustness and generalizability, helping overcome data fragmentation that often limits cross-context learning (Odetayo & Haruna, 2024).

In summary, it is evident that artificial intelligence and intelligent automation can enhance aviation continuity by sustaining critical operations during staffing shortages. AI and automation consistently demonstrate the ability to enhance predictive accuracy, streamline decision-making, and reduce controller workload (Westin et al., 2020; Odetayo & Haruna, 2024). Yet studies caution that these systems require robust human oversight, explainable interfaces, and reliable update cycles, conditions that deteriorate during funding shortfalls or staffing gaps (Smith & Baumann, 2020). International ATM research shows that decision-support systems perform best under stable governance and continuous monitoring, both of which were compromised during the 2025 shutdown. Consequently, AI cannot be viewed as a stand-alone solution but rather as a component of a broader socio-technical ecosystem, where automation supports, but does not replace, human judgment and institutional capacity. All of these have important implications for both practice and policy.

Cybersecurity and Continuity of Operations

The aviation ecosystem faces various threats and attack vectors, including credential-based incidents, unauthorized access (mainly data theft), denial-of-service (DoS) attacks, and operational disruption (Eleimat & Őszi, 2025; Florido-Benítez, 2024). These cybersecurity incidents can endanger safety-critical functions, such as flight control and communication (Eleimat & Őszi, 2025). The continued dependence on legacy systems intensifies cybersecurity risks, exposing the vital aviation infrastructure to heightened vulnerability and potential exploitation (Eleimat & Őszi, 2025).

Furthermore, technologies designed to enhance aviation safety can simultaneously undermine it if cybersecurity is not embedded from the beginning (Eleimat & Őszi, 2025). While modernization programs like NextGen can improve performance and coordination, they can also introduce new digital exposure points within air traffic management, especially weaknesses in authentication and data integrity (Brooker, 2008; Darr et al., 2008; Eleimat & Őszi, 2025). As an example, the integration of new satellite navigation and automation technologies expands the aviation system's attack surface beyond the vulnerabilities present in legacy systems (United States Government Accountability Office, 2015).

Airports are focal points of risk in an increasingly interconnected transport ecosystem (Florido-Benítez, 2024). It is estimated that major airport incidents can impose losses of US$1 million per peak-hour disruption (Florido-Benítez, 2024). With the increasing implementation of smart airports, heightened connectivity also expands the attack surface, making them more susceptible to cyber threats. Interconnected systems heighten cybersecurity and privacy vulnerabilities, requiring robust standards for device authentication, network segmentation, and data governance (Abeyratne, 2020). The sector's deepening dependence on IoT, cloud platforms, AI, digital twins, and edge computing not only multiplies attack surfaces but also complicates the adoption of cybersecurity defenses (Florido-Benítez, 2024). IoT integration and automation of airports has created complex networks that demand robust data governance, cybersecurity training, and interagency collaboration (Eleimat & Őszi, 2025).

To mitigate these risks, cyber resilience must be treated as a core element of aviation safety and governance rather than a technical afterthought (Eleimat & Őszi, 2025). Robust cybersecurity measures, including network segmentation, secure system design, regular penetration testing, intrusion detection and prevention (IDPS), and comprehensive cyber awareness and training programs for all airport personnel are crucial (Eleimat & Őszi, 2025). The development of comprehensive cybersecurity threat models combined with collaborative, continuous threat intelligence sharing would facilitate the systematic identification of potential threats and vulnerabilities, thereby strengthening system resilience through proactive risk mitigation (Eleimat & Őszi, 2025; United States Government Accountability Office, 2015). From a cyber operations perspective, a government shutdown can further weaken cyber defenses if monitoring and patching schedules are delayed due to employee shortages. This highlights the need for automated security monitoring and AI-driven threat detection that operate even with minimal staffing.

Zero-trust architectures and cloud failover systems can help maintain secure networks and communication between essential personnel during crises. As an example, a layered network model, consisting of three interdependent layers: traffic layer (representing air traffic dynamics at the level of major flows and control mechanisms), the cyber layer (abstractly modeling the information exchanges among key operational stakeholders), and the weather layer (including forecasted severe weather conditions and their corresponding effects on air traffic and system capacity), can enable integrated analysis of operational, informational, and environmental interdependencies within the air traffic management system (Roy & Sridhar, 2016).

Identity and Access Management (IAM) related technologies can provide additional security for aviation operations. The recent convergence of biometrics, blockchain, and AI represents a new era of privacy-aware automation, where convenience must be balanced with data protection and ethical oversight (Abeyratne, 2020). Blockchain's adoption presents significant challenges, particularly surrounding jurisdictional uncertainty, user anonymity, and questions of legal responsibility, which must be addressed before it can be fully integrated into global aviation systems (Eleimat & Őszi, 2025).

Inconsistent international regulations further undermine coordinated response capabilities, elevating cybersecurity from a merely technical problem to a strategic governance challenge requiring alignment among regulators, operators, and technology providers (Eleimat & Őszi, 2025). Harmonized, interoperable cybersecurity standards across airports and carriers could shift aviation information security from reactive incident response toward anticipatory risk reduction (Florido-Benítez, 2024). Technical evolution, therefore, must be supported by policy frameworks that keep pace with adversary innovation (Florido-Benítez, 2024).

This necessitates a multi-layered cybersecurity strategy that integrates policy, training, and technology into the broader aviation safety architecture (Eleimat & Őszi, 2025). Cybersecurity considerations must be embedded across the entire system design lifecycle (from conceptual design and implementation to operation and maintenance) and decision-making processes to ensure resilience and operational integrity in the evolving airspace environment, and for a more holistic approach to risk management (Eleimat & Őszi, 2025; United States Government Accountability Office, 2015). Cybersecurity must transition from a reactive compliance requirement to a proactive safety function: one that enhances system integrity, operational continuity, and passenger trust across the global aviation network (Eleimat & Őszi, 2025).

Sustained collaboration among government agencies, airlines, manufacturers, and airport authorities, coupled with investments in research and workforce development to close expertise gaps, should be a priority in the aviation context (Eleimat & Őszi, 2025). Technology investments require coordinated governance, threat-informed risk assessments, and operator training (Florido-Benítez, 2024). The adoption of standardized cybersecurity frameworks and greater transparency through mandatory incident reporting, could facilitate this collaboration (Eleimat & Őszi, 2025).

The literature is clear that aviation's growing digital interdependence expands the attack surface across airports, aircraft, and ATC systems (Florido-Benítez, 2024; Eleimat & Őszi, 2025). Empirical studies show that shutdown conditions amplify cyber risk by delaying patch cycles, reducing monitoring capacity, and weakening institutional response readiness (United States Government Accountability Office, 2015). Researchers disagree on the optimal mix of zero-trust architectures, threat modeling, and distributed monitoring, but concur that modernization cannot succeed without integrating cybersecurity into system design. Cybersecurity, therefore, is as an essential layer in aviation resilience.

Communication and Data Link Technologies

Communication is the backbone of aviation safety and efficiency, serving as the critical interface between human operators, technological systems, and organizational coordination. Effective communication ensures situational awareness across pilots, air-traffic controllers, maintenance personnel, and automated systems, enabling rapid information exchange and decision-making under dynamic conditions (Federal Aviation Administration [FAA], 2023). Miscommunication, data latency, or degraded links within this network can produce cascading consequences ranging from delays and operational inefficiencies to safety-critical incidents, which is why modern air-traffic modernization efforts emphasize robust, resilient communications, navigation, and surveillance systems and standardized procedures (Baugh & Stolzer, 2018; FAA, 2023; Yang et al., 2023). Secure and reliable communication channels, supported by standardized protocols, encrypted data links, and real-time information sharing, are therefore essential to maintaining operational integrity and enabling coordinated responses to outages, cyber incidents, or policy disruptions.

Information-sharing enhancements can target a significant limitation of air traffic: the serial, verbal, and error-prone nature of traditional air–ground communication (Baugh & Stolzer, 2018; FAA, 2023; Yang et al., 2023). These solutions have proven effective when communication infrastructure is operational but requires greater efficiency and accuracy. The adoption of mobile device–based approaches that leverage commercial products and Internet Protocol (IP) networks offers additional resilience by operating through infrastructure external to government systems, thereby maintaining critical functionality during periods of government operational disruption.

A recent proposal has explored the use of commercial mobile devices and Internet Protocol (IP) networks to mitigate these core communication vulnerabilities within the air traffic management environment. The Info-Centric National Airspace System (ICN) concept exemplifies this approach by employing native iOS applications and Progressive Web Applications (PWAs) hosted within secure virtual machine environments (Menzenski et a., 2023). These platforms facilitate the electronic exchange of Instrument Flight Rules (IFR) clearances, releases, and cancellations; the negotiation of Call for Release (CFR) times; and the issuance, receipt, acceptance, and monitoring of taxi route conformance (Menzenski et a., 2023). By replacing traditional voice-based coordination with authenticated digital transactions, the ICN approach reduces the time demands of verbal exchanges, minimizes the risk of read-back errors, and enhances data security through controlled, identity-verified connections (Menzenski et a., 2023). These types of technologies can be extremely efficient in situations with staffing challenges, such as in the case of the 2025 shutdown that forced many overworked air traffic controllers to stay on shift, when errors or lack of clarity in verbal exchanges can pose significant risks to passengers.

Mobile device and data link technologies that leverage commercial infrastructure can preserve critical information exchange even when government systems are degraded. The electronic transmission of clearances and taxi routes reduces reliance on serial, verbal communication, eliminating common bottlenecks that intensify during staffing shortages. Specialized platforms for data exchange facilitate the real-time sharing of scheduling and traffic management information between the FAA and airlines. This capability supports coordinated decision-making while minimizing controller workload and has demonstrated operational effectiveness without adverse impacts, suggesting strong resilience to staffing fluctuations.

In summary, research shows that digital communication systems, IP-based datalink platforms, and mobile-device exchange tools reduce verbal errors, speed coordination, and maintain situational awareness under high workload (Menzenski et al., 2023; Yang et al., 2023). However, they also rely on robust authentication, reliable networks, and continuous monitoring, elements that become strained during shutdowns or staffing shortages (Alhalabi et al., 2025). International ATM environments demonstrate that these systems are most resilient when coupled with distributed architectures and harmonized security frameworks. Thus, digital communication technologies offer meaningful mitigation benefits but must be embedded in a broader, resilient system design. Their role in the layered mitigation framework therefore should be embedded in the broader digital coordination layer of aviation information systems.

Human Factors in Aviation Technology

It is well known that organizational pressures, physiological stressors, and communication breakdowns can compromise both airworthiness and operational safety (Olaganathan, 2024). Organizational resilience in aviation, therefore, is highly dependent on understanding human behavior. Safety incidents often originate from latent human-system interactions, including workload pressures, ambiguous task sequencing, and cognitive fatigue (Haruna & Taiwo, 2024; Olaganathan, 2024). Additionally, human-related variables (such as crew experience, fatigue, and decision-making under pressure) along with aircraft age and operational complexity, are among the strongest predictors of accident severity (Odetayo & Haruna, 2024). Considering the significant human impacts of a shutdown, resulting in increased overtime expectations from flight controllers, designing aviation information systems with human factors in mind could significantly decrease these negative impacts. Enhancing air traffic control resilience requires continuous training, strong team coordination, data-driven learning, well-defined contingency procedures, and automation technologies designed to complement (rather than replace) human judgment (Smith & Baumann, 2020)

Embedding human factors principles into quality processes allows maintenance organizations to anticipate and mitigate errors before they escalate into operational failures (Haruna & Taiwo, 2024). Human-factors-based frameworks can detect latent organizational weaknesses (such as fatigue, communication breakdowns, or training gaps) that traditional technical inspections often overlook (Haruna & Taiwo, 2024). These human factors integrations can result in measurable reductions in maintenance errors, improved safety culture, and heightened situational awareness across shifts (Haruna & Taiwo, 2024). Further technological innovation, such as predictive maintenance analytics and robotic inspections, can offer new ways to support human performance management, especially when organizations are understaffed (Olaganathan, 2024).

Aviation systems, therefore, must be considered in a socio-technical systems perspective, where human performance, environmental conditions, and technological tools jointly determine reliability outcomes (Olaganathan, 2024). Aviation resilience is both technical and human: information systems should support, not replace, human judgment during crises. Human-automation frameworks can enhance adaptability when controller staffing drops below safe thresholds. Aviation regulators and maintenance organizations must evolve from reactive processes to human-centered workflows for anticipatory safety management to strengthen the reliability of the air transportation system. Regulatory agencies should further assess workforce attitudes and identify gaps between official policy and lived experience of controllers, pilots, and other aviation workers (Walden & Thomas, 2025).

Summary of Findings: The Layered Mitigation IS Framework for Crisis Scenarios

The synthesis of this analysis indicates that for government shutdown scenarios, a layered mitigation strategy of information systems offers the most effective means of sustaining operational resilience. The suggested improvements can be grouped into four overarching domains to make up these 4 layers (depicted in Figure 1): infrastructure integration and resilience, an integrated digital coordination layer (which includes decision-support systems, automation, and information-sharing), cybersecurity advancements, and human-system integration.

Figure 1.The layered mitigation framework of information systems for aviation resilience.

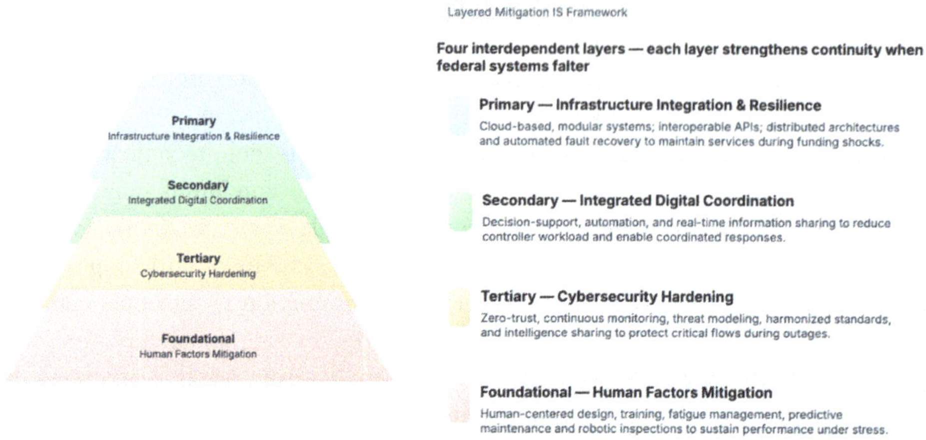

Primary Layer – Infrastructure Integration and Resilience

Infrastructure resilience in the new era of aviation depends on the industry's ability to modernize legacy systems and design architectures that remain functional under fiscal, technical, or operational stress. The 2025 government shutdown revealed how centralized funding models and aging communication networks create systemic vulnerabilities, highlighting the need for redundant, cloud-based, and modular infrastructures capable of sustaining essential services even amid disruption. Integrating IoT, AI, and big data analytics can enhance predictive management, real-time decision-making, and cross-agency coordination, but these technologies must be governed through frameworks that embed cyber-physical resilience from the outset. Moving forward, infrastructure design should prioritize distributed systems, automated fault recovery, and interoperable data governance, ensuring that air traffic operations, maintenance, and passenger services remain agile and secure.

Interagency data integration is essential to sustaining operational continuity and safety in the increasingly networked aviation ecosystem. Application Programming Interfaces (APIs) and standardized data exchange protocols enable seamless interoperability among agencies and aviation players, ensuring that critical safety and situational awareness data remain accessible even if one agency's internal systems are compromised or offline. Such interconnected frameworks reduce the risk of information silos and allow for real-time decision-making across institutional boundaries. Establishing cross-agency contingency systems, supported by shared cloud infrastructures and synchronized communication platforms, can prevent fragmented responses during crises such as shutdowns, cyber incidents, or system outages. Ultimately, building resilient aviation infrastructure and embedding interagency coordination through data integration is not merely a technical enhancement but a strategic imperative for maintaining aviation safety, resilience, and public trust in an increasingly digital airspace.

Secondary Layer – Integrated Digital Coordination

The convergence of automation, decision-support systems, and information-sharing infrastructure forms a unified digital coordination layer that supports modern aviation resilience. When these technologies operate in concert, they enable continuous situational awareness, rapid data-driven decision-making, and adaptive responses to disruptions. Automation streamlines operational and administrative processes, decision-support tools provide analytical insight and predictive capabilities, and shared data infrastructures ensure that critical information flows seamlessly across agencies and systems. Together, this integrated layer enhances organizational agility, mitigates human and systemic vulnerabilities, and establishes the foundation for a more proactive, interconnected aviation ecosystem.

Tertiary Layer – Cybersecurity Hardening

Cybersecurity must be embedded across the entire system lifecycle, shifting from reactive compliance to a proactive safety function supported by automation, continuous monitoring, and zero-trust architectures. Modernizing legacy infrastructure through cloud-based, modular, and redundant systems is essential to maintaining operational continuity during funding or staffing disruptions. Adopting structured threat modeling and implementing network-level protections for vulnerable data flows can prevent opportunistic cyberattacks during shutdowns, when monitoring and response capabilities may be constrained. In addition, the aviation sector should pursue harmonized, interoperable cybersecurity standards and governance frameworks that align regulatory oversight with technological innovation. Finally, multi-layered collaboration among agencies, airlines, and manufacturers, supported by workforce development, threat intelligence sharing, and mandatory incident reporting, will enable a more agile, anticipatory approach to risk management in the digital aviation ecosystem.

Foundational Layer – Human Factors Mitigation

To enhance aviation safety, resilience, and technological agility, organizations must explicitly integrate human factors principles into the system design, operational workflows, and oversight of interconnected systems. Continuous training, clear communication protocols, and automation tools that support rather than replace human judgment are essential for sustaining performance under stress and workforce shortages. Regulatory and organizational governance structures should adopt human-centered, anticipatory safety management frameworks capable of identifying latent vulnerabilities, such as fatigue, communication breakdowns, and training deficiencies, before they escalate into operational failures. Additionally, predictive maintenance analytics and robotic inspection systems should be leveraged to strengthen human performance and reduce error rates, especially during times of staffing disruption. Ultimately, aviation governance must embrace a socio-technical systems perspective, aligning policy, technology, and workforce wellbeing to ensure that modernization initiatives enhance, not compromise, safety, adaptability, and organizational trust.

Collectively, the findings across infrastructure, digital coordination, cybersecurity, and human factors demonstrate that no single technology or policy intervention is sufficient to sustain aviation continuity under shutdown conditions. Instead, resilience emerges from the interaction of distributed technical architectures, adaptive workforce processes, and governance structures capable of supporting continuous modernization. The layered framework advanced here integrates these insights into an applied, socio-technical approach to aviation resilience. This directly answers the central research question by identifying the IS improvements most capable of mitigating shutdown-induced disruptions.

CONCLUSIONS

The analysis across infrastructure, digital coordination, cybersecurity, and human factors demonstrates that aviation resilience during governance disruptions emerges from the interaction of tightly coupled socio-technical elements rather than from any single technological upgrade. The 2025 U.S. government shutdown served as a stress test for the nation's aviation infrastructure, exposing the fragility of legacy systems and the cascading operational, human, and cybersecurity vulnerabilities that emerge when federal functions halt. Through a socio-technical systems lens, this study demonstrated that sustaining aviation continuity under such extreme conditions requires more than technical upgrades; it demands systemic redesigns that align people, processes, and technology. Information systems must be viewed not as isolated tools but as integral components of a resilient governance ecosystem capable of maintaining safety, coordination, and trust even amid fiscal and political uncertainty.

This study shows that the shutdown's most disruptive effects (reduced staffing, delayed safety checks, suspended modernization work, and communication bottlenecks) could have been mitigated through distributed cloud architectures, automated digital coordination tools, redundant communication and data-link channels, and proactive cybersecurity monitoring frameworks. These systems do not eliminate the operational consequences of a shutdown, but they substantially reduce the risk of cascading failures by providing continuity in information flow, decision support, and safety oversight.

The layered mitigation framework proposed in this paper (encompassing infrastructure modernization, integrated digital coordination, cybersecurity hardening, and human factors optimization), highlights that organizational agility in aviation depends on interdependence and redundancy. To reduce operational disruptions, aviation information systems should prioritize greater interoperability, the development of integrated delay prediction platforms, and more adaptive data-sharing frameworks. Future aviation systems must incorporate modular architectures, cloud-based redundancy, and automated recovery mechanisms to ensure operational continuity during funding disruptions. Likewise, decision-support automation, AI-assisted communication systems, and blockchain-enabled data integrity can reinforce coordination across agencies and private stakeholders, reducing dependency on vulnerable verbal and manual processes.

Equally vital is the human dimension. Investing in workforce well-being, training, and cognitive readiness transforms technology from a potential failure point into an enabler of adaptive performance. By embedding human factors engineering into design and governance, the aviation industry can strengthen both the safety culture and the resilience of their operations. Sustained training programs, well-defined contingency procedures, and integration of human factors in design decisions ensure that controllers can effectively manage air traffic during reduced staffing. This foundation mitigates the risk of compounding technical and human-factor vulnerabilities during crisis conditions.

Ultimately, the 2025 shutdown demonstrates that organizational agility cannot rely on technology alone; it depends on the coordinated evolution of innovation, governance, and workforce adaptability. Future aviation systems must function as integrated socio-technical environments: designed to anticipate disruptions, apply lessons learned from crises, and adjust operational processes in real time to maintain public safety and operational continuity. Aviation resilience requires socio-technical alignment, where robust information systems, supportive governance structures, and empowered human operators function together to maintain safety, continuity, and public trust even under extreme operational stress.

As with any qualitative interpretive analysis, this study carries several limitations. The findings are shaped by the availability of documented shutdown effects, contemporary aviation research, and international technical reports, and should therefore be interpreted as a conceptual model rather than a predictive evaluation. Because this analysis focuses primarily on U.S. aviation governance and available documentation from a single shutdown event, the findings may not fully generalize to international contexts with different institutional structures or funding mechanisms. The study is also limited by the uneven availability of empirical data and post-incident reporting, which constrains the ability to fully assess the performance of specific information system components during the shutdown.

RECOMMENDATIONS FOR FUTURE RESEARCH

Future research should expand empirical analysis of aviation information systems under crisis conditions to better quantify how specific technologies (such as AI-assisted decision tools, blockchain-based coordination systems, and cloud redundancy architectures) impact operational resilience during funding or staffing disruptions. Comparative studies across international aviation authorities could reveal governance models and policy frameworks that enable faster recovery and improved cross-agency coordination during government shutdowns or similar crises.

Further studies are needed to explore the integration of socio-technical systems (STS) theory in aviation modernization initiatives, particularly focusing on how workforce culture, communication structures, and automation interact to shape resilience outcomes. Research should also examine human factors in digital aviation environments, identifying how training, fatigue management, and decision-support systems can be optimized to sustain performance during prolonged disruptions.

Finally, cybersecurity resilience in aviation warrants ongoing investigation, particularly in developing predictive, AI-driven models that detect and mitigate cyber threats when normal monitoring operations are interrupted. Longitudinal studies assessing the cumulative impact of repeated shutdowns or funding interruptions on safety, maintenance, and workforce retention could provide the evidence base necessary for policy and technology design that ensures continuity and public trust in critical aviation infrastructure.

REFERENCES

Abeyratne, R. (2020). *Aviation in the digital age: Legal and regulatory aspects.* Springer., DOI: 10.1007/978-3-030-48218-3

Agbolosu-Amison, S., & Mondoloni, S. (2012). Modeling system-wide predictability and associated air carrier benefits. *Proceedings of the 11th AIAA Aviation Technology, Integration, and Operations (ATIO) Conference*, AIAA. DOI: 10.2514/6.2011-6810

Alhalabi, D., Alawida, M., & Hasan, R. (2025). How secure is CPDLC? A comprehensive review of cyber threats and defense mechanisms in aviation communication. *Journal of Transportation Security, 18*(1), 23. Advance online publication. DOI: 10.1007/s12198-025-00312-z

Baugh, B. S., & Stolzer, A. J. (2018). Language-related communications challenges in general aviation operations and pilot training. *International Journal of Aviation, Aeronautics, and Aerospace, 5*(4). Advance online publication. DOI: 10.15394/ijaaa.2018.1271

Baxter, G., & Sommerville, I. (2011). Socio-technical systems: From design methods to systems engineering. *Interacting with Computers, 23*(1), 4–17. DOI: 10.1016/j.intcom.2010.07.003

Bostrom, R. P., & Heinen, J. S. (1977). MIS problems and failures: A socio-technical perspective, Part I: The causes. *Management Information Systems Quarterly, 1*(3), 17–32. DOI: 10.2307/248710

Brooker, P. (2008). SESAR and NextGen: Investing in new paradigms. *Journal of Navigation, 61*(2), 195–208. DOI: 10.1017/S0373463307004596

Cherns, A. (1976). The principles of sociotechnical design. *Human Relations, 29*(8), 783–792. DOI: 10.1177/001872677602900806

Cherns, A. (1987). Principles of sociotechnical design revisited. *Human Relations, 40*(3), 153–161. DOI: 10.1177/001872678704000303

Cokorilo, O. (2020). Urban air mobility: Safety challenges. *Transportation Research Procedia, 45*, 21–29. DOI: 10.1016/j.trpro.2020.02.058

Cook, D., Mayer, R., & Doya, G. (2023). Crises and the resilience of the aviation industry: A literature review. *Transportation Research Interdisciplinary Perspectives, 27*, 101182. Advance online publication. DOI: 10.1016/j.trip.2024.101182

Cooper, R., & Foster, M. (1971). Sociotechnical systems. *The American Psychologist, 26*(5), 467–474. DOI: 10.1037/h0031539

Darr, S., Ricks, W., & Lemos, A. K. (2008). Safer systems: A NextGen aviation safety strategic goal. In *Proceedings of 2008 IEEE/AIAA 27th Digital Avionics Systems Conference,* (pp. 2.A.1-1 - 2.A.1-8.). IEEE. DOI: 10.1109/DASC.2008.4702772

Dave, K. (2025). Modernizing U.S. air traffic control: The promise and pitfalls of NextGen implementation + comprehensive policy recommendations. *SSRN*. DOI: 10.2139/ssrn.5550998

Davis, M. C., Challenger, R., Jayewardene, D. N. W., & Clegg, C. W. (2014). Advancing socio-technical systems thinking: A call for bravery. *Applied Ergonomics, 45*(2), 171–180. DOI: 10.1016/j.apergo.2013.02.009

Dixon-Woods, M., Agarwal, S., Jones, D., Young, B., & Sutton, A. (2006). Synthesising qualitative and quantitative evidence: A review of possible methods. *Journal of Health Services Research & Policy, 10*(1), 45–53. DOI: 10.1177/135581960501000110

Eleimat, M., & Őszi, A. (2025). Cybersecurity in aviation: Exploring the significance, applications, and challenges of cybersecurity in the aviation sector. *Periodica Polytechnica Transportation Engineering, 53*(2), 169–183. DOI: 10.3311/PPtr.37153

EUROCONTROL. (2023). *EUROCONTROL Aviation Outlook 2050.* https://www.eurocontrol.int/publication/eurocontrol-aviation-outlook-2050

Federal Aviation Administration. (2023). *NextGen annual report, fiscal year 2023.* U.S. Department of Transportation. https://www.faa.gov/nextgen/NextGen-Annual-Report-2023.pdf

Federal Aviation Administration. (2025, November 6). *DOT & FAA announce temporary 10% reduction in flights at 40 airports.* https://www.faa.gov/newsroom/dot-faa-announce-temporary-10-reduction-flights-40-airports

Florido-Benítez, L. (2024). The types of hackers and cyberattacks in the aviation industry. *Journal of Transportation Security, 17*(1), 13. Advance online publication. DOI: 10.1007/s12198-024-00281-9

Gu, Y., Wiedemann, M., Freestone, R., Rothe, H., & Stevens, N. (2024). The impacts of shock events on airport management and operations: A systematic literature review. *Transportation Research Interdisciplinary Perspectives, 27*, 101182. Advance online publication. DOI: 10.1016/j.trip.2024.101182

Haruna, A. D., & Taiwo, O. O.Ayegba David HarunaOlugbenga Olayinka Taiwo. (2024). Enhancing aviation maintenance oversight through proactive quality auditing and human factors integration. *World Journal of Advanced Engineering Technology and Sciences, 13*(1), 1180–1199. DOI: 10.30574/wjaets.2024.13.1.0419

International Civil Aviation Organization. (n.d.). *Global Air Navigation Plan (GANP).* https://www.icao.int/global-air-navigation-plan-ganp

Jin, L., Jain, A., Shah, A., & Sykes, R. (2024). Government funding gap impacts on commercial aviation safety: President Carter through Trump (1978-2020). *International Journal of Aviation Research, 16*(1).

Kaminski, J. (2022). Editorial. Theory applied to informatics: Socio-Technical Theory. *Canadian Journal of Nursing Informatics, 17*(3-4). https://cjni.net/journal/?p=10442

Menzenski, J., Baumgartner, D. M., Cheng, J., Diffenderfer, P. A., Helleberg, J., Mykityshyn, A., & Wilkins, S. A. (2023). Airspace user–air traffic control information exchange using mobile devices to enhance the future info-centric national airspace system. *Proceedings of the 42nd IEEE/AIAA Digital Avionics Systems Conference (DASC).* IEEE. DOI: 10.1109/DASC58513.2023.10311312

Miles, M. B., Huberman, A. M., & Saldaña, J. (2014). *Qualitative data analysis: A methods sourcebook* (3rd ed.). Sage.

Mumford, E. (2006). The story of socio-technical design: Reflections on its successes, failures and potential. *Information Systems Journal, 16*(4), 317–342. DOI: 10.1111/j.1365-2575.2006.00221.x

Odetayo, T., & Haruna, A. D. (2024). Assessment of aviation accident datasets in severity prediction through artificial intelligence. *Journal of Air Transport Management, 115*, 102531. Advance online publication. DOI: 10.1016/j.jairtraman.2023.102531

Olaganathan, R. (2024). Human factors in aviation maintenance: Understanding errors, management, and technological trends. *Global Journal of Engineering and Technology Advances, 18*(2), 92–101. DOI: 10.30574/gjeta.2024.18.2.0021

Pasmore, W., Winby, S., Mohrman, S. A., & Vanasse, R. (2019). Reflections: Sociotechnical systems design and organization change. *Journal of Change Management, 19*(2), 67–85. DOI: 10.1080/14697017.2018.1553761

Roy, S., & Sridhar, B. (2016). Cyber-threat assessment for the air traffic management system: A network controls approach. *AIAA Aviation and Aeronautics Forum and Exposition.* AIAA. https://ntrs.nasa.gov/citations/20180000393

Smith, P. J., & Baumann, E. (2020). Human-automation teaming: Unintended consequences of automation on user performance. *Proceedings of the IEEE International Conference on Human-Machine Systems,* 1–9. IEEE. DOI: 10.1109/DASC50938.2020.9256418

Targeted News Service. (2025, October 30). WATCH: Davids discusses impact of government shutdown on aviation safety, workforce. Retrieved from ProQuest database. https://www.proquest.com/wire-feeds/watch-davids-discusses-impact-government-shutdown/docview/3267096786/se-2

. Trist, E. L., & Bamforth, K. W. (1951). Some social and psychological consequences of the Longwall Method of coal-getting: An examination of the psychological situation and defences of a work group in relation to the social structure and technological content of the work system. *Human Relations, 4*(1), 3-38. (Original work published 1951)DOI: 10.1177/001872675100400101

United States Government Accountability Office. (2015). *Air traffic control: FAA needs a more comprehensive approach to address cybersecurity as agency transitions to NextGen.* https://heinonline.org/HOL/Page?handle=hein.gao/gaobaaiua0001&id=1&collection=gao&index=

Walden, A., & Thomas, J. (2025). Unveiling the narrative around pilot mental health and aviation – A content analysis of FAA and mental-health-related social-media content. *Collegiate Aviation Review International, 43*(1), 19–35. https://ojs.library.okstate.edu/osu/index.php/CARI/article/view/9997/8944

Walsham, G. (1995). Interpretive case studies in IS research: Nature and method. *European Journal of Information Systems*, *4*(2), 74–81. DOI: 10.1057/ejis.1995.9

Walsham, G. (2006). Doing interpretive research. *European Journal of Information Systems*, *15*(3), 320–330. DOI: 10.1057/palgrave.ejis.3000589

Welsh, T., & Benkhelifa, E. (2020). On resilience in cloud computing: A survey of techniques across the cloud domain. *ACM Computing Surveys*, *53*(3), 59. Advance online publication. DOI: 10.1145/3388922

Westin, C., Hilburn, B., Borst, C., van Kampen, E.-J., & Bång, M. (2020). Building transparent and personalized AI support in air traffic control. In *IEEE/AIAA 39th Digital Avionics Systems Conference (DASC)*. DOI: 10.1109/DASC50938.2020.9256708

Yamat, R. (2025, October 15). The government shutdown is putting a renewed spotlight on the cracks in the US aviation system. *The Canadian Press*. https://www.proquest.com/wire-feeds/government-shutdown-is-putting-renewed-spotlight/docview/3262021655/se-2

Yang, H.-H., Chang, Y.-H., & Chou, Y.-H. (2023). Subjective measures of communication errors between pilots and air traffic controllers. *Journal of Air Transport Management*, *112*, 102461. DOI: 10.1016/j.jairtraman.2023.102461

Chapter 3
Digital Transformation in Government Agencies:
Overcoming Bureaucracy, Fragmentation, and Security Risks

Lord Dordunoo
http://orcid.org/0009-0007-7395-2677
Marymount University, USA

ABSTRACT

Digital transformation in government agencies can enhance service delivery, transparency, and operational efficiency. Yet, efforts are often hindered by entrenched bureaucracy, fragmented IT systems, and cybersecurity risks. This chapter critically examines the intersection of digital modernization and public administration, identifying key institutional, cultural, and technical barriers that hinder effective implementation. Drawing on over 30 peer-reviewed sources, it integrates strategic planning and change management frameworks, most notably Kotter's 8-Step Model and the Digital Government Maturity Model, to explore how agencies can implement secure, resilient, and citizen-centered reforms. Case studies illustrate how governments have navigated resistance, fostered interagency collaboration, and safeguarded data integrity. Situating digital transformation within governance innovation and ethical risk management, this chapter offers both theoretical insight and practical guidance for sustainable public-sector modernization.

INTRODUCTION

Digital transformation is fundamentally reshaping how government agencies operate, communicate, and deliver services to the public. As digital technologies

DOI: 10.4018/979-8-2600-1021-1.ch003

evolve rapidly, public institutions face growing pressure to modernize legacy systems, streamline service delivery, and meet rising expectations for transparency, responsiveness, and digital accessibility (Mergel et al., 2019; OECD, 2019). Unlike the private sector, however, government agencies must navigate a complex landscape marked by bureaucratic inertia, rigid policy constraints, siloed organizational structures, and diverse stakeholder demands (Lindgren et al., 2019; Ubaldi et al., 2019; Wirtz et al., 2018). Although governments are making substantial investments in digital infrastructure, transformation initiatives frequently falter due to institutional fragmentation, leadership turnover, resistance to change, and inconsistent cybersecurity protocols (Kuhlmann & Heuberger, 2021; Wirtz et al., 2018).

Historically, public-sector modernization efforts have been hindered by hierarchical administrative structures and incompatible information systems that impede agency coordination. These structural barriers delay implementation and diminish service delivery quality and consistency (Hinings et al., 2018). Research increasingly emphasizes that successful digital transformation requires more than technology upgrades. It demands fundamental shifts in organizational culture, governance norms, leadership mindset, and citizen engagement (Kuhlmann & Heuberger, 2021; Wirtz et al., 2018). Public agencies must address not only the what of digital platforms and services but also the how and why, including change management, workforce readiness, and ethical considerations such as algorithmic fairness and data stewardship (Engin et al., 2025; Zwitter & Boisse-Despiaux, 2018).

The COVID-19 pandemic accelerated the urgency of digital transformation and exposed the limitations of analog systems within many government institutions (Boehm et al., 2020). During the crisis, numerous agencies struggled to scale remote services, coordinate real-time data, or protect sensitive information, revealing gaps in cybersecurity readiness, procurement agility, and interagency interoperability (Bernardez Molina et al., 2023). However, the pandemic also demonstrated that governments could act swiftly under pressure, as evidenced by rapid deployments of virtual courtrooms, online health portals, and emergency digital outreach platforms (Boehm et al., 2020). These developments highlight that digital transformation is no longer optional, but rather, it is foundational to building agile, resilient, and citizen-centered public institutions equipped to handle contemporary challenges. For example, the United States Digital Service (USDS), a team of technologists embedded in federal agencies, played a key role in rapidly scaling digital services during the COVID-19 crisis, including virtual service portals and online benefit access tools (UNITED STATES DIGITAL SERVICES, 2024).

This chapter critically examines the institutional, structural, and technological challenges that hinder digital transformation in government agencies. Drawing on over 25 scholarly sources, it integrates leading strategic planning and change management frameworks, notably the Digital Government Maturity Model (DGMM) and Kotter's 8-Step Change Model, to explore how public entities can overcome bureaucracy, bridge institutional silos, and address cybersecurity risks (Kotter, 1996; Renteria et al., 2019; Ubaldi et al., 2019). The chapter is organized into four parts: (1) a review of recent developments and barriers in public-sector digitalization; (2) a definition of the core problem and proposed goals; (3) the application of evidence-based strategic and change models; and (4) a synthesis of actionable recommendations supported by global case studies. Linking interdisciplinary theory with practical governance challenges, the chapter contributes to the evolving discourse on digital public administration and provides a roadmap for responsible, scalable, and inclusive government modernization.

Problem Statement

Despite the transformative potential of digital technologies, many government agencies struggle to implement coherent, inclusive, and sustainable modernization strategies. At the heart of the challenge lies the deeply entrenched nature of bureaucratic processes, fragmented digital infrastructures, and siloed administrative cultures, all limiting cross-functional collaboration and innovation (Lindgren et al., 2019; Ubaldi et al., 2019). Numerous agencies still rely on outdated legacy systems that are not only expensive to maintain but also incompatible with newer technologies, creating inefficiencies, redundancies, and poor user experiences for both employees and citizens (Mergel et al., 2019). These technical limitations often reinforce institutional inertia, where resistance to change becomes embedded in daily operations and decision-making hierarchies (Hinings et al., 2018; Kuhlmann & Heuberger, 2021).

Recent studies have shown that the long-term costs of maintaining legacy systems can significantly outweigh the investments required for modernization. For instance, the U.S. Government Accountability Office (GAO) reported that some agencies spend over 80% of their IT budgets on operations and maintenance of outdated systems (GAO, 2023). These legacy systems often expose agencies to security risks and limit interoperability, leading to indirect costs such as service delays and compliance failures. In contrast, agencies that have invested in cloud-native or modular platforms, such as the VA's transition to cloud-based benefits processing, have demonstrated significant cost savings and improved service delivery (UNITED STATES DIGITAL SERVICES, 2024). A complete cost-benefit analysis must, therefore, account for both technical and institutional gains, not just upfront spending.

Security vulnerabilities and regulatory ambiguities compound the digital transformation problem in the public sector. As agencies increasingly rely on cloud platforms, mobile services, and interconnected databases, they face heightened exposure to cyberattacks, data breaches, and operational disruptions (Bernardez Molina et al., 2023; Zwitter & Boisse-Despiaux, 2018). However, many public institutions lack uniform cybersecurity frameworks or clearly defined protocols for digital risk management, leading to uneven levels of preparedness across departments and levels of government (OECD, 2019). Furthermore, the rapid pace of digital innovation has outstripped many agencies' capacity to develop digital skills internally, leading to workforce gaps in data governance, artificial intelligence, and cyber threat detection (Engin et al., 2025; Reyna et al., 2018). Addressing the workforce-skills deficit is critical for sustaining digital transformation. Many agencies lack access to talent in high-demand fields such as cloud security, user experience design, and data science. Programs like the Presidential Innovation Fellows and state-level digital academies offer promising models for recruitment and upskilling. However, without institutional incentives, career mobility, and flexible hiring authorities, public agencies struggle to compete with the private sector for top talent (Engin et al., 2025). Given these persistent barriers, the primary goal of this chapter is to explore how government agencies can strategically overcome bureaucratic resistance, institutional fragmentation, and security vulnerabilities in their digital transformation efforts. Achieving this goal requires a multidimensional approach that moves beyond technological deployment to embrace systemic reform, interagency collaboration, agile procurement, ethical data governance, and continuous stakeholder engagement (Kuhlmann & Heuberger, 2021; Mergel et al., 2019). Leadership commitment and structured change management are critical enablers for fostering a culture of innovation and accountability across public institutions (Kotter, 1996; Wirtz et al., 2018).

Addressing the core problem is not merely about acquiring better digital tools but transforming the institutional environment in which those tools are deployed. This requires public agencies to move beyond isolated technology upgrades and pursue holistic reforms that embed digital capabilities within everyday governance structures (Comella-Dorda et al., 2020). These reforms include clarifying roles and responsibilities across departments, modernizing procurement frameworks to support agile innovation, ensuring compliance with evolving data protection laws, and aligning digital initiatives with long-term governance and equity objectives (Bailey et al., 2019; Kaplan et al., 2020; Ubaldi et al., 2019; Wirtz et al., 2018). Emphasizing technical and cultural dimensions of change, this chapter argues that digital transformation in government must be approached as an integrated strategy focused on institutional resilience, public trust, and democratic accountability. As demonstrated by USDS, effective transformation also involves rethinking institutional design, streamlining procurement, and integrating digital ethics into operations through tools such as the Digital Services Playbook and TechFAR Handbook (UNITED STATES DIGITAL SERVICES, 2024). Agile procurement frameworks, such as modular contracting and outcome-based specifications, have been successfully piloted to address legacy procurement inefficiencies. The TechFAR Handbook emphasizes iterative purchasing aligned with agile development cycles, enabling faster innovation without sacrificing compliance. However, inconsistent application across agencies and resistance from traditional procurement offices limit their scalability. To overcome these constraints, some jurisdictions have established procurement innovation labs and cross-functional review panels to streamline the evaluation and vendor engagement process.

Significance Statement

The significance of digital transformation in government extends beyond operational efficiency; it is foundational to institutional legitimacy, public trust, and democratic responsiveness in the 21st century. As governments serve increasingly diverse and digitally literate populations, failure to modernize public services can deepen inequalities, reduce access to essential programs, and reinforce public perceptions of inefficiency and detachment (OECD, 2019; Wirtz et al., 2018). Outdated digital systems and bureaucratic inertia have already contributed to delays in benefits processing, inconsistent service delivery, and poor citizen experiences across many jurisdictions (Lindgren et al., 2019). These issues are particularly acute during times of crisis, such as the COVID-19 pandemic, when agile, integrated, and secure systems become critical for mobilizing resources, disseminating information, and ensuring continuity of governance.

Despite growing recognition of the need for integrated digital services, governments worldwide continue to struggle with outdated infrastructure and fragmented delivery systems. According to the OECD Digital Government Index, only 36% of surveyed countries had integrated service delivery platforms across sectors by 2021, reflecting limited progress in cross-agency digital coordination (OECD, 2023). Similarly, the U.S. Federal IT Dashboard reports that the federal government allocates more than $65 billion annually to maintaining legacy and operational IT systems under the Operations & Maintenance (O&M) category, accounting for roughly two-thirds of its $102 billion IT budget in FY 2025 (U.S. Office of Management and Budget, 2024). These figures underscore the urgency of redirecting public-sector investment from sustaining outdated technologies toward scalable, interoperable, and user-centered digital platforms.

Figure 1. illustrates U.S. federal IT spending from 2021 to 2025, showing that Operations & Maintenance (O&M) consistently dominates the budget, exceeding $65 billion annually, while Development, Modernization, and Enhancement (DME) receives significantly less funding, highlighting a persistent modernization gap.

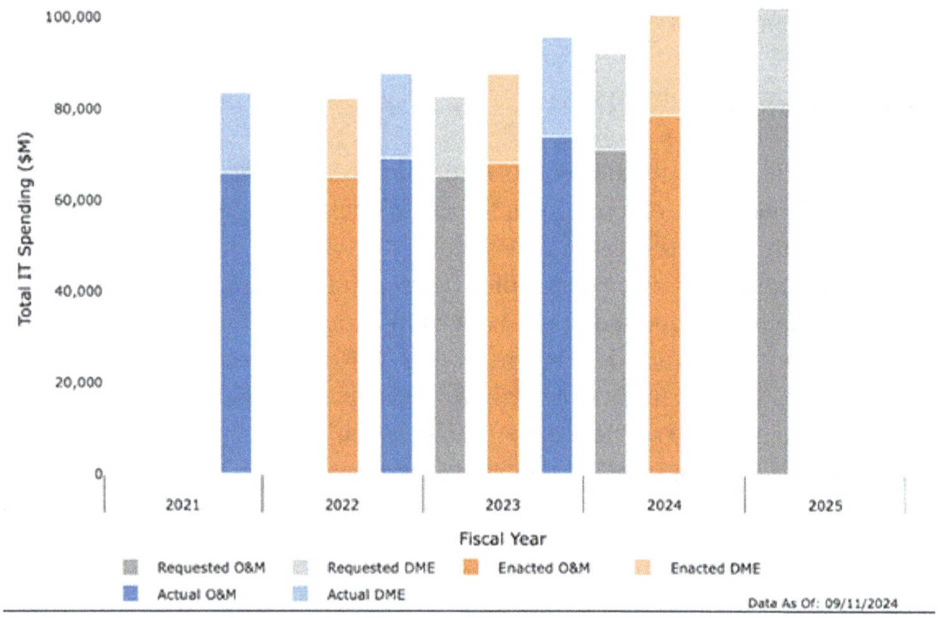

Source: U.S. Office of Management and Budget, Federal IT Dashboard (2024).

From a strategic and operational perspective, digital failure also threatens government effectiveness at a structural level. Agencies that lag in adopting interoperable platforms and secure data systems can often not participate in collaborative policymaking, intergovernmental service integration, or real-time emergency response networks (Mergel et al., 2019; Ubaldi et al., 2019). This digital fragmentation limits the public sector's ability to make evidence-based decisions, protect sensitive citizen data, and deliver consistent services across regions and demographics (Bernardez Molina et al., 2023). Moreover, vulnerabilities in cybersecurity infrastructure can expose governments to ransomware attacks, surveillance threats, and loss of operational control, undermining the reliability and credibility of digital public institutions (Engin et al., 2025; Wirtz et al., 2018). The work of USDS demonstrates that when agencies adopt user-centered design and cross-functional collaboration, outcomes can be dramatically improved, as seen in the redesigned VA.gov, which increased public trust and streamlined access for veterans (UNITED STATES DIGITAL SERVICES, 2024).

The broader implications of ethical digital transformation also intersect with governance equity and social inclusion issues. When implemented responsibly, digital tools can help reduce marginalized communities' barriers, increase resource allocation transparency, and support participatory decision-making (Kuhlmann & Heuberger, 2021). Conversely, when deployed without inclusive design or accountability safeguards, technology can amplify existing inequities, automate bias, and erode citizen rights, especially in data-intensive systems that lack transparency or oversight (Wirtz et al., 2018; Zwitter & Boisse-Despiaux, 2018). Digital modernization must be viewed as a technical upgrade and a public value proposition rooted in democratic ethics, human rights, and institutional renewal (Hinings et al., 2018; OECD, 2019).

Government digital transformation's ethical, political, and strategic stakes are high. Governments that proactively invest in internal capacity-building, meaningful stakeholder engagement, and sustained cross-sector collaboration are more likely to develop resilient, inclusive, and future-ready public services (Carson et al., 2024). Conversely, failure to act decisively risks deepening institutional fragmentation, eroding public trust, widening digital divides, and diminishing the legitimacy of democratic governance. Therefore, transforming public digital infrastructure is not merely a modernization priority; it is a foundational governance imperative essential to maintaining transparency, equity, and civic accountability in the digital.

Methodology

This chapter employs an exploratory qualitative case study methodology to investigate digital transformation's ethical, organizational, and technical dimensions within government agencies. A qualitative case study approach is well-suited to examining digital reform's complex and context-dependent nature in public administration, where variables such as institutional culture, political leadership, and legacy systems interact in multifaceted ways (Yin, 2017). Unlike quantitative methods, which may overlook nuances in implementation and behavior, qualitative case studies provide rich, detailed accounts of how transformation unfolds within specific agencies and policy contexts (Mergel et al., 2019; Wirtz et al., 2018). This design allows researchers to explore challenges and how and why they persist in real-world environments, making it ideal for evaluating multidimensional government reforms.

Historically, the case study method has proven particularly effective in public sector research focused on digital modernization. Scholars have used it to explore barriers to e-government implementation, assess change management strategies, and evaluate cross-agency digital coordination (Kuhlmann & Heuberger, 2021; Lindgren et al., 2019). For example, studies examining failures in digital service integration often point to poor interagency governance, leadership instability, or inadequate user engagement factors that are usually invisible in statistical datasets but critical to successful reform (Ubaldi et al., 2019). These qualitative insights help reveal how competing institutional mandates, resource constraints, and political pressures interact to shape digital outcomes across diverse administrative contexts.

This chapter supports the case study methodology by synthesizing peer-reviewed scholarly literature. These sources span multiple disciplines, including public administration, information systems, cybersecurity, change management, and digital ethics, reflecting the inherently interdisciplinary nature of digital government research. Articles were selected through a rigorous review of academic databases, policy reports, and practitioner literature to ensure relevance and contemporary applicability. Key themes analyzed include organizational fragmentation, data interoperability, leadership dynamics, and ethical governance, all central to understanding both barriers and opportunities for reform (Wirtz et al., 2018; Zwitter & Boisse-Despiaux, 2018).

Two complementary frameworks guide the analytical lens of this chapter. First, the Digital Government Maturity Model (DGMM) assesses institutional readiness across core domains such as technology infrastructure, user-centric service design, data integration, and digital culture (OECD, 2019; Renteria et al., 2019; Ubaldi et al., 2019). The DGMM enables a structured evaluation of where government agencies stand in their transformation journey and helps identify critical capability gaps. Second, Kotter's 8-Step Change Model provides a process-oriented roadmap for understanding how leadership, vision, and internal communication strategies can overcome bureaucratic resistance and support long-term institutional change (Kotter, 1996; Kuhlmann & Heuberger, 2021). These models work in tandem to connect organizational strategy with behavioral change, offering a dual lens on both technical and human transformation.

Synthesizing real-world examples, strategic frameworks, and empirical insights, this methodology allows for a holistic evaluation of the factors that shape digital transformation outcomes in the public sector. The case study approach supports the thematic interpretation of recurring challenges such as procurement rigidity, outdated governance frameworks, cybersecurity fragmentation, and digital skill shortages while identifying innovation accelerators and enabling conditions for reform (Bernardez Molina et al., 2023; Hinings et al., 2018). This methodological structure ensures the research remains grounded in current practice and academic theory. It supports the chapter's goal of producing actionable, evidence-based strategies for ethically grounded, scalable, and future-oriented digital modernization in public governance.

LITERATURE REVIEW

Overview

Digital transformation in government has emerged as a central priority in contemporary public administration, intersecting with demands for transparency, efficiency, and equitable service delivery. While early e-government research focused on technology adoption, recent studies have emphasized institutional complexity, ethical accountability, and strategic planning (Mergel et al., 2019; Wirtz et al., 2018). The rapid acceleration of digital reform, especially in response to COVID-19, has intensified scholarly interest in how bureaucratic structures, cybersecurity risks, and leadership gaps affect transformation outcomes (OECD, 2019). Drawing on peer-reviewed articles, this section synthesizes current literature across four core themes to frame digital government modernization's institutional, cultural, and technological dynamics.

Bureaucratic Resistance and Organizational Inertia

Bureaucratic resistance is one of the most cited barriers to digital transformation in the public sector. Government institutions built around hierarchical structures and risk-averse cultures often struggle to adopt the flexibility and speed that digital systems require (Kuhlmann & Heuberger, 2021; Lindgren et al., 2019). Public servants may fear technology-induced job displacement or lack clarity on their roles within new systems, fostering organizational inertia. In addition, civil servants may view digital initiatives as top-down impositions rather than opportunities for innovation, further reducing engagement. In many jurisdictions, this resistance persists even when clear policy mandates and funding streams are in place, suggesting that more profound cultural transformation is required beyond procedural reforms (Gil-Garcia et al., 2017; Janssen & van der Voort, 2020).

Leadership turnover, political instability, and shifting policy priorities further complicate transformation continuity. These external pressures make it challenging to maintain consistent reform agendas and often interrupt implementation before systems can reach maturity. Research shows that digital initiatives often stall after pilot phases due to limited executive sponsorship or short-term thinking (Bernardez Molina et al., 2023). Resistance is also exacerbated by low digital literacy across senior civil service ranks, where skepticism toward algorithmic decision-making or cloud infrastructure persists (Wirtz et al., 2018). To counteract this, several scholars advocate for distributed leadership models and innovation-oriented training programs that empower frontline staff while securing top-level endorsement (Hinings et al., 2018; Mergel et al., 2019).

Cultural reform must be explicitly addressed within digital strategies. Studies suggest that fostering a learning-oriented, feedback-rich environment enables greater receptivity to new technologies and agile workflows (Boehm et al., 2020). Organizations encouraging knowledge sharing and experimentation are more likely to overcome status quo bias and cultivate internal change agents. Leaders who frame transformation as mission-driven and inclusive rather than compliance-focused help shift perceptions and reduce passive resistance (Battilana & Casciaro, 2021). Thus, the literature underscores that digital transformation is ultimately a change management challenge, where cultural alignment is as critical as technical deployment.

Institutional Fragmentation and Interoperability Challenges

Institutional fragmentation remains one of the most persistent and complex barriers to digital transformation in the public sector. Many government agencies operate within siloed administrative structures, each maintaining independent digital systems, procurement procedures, and data protocols that hinder cross-functional integration (Ubaldi et al., 2019). This separation results in duplicative IT investments, increased operational costs, and fragmented service experiences for citizens who must navigate multiple departments to access related services (OECD, 2020). Fragmentation also limits institutional learning, as agencies lack shared platforms for monitoring, evaluation, or collaborative problem-solving (Zwitter & Boisse-Despiaux, 2018). For instance, in Vietnam, the absence of a centralized digital authority has led to overlapping mandates among various agencies, impeding cohesive digital transformation efforts (World Bank, 2021). Similarly, a study on the Norwegian Court Administration highlights that sector-wide transformation is necessary, as isolated digital initiatives often falter without coordinated efforts across institutions (Tangi et al., 2020). Moreover, the OECD emphasizes that fragmented governance structures can undermine the scalability and sustainability of digital government strategies (OECD, 2016).

While interoperability is often framed as a technical issue, the literature emphasizes that it is equally organizational and political. Public agencies typically operate under distinct legal mandates, funding mechanisms, and accountability frameworks, which complicate the development of shared digital infrastructure (Wirtz et al., 2018). Even when compatible data standards and architectures exist, political will, turf protection, and fears about losing autonomy frequently obstruct implementation (Wirtz et al., 2018). These structural dynamics reduce opportunities for coordination and make digital reform efforts highly inconsistent across departments or levels of government. For instance, the European Interoperability Framework highlights that differences in government structures and citizen-state interaction models across EU Member States pose significant challenges to interoperability (European Commission, 2017). Legacy systems and lack of shared standards impede seamless data exchange in many governments worldwidc (Boyce, 2024). Moreover, organizational silos and resistance to change further exacerbate interoperability issues, as agencies often prioritize their autonomy over collaborative efforts.

Efforts to resolve interoperability barriers have yielded mixed results, often depending on governance models and leadership commitment. Case studies from countries like Estonia and Denmark show that whole-of-government strategies anchored in strong central coordination can significantly improve service integration and user experience (OECD, 2019). These governments implemented national digital identity systems and unified APIs that allow secure, seamless data exchange while preserving agency-level responsibilities. However, such models require sustained political backing, legal harmonization, and cross-sector stakeholder engagement to be effective and equitable (Engin et al., 2025).

The literature suggests that overcoming fragmentation demands more than technical fixes; it requires rethinking institutional design and public value alignment. Interagency working groups, federated data governance frameworks, and collaborative budgeting practices can foster a culture of cooperation and transparency (Ubaldi et al., 2019). Moreover, adopting user-centered design principles across all service domains encourages a shift from department-centric logic to integrated service delivery models. Without addressing these institutional conditions, digital transformation will remain disjointed, limiting its capacity to deliver equitable and efficient outcomes across the public sector.

Cybersecurity and Ethical Data Governance

As government agencies digitize more of their infrastructure and services, cybersecurity has emerged as a critical pillar of digital transformation. Public institutions hold vast amounts of sensitive data, from tax records and health information to biometric identifiers, making them prime targets for cyberattacks and ransomware (Zwitter & Boisse-Despiaux, 2018). However, many government systems remain outdated, under-resourced, and inconsistently protected across departments, leaving significant vulnerabilities (OECD, 2019). Scholars emphasize that cybersecurity should be embedded early in digital planning, not as a secondary concern or post-deployment add-on (Wirtz et al., 2018).

Inadequate cybersecurity also undermines public trust, particularly when data breaches expose citizens to identity theft, surveillance, or discriminatory profiling. Legal frameworks such as the GDPR in Europe and equivalent regulations in other regions provide guidelines on data protection, but compliance across agencies varies widely in practice (Wirtz et al., 2018). Moreover, inconsistencies in cyber-readiness are compounded by fragmented IT governance, unclear accountability for security lapses, and a shortage of skilled cybersecurity personnel in the public sector (Cracknell et al., 2020). To mitigate these risks, scholars call for investment in modern security architecture, cross-agency coordination protocols, and ongoing cyber hygiene training for public servants (Zwitter & Boisse-Despiaux, 2018).

Alongside technical security, the ethical governance of data collection, usage, and retention presents equally urgent challenges. Governments increasingly rely on predictive analytics, behavioral tracking, and algorithmic decision-making to deliver public services, yet these tools raise concerns about transparency, consent, and fairness (Lindgren et al., 2019). For example, automated welfare distribution systems or law enforcement systems may entrench existing inequalities if not carefully designed and monitored (Kuhlmann & Heuberger, 2021). Ethical lapses in data governance risk reputational damage and civil rights violations and reduce citizens' willingness to engage with digital services altogether (Hinings et al., 2018).

The literature strongly supports adopting privacy-by-design frameworks and participatory data governance strategies essential to ethical digital transformation. Public agencies are increasingly encouraged to conduct algorithmic impact assessments, establish independent data ethics boards, and co-develop data governance charters with civil society stakeholders to ensure legitimacy and inclusiveness (Wirtz et al., 2018). These strategies not only promote transparency and democratic accountability but also foster public trust in digital government initiatives by demonstrating respect for individual rights and social equity. Cybersecurity and ethical data governance must be treated as foundational principles on par with cost-efficiency or service delivery if digital transformation in government is to be sustainable, inclusive, and publicly accountable.

Beyond data privacy, ethical digital transformation entails addressing algorithmic bias and digital exclusion, as well as ensuring procedural transparency. For example, automated decision systems in welfare eligibility or predictive policing must be subject to public audit and inclusive oversight. Participatory frameworks that integrate the voices of civil society, particularly those from marginalized communities, can help surface unintended harms. Ethical frameworks should evolve in tandem with digital systems, ensuring that innovation does not come at the expense of public accountability or democratic value (Taylor et al., 2017).

Strategic Planning and Change Management in the Public Sector

Strategic planning is essential for guiding digital transformation in government agencies, especially in environments characterized by legal complexity, resource constraints, and overlapping stakeholder mandates. Frameworks like the Digital Government Maturity Model (DGMM) have emerged as critical tools for assessing institutional readiness and charting a path from fragmented digital efforts to coherent, citizen-centered systems (OECD, 2019; Renteria et al., 2019; Ubaldi et al., 2019). The DGMM evaluates agencies across core dimensions such as infrastructure modernization, data integration, user-centered service design, and digital leadership, allowing decision-makers to align reform initiatives with measurable outcomes (Renteria et al., 2019. Agencies that apply the DGMM systematically can better prioritize investments, benchmark progress, and communicate value to political leaders and the public (Nerima & Ralyté, 2021; Renteria et al., 2019).

Equally important is the role of change management in ensuring that digital transformation is technically successful and culturally embedded. Kotter's 8-Step Change Model remains one of the most widely applied frameworks in public administration for this purpose, offering a structured process that begins with creating a sense of urgency and culminates in anchoring new practices within organizational culture (Kotter, 1996; Kuhlmann & Heuberger, 2021). The model emphasizes leadership engagement, transparent communication, and short-term wins factors that help to overcome resistance and build momentum. Studies show agencies using Kotter's model are more likely to maintain reform continuity beyond leadership transitions and adapt flexibly to emerging challenges (Bernardez Molina et al., 2023).

Figure 2. Kotter's 8-Step Change Model for Leading Organizational Transformation

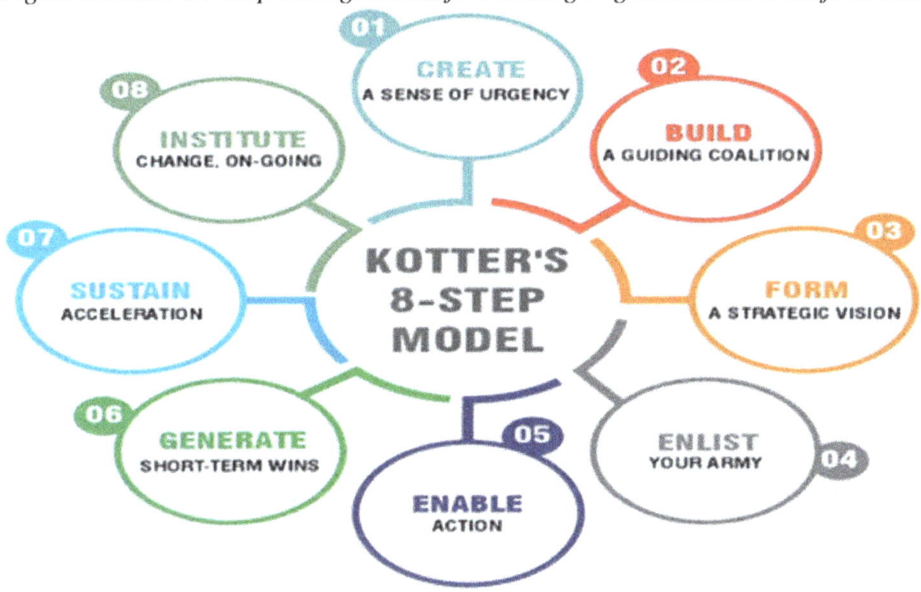

When integrated, strategic planning and change management frameworks create a powerful dual approach to transformation. While the DGMM provides the structural and diagnostic lens needed to assess institutional capabilities, Kotter's model offers the behavioral roadmap for mobilizing people and reshaping culture (Hinings et al., 2018; Kotter, 1996). USDS exemplifies how strategic planning and agile implementation can work in tandem to achieve effective results. Through structured tools such as the USDS Digital Services Playbook, design systems, and modular procurement guidance, the agency has helped organizations like the Social Security Administration (SSA), Department of Veterans Affairs (VA), and Department of Homeland Security (DHS) transition from legacy systems to scalable, secure platforms (UNITED STATES DIGITAL SERVICES, 2024). Scholars argue that combining these approaches enables public agencies to implement reform efforts that are both technically robust and socially legitimate (Wirtz et al., 2018). In an era of rapid technological change and heightened scrutiny of government performance, this holistic perspective is especially critical to achieving scalable, ethical, and resilient digital systems.

Moreover, the literature emphasizes that digital transformation should not be a one-off project but a continuous cycle of innovation and learning. Agencies that institutionalize strategic review mechanisms, stakeholder feedback loops, and adaptive governance practices are better positioned to respond to evolving technologies and citizen needs (Engin et al., 2025; UNDP, 2022). Research further highlights that anticipatory governance, including regulatory foresight and iterative policy experimentation, is essential for creating institutions that can adapt to uncertainty and technological disruptions (Ahern, 2025; Rudmark, & Andersson, 2021). Therefore, strategic planning must account for long-term vision and short-term adaptability, ensuring reforms remain relevant and resilient. This dynamic, feedback-informed governance model is central to sustaining trust and effectiveness in a digitally enabled public sector.

Recommendations

This chapter proposes ten actionable recommendations grounded in strategic frameworks, empirical case studies, and contemporary public administration research to achieve scalable, ethical, and sustainable digital transformation in government agencies. These recommendations align with the Digital Government Maturity Model and Kotter's 8-Step Change Model, ensuring a balanced focus on structural reform and organizational behavior.

1. Establish a Central Digital Transformation Office: Government agencies should create or strengthen dedicated digital transformation units that coordinate strategy, manage change, and align department efforts. Central offices improve institutional coherence and are shown to accelerate reform when granted budgetary authority

and reporting access to top leadership (Mergel et al., 2019; OECD, 2019). The USDS provides a successful model for this type of centralized transformation unit. Its embedded multidisciplinary teams have delivered measurable improvements in service delivery, procurement, and interagency coordination across more than 30 federal initiatives (UNITED STATES DIGITAL SERVICES, 2024).

2. Adopt the Digital Government Maturity Model (DGMM): The DGMM should serve as a foundational planning and evaluation tool for public agencies seeking to benchmark progress and identify gaps across infrastructure, service design, and organizational culture (Renteria et al., 2019; Ubaldi et al., 2019). Agencies using DGMM insights to drive decision-making are more likely to implement phased, scalable reforms aligned with long-term policy goals.
3. Apply Kotter's 8-Step Change Model: Integrating change management strategies is crucial for overcoming internal resistance and fostering a supportive reform culture. Agencies that apply Kotter's model report higher employee buy-in, more substantial leadership alignment, and greater continuity across political transitions (Bernardez Molina et al., 2023; Kuhlmann & Heuberger, 2021).
4. Standardize Interoperability Frameworks: Interoperability should be treated as a technical and governance priority. Implementing standardized APIs, data models, and cross-agency platforms enables seamless information exchange, reduces duplication, and enhances service continuity (Wirtz et al., 2018).
5. Invest in Cybersecurity Infrastructure and Talent: Agencies must treat cybersecurity as foundational, not supplemental. Investments should include updated hardware, threat detection systems, and specialized training programs for IT personnel and general staff (Zwitter & Boisse-Despiaux, 2018). Zero-trust architectures and multi-layered incident response protocols are particularly recommended.
6. Implement Privacy-by-Design and Ethical Governance: Public trust requires transparent and rights-respecting data practices. Agencies should conduct algorithmic impact assessments, involve citizens in data governance decisions, and publish clear privacy frameworks to ensure compliance with legal standards and ethical norms (Lindgren et al., 2019; Wirtz et al., 2018).
7. Create Cross-Functional Digital Teams: Cross-disciplinary collaboration strengthens the relevance and feasibility of digital initiatives. Teams that include technologists, service designers, policy analysts, and legal advisors ensure that digital services are usable and compliant (Hinings et al., 2018).
8. Deliver Continuous Digital Skills Training: Digital literacy must extend beyond IT departments. Training programs should be embedded into professional development pathways and tailored to the needs of public administrators, enabling better implementation, oversight, and user engagement (Engin et al., 2025; Lindgren et al., 2019).

9. Foster Stakeholder Engagement and Co-Creation: Participatory design ensures digital services reflect public needs and values. Agencies should formalize citizen feedback loops, partner with civil society groups, and leverage co-creation to build legitimacy and prevent unintended harm (Wirtz et al., 2018).
10. Publish Open Digital Transformation Dashboards: Transparency builds accountability. Publicly available dashboards tracking progress, cybersecurity performance, and user satisfaction provide stakeholders with valuable insights while creating incentives for ongoing improvement (Boehm et al., 2020; OECD, 2019; Zwitter & Boisse-Despiaux, 2018).

To improve usability for practitioners, the following table visually aligns each strategic recommendation with the relevant domains of the Digital Government Maturity Model (DGMM) and stages of Kotter's 8-Step Change Model. This mapping supports implementation by clarifying how each recommendation addresses both structural capabilities and behavioral change processes within public institutions.

Strategic Recommendation DGMM Domain Alignment Kotter Stage Alignment

Table 1. Strategic Alignment of 10 Recommendations with DGMM and Kotter's Change Model

1. Establish a Central Digital Transformation Office	Leadership, Digital Strategy	Step 1: Create Urgency Step 2: Form a Guiding Coalition
2. Adopt the Digital Government Maturity Model (DGMM)	All Domains (Maturity Benchmarking)	Step 4. Communicate the Vision
3. Apply Kotter's 8-Step Change Model	Behavioral/Change Process	All Steps (Framework-Level Guidance)
4. Standardize Interoperability Frameworks	Data Integration, ICT Infrastructure	Step 6: Generate Short-Term Wins
5. Invest in Cybersecurity Infrastructure and Talent	ICT Infrastructure, Risk Management	Step 5: Empower Broad-Based Action
6. Implement Privacy-by-Design and Ethical Governance	Ethical Governance, Digital Rights	Step 7: Consolidate Gains and Produce More Change
7. Create Cross-Functional Digital Teams	Organizational Culture, Talent	Step 4: Communicate the Vision Step 5: Empower Action
8. Deliver Continuous Digital Skills Training	Organizational Culture, Talent	Step 5: Empower Action

continued on following page

Table 1. Continued

9. Foster Stakeholder Engagement and Co-Creation	Stakeholder Engagement	Step 3: Create a Vision for Change Step 8: Generate Short-Term Wins
10. Publish Open Digital Transformation Dashboards	Digital Strategy, Monitoring & Evaluation	Step 6: Generate Short-Term Wins

These recommendations provide a comprehensive roadmap for public leaders committed to building digital governments that are not only technologically advanced but also equitable, secure, and resilient.

CONCLUSION

Digital transformation in government agencies is no longer aspirational; it is imperative. As public expectations evolve and crises such as the COVID-19 pandemic expose the limitations of analog systems, the urgency to modernize state institutions has become indisputable (Mergel et al., 2019; OECD, 2019). However, as this chapter has shown, digital transformation is not solely a technical challenge; it is a complex institutional endeavor that demands sustained leadership, cultural adaptation, and ethical stewardship. Entrenched bureaucracy, fragmented IT infrastructure, and inconsistent cybersecurity practices all contribute to digital inertia, threatening service equity, operational efficiency, and citizen trust.

To overcome these systemic barriers, public agencies must move beyond ad hoc digitization and embrace strategic, values-driven reform. Drawing from the Digital Government Maturity Model and Kotter's 8-Step Change Model, this chapter has emphasized the need for integrated frameworks that blend long-term planning with participatory change processes (Kotter, 1996; Ubaldi et al., 2019). Transformation efforts that fail to address change's technological and human dimensions risk deepening institutional fragmentation and exacerbating public distrust. Conversely, agencies that invest in workforce capacity, cross-functional collaboration, and ethical governance can unlock the full potential of digital technologies to create agile, inclusive, and resilient public systems.

Ten actionable recommendations were presented to guide this shift toward sustainable digital transformation:

1. Establish a centralized digital transformation office to ensure leadership and coherence.
2. Adopt the Digital Government Maturity Model (DGMM) for strategic alignment and progress tracking.

3. Apply Kotter's 8-Step Change Model to build organizational support and momentum.
4. Standardize interoperability frameworks to enable integrated service delivery.
5. Invest in cybersecurity infrastructure and workforce readiness to mitigate digital risks.
6. Implement privacy-by-design and ethical data governance to protect citizen rights.
7. Create cross-functional digital teams for holistic and inclusive solution development.
8. Deliver continuous digital skills training to future-proof the public workforce.
9. Foster stakeholder engagement and co-creation for more democratic innovation.
10. Publish open data dashboards to increase transparency and accountability.

These recommendations are rooted in contemporary research and real-world lessons from government innovation efforts worldwide (Wirtz at al., 2018; Zwitter & Boisse-Despiaux, 2018). Together, they offer a replicable framework that can guide institutions through the complexities of digital modernization while safeguarding core democratic values. In conclusion, Governments must adopt emerging technologies and transform the institutional environments in which those technologies operate. The success of initiatives led by the United States Digital Service reaffirms that transformation is feasible even within the most complex public institutions. Its practices serve as a replicable template for ethical, user-centered, and scalable modernization across diverse government contexts (UNITED STATES DIGITAL SERVICES, 2024). Bureaucracy and fragmentation may be deeply entrenched, but with strategic vision, ethical leadership, and inclusive governance, public agencies can lead a new era of digital democracy. The future of government lies in its capacity to evolve not merely by upgrading software or systems but by fundamentally reimagining its structures, cultures, and commitments in service of the public good.

REFERENCES

Ahern, D. (2025). The new anticipatory governance culture for innovation: Regulatory foresight, regulatory experimentation and regulatory learning. *European Business Organization Law Review, 26*(2), 241–283. Advance online publication. DOI: 10.1007/s40804-025-00348-7

Bailey, T., Barriball, E., Dey, A., & Sankur, A. (2019). *A practical approach to supply-chain risk management.* Digital McKinsey and Global Risk Practice. McKinsey & Company

Battilana, J., & Casciaro, T. (2021). *Power, for all: How it really works and why it's everyone's business.* Simon & Schuster.

Bernardez Molina, S., Nespoli, P., & Gómez Mármol, F. (2023). *Tackling cyberattacks through AI-based reactive systems: A holistic review and future vision.* https://arxiv.org/abs/2312.06229

Boehm, J., Curcio, N., Merrath, P., Shenton, L., & Stähle, T. (2020). *The risk-based approach to cybersecurity.* Digital McKinsey and Global Risk Practice. McKinsey & Company.

Boyce, E. (2024). *Interoperability: Seamless data exchange for government transformation.* Retrieved from https://publicsectornetwork.com/insight/discover-the-knowledge-that-drives-innovation

Carson, R., Pandey, P., Lekhi, A., Keyal, A., Fishman, T., & Chew, B. (2024). *Government's resilience imperative.* Deloitte Center for Government Insights.

Comella-Dorda, S., Kaplan, J., Lau, L., & McNamara, N. (2020). Agile, reliable, secure, compliant IT: Fulfilling the promise of DevSecOps. Digital McKinsey and Global Risk Practice. McKinsey & Company.

Cracknell, R., Kaplan, J., Richter, W., Shenton, L., & Stewart, C. (2020). *Cybersecurity in a digital era.* Digital McKinsey and Global Risk Practice. McKinsey & Company.

Engin, Z., Crowcroft, J., Hand, D., & Treleaven, P. (2025). *The Algorithmic State Architecture (ASA): An integrated framework for AI-enabled government.* https://doi.org//arXiv.2503.08725DOI: 10.48550

European Commission. (2017). *European Interoperability Framework: Implementation Strategy.* Retrieved from https://eur-lex.europa.eu/legal-content/EN/TXT/HTML/?uri=CELEX:52017DC0134

Gil-Garcia, J. R., Dawes, S. S., & Pardo, T. A. (2017). Digital government and public management research: Finding the crossroads. *Public Management Review*, *20*(3), 1–14. DOI: 10.1080/14719037.2017.1327181

Hinings, B., Gegenhuber, T., & Greenwood, R. (2018). Digital innovation and transformation: An institutional perspective. *Information and Organization*, *28*(1), 52–61. DOI: 10.1016/j.infoandorg.2018.02.004

Janssen, M., & van der Voort, H. (2020). Agile and adaptive governance in crisis response: Lessons from the COVID-19 pandemic. *International Journal of Information Management*, *55*, 102180. DOI: 10.1016/j.ijinfomgt.2020.102180 PMID: 32836637

Kaplan, J., Richter, W., & Ware, D. (2020). *Cybersecurity: Linchpin of the digital enterprise*. Digital McKinsey and Global Risk Practice. McKinsey & Company

Kotter, J. P. (1996). *Leading Change*. Harvard Business School Press.

Kuhlmann, S., & Heuberger, M. (2021). Digital transformation going local: Implementation, impacts and constraints from a German perspective. *Public Money & Management*, *43*(3), 1–9. DOI: 10.1080/09540962.2021.1939584

Lindgren, I., Madsen, C. Ø., Hofmann, S., & Melin, U. (2019). Close encounters of the digital kind: A research agenda for the digitalization of public services. *Government Information Quarterly*, *36*(3), 427–436. DOI: 10.1016/j.giq.2019.03.002

Mergel, I., Edelmann, N., & Haug, N. (2019). Defining digital transformation: Results from expert interviews. *Government Information Quarterly*, *36*(4), 101385. DOI: 10.1016/j.giq.2019.06.002

Nerima, M., & Ralyté, J. (2021). Towards a digital maturity balance model for public organizations. In Cherfi, S., Perini, A., & Nurcan, S. (Eds.), *Research Challenges in Information Science. RCIS 2021. Lecture Notes in Business Information Processing* (Vol. 415). Springer., DOI: 10.1007/978-3-030-75018-3_20

OECD. (2016). *Digital government strategies for transforming public services in the welfare areas*. OECD Publishing. Retrieved from https://www.oecd.org/gov/digital-government/Digital-Government-Strategies-Welfare-Service.pdf

OECD (2019). *Digital government review of Sweden: Towards a data-driven public sector*. OECD Digital Government Studies. OECD Publishing. DOI: 10.1787/4daf932b-en

OECD. (2020). *Digital government index: 2019 Results*. OECD Public Governance Policy Papers, No. 03. OECD Publishing. DOI: 10.1787/14e1c5e8-en-fr

OECD. (2023). *Digital government index.* Retrieved from https://www.oecd.org/en/publications/2023-oecd-digital-government-index_1a89ed5e-en.html

Renteria, C., Gil-Garcia, J. R., & Pardo, T. A. (2019). Toward an enabler-based digital government maturity framework: A Preliminary proposal based on theories of change. *In Proceedings of the 12th International Conference on Theory and Practice of Electronic Governance (ICEGOV2019), Melbourne, VIC, Australia, April 3-5, 2019*, 10 pages. https://doi.org/DOI: 10.1145/3326365.33264190

Reyna, A., Martín, C., Chen, J., Soler, E., & Díaz, M. (2018). On blockchain and its integration with IoT. Challenges and opportunities. *Future Generation Computer Systems, 88*, 173–190. DOI: 10.1016/j.future.2018.05.046

Rudmark, D., & Andersson, M. (2021). Feedback loops in open data ecosystems. *IEEE Software, 1*(39), 43–47.

Tangi, L., Janssen, M., Benedetti, M., & Noci, G. (2020). Barriers and drivers of digital transformation in public organizations: Results from a survey in the Netherlands. *Lecture Notes in Computer Science, 12219*, 42–56. Advance online publication. DOI: 10.1007/978-3-030-57599-1_4

Taylor, L., Floridi, L., & van der Sloot, B. (2017). *Group privacy: New challenges of data technologies.* Springer., DOI: 10.1007/978-3-319-46608-8

Ubaldi, B., van Ooijen, C., & Welby, B. (2019). *Digital government review of Sweden: Towards a data-driven public sector.* OECD Digital Government Studies. OECD Publishing. DOI: 10.1787/19934351

United Nations Development Programme (UNDP). (2022). *Digital strategy.* 2022-2025. Retrieved from https://www.undp.org/digital/Digital-Strategy

United States Digital Services (USDS). (2024). 2024 *Impact report.* Retrieved from https://www.usds.gov/resources/USDS-2024-Impact-Report.pdf

United States Government Accountability Office. (2023). *Agencies need to continue addressing critical legacy systems* (GAO-23-106821). Retrieved from https://www.gao.gov/products/gao-23-106821

United States Office of Management and Budget. (2024). *Federal IT dashboard.* Retrieved from https://www.itdashboard.gov/itportfoliodashboard

Wirtz, B. W., Weyerer, J. C., & Geyer, C. (2018). Artificial Intelligence and the public sector: Applications and Challenges. *International Journal of Public Administration, 42*(7), 596–615. DOI: 10.1080/01900692.2018.1498103

World Bank. (2021). *Digital government transformation in Vietnam: Global lessons and policy implications*. Retrieved from https://documents1.worldbank.org/curated/en/099235103032229053/pdf/P16734904490250bd0b6830feee7a77690c.pdf

Yin, R. K. (2017). *Case study research and applications: Design and methods* (6th ed.). SAGE Publications.

Zwitter, A., & Boisse-Despiaux, M. (2018). Blockchain for humanitarian action and development aid. *Journal of International Humanitarian Action*, *3*(16), 1–7. DOI: 10.1186/s41018-018-0044-5

Chapter 4
Exploring the Risk Management Psychology of Insider Cybersecurity Threats in Complex Organizations

Terrence D. Duncan
Liberty University, USA

Darrell Norman Burrell
http://orcid.org/0000-0002-4675-9544
Marymount University, USA

Adina Lundy
http://orcid.org/0000-0001-7564-2110
University of Rhode Island, USA

Calvin Nobles
http://orcid.org/0000-0003-4002-1108
University of Maryland Global Campus, USA

Teresa Manfreda-Foley
http://orcid.org/0009-0002-9136-9673
Marymount University, USA

Samantha Thibodeau
http://orcid.org/0009-0000-4639-9166
Marymount University, USA

Phillip Reed
http://orcid.org/0009-0000-1266-0151
Marymount University, USA

Gregory K. Karl Smith
http://orcid.org/0009-0000-5122-2250
Marymount University, USA

Jessica Parker
http://orcid.org/0009-0008-9574-3275
Marymount University, USA

Hilda Eke
http://orcid.org/0009-0006-2021-178X
Marymount University, USA

Laura A. Jones
http://orcid.org/0000-0002-0299-370X
Capitol Technology University, USA

Kim L. Brown-Jackson
http://orcid.org/0000-0001-9231-2076
Claremont Lincoln University, USA

DOI: 10.4018/979-8-2600-1021-1.ch004

Won Kang Song
http://orcid.org/0009-0004-8644-4987
Capitol Technology University, USA

Julia DeFrance
http://orcid.org/0009-0005-8105-2594
Marymount University, USA

Kylei L. Conti
http://orcid.org/0009-0009-0495-6601
Marymount University, USA

ABSTRACT

Insider cybersecurity threats represent a critical and underexamined risk within healthcare organizations, where traditional security strategies remain overly focused on technical controls rather than human behavior. This case study examines insider threats through the integrated lenses of criminal psychology and organizational psychology, emphasizing how organizational culture, employee motivation, moral disengagement, and perceived injustice contribute to counterproductive work behaviors. Using a management consulting intervention framework, the study synthesizes interdisciplinary literature to identify behavioral, cultural, and technological drivers of insider misconduct, including malicious, negligent, and opportunistic actions. The analysis highlights the limitations of conventional detection mechanisms and underscores the necessity of psychologically informed strategies that integrate AI-driven behavioral analytics, ethical leadership, training, and cultural transformation.

INTRODUCTION

This case study examines a severe insider-driven cybersecurity breach at Quest Wellness Hospital Consortium (QWHC), a pseudonymous healthcare organization used to protect the identity and privacy of the actual institution involved. Internal investigations revealed that a coordinated group of employees exploited legitimate system access privileges to extract electronic health records and associated financial data, subsequently monetizing this information through dark web marketplaces. Once the breach became public through major media outlets, the incident escalated from an internal security failure into a large-scale organizational crisis characterized by reputational collapse, regulatory scrutiny, and widespread erosion of public trust. Approximately sixty-five percent of patient records were compromised, exposing individuals to identity theft, financial fraud, social stigmatization, and long-term psychological harm; consequences that persist well beyond immediate monetary losses.

From a criminal and organizational psychology perspective, the scope and persistence of the breach strongly suggest systemic cultural and behavioral dysfunction rather than isolated deviant acts (Jones & Burrell, 2025; Burrell et al., 2023). Insider cybercrime rarely originates from sudden moral failure; instead, it evolves within organizational environments where ethical boundaries are ambiguously defined, oversight is inconsistent, and employees experience psychological distancing from the consequences of their actions (Jones & Burrell, 2025; Burrell, 2024; Burrell et al., 2022; Burrell et al., 2023; Huff et al., 2023). In this case, estimated patient losses between twenty and fifty million dollars represent only the measurable financial impact. The deeper damage lies in the moral injury inflicted upon patients who entrusted QWHC with profoundly sensitive information and upon employees whose professional identities are destabilized by association with institutional wrongdoing.

The public reaction further illustrates the psychological dimensions of organizational betrayal. The rapid spread of the hashtag #boycottQWHC reflects collective moral outrage driven by perceived violations of trust, particularly salient in healthcare contexts where patients assume fiduciary responsibility and ethical stewardship. As patient volumes declined precipitously, from approximately six hundred daily visits to fewer than forty, the organization entered a legitimacy crisis that compounded operational instability. Internally, the presence of federal investigators, regulatory auditors, and media scrutiny intensified employee anxiety, defensive silence, and mistrust toward leadership. These responses align with well-documented organizational psychology patterns in crisis settings, where uncertainty, fear of reprisal, and perceived injustice contribute to disengagement and further ethical erosion. The unfolding crisis at QWHC therefore represents not only a failure of HIPAA compliance but a profound collapse of ethical culture, psychological safety, and behavioral governance.

Traditional cybersecurity architectures are largely designed to detect anomalous external intrusion attempts, yet they frequently fail to identify threats originating from individuals who operate within trusted organizational boundaries (Jones & Burrell, 2025; Burrell, 2024; Burrell et al., 2022; Burrell et al., 2023; Huff et al., 2023). From an organizational psychology perspective, this limitation reflects a deeper cultural assumption that trust and employment status are proxies for ethical alignment, an assumption that becomes increasingly fragile in digitally dense and high-pressure healthcare environments.

Malicious insiders represent the most overtly criminal manifestation of insider threats, yet their behavior is best understood as an interaction between individual motivation and organizational context rather than as isolated deviance. These individuals intentionally exploit legitimate credentials to access, manipulate, or exfiltrate sensitive data, often motivated by financial gain, perceived injustice, or retaliatory impulses (Jones & Burrell, 2025; Burrell, 2024). Their psychological advantage lies not in technical superiority but in familiarity with internal systems, informal workarounds, and cultural blind spots. Real-world healthcare breaches illustrate how disgruntled employees, denied promotions or facing disciplinary action, have sold patient records or proprietary data to competitors, rationalizing their actions as compensation for perceived organizational betrayal. Such behavior reflects moral disengagement processes reinforced by cultures that fail to address grievances transparently or equitably.

Careless insiders constitute the most prevalent yet frequently underestimated category of insider threats, emerging not from malicious intent but from cognitive overload, complacency, and normalized policy deviations. In healthcare organizations like QWHC, employees routinely operate under time pressure, emotional strain, and competing priorities, conditions that significantly increase susceptibility to error. Clicking malicious links, misplacing unsecured devices, or bypassing authentication protocols often reflects adaptive behavior within dysfunctional systems rather than individual irresponsibility (Jones & Burrell, 2025; Burrell, 2024). Organizational cultures that emphasize speed and productivity over procedural fidelity inadvertently reinforce these behaviors, transforming individual mistakes into systemic vulnerabilities (Hart, 2025). High-profile ransomware incidents triggered by phishing emails in hospital networks exemplify how careless actions, when culturally tolerated, can escalate into catastrophic organizational crises.

The phenomenon commonly described as the "mole" further complicates insider threat management by exploiting organizational trust structures rather than formal employment boundaries. These actors originate outside the organization but acquire insider-level access through impersonation, social engineering, or strategic hiring with concealed malicious intent (Jones & Burrell, 2025; Burrell, 2024). From a criminal psychology standpoint, such actors leverage institutional assumptions about legitimacy and belonging, often embedding themselves within teams long enough to learn workflows and identify exploitable weaknesses. Healthcare systems, which frequently rely on contractors, vendors, and temporary staff, are particularly vulnerable when background checks, access controls, and cultural integration processes are inconsistently applied.

While insider threats are often categorized by intent or method, their persistence is most accurately explained by organizational culture. At QWHC, as in many healthcare institutions, insider risks were amplified by cultural conditions that privileged trust over verification and operational continuity over ethical scrutiny. Cultures that discourage reporting, minimize near-miss incidents, or frame cybersecurity as a purely technical responsibility inadvertently create psychological distance between employees and the consequences of their actions.

PROBLEM ANALYSIS

The healthcare sector's rapid digital transformation has fundamentally altered how medical information is created, stored, and accessed, introducing both operational efficiencies and novel psychological vulnerabilities (Chernyshev et al., 2018). The adoption of electronic health records, cloud-based infrastructures, and Internet of Medical Things (IoMT) technologies has expanded the attack surface not only for external adversaries but also for internal actors whose authorized access enables misconduct with minimal technical sophistication (Seh et al., 2020). Within this environment, cybersecurity risk becomes inseparable from employee cognition, motivation, and moral reasoning (Burrell, 2024).

Insider offenders in healthcare settings frequently differ from stereotypical cybercriminals. Rather than possessing advanced hacking skills, they rely on familiarity, trust, and routine access (Jones & Burrell, 2025; Burrell et al., 2023). Criminal psychology research (Jones & Burrell, 2025; Burrell et al., 2023) suggests that such individuals often engage in gradual moral disengagement, rationalizing misconduct through cognitive distortions such as entitlement ("I am underpaid"), neutralization ("no one is directly harmed"), or diffusion of responsibility ("everyone cuts corners"). At QWHC, the coordinated nature of the data exfiltration indicates social reinforcement among offenders, where group dynamics normalize unethical behavior and reduce individual guilt through shared participation.

Organizational culture plays a decisive role in enabling this progression from ethical discomfort to deliberate criminality (Huff et al., 2023). When leadership prioritizes efficiency over accountability, tolerates minor policy violations, or fails to enforce consequences consistently, employees internalize a permissive ethical climate. Over time, such climates foster what organizational psychologists describe as ethical fading, wherein moral considerations recede from decision-making processes (Jones & Burrell, 2025; Burrell et al., 2023). In these environments, protected health information becomes psychologically reframed as an abstract digital asset rather than as an extension of vulnerable human lives.

The motivations driving insider offenders are rarely singular (Jones & Burrell, 2025; Burrell et al., 2023; Huff et al., 2023). Financial stress, perceived organizational injustice, burnout, and identity conflict frequently intersect. Healthcare workers experiencing chronic workload pressure and emotional exhaustion may develop resentment toward institutions they perceive as exploitative or indifferent. In this psychological state, illicit data sales can be reframed as compensatory justice rather than criminal theft. Similar real-world cases, such as hospital employees selling patient data for relatively modest sums, demonstrate that insider cybercrime often reflects opportunistic exploitation amplified by weak ethical reinforcement rather than premeditated criminal intent.

The consequences of insider-driven data breaches extend far beyond immediate regulatory penalties or remediation costs (Jones & Burrell, 2025; Burrell et al., 2023). Patients suffer enduring psychological harm, including anxiety, loss of dignity, and fear of discrimination, while organizations experience cascading losses in trust, workforce morale, and stakeholder confidence (Seh et al., 2020). For QWHC, the breach has triggered regulatory scrutiny, potential litigation, and long-term reputational damage that threatens institutional survival. More critically, it has exposed the inadequacy of treating cybersecurity as a purely technical challenge.

Preventing future insider threats requires a psychologically informed approach that integrates organizational culture, employee behavior, and ethical leadership into cybersecurity governance (Jones & Burrell, 2025; Burrell et al., 2023). Technical controls, while necessary, are insufficient in isolation. Without intentional change management strategies that reinforce ethical identity, cultivate psychological safety, address burnout, and align incentives with moral accountability, insider risks will persist (Jones & Burrell, 2025; Burrell et al., 2023). The urgency of this case lies in its demonstration that cybersecurity failures in healthcare are, at their core, failures of organizational psychology, failures that demand cultural transformation as much as technological defense.

PURPOSE OF THE INQUIRY

The purpose of this inquiry is to examine cybersecurity insider threats within healthcare and biotechnology organizations through the integrated lenses of criminal psychology and organizational psychology, with a particular focus on the behavioral mechanisms that give rise to worker misconduct. This study seeks to move beyond predominantly technical explanations of insider threats by analyzing how motivational dynamics, moral disengagement, organizational culture, and perceived risk influence employee decision-making related to cybersecurity. By using a case-study approach oriented toward management consulting intervention, this inquiry aims to identify psychologically informed strategies that healthcare organizations can employ to mitigate insider threats, enhance ethical accountability, and align cybersecurity practices with human behavior rather than assuming compliance through technical controls alone.

SIGNIFICANCE OF THE INQUIRY

The significance of this inquiry lies in addressing a critical and underexplored gap between the growing prevalence of insider cybersecurity incidents and the persistent underestimation of their likelihood and impact by organizational leaders. Despite widespread evidence that a majority of organizations experience cybersecurity incidents, many decision-makers continue to deprioritize cybersecurity risks, reflecting cognitive biases such as optimism bias and normalcy bias that are deeply rooted in organizational psychology (Fruhlinger, 2020). This disconnect is further compounded by a global shortage of cybersecurity professionals and a workforce that frequently enters the field without formal technical training, increasing reliance on human judgment in high-risk environments (Dobson, 2018).

Moreover, the economic and psychological costs of insider threats and counterproductive work behaviors are substantial, extending beyond direct financial loss to include diminished morale, reduced productivity, and erosion of trust (Jones & Burrell, 2025). In healthcare settings, where the consequences of data misuse directly affect patient well-being and institutional legitimacy, the stakes are uniquely high (Burrell, 2024). This inquiry is significant because it reframes insider cybersecurity threats as a people-centered organizational risk, emphasizing that sustainable mitigation requires cultural, behavioral, and leadership interventions rather than purely technical solutions (Burrell et al., 2023; Huff et al., 2023). By foregrounding the psychology of employee behavior, this research contributes to a more holistic and ethically grounded understanding of cybersecurity risk management.

NATURE OF THE INQUIRY

The nature of this inquiry is qualitative, interpretive, and exploratory, employing a case-study methodology to synthesize insights from interdisciplinary literature spanning healthcare cybersecurity, insider threat research, criminal psychology, organizational behavior, and management consulting. Rather than testing a single hypothesis, the inquiry seeks to construct a comprehensive conceptual understanding of how insider threats emerge, escalate, and persist within organizational systems shaped by culture, leadership, and human motivation.

This inquiry is practice-oriented, designed to inform real-world management consulting interventions by integrating empirical findings and theoretical frameworks into a coherent narrative that highlights behavioral risk factors and culturally embedded vulnerabilities. Emphasis is placed on understanding insider threats as dynamic processes influenced by organizational norms, perceived injustice, role ambiguity, and moral cognition, particularly in environments where cybersecurity expertise is limited and responsibility is diffusely distributed. Through this approach, the inquiry aims to advance both scholarly dialogue and professional practice by encouraging greater attention to the human dimensions of cybersecurity in healthcare organizations.

INTRODUCTION AND CONTEXTUAL FRAMING

Quest Wellness Hospital Consortium (QWHC) is a pseudonymous healthcare organization used in this case study to protect the identity and legal privacy of the actual institution examined. The organization experienced a severe insider-driven cybersecurity breach that exposed a fundamental misconception common in healthcare security strategy: the belief that insider risk is defined solely by employment status. While cybersecurity is traditionally anchored in the protection of confidentiality, integrity, and availability of information, these objectives cannot be meaningfully achieved without a psychologically informed understanding of who qualifies as an "insider" and how organizational culture shapes employee behavior (Wilder, 2022). In complex healthcare ecosystems such as QWHC, insiders extend beyond salaried staff to include contractors, volunteers, vendor partners, and even patients accessing electronic portals, each carrying distinct psychological motivations, access privileges, and behavioral risk profiles.

PSYCHOLOGICAL DIMENSIONS OF INSIDER STATUS AND ACCESS ENTITLEMENT

From an organizational psychology perspective, insider threats emerge at the intersection of access entitlement and moral decision-making rather than formal role designation. Healthcare environments rely heavily on trust-based access models, granting individuals extensive privileges to expedite care delivery and operational efficiency. However, when access is decoupled from continuous ethical reinforcement and behavioral accountability, psychological distance from harm increases. Individuals begin to perceive sensitive data as abstract digital assets rather than representations of human vulnerability. Real-world breaches across hospital systems illustrate that insiders rarely "hack" systems; instead, they exploit routine access in environments where ethical vigilance has faded and oversight mechanisms are inconsistently enforced.

BEHAVIORAL PATHWAYS TO COUNTERPRODUCTIVE WORK BEHAVIORS

Insider cybersecurity incidents at QWHC align closely with the framework of Counterproductive Work Behaviors (CWBs), defined as volitional actions that harm organizational functioning, stakeholder well-being, or both (Spector & Fox, 2002). According to Wilder (2022), insider-driven data exposure typically manifests through three psychologically distinct pathways: accidental, negligent, and malicious behavior. Accidental exposure often reflects cognitive overload, inadequate training, or poor usability design, where employees lack the situational awareness necessary to navigate complex systems safely. Negligent behavior emerges when individuals knowingly bypass policies, frequently rationalized by time pressure, normalization of deviance, or perceived organizational indifference. Malicious behavior represents the most severe form, characterized by intentional misuse of access for personal gain, retaliation, or ideological motives.

CRIMINAL PSYCHOLOGY OF MALICIOUS INSIDER OFFENDERS

Malicious insider behavior is best understood through the lens of criminal psychology rather than technical failure alone. Employees who intentionally exfiltrate data often engage in moral disengagement, reframing their actions through justifications such as perceived unfair compensation, lack of recognition, or belief that the organization itself is unethical. Group-based offending, as observed in coordinated insider breaches, further diffuses responsibility and reinforces deviant norms. Comparable real-world cases involving hospital employees selling patient records for modest financial returns demonstrate that insider cybercrime is frequently opportunistic rather than sophisticated, driven by situational access combined with weak ethical culture rather than advanced criminal intent.

SABOTAGE, TRUST EROSION, AND ORGANIZATIONAL HARM

Sabotage represents one of the most destructive yet underacknowledged forms of counterproductive work behavior in organizational settings (Spector & Fox, 2002). In cybersecurity contexts, sabotage may include deliberate system compromise, intentional data corruption, or facilitation of external breaches. The consequences extend far beyond immediate technical remediation costs. Organizations must absorb expenditures related to forensic investigations, system rebuilding, regulatory penalties, and potential litigation, while simultaneously addressing declines in employee morale and public trust. When leadership fails to detect, deter, or respond decisively to sabotage, employees internalize a message of tolerance or helplessness, accelerating ethical decay and disengagement across the workforce.

WORK MOTIVATION AND THE PATHWAY TO COUNTERPRODUCTIVE WORK BEHAVIORS

Scholarly efforts to conceptualize motivation have evolved considerably, reflecting its multidimensional, situational, and temporally dynamic nature (Jones & Burrell, 2025; Burrell, 2024; Burrell et al., 2022; Burrell et al., 2023; Huff et al., 2023). Within this case study, motivation is examined not as a static personality trait but as an adaptive psychological force shaped by organizational culture, perceived fairness, and access-related opportunity. This distinction is critical, as insider cyber threats frequently emerge not from inherent deviance but from motivational shifts influenced by systemic organizational conditions.

In workplace psychology, motivation is commonly understood as the constellation of internal and external forces that initiate, direct, and sustain work-related behavior over time (Pinder, 2008). This conceptualization is particularly salient when analyzing counterproductive work behaviors (CWBs), as it highlights how employee actions are goal-oriented and contextually responsive rather than impulsive anomalies. At QWHC, insider misconduct involving unauthorized data access can be interpreted as behavior driven by unmet psychological needs, perceived injustice, or instrumental goals rather than spontaneous criminal intent. Viewing CWBs through a motivational lens enables management consultants to diagnose not only what behaviors occurred but why employees found those behaviors psychologically viable or even justified within the organizational environment.

MORAL DISENGAGEMENT AND THE NORMALIZATION OF ETHICAL VIOLATIONS

Criminal psychology research underscores the role of moral disengagement in transforming ethically prohibited actions into psychologically permissible ones. Bandura (2002, 2016) demonstrated that individuals who engage in moral disengagement gradually reinterpret their misconduct as ordinary or defensible, particularly in environments lacking consistent ethical reinforcement. Within healthcare settings, this process may involve reframing patient data as impersonal information assets, employing euphemistic language to minimize perceived harm, or dehumanizing affected individuals by viewing them as abstract system entries rather than vulnerable patients. In the absence of robust ethical training and leadership modeling, these cognitive distortions can become culturally embedded, enabling insider misconduct to persist undetected and unchallenged.

CRISIS STATES, DISGRUNTLEMENT, AND INSIDER THREAT ESCALATION

Historically, workplace violence, revenge, and cybersecurity misconduct were treated as distinct organizational risks, often managed through separate investigative frameworks (Gelles, 2016). Contemporary insider threat programs, however, increasingly recognize that these behaviors share common psychological antecedents rooted in perceived injustice, identity threat, and crisis escalation. Employees who feel chronically undervalued, unfairly treated, or professionally marginalized may enter prolonged psychological crisis states, during which emotional regulation and moral attentiveness are significantly compromised (Shields et al., 2015). In such states, individuals may seek symbolic or instrumental retaliation against the organization, targeting information systems, reputational assets, or operational continuity as a means of restoring perceived balance or agency.

REVENGE AS A MOTIVATIONAL CONSTRUCT IN INSIDER CYBERCRIME

Revenge occupies a prominent yet frequently misunderstood position in discussions of workplace misconduct. While media narratives often associate revenge with overt violence, organizational research consistently demonstrates that retaliatory behaviors are more commonly expressed through covert, nonviolent actions such as data theft, sabotage, or intentional noncompliance (Tripp & Bies, 2009). Scholars conceptualize revenge as a response to perceived violations of fairness or social norms, wherein individuals seek to impose costs on those they deem responsible (Bies et al., 1997; Folger & Skarlicki, 2005). Within cybersecurity contexts, this may manifest as an employee exploiting privileged access to disclose sensitive information after being denied a promotion or disciplined in a manner perceived as unjust.

ORGANIZATIONAL CULTURE AS A RISK AMPLIFIER OR PROTECTIVE MECHANISM

At QWHC, the insider breach underscores how organizational culture functions either as a risk amplifier or a protective mechanism. Cultures that prioritize productivity over accountability, silence over transparency, and compliance theater over ethical ownership inadvertently cultivate environments where CWBs thrive. In contrast, psychologically healthy cultures reinforce shared responsibility, encourage ethical voice, and integrate cybersecurity awareness into professional identity. Management consulting interventions must therefore move beyond technical controls to address leadership behavior, incentive structures, burnout, and moral cognition. Without cultural recalibration, cybersecurity policies remain symbolic rather than behavioral, leaving organizations vulnerable to recurring insider threats.

URGENCY AND IMPLICATIONS FOR MANAGEMENT CONSULTING INTERVENTION

The urgency of insider cybersecurity threats in healthcare lies in their human origin and human impact. Data breaches compromise not only financial assets but patient dignity, psychological safety, and institutional legitimacy. For QWHC, restoring trust requires more than system upgrades; it demands a deliberate transformation of organizational culture, ethical leadership, and employee engagement. Management consulting interventions grounded in organizational and criminal psychology are uniquely positioned to diagnose behavioral risk patterns, redesign accountability mechanisms, and realign cultural norms. Without such interventions, healthcare organizations risk perpetuating environments where insider misconduct is not an anomaly but an emergent property of the system itself.

PRACTICAL SOLUTIONS FOR INSIDER CYBERSECURITY RISK REDUCTION

1. **Implement AI-Enabled User and Entity Behavior Analytics (UEBA)** Deploy machine-learning systems that establish individual behavioral baselines and detect anomalies across login behavior, data access, task patterns, and work hours. These systems should correlate behavioral and digital indicators to detect early-stage moral disengagement before malicious action occurs.
2. **Adopt Dynamic, Risk-Adaptive Access Controls** Move beyond static role-based access by dynamically adjusting privileges based on behavioral risk scores that integrate anomalous activity, job stress indicators, and policy violations. This approach aligns access entitlement with psychological state rather than job title alone.
3. **Establish Continuous Employee Sentiment and Climate Monitoring** Use anonymized AI-driven sentiment analysis of surveys, exit interviews, and organizational feedback channels to identify emerging patterns of dissatisfaction, injustice perception, or disengagement that often precede insider misconduct.
4. **Create a Formal Insider Threat Behavioral Risk Index** Develop an internally governed index combining behavioral indicators (resentment, policy circumven-

tion) and digital signals (off-hours access, data hoarding) to support consistent, evidence-based decision-making rather than ad hoc suspicion.

5. **Deploy Deception Technologies Strategically** Use decoy credentials, honey files, and false repositories to detect intentional data exploration. Interaction with deception assets should trigger high-confidence alerts, distinguishing malicious intent from accidental error.
6. **Redesign Cybersecurity Training Around Moral Cognition** Shift training from rule memorization to psychologically informed modules addressing moral disengagement, rationalization, and normalization of deviance, supported by real-world healthcare breach case studies.
7. **Introduce Scenario-Based Insider Threat Simulations** Conduct live simulations where employees face ethically ambiguous situations involving time pressure, access temptation, or perceived unfairness, reinforcing ethical decision-making under realistic conditions.
8. **Form Multidisciplinary Insider Threat Governance Teams** Integrate cybersecurity, HR, legal, compliance, and organizational psychology expertise into a single insider threat program to ensure behavioral signals are interpreted holistically and proportionately.
9. **Embed Organizational Psychologists in Cybersecurity Strategy** Leverage psychologists to analyze workforce stressors, identity conflict, burnout, and grievance patterns that elevate insider threat risk, translating findings into preventive interventions.
10. **Align Cybersecurity KPIs with Cultural Metrics** Measure success not only through reduced incidents but through indicators such as ethical reporting rates, training engagement quality, and reductions in policy circumvention.
11. **Standardize Fair and Transparent Policy Enforcement** Ensure cybersecurity and misconduct policies are applied consistently across roles and hierarchies to reduce perceptions of injustice that fuel retaliatory CWBs.
12. **Enhance Psychological Safety for Ethical Voice** Create protected channels for reporting concerns, grievances, and near-miss security incidents without fear of retaliation, reducing covert escalation pathways.
13. **Implement Structured Offboarding and Transition Monitoring** Apply heightened behavioral and access monitoring during resignation, termination, or role changes, paired with supportive communication to reduce revenge-motivated misconduct.
14. **Introduce Manager Training on Behavioral Risk Recognition** Train supervisors to recognize early warning signs such as withdrawal, excessive enthusiasm, resentment, or boundary-pushing behavior, and respond with support rather than punishment.

15. **Use AI to Correlate Behavioral and Digital Signals Across Silos** Break down data silos by integrating HR systems, access logs, network activity, and incident reports into unified analytic dashboards for insider threat detection.
16. **Reduce Cognitive Overload Through Secure-by-Design Workflows** Redesign systems to minimize workarounds, excessive permissions, and usability friction that normalize policy violations and increase careless insider risk.
17. **Institute Mandatory Ethical Refresh Cycles for High-Access Roles** Require recurring ethics and accountability reviews for employees with privileged access, emphasizing stewardship of patient data as a moral responsibility.
18. **Leverage Predictive Analytics for Insider Risk Forecasting** Use longitudinal data to identify combinations of stress, access expansion, and behavioral drift that historically precede insider incidents.
19. **Create Clear Intellectual Property Ownership Education Programs** Educate employees on IP boundaries, data ownership, and legal consequences to reduce rationalization and accidental misuse of sensitive information.
20. **Integrate Insider Threat Metrics into Executive Risk Reporting** Ensure insider threat risk is regularly reviewed at the executive and board level, reframing it as a strategic organizational risk rather than an IT issue.
21. **Conduct Regular Cultural Risk Audits** Assess norms around shortcuts, silence, fairness, and accountability to identify cultural conditions that enable CWBs.
22. **Implement Graduated Intervention Protocols** Develop tiered response models that range from coaching and support to restriction and investigation, avoiding overly punitive responses to early-stage risk indicators.
23. **Use AI-Assisted Workload and Burnout Monitoring** Monitor excessive overtime, task overload, and role strain—particularly among cybersecurity and clinical staff—to mitigate burnout-related errors and resentment.
24. **Align Incentive Structures with Ethical Cyber Behavior** Reward proactive reporting, policy adherence, and ethical leadership behaviors rather than only productivity metrics that encourage corner-cutting.
25. **Position Insider Threat Prevention as Cultural Transformation** Frame insider threat mitigation as an ongoing organizational change initiative focused on trust, fairness, accountability, and human behavior; recognizing that insider risk is an emergent property of culture, not a technical anomaly.

CONCLUSION AND IMPLICATIONS

This inquiry demonstrates that insider cybersecurity threats in healthcare organizations are not anomalous technical failures but foreseeable outcomes of organizational systems that insufficiently integrate psychological, cultural, and ethical considerations into risk management. Insider misconduct emerges not merely from individual malfeasance, but from the interaction between access entitlement, motivational strain, moral disengagement, and organizational climates that normalize deviation while discouraging ethical voice. When trusted insiders exploit legitimate access, the breach reflects a deeper systemic failure, one rooted in governance, leadership, and culture rather than technology alone.

From a theoretical perspective, this study advances insider threat scholarship by synthesizing criminal psychology and organizational psychology into a unified explanatory framework. It reinforces the premise that moral disengagement, perceived injustice, and normalization of deviance function as critical psychological mechanisms through which routine access becomes criminal opportunity. By framing insider incidents as a subset of counterproductive work behaviors shaped by motivation and context, the inquiry challenges approaches that treat insider threats as isolated acts of individual deviance or purely technical vulnerabilities. Instead, it positions insider risk as an emergent organizational property shaped by leadership priorities, cultural norms, and behavioral reinforcement structures.

The practical implications for healthcare leadership and management consulting are substantial. First, cybersecurity must be reframed as a people-centered enterprise risk rather than a narrowly technical function. While advanced monitoring and detection technologies are necessary, they are insufficient without parallel investments in ethical leadership, psychological safety, and cultural accountability. Organizations that tolerate burnout, inconsistent policy enforcement, or opaque decision-making inadvertently create conditions that facilitate resentment, rationalization, and covert retaliation.

Second, insider threat prevention should be understood as a continuous organizational change process rather than a compliance-driven initiative. Effective mitigation requires multidisciplinary governance that integrates cybersecurity expertise with human resources, legal oversight, and organizational psychology. Such integration enables early identification of behavioral risk indicators and supports graduated, proportionate interventions that emphasize support and correction before misconduct escalates into criminal action. This approach also mitigates the risk of over-surveillance, preserving employee trust while enhancing security outcomes.

Third, the ethical implications are particularly pronounced in healthcare settings. Patient data is not merely an information asset but a representation of personal vulnerability, dignity, and trust. Insider breaches therefore constitute a form of institutional betrayal with enduring psychological consequences for patients and communities. Organizations that allow ethical fading to occur fail not only in regulatory compliance but in their fiduciary and moral obligations. Financial remediation and technical upgrades, while necessary, cannot fully repair the erosion of trust that follows such violations.

Finally, this inquiry highlights the strategic risk of executive disengagement from insider threat governance. Treating insider risk as an operational or IT concern obscures its cultural origins and limits organizational learning. When leadership embeds insider threat metrics into enterprise risk reporting, aligns incentives with ethical behavior, and models accountability, cybersecurity stewardship becomes integrated into professional identity rather than perceived as external enforcement.

In sum, insider cybersecurity threats in healthcare are neither inevitable nor random. They are highly probable in organizations that neglect the human dimensions of security and comparatively rare in those that cultivate ethical clarity, psychological safety, and behavioral accountability. Sustainable prevention depends on cultural transformation informed by psychological insight and ethical leadership. Reframing insider threat mitigation as a function of organizational health rather than technical control offers a pathway toward resilient, trust-centered cybersecurity governance in healthcare and other high-risk sectors.

RECOMMENDATIONS FOR FUTURE RESEARCH

Action Research in Organizational Cybersecurity Culture

Future research should employ action research methodologies to directly examine and influence insider cybersecurity risk within healthcare and biotechnology organizations. Action research is particularly well suited to insider threat studies because it allows researchers and practitioners to collaborate in diagnosing behavioral risks, implementing interventions, and iteratively refining solutions in real organizational contexts. Through cycles of planning, action, observation, and reflection, researchers can evaluate how interventions such as AI-driven behavioral analytics, ethical leadership training, and psychological safety initiatives alter employee behavior and organizational culture over time.

This approach would be especially valuable in examining how insider threat mitigation strategies interact with employee perceptions of fairness, trust, and surveillance. Action research can capture how cultural resistance or acceptance evolves as organizations shift from purely technical controls to people-centered cybersecurity governance. Given the dynamic nature of insider threats and the complexity of healthcare environments, action research offers a practical pathway for generating evidence-based interventions that are both theoretically grounded and operationally viable.

Benchmarking Studies Across Healthcare and High-Risk Industries

Benchmarking research is recommended to compare insider threat prevention practices across healthcare organizations and other high-risk sectors such as finance, energy, and defense. Such studies can identify best practices in integrating behavioral analytics, access governance, and cultural interventions while highlighting gaps unique to healthcare settings. Benchmarking allows researchers to assess how variations in organizational culture, leadership models, and workforce composition influence the effectiveness of insider threat programs.

Future benchmarking efforts should examine both technical and behavioral dimensions, including how organizations measure insider risk, respond to early warning indicators, and balance security with employee trust. Comparative analysis can also illuminate how mature insider threat programs incorporate criminal psychology principles, multidisciplinary governance, and executive oversight. These insights would provide healthcare leaders and management consultants with empirically grounded reference points for designing and scaling insider threat interventions.

Qualitative Focus Group Research on Employee Perceptions and Moral Reasoning

Qualitative focus group research is strongly recommended to deepen understanding of employee perceptions, moral reasoning processes, and lived experiences related to cybersecurity policies and insider threat monitoring. Focus groups can reveal how employees interpret organizational signals about trust, accountability, and ethical responsibility, factors that are often invisible in quantitative security metrics. Such research is particularly important for uncovering how moral disengagement, normalization of deviance, and perceived injustice develop within organizational cultures.

By engaging employees across roles, access levels, and departments, focus group studies can identify psychological stressors, ambiguities in policy communication, and unintended consequences of surveillance technologies. These insights can inform the design of training programs, communication strategies, and governance frameworks that reduce resistance while strengthening ethical alignment. In healthcare contexts, where professional identity and patient trust are central, qualitative research offers a critical lens for understanding how insider threat mitigation strategies affect both behavior and organizational legitimacy.

REFERENCES

Bandura, A. (2002). Selective moral disengagement in the exercise of moral agency. *Journal of Moral Education, 21*(2), 101–120. DOI: 10.1080/0305724022014322

Bandura, A. (2016). Moral disengagement: How people do harm and live with themselves. *Business Ethics Quarterly, 26*(3), 426–429. DOI: 10.1017/beq.2016.37

Bies, R., Tripp, T., & Kramer, R. (1997). At the breaking point: Cognitive and social dynamics of revenge in organizations. In Giacalone, R. A., & Greenberg, J. (Eds.), *Antisocial behavior in organizations* (pp. 18–36). Sage., https://psycnet.apa.org/record/1997-97285-002

Burrell, D. N. (2024). Understanding Cognitive and Behavioral Psychological Factors that Lead to Cybersecurity Breaches in Healthcare. *RAIS Journal for Social Sciences, 8*(2), 43-53. https://ideas.repec.org/a/smo/jornl1/v8y2024i2p43-53.html

Burrell, D. N., Nobles, C., Cusak, A., Jones, L. A., Wright, J. B., Mingo, H. C., Ferreras-Perez, J., Khanta, K., Shen, P., & Richardson, K. (2023). Cybersecurity and Cyberbiosecurity Insider Threat Risk Management. In Adedoyin, F., & Christiansen, B. (Eds.), *Handbook of Research on Cybersecurity Risk in Contemporary Business Systems* (pp. 121–136). IGI Global Scientific Publishing., DOI: 10.4018/978-1-6684-7207-1.ch006

Burrell, D. N., Sabie-Aridi, A. S., Shufutinsky, A., Wright, J. B., Nobles, C., & Dawson, M. (2022). Exploring Holistic Managerial Thinking to Better Manage Healthcare Cybersecurity. [IJHSTM]. *International Journal of Health Systems and Translational Medicine, 2*(1), 1–13. DOI: 10.4018/IJHSTM.300337

Chernyshev, M., Zeadally, S., & Baig, Z. (2018). Healthcare data breaches: Implications for digital forensic readiness. *Journal of Medical Systems, 43*(1), 7. Advance online publication. DOI: 10.1007/s10916-018-1123-2 PMID: 30488291

Dobson, S. (2018). Cybersecurity talent hard to find: Report. *Canadian HR Reporter, 31*(9), *3-18.* https://www.hrreporter.com/focus-areas/recruitment-and-staffing/cybersecurity-talent-hard-to-find-report/299496

Folger, R., & Skarlicki, D. P. (2005). Beyond counterproductive work behavior: Moral emotions and deontic retaliation versus reconciliation. In Fox, S., & Spector, P. E. (Eds.), *Counterproductive work behavior: Investigations of actors and targets* (pp. 83–106). American Psychological Association., DOI: 10.1037/10893-004

Fruhlinger, J. (2020, March 9). Top cybersecurity facts, figures, and statistics. *CSO Online*. https://www.csoonlinc.com/article/3153707/top-cybersecurity-facts-figures-and-statistics.html

Gelles, M. (2016). *Insider threat: Prevention, detection, mitigation, and deterrence*. Elsevier., DOI: 10.1016/B978-0-12-802410-2.00015-0

Hart, G. (2025). Conceptual Explorations Of Employee Coaching For Generation Z Sales Professionals. *Land Forces Academy Review, 30*(1), 118-133. https://reference-global.com/download/article/10.2478/raft-2025-0012.pdf

Huff, A. J., Burrell, D. N., Nobles, C., Richardson, K., Wright, J. B., Burton, S. L., Jones, A. J., Springs, D., Omar, M., & Brown-Jackson, K. L. (2023). Management practices for mitigating cybersecurity threats to biotechnology companies, laboratories, and healthcare research organizations. In *Applied Research Approaches to Technology, Healthcare, and Business* (pp. 1-12). IGI Global. https://www.igi-global.com/chapter/management-practices-for-mitigating-cybersecurity-threats-to-biotechnology-companies-laboratories-and-healthcare-research-organizations/331637

Jones, L. A., & Burrell, D. N. (2025). Illegal Cybersecurity Threats Created by Organizational Arsonists in Healthcare Organizations. *Law. Economics and Society, 1*(1), 93–p93. https://j.ideasspread.org/index.php/les/article/view/1427

Pinder, C. C. (2008). *Work motivation in organizational behavior*. Psychology Press., DOI: 10.4324/9781315734606

Ramluckan, T., Van Niekerk, B., & Martins, I. (n.d.). A change management perspective to implementing a cyber security culture. *In ECCWS 2020 20th European Conference on Cyber Warfare and Security* (, 442-448. https://books.google.com/books?hl=en&lr=&id=lB4EEAAAQBAJ&oi=fnd&pg=PA442&dq=Ramluckan,+T.,+Van+Niekerk,+B.,+%26+Martins,+I.+(n.d.).+A+change+management+perspective+to+implementing+a+cyber+security+culture.+In+ECCWS+2020+20th+European+Conference+on+Cyber+Warfare+and+Security+(,+442-448.&ots=zhgyJUSTzM&sig=QBhDAsQ88v3IeMGZvStJuqI1eqQ#v=onepage&q&f=false

Seh, A. H., Zarour, M., Alenezi, M., Sarkar, A. K., Agrawal, A., Kumar, R., & Ahmad Khan, R. (2020). Healthcare data breaches: Insights and implications. *Health Care, 8*(2), 133. DOI: 10.3390/healthcare8020133 PMID: 32414183

Shields, D., Funk, C., & Bredemeier, B. L. (2015). Predictors of moral disengagement in sport. *Journal of Sport & Exercise Psychology, 37*(6), 646–658. DOI: 10.1123/jsep.2015-0110 PMID: 26866772

Smith, D. (2022). *Fraud and corruption: Cases and materials.* Springer Nature. https://link.springer.com/book/10.1007/978-3-031-10063-5

Spector, P. E., & Fox, S. (2002). An emotion-centered model of voluntary work behavior: Some parallels between counterproductive work behavior and organizational citizenship behavior. *Human Resource Management Review, 12*(2), 269–292. DOI: 10.1016/S1053-4822(02)00049-9

Tripp, T. M., & Bies, R. J. (2009). *Getting even: The truth about workplace revenge—and how to stop it.* John Wiley & Sons.

Wilder, J. (2022, April 27). HHS Warns of Insider Threats in the Healthcare Sector. *Healthcare Innovation.* https://www.hcinnovationgroup.com/cybersecurity/data-breaches/news/21265719/hhs-warns-of-insider-threats-in-the-healthcare-sector

Chapter 5
Financial Cybersecurity: A Critical Review of Software Supply Chain Attacks

Lawrence Ejime Iweriebor
http://orcid.org/0009-0004-4812-3787
Capitol Technology University, USA

Eugene Lewis
http://orcid.org/0000-0002-2956-0760
Capitol Technology University, USA

ABSTRACT

This study analyzes software supply chain attacks in financial cybersecurity using a qualitative literature review and case studies. It integrates cybersecurity, supply chain, and financial risk concepts to address sector-specific gaps in taxonomy and mitigation. Findings show attackers exploit trust in software distribution: 61% of malicious packages use typosquatting and 56% activate at install time, with average dwell times of 209 days and 49% employing obfuscation (Ohm et al., 2020). Interconnected financial and cyber-physical systems heighten systemic risk (Yeboah-Ofori & Islam, 2019). While neural networks outperform alternative classifiers, detection still struggles with obfuscation and conditional execution (Li, 2024). The study concludes that perimeter-centric defenses are insufficient and calls for integrated controls—vendor assurance, provenance verification, advanced detection, and incident response, aligned with regulatory requirements (Alshammari & Singh, 2025).

DOI: 10.4018/979-8-2600-1021-1.ch005

INTRODUCTION

The rapid digitization of financial services has reshaped the attack surface, exposing institutions to risks that originate well beyond their own networks. As banks and FinTechs assemble products from third-party libraries, cloud platforms, continuous integration and delivery pipelines, and other external services, each dependency becomes a potential entry point that attackers can target (Yeboah-Ofori et al., 2021). Adversaries increasingly exploit these trust relationships, inserting malicious code into legitimate update channels, compromising build systems, or abusing managed service providers to gain privileged access to production systems and sensitive financial data (Yeboah-Ofori et al., 2021). Observed incidents show that compromise of a single upstream vendor can cascade into dozens or hundreds of downstream institutions and create direct consequences for operations, regulatory exposure, and confidence in data integrity (Ohm et al., 2020).

Because the financial sector plays an essential role in global economic stability, it remains an attractive target for cybercriminals, state-aligned actors, and other malicious entities (Yeboah-Ofori et al., 2021). This study examines software supply chain attacks in the financial sector, tracing how they emerge, how they spread, and why traditional security models centered on perimeter defense and endpoint protection are no longer sufficient in environments that depend on shared vendors, rapid release cycles, and high-value payment and settlement functions.

This chapter proceeds by defining the purpose and scope of the study, establishing the theoretical and conceptual framework that links software supply chain compromise to systemic financial risk, reviewing the historical and current literature on attack techniques and regulatory exposure, explaining the qualitative integrative methodology used to synthesize that literature and associated case evidence, presenting findings across technical, organizational, and systemic layers, and concluding with actionable recommendations for institutional leadership, financial market infrastructures, and regulators.

PURPOSE OF THE STUDY

The purpose of this qualitative integrative review is to analyze how software supply chain attacks manifest in the financial sector, explain why they are uniquely dangerous in high-dependency, high-uptime environments, and develop mitigation strategies that reflect the systemic importance of payment, clearing, and settlement infrastructure. Software supply chain attacks are a fast-growing and high-impact threat vector because adversaries compromise trusted vendors, update channels, and development tooling rather than attacking a financial institution directly. Traditional controls often underestimate this layered risk and therefore leave critical gaps. The expanding reliance on third-party components and open-source libraries enlarges the attack surface, creating numerous points of entry for adversaries who exploit implicit trust in software distribution channels. In one study of 174 malicious packages, 61% used typosquatting to infiltrate legitimate repositories and reach downstream users (Ohm et al., 2020). Because financial systems are tightly interconnected, compromise of a single upstream dependency can create operational loss, data exposure, and reputational harm across multiple institutions at once. Detection is also difficult. Attackers increasingly deploy code that remains dormant or only activates under specific runtime conditions, which delays discovery and complicates incident response (Ohm et al., 2020).

These pressures are intensified by continuing digital transformation in financial institutions. Cloud adoption, open banking interfaces, and continuous integration and delivery mean that code is assembled and deployed faster than it can be fully reviewed. Governance and procurement controls have not always kept pace with this tempo. As a result, production environments often inherit dependencies whose security posture is only partially understood, especially when those dependencies are maintained by niche vendors or individual open-source maintainers. This accelerates exposure, widens the window for compromise, and weakens boundary-focused defenses (Alshammari & Singh, 2025; Ohm et al., 2020; Yeboah-Ofori & Islam, 2019).

The purpose of this study is to analyze how software supply chain attacks manifest in the financial sector, explain why they are uniquely dangerous in high-dependency, high-uptime environments, and develop mitigation strategies that reflect the systemic importance of modern payment, clearing, and settlement infrastructure. The analysis aims to provide guidance relevant to executive leadership, security and risk teams, regulators, and market operators responsible for financial stability.

RESEARCH QUESTIONS

This study is guided by four core research questions. First, in what specific ways do software supply chain attacks infiltrate financial institutions and critical financial market infrastructures, including payment, clearing, and settlement systems? Second, how do organizational practices within these institutions, including vendor governance, change control, escalation authority, and incident response tempo, influence both the likelihood of compromise and the duration of an attacker's persistence? Third, how can a compromise of a single vendor, dependency, or privileged update channel propagate beyond the initially affected institution and generate liquidity stress, settlement disruption, or loss of confidence across the financial system?

Finally, which governance, architectural, and supervisory measures emerge from the literature as most aligned with mitigating these risks in practice?

NATURE OF THE STUDY

This study addresses a critical gap in financial cybersecurity by focusing on software supply chain attacks as both a technical and systemic problem. The financial sector historically treated cyber incidents as institutional outages or fraud events. But attacks such as large-scale poisoned updates illustrate that a single corrupted component can trigger simultaneous operational disruption, regulatory penalties, and reputational harm across many dependent organizations. The same pattern is visible in financial platforms today: a breach at one vendor can instantly become a shared crisis for every institution that relies on that vendor's code or services.

Emerging technologies such as AI-driven analytics, blockchain settlement infrastructure, and embedded finance intensify this challenge by introducing additional vendors, shared data models, and privileged runtime services. Integration of these components often happens under competitive pressure to ship quickly, not under conservative assurance regimes. That dynamic raises the likelihood that compromise in one shared component will produce cross-institution consequences even when no bank is directly targeted (Yeboah-Ofori & Islam, 2019).

Accordingly, the study is structured as an integrative review and synthesis. It links technical exploit paths to organizational governance failures and then to potential systemic amplification in payments, liquidity, data integrity, and confidence. This framing reflects growing recognition among macroprudential and supervisory bodies that cyber risk is no longer only an internal IT problem but a channel for system-wide financial stress capable of triggering liquidity freezes, runs, and loss of confidence (European Systemic Risk Board, 2020; Eisenbach et al., 2020; Board of Governors of the Federal Reserve System, 2022).

THEORETICAL AND CONCEPTUAL FRAMEWORK

This study models software supply chain risk as the interaction of three layers: technical compromise, organizational governance, and systemic interdependence. To make that interaction explicit, the analysis draws on four established frameworks: the National Institute of Standards and Technology Risk Management Framework (RMF), Zero Trust Architecture, the OCTAVE risk assessment method, and the Observe-Orient-Decide-Act (OODA) decision cycle. Together these frameworks clarify how financial institutions can categorize, prioritize, detect, and contain supply chain threats while meeting supervisory expectations (Joint Task Force, 2018; Rose, Borchert, Mitchell, & Connelly, 2020; Alberts, Behrens, Pethia, & Wilson, 1999; Priambodo, Pramadi, Briliyanti, Hasbi, & Yahya, 2022).

The NIST Risk Management Framework (RMF) defines a disciplined, lifecycle process for categorizing information systems, selecting and implementing security controls, assessing those controls, authorizing system operation, and continuously monitoring risk (Joint Task Force, 2018). RMF links system-level controls to organizational risk tolerance and executive accountability. In the financial sector, this mapping is essential. Banks, payment processors, and other regulated firms must show supervisors that not only their own systems, but also critical vendors and hosted services, meet governance, control, and monitoring expectations. Under RMF, every externally sourced software component that processes, stores, or transmits regulated financial data must be categorized, assigned controls, assessed, and continuously monitored. That requirement turns software supply chain exposure from an ad hoc procurement concern into an auditable element of formal risk governance.

Zero Trust Architecture rejects the assumption that code, users, or devices deserve implicit trust simply because they are inside a network boundary. Instead, access to resources is continuously authenticated, authorized, and evaluated based on context such as workload behavior and data sensitivity (Rose et al., 2020). For supply chain risk, Zero Trust matters because it limits how far an intrusion can spread when – not if – a poisoned vendor component runs in production. Even code that arrives through a historically trusted channel is not allowed to freely move laterally, extract sensitive payment data, or call privileged services without being challenged again. This aligns directly with observed attacker strategies that rely on abusing trusted update channels to gain privileged access.

The OCTAVE methodology (Operationally Critical Threat, Asset, and Vulnerability Evaluation) emphasizes identifying the organization's most critical assets, mapping the threats and vulnerabilities associated with those assets, and prioritizing mitigation based on business impact (Alberts et al., 1999). OCTAVE is especially relevant to financial services because not all assets are equally important to financial stability. A marketing database is not systemically comparable to payment instructions, settlement records, or balance data. OCTAVE pushes institutions to rank which dependencies – including external software suppliers – are operationally critical to liquidity, settlement finality, and regulatory obligations. That ranking is the precondition for credible board-level risk appetite statements and recovery planning.

The Observe-Orient-Decide-Act (OODA) loop is an iterative decision model adapted for cybersecurity operations in high-tempo environments (Priambodo et al., 2022). OODA frames incident response as a continuous cycle: quickly observe signals of compromise, orient by interpreting those signals in context, decide on a course of action, and act to contain and recover. In finance, this tempo is essential.

Financial market infrastructures are expected to restore critical services within hours – often within a two-hour recovery time objective – even after extreme cyber attacks (CPMI-IOSCO, 2016). Embedding OODA into security operations centers and crisis management playbooks allows institutions and market infrastructures to make containment and liquidity decisions fast enough to prevent an operational disruption from escalating into a confidence shock.

Taken together, RMF, Zero Trust, OCTAVE, and OODA form a layered conceptual model. RMF provides governance discipline and continuous monitoring for both first-party and vendor systems. Zero Trust constrains how a compromised component can behave if it reaches production. OCTAVE ties technical controls to business-critical assets and the institution's risk appetite. OODA operationalizes crisis response at the speed demanded by payments, trading, and settlement. This integrated model structures the literature review, informs the case analysis, and grounds the recommendations for financial institutions and regulators.

LITERATURE REVIEW AND BACKGROUND

Historical Evolution

Early financial cybersecurity programs were built around perimeter defense, fraud monitoring, and disaster recovery. Those programs assumed that the most credible threat was an external intruder trying to penetrate the institution's own network, or a localized outage caused by hardware failure. As financial firms digitized core operations and outsourced functionality to specialized vendors, that assumption weakened. Attackers increasingly bypassed hardened perimeters by compromising software suppliers, managed service providers, and open-source libraries that financial institutions consume by default. This marks a shift from direct intrusion toward exploitation of trust relationships embedded in the software development and deployment pipeline (Ohm et al., 2020; Yeboah-Ofori & Islam, 2019).

Supervisory bodies and market operators now recognize that these attacks are not isolated IT problems but potential triggers for market-wide stress. Guidance for financial market infrastructures issued by the Committee on Payments and Market Infrastructures and the International Organization of Securities Commissions emphasizes that cyber resilience is inseparable from operational resilience and financial stability (CPMI-IOSCO, 2016). That guidance highlights that clearing and settlement systems concentrate risk, and that a successful cyber attack on one such infrastructure could transmit liquidity shocks across markets. In parallel, macroprudential authorities in Europe describe how a cyber incident could escalate from a localized operational outage into a liquidity freeze, a run on institutions perceived as exposed, and ultimately a systemic crisis if confidence in data integrity were lost (European Systemic Risk Board, 2020). This reframed cyber risk – including software supply chain compromise – as a channel for systemic financial instability.

Current Attack Techniques

Several attack techniques dominate contemporary software supply chain compromise. Adversaries inject malicious code into legitimate build and distribution infrastructure, rather than attempting noisy direct intrusions. By inserting altered packages, modified libraries, or backdoored updates into trusted repositories and update servers, attackers inherit the credibility of the upstream vendor and ride that trust directly into production environments inside financial institutions. In one study of 174 malicious packages, attackers most commonly registered look-alike package names – a technique known as typosquatting – to trick developers and automated build systems into installing a poisoned dependency (Ohm et al., 2020). Once executed, these packages harvested credentials, exfiltrated API keys, injected skimmers, or established remote access channels that could enable fraudulent activity within financial systems (Ohm et al., 2020).

These attacks often unfold in stages. Attackers quietly collect credentials and environment details, alter build configurations or continuous integration and delivery pipelines, and then trigger activation only after the malicious code reaches high-value financial workloads. Attackers deliberately design these payloads to blend into normal development and maintenance flows. They exploit the assumption that signed updates and internal build pipelines are inherently trustworthy. This staged approach complicates detection, prolongs attacker dwell time, and expands the potential spread once activation occurs. Supply chain compromise can enable movement into payment processing systems, exposure of client data, manipulation of transaction logic, or insertion of fraudulent instructions into back-office systems that settle real funds.

A majority of observed malicious packages aim to capture credentials or deploy remote access mechanisms that allow persistent control over downstream systems (Ohm et al., 2020; Yeboah-Ofori & Islam, 2019; Li, 2024). These behaviors align with strategic objectives seen in both financially motivated attackers and state-aligned actors: long-term, stealthy access to high-value systems rather than immediate smash-and-grab theft. Persistent access enables data exfiltration, manipulation of transaction workflows, or quiet positioning for future disruption at a moment of market or geopolitical significance.

Systemic and Regulatory Risk in Finance

Systemic risk emerges because modern finance is a tightly coupled, real-time network of institutions, vendors, data feeds, and market infrastructures. A cyber event at one node can propagate quickly through payment rails, liquidity channels, and shared service providers. Researchers at the Federal Reserve Bank of New York show that if one of the largest U.S. banks cannot send payments, liquidity stress spreads almost immediately to other banks that depend on incoming payments to fund their own obligations. The result can be a freeze in intraday funding markets even among firms that were never directly attacked (Eisenbach et al., 2020). Macroprudential authorities warn that such a disruption could cascade into market dysfunction, forced asset sales, and broader confidence shocks (European Systemic Risk Board, 2020; Board of Governors of the Federal Reserve System, 2022).

From a supervisory standpoint, cyber risk therefore resembles – and in some ways exceeds – traditional forms of operational risk. Unlike most physical outages, a malicious software update can corrupt data across many institutions at once. Unlike market or credit risk, capital buffers alone cannot restore corrupted records or restart an immobilized settlement platform (Board of Governors of the Federal Reserve System, 2022). Financial market infrastructures are expected to resume critical services within hours, often within a two-hour recovery time objective, even after extreme cyber attacks (CPMI-IOSCO, 2016). These expectations elevate software supply chain security from a procurement issue to a core element of financial stability policy.

GAPS IN THE RESEARCH

Despite growing recognition of software supply chain security as a strategic risk, most academic and industry work still treats it as an implementation detail of cybersecurity programs. The literature frequently documents individual breaches, maps attacker techniques, or recommends secure development practices. Far less work frames supply chain compromise as a deliberate pathway for adversaries to trigger systemic financial disruption. In particular, research still rarely links software dependency poisoning to liquidity contagion, payment-system concentration, or macroprudential stress amplification (Eisenbach et al., 2020; European Systemic Risk Board, 2020).

Research also has not yet produced widely accepted methods for embedding supply chain risk into board-level risk appetite statements, liquidity stress tests, recovery time objectives, or supervisory reporting obligations. Questions such as who owns remediation of a poisoned vendor component, how quickly incident information must be shared with regulators and counterparties, and how to quantify cross-institution spread remain unsettled. This study addresses those gaps by integrating technical analysis, governance expectations, and macro-level stability concerns to inform both practitioners and policymakers.

Summary Table

Table 1. Summary of Dominant Software Supply Chain Attack Patterns, Impacts, and Governance Implications in the Financial Sector

Attack Vector	How the Vector Works	Observed Impact in Financial / Critical Infrastructures	Governance / Supervisory Implication
Typo squatting / Malicious Package Injection	Attacker publishes a package with a nearly identical name to a trusted dependency; developers or automated build systems pull the poisoned package.	Credential theft, data exfiltration, persistent access to downstream systems. In one study, this accounted for most malicious packages and many remained undetected for extended periods (Ohm et al., 2020).	Requires continuous supplier verification, provenance checking, and runtime controls that do not assume trust based on source alone (Rose et al., 2020; Joint Task Force, 2018).
Compromised Build / Update Channel	Attacker gains access to a vendor's CI/CD or update mechanism and ships a signed but modified update to all downstream institutions.	Simultaneous compromise of many institutions that depend on the vendor; potential disruption of payment processing or settlement; treated as a systemic operational resilience issue by supervisors (CPMI-IOSCO, 2016; European Systemic Risk Board, 2020).	Demands RMF-style classification of vendor code as 'in scope,' explicit control ownership, and board-level recovery and communication plans aligned with supervisory expectations (Joint Task Force, 2018; CPMI-IOSCO, 2016).
Maintainer / Insider Social Engineering	Attacker convinces or replaces an upstream maintainer, quietly inserts malicious logic into a legitimate component, and leverages inherited trust.	Privileged execution that appears 'normal,' enabling very long dwell time and hard-to-detect data theft or transaction manipulation (Ohm et al., 2020; Yeboah-Ofori & Islam, 2019).	Requires OCTAVE-style identification of which upstream components are operationally critical for liquidity, settlement finality, and balance integrity, so they receive board attention and monitoring (Alberts et al., 1999).
Systemic Propagation via Payment and Settlement Infrastructure	A compromised dependency disrupts payment messaging or corrupts balance data at a major institution, causing downstream liquidity stress for counterparties.	Potential market-wide liquidity freezes and confidence loss even at firms not directly attacked; may trigger runs or require central bank intervention (Eisenbach et al., 2020; Board of Governors of the Federal Reserve System, 2022).	Requires OODA-speed coordinated response exercises with payment utilities, regulators, and central banks, with recovery time objectives consistent with FMI cyber resilience expectations (Priambodo et al., 2022; CPMI-IOSCO, 2016).

Across the reviewed sources and case evidence, several themes emerge. Adversaries weaponize trust by inserting malicious code into software pipelines that financial institutions already rely on. Organizational blind spots, fragmented ownership of vendor code, unclear escalation paths, and uneven monitoring of deployment pipelines – allow these intrusions to persist. The structure of modern finance can then amplify what begins as a technical compromise into a macro-level event by disrupting payment finality, eroding confidence in balances, or forcing emergency liquidity interventions. The standalone summary table that follows groups these themes by attack vector, mechanism, observed impact in financial infrastructures, and governance or supervisory implications.

Table 1 consolidates the dominant software supply chain attack patterns identified in the literature and maps each pattern to both systemic financial impact and supervisory expectation. It is intended to support senior leadership, regulators, and financial market infrastructure operators by linking concrete attack techniques to liquidity stress, settlement disruption, and governance obligations (Ohm et al., 2020; Alberts et al., 1999; Joint Task Force, 2018; CPMI-IOSCO, 2016; European Systemic Risk Board, 2020; Eisenbach et al., 2020; Rose et al., 2020; Priambodo et al., 2022; Board of Governors of the Federal Reserve System, 2022).

METHODOLOGY

Search Strategy and Selection

This study combines a qualitative literature review with targeted analysis of high-impact incidents that illustrate software supply chain compromise in, or directly relevant to, financial services. Peer-reviewed journal articles, conference proceedings, and authoritative publications from standard-setting bodies and financial supervisors were collected and analyzed for key findings, methods, and theoretical contributions (Joint Task Force, 2018; Rose et al., 2020; CPMI-IOSCO, 2016; European Systemic Risk Board, 2020; Board of Governors of the Federal Reserve System, 2022). Inclusion criteria emphasized relevance to software supply chain threats, financial-sector impact, systemic risk transmission, or operational resilience requirements.

Sources were included if they described software supply chain compromise or attempted compromise; analyzed attack vectors involving software dependencies, vendor code, or privileged update channels; and addressed either the financial sector directly or an infrastructure domain with direct financial interdependence, such as payments, clearing, or settlement. Articles and reports that focused solely on generic malware, consumer fraud, or non-financial critical infrastructure were excluded unless they provided transferable insight into supply chain attack mechanics or rapid incident response tempo. After screening, accepted sources were coded thematically around recurring patterns: attack vectors; persistence and dwell time; governance and organizational failures; and systemic or regulatory implications. These themes structure the Findings and Results section of this study (Ohm et al., 2020; Yeboah-Ofori & Islam, 2019; Eisenbach et al., 2020).

Case Study Selection

Case studies were selected when they provided detailed insight into how adversaries inserted themselves into trusted pipelines, how compromised components moved into production financial environments, and how defenders detected and contained the intrusion. Incidents in which attackers leveraged poisoned software updates, manipulated build infrastructure, or abused privileged vendor access were favored because they expose the specific trust failures that define supply chain attacks. These cases also illustrate how quickly a localized breach can become a multi-institution event through shared payment rails and liquidity dependencies. Where public post-incident reporting was limited, supervisory analyses and central bank research were used to infer likely systemic consequences, such as intraday liquidity stress caused by a payment system outage (Eisenbach et al., 2020; Board of Governors of the Federal Reserve System, 2022).

LIMITATIONS

This methodology has limitations. Publicly disclosed case studies often omit forensic detail, attacker tradecraft, and timing. Many findings remain confidential or classified, especially when nation-state actors or critical market infrastructures are involved. As a result, some conclusions about systemic impact rely on supervisory simulations and macroprudential scenario analyses rather than on fully disclosed real-world failures (European Systemic Risk Board, 2020; Eisenbach et al., 2020). The threat landscape is also dynamic. Attacker tooling, organizational practices, and supervisory expectations evolve quickly, which affects how long any single set of controls or recommendations will remain sufficient.

FINDINGS AND RESULTS

The technical vectors observed across the literature and case studies follow a recurring pattern. Attackers compromise upstream code or tooling, distribute the modified component through legitimate channels, and leverage the inherited trust of that channel to obtain privileged execution inside downstream financial institutions. Many payloads seek credential theft, installation of remote command beacons, or subtle manipulation of transaction logic. In one large sample of malicious packages, typosquatting accounted for the majority of injection methods (Ohm et al., 2020). By masquerading as legitimate dependencies, these packages captured developer credentials and API keys that could later be used to access payment workflows, account data, or regulatory reporting systems, creating direct opportunities for fraud and data exfiltration.

Organizational and human factors repeatedly enable these technical vectors. Financial institutions often treat vendor-provided software, managed service providers, and internal deployment infrastructure as trusted zones. When procurement, security engineering, and operations teams have fragmented responsibilities, no single owner has complete visibility into where third-party code runs, what privileges it holds, or how quickly a compromise must be escalated. Delayed patching, credential reuse across development and production, and informal exceptions to change-control processes all widen the window attackers can exploit (Yeboah-Ofori & Islam, 2019).

The frameworks described above map directly to these gaps. RMF requires institutions to categorize every system and supplier by criticality, assign accountable control owners, assess those controls, and continuously monitor deviations (Joint Task Force, 2018). OCTAVE extends this discipline by forcing explicit prioritization of assets such as payment messages, settlement records, and customer balance data (Alberts et al., 1999). Zero Trust requires that even code obtained through trusted channels continue to be authenticated, authorized, and behaviorally evaluated before it can access high-value data or services (Rose et al., 2020). Finally, the OODA loop highlights that defenders must be able to observe anomalies in deployment pipelines or vendor behavior, orient those anomalies against business-critical assets, decide on containment actions, and act in minutes rather than hours (Priambodo et al., 2022). Together, these approaches recast supply chain security as an executive governance problem, not only a patching task.

The systemic impact dimension reflects how quickly a localized compromise can escalate into a macro-level event. Clearinghouses, payment systems, and core banking platforms are deeply interdependent. A poisoned software update that halts payment messaging in one large institution can delay high-value transfers, which in turn deprives counterparties of expected liquidity. Researchers have shown that if a top-tier U.S. bank cannot send payments, the resulting liquidity shortfalls can impair a significant share of the sector by assets within a single business day (Eisenbach et al., 2020). Supervisory analyses warn that such a disruption could trigger runs, market freezes, or forced asset sales even at institutions that were never directly breached (European Systemic Risk Board, 2020; Board of Governors of the Federal Reserve System, 2022).

Because financial market infrastructures are expected to restore critical operations quickly – often within a two-hour target even under extreme cyber stress (CPMI-IOSCO, 2016) – senior leadership and boards cannot treat supply chain incidents as routine vendor issues. An upstream compromise that corrupts data used to settle trades, route high-value payments, or record balances is not simply an IT outage. It is an event with potential to undermine confidence in account integrity, disrupt liquidity, and force extraordinary central bank support to stabilize markets.

CONCLUSION

Software supply chain attacks now represent a structural threat to the stability, integrity, and credibility of modern financial services. Adversaries no longer need to penetrate a bank's perimeter directly. Instead, they weaponize trusted software pipelines, exploit implicit trust in vendor updates, and use that trust to gain privileged access to systems that process payments, record balances, and satisfy regulatory reporting obligations. Because these functions underpin liquidity and confidence, a successful supply chain intrusion can produce not only operational disruption but also systemic financial stress.

First, financial institutions and market infrastructures must institutionalize continuous supplier verification. This requires applying RMF-style categorization, control selection, assessment, authorization, and continuous monitoring to every externally sourced component that touches regulated data or critical transaction flows (Joint Task Force, 2018). In practice, this means treating vendor code, managed service providers, and open-source dependencies as in-scope systems that demand the same rigor as internally developed applications. It also means maintaining an authoritative software bill of materials and automated attestation that updates have not been altered in transit.

Second, institutions must adopt Zero Trust principles as the runtime enforcement layer for supply chain defense. Rather than assuming that code signed by a vendor is safe, Zero Trust requires continuous authentication and authorization for every request, granular least privilege, and segmentation of high-value assets such as payment messaging gateways and settlement databases (Rose et al., 2020). This architectural posture limits how far an intrusion can spread when a poisoned dependency executes in production.

Third, boards and senior risk committees must explicitly incorporate software supply chain scenarios into enterprise risk appetite statements, liquidity stress testing, recovery time objectives, and regulatory communication playbooks. OCTAVE provides a structured way to identify which assets – for example, high-value payment instructions, securities settlement records, or customer balance data – are operationally critical and to align investment and escalation authority with their systemic importance (Alberts et al., 1999). Elevating supply chain compromise to a board-visible scenario alongside credit, market, and liquidity risk ensures it is resourced accordingly and that extraordinary recovery actions are pre-authorized.

Fourth, institutions and supervisors must rehearse coordinated, time-bounded cyber crisis drills that follow an OODA-style cadence: observe abnormal behavior in a shared vendor or payment utility, orient that signal against liquidity and settlement dependencies, decide on containment and communication actions, and act within minutes, not days (Priambodo et al., 2022). CPMI-IOSCO guidance already expects financial market infrastructures to be able to resume critical operations rapidly, often within a two-hour recovery time objective, even under extreme cyber stress (CPMI-IOSCO, 2016). Embedding this tempo into joint exercises with regulators and counterparties reduces the probability that a software supply chain incident will cascade into a systemic liquidity event (European Systemic Risk Board, 2020; Board of Governors of the Federal Reserve System, 2022).

These recommendations extend beyond any single firm. Because critical payment, clearing, and settlement functions are concentrated in a relatively small number of financial market infrastructures and large service providers, cyber resilience is partly a collective good. CPMI-IOSCO emphasizes that these infrastructures must coordinate with their participants, technology partners, and relevant authorities to strengthen resilience across the entire ecosystem, not just within their own perimeter (CPMI-IOSCO, 2016). Macroprudential authorities similarly argue that systemic cyber preparedness requires joint planning for communication, liquidity support, and data integrity restoration if a supply chain attack compromises critical services (European Systemic Risk Board, 2020; Board of Governors of the Federal Reserve System, 2022).

RECOMMENDATIONS FOR FUTURE RESEARCH

Several avenues for future research emerge from this analysis. One priority is extending quantitative models of financial contagion to explicitly incorporate software supply chain compromise. Existing work shows how payment-system outages at a single major institution can transmit funding stress to other institutions that were never directly attacked (Eisenbach et al., 2020). Comparable models are still rare for scenarios in which malicious code silently propagates through shared vendors or poisoned dependencies and interferes with payment execution, settlement finality, or balance integrity across multiple institutions at once.

Another priority is translating supply chain defense into operational doctrine. Security teams need measurable frameworks for continuous supplier assurance, provable software bill of materials integrity, and Zero Trust enforcement in deployment pipelines. Boards and regulators, in turn, need standardized escalation triggers and disclosure timelines for software supply chain incidents that could impair liquidity, settlement, or customer balance integrity. Research should also continue to track how attackers evolve their tradecraft – including automated code generation and adaptive credential theft – to ensure that financial-sector defenses evolve at least as quickly as software supply chain threats (Li, 2024; Alshammari & Singh, 2025).

Future work should adopt mixed-methods approaches that integrate quantitative modeling of systemic financial impact with qualitative analysis of institutional decision-making and governance. Quantitatively, there is a need to extend payment-system contagion modeling to scenarios in which malicious dependencies corrupt data or delay payments across multiple firms simultaneously, measuring propagation speed, liquidity stress, data integrity loss, and recovery timelines under supervisory expectations that core services resume quickly (CPMI-IOSCO, 2016; European Systemic Risk Board, 2020; Eisenbach et al., 2020). Qualitatively, future work should examine how institutions assign ownership for third-party code risk, escalate under uncertainty, and coordinate with supervisors in real time. Combining these perspectives is necessary because software supply chain compromise operates simultaneously at technical, organizational, and systemic levels, and neither quantitative contagion modeling nor governance interviews alone is sufficient to capture that full dynamic.

REFERENCES

Alberts, C. J., Behrens, S. G., Pethia, R. D., & Wilson, W. R. (1999). Operationally critical threat, asset, and vulnerability evaluation (OCTAVE) framework, version 1.0. DOI: 10.21236/ADA367718

Alshammari, B., & Mahinderjit Singh, M. (2025). A systematic literature review on tackling cyber threats for cyber logistic chain and conceptual frameworks for robust detection mechanisms. *IEEE Access : Practical Innovations, Open Solutions*, *13*, 67661–67692. DOI: 10.1109/ACCESS.2025.3552689

Board of Governors of the Federal Reserve System. (2022). *Implications of cyber risk for financial stability*. Federal Reserve Board. Retrieved October 26, 2025, from https://www.federalreserve.gov/econres/notes/feds-notes/implications-of-cyber-risk-for-financial-stability-20220512.html

Board of the International Organization of Securities Commissions. (2016). *Committee on Payments and Market Infrastructures*. Bank for International Settlements. https://www.bis.org/cpmi/publ/d146.pdf?utm_source=chatgpt.com

Eisenbach, T. M., Kovner, A., & Lee, M. J. (2020). Cyber risk and the U.S. financial system: A pre-mortem analysis. SSRN *Electronic Journal*. DOI: 10.2139/ssrn.3522710

Li, S. (2024). Comparative analysis of predicting malware attack trends in cyber supply chain using multiple classification models. *IEEE Access : Practical Innovations, Open Solutions*, •••, 1–1. DOI: 10.1109/ACCESS.2024.3471802

NIST. (2025). *NIST risk management framework*. NIST Computer Security Resource Center | CSRC. Retrieved October 26, 2025, from https://csrc.nist.gov/projects/risk-management?utm_source=chatgpt.com

Ohm, M., Plate, H., Sykosch, A., & Meier, M. (2020). Backstabber's knife collection: A review of open source software supply chain attacks. *Lecture Notes in Computer Science*, *12223*, 23–43. DOI: 10.1007/978-3-030-52683-2_2

Priambodo, D. F., Pramadi, Y. R., Briliyant, O. C., Hasbi, M., & Yahya, M. A. (2022). Observe-Orient-Decide-Act (OODA) for cyber security education. *International Journal of Advanced Computer Science and Applications*, *13*(10). Advance online publication. DOI: 10.14569/IJACSA.2022.0131031

Rose, S., Borchert, O., Mitchell, S., & Connelly, S. (2020). *Zero trust architecture*. NIST Computer Security Resource Center | CSRC. https://csrc.nist.gov/pubs/sp/800/207/final

Yeboah-Ofori, A., & Islam, S. (2019). Cyber security threat modeling for supply chain organizational environments. *Future Internet*, *11*(3), 63. DOI: 10.3390/fi11030063

Yeboah-Ofori, A., Islam, S., Lee, S. W., Shamszaman, Z. U., Muhammad, K., Altaf, M., & Al-Rakhami, M. S. (2021). Cyber threat predictive analytics for improving cyber supply chain security. *IEEE Access : Practical Innovations, Open Solutions*, *9*, 94318–94337. DOI: 10.1109/ACCESS.2021.3087109

Chapter 6

Exploring the Organizational Strategic Complexities of Managing Human Behavioral Risks in Banking Cybersecurity

Marlena Daryousef
http://orcid.org/0000-0001-9513-501X
Golden Gate University, USA

Darrell Norman Burrell
http://orcid.org/0000-0002-4675-9544
Marymount University, USA

Calvin Nobles
http://orcid.org/0000-0003-4002-1108
University of Maryland Global Campus, USA

Maurice Dawson
http://orcid.org/0000-0003-4609-3444
Illinois Institute of Technology, USA

Sharon Burton
http://orcid.org/0000-0003-1653-9783
Embry-Riddle Aeronautical University, USA

Laura A. Jones
http://orcid.org/0000-0002-0299-370X
Capitol Technology University, USA

Jessica Parker
http://orcid.org/0009-0008-9574-3275
Marymount University, USA

Phillip Reed
http://orcid.org/0009-0000-1266-0151
Marymount University, USA

Natasha Harris
http://orcid.org/0009-0002-1745-7966
Marymount University, USA

Hilda Eke
http://orcid.org/0009-0006-2021-178X
Marymount University, USA

DOI: 10.4018/979-8-2600-1021-1.ch006

KerriLaine Prunella
http://orcid.org/0009-0001-0177-3545
Marymount University, USA

Kylei L. Conti
http://orcid.org/0009-0009-0495-6601
Marymount University, USA

Stacey Morin
http://orcid.org/0000-0003-2935-8332
Marymount University, USA

Julia DeFrance
http://orcid.org/0009-0005-8105-2594
Marymount University, USA

ABSTRACT

This study examines cybersecurity risk through an in-depth case analysis of HomeTown Bank, a regional financial institution that experienced two significant breaches driven by insider misconduct and employee error. Using a management consulting intervention grounded in root cause analysis, the study identifies human behavior and organizational culture, not technical deficiencies, as the primary sources of vulnerability. Findings demonstrate that insufficient cybersecurity awareness, weak cultural ownership of risk, and limited use of behavioral analytics enabled both malicious and unintentional actions to escalate into enterprise-level incidents. The study illustrates the value of case-based inquiry for generating actionable, human-centered insights that bridge theory and practice in cybersecurity risk management

INTRODUCTION

HomeTown Bank, a pseudo name for the actual organization to protect the privacy of the actual organization), a regional financial institution operating in the Midwest, experienced two significant cybersecurity incidents that underscore the central role of human behavior in modern cyber risk. The first incident involved a disgruntled employee who deliberately exfiltrated and sold sensitive customer data on the dark web. The second breach resulted from an employee inadvertently clicking on a malicious phishing link, which enabled attackers to gain unauthorized access to internal systems and customer information.

While the technical vulnerabilities exploited in these breaches were consequential, the more profound exposure lay in the bank's insufficient attention to human-centered cybersecurity risks. The incidents revealed systemic weaknesses in employee oversight, behavioral monitoring, and organizational preparedness. Compounding the technical and operational failures was HomeTown Bank's ineffective response strategy. The organization delayed customer notification and failed to communicate transparently, exacerbating reputational damage and increasing the likelihood of regulatory penalties for noncompliance with data protection requirements. As a result, customer attrition accelerated, with clients migrating to competitors perceived as more trustworthy and technologically resilient.

From a business perspective, these events demonstrate that cybersecurity failures are not isolated IT problems but enterprise-level risks that directly affect revenue stability, customer loyalty, and long-term brand equity.

PROBLEM STATEMENT

HomeTown Bank's cybersecurity failures highlight a critical gap in its risk management framework: the inability to anticipate, detect, and mitigate cyber threats driven by insider behavior and social engineering. The root causes extend beyond technical shortcomings and include inadequate employee training, limited use of behavioral analytics, weak insider threat detection mechanisms, and an organizational culture that underestimated human-driven cyber risk.

The bank's reliance on traditional perimeter-based security controls proved insufficient in an environment where employees serve as both the first line of defense and the most frequent point of failure. The insider data theft incident revealed the absence of continuous monitoring and AI-driven anomaly detection capable of identifying unusual access patterns, privilege misuse, or behavioral deviations. Similarly, the phishing-related breach exposed gaps in employee awareness programs and a lack of adaptive training mechanisms designed to respond to evolving social engineering tactics.

Without a comprehensive strategy that integrates human risk into cybersecurity design, HomeTown Bank remains vulnerable to repeat incidents. Addressing these deficiencies is essential not only to protect sensitive data but also to meet regulatory obligations, preserve stakeholder trust, and sustain competitive positioning in an increasingly digital banking environment.

STRATEGIC GOAL IN ADDRESSING THE PROBLEM

Insider threats and social engineering attacks represent a disproportionate risk to financial institutions because they exploit predictable cognitive biases, routine behaviors, and organizational norms. Failure to address these risks carries substantial financial and strategic consequences, including direct remediation costs, regulatory fines, legal exposure, and enduring reputational harm.

A holistic risk management approach is required, one that combines advanced technologies with organizational and cultural interventions. From a practical business standpoint, artificial intelligence can play a pivotal role in this transformation. AI-enabled user and entity behavior analytics (UEBA), for example, can continuously assess employee activity to detect anomalies that may indicate malicious intent or compromised credentials. Financial institutions such as JPMorgan Chase and HSBC have publicly disclosed investments in AI-based monitoring systems to identify insider threats and reduce false positives while maintaining employee productivity.

However, technology alone is insufficient. Effective implementation depends on aligning AI tools with clear governance structures, transparent policies, and ethical oversight to avoid eroding employee trust. Continuous, role-specific training programs, enhanced through AI-driven personalization, can reinforce secure behaviors while adapting to emerging threat patterns. Equally important are well-defined incident response and communication protocols that enable rapid, compliant, and transparent engagement with regulators and customers when breaches occur.

Case studies occupy a uniquely powerful position in academic inquiry because they function as an intellectual bridge between theory and practice. In the context of complex organizational problems, such as cybersecurity risk, human behavior, and AI-enabled decision-making, case studies provide the contextual depth necessary to understand how abstract concepts manifest in real-world environments. Unlike purely theoretical or highly abstract studies, case-based research embeds analysis within lived organizational realities, where competing incentives, cultural norms, regulatory pressures, and human limitations interact in ways that cannot be fully captured through generalized models alone.

VALUE OF CASE STUDIES IN EXAMINING COMPLEX ORGANIZATIONAL SYSTEMS

Modern organizations operate as socio-technical systems in which technology, human behavior, governance, and culture are tightly interwoven. Case studies allow researchers to examine these interdependencies holistically rather than isolating variables in artificial settings. For example, the HomeTown Bank case demonstrates how cybersecurity failures emerge not solely from technical weaknesses, but from a convergence of employee behavior, leadership decisions, organizational culture, and crisis response practices. This layered complexity is precisely what makes real-world organizational problems resistant to simple, abstract solutions.

By grounding analysis in a specific organizational context, case studies make visible the nonlinear dynamics that characterize enterprise risk. They reveal how small human decisions, such as clicking a phishing link or failing to escalate concerns, can cascade into systemic failures with strategic consequences. Abstract studies often assume rational actors, stable environments, and clean data, whereas case studies expose ambiguity, imperfect information, and cognitive bias as defining features of organizational life.

ROLE OF CASE STUDIES IN ADVANCING THEORY AND PRACTICE

Case studies play a dual role: they refine theory while simultaneously informing practice. From a scholarly perspective, they test theoretical frameworks under real conditions, revealing where existing models are incomplete, overly deterministic, or disconnected from operational realities. In cybersecurity and risk management research, case studies challenge technology-centric assumptions by demonstrating that risk frequently originates at the human–organizational interface rather than within code or infrastructure alone.

From a practical standpoint, case studies translate academic insights into forms that decision-makers can recognize and apply. Executives, regulators, and risk professionals are more likely to engage with research that mirrors the complexity they face daily. The HomeTown Bank case, for instance, illustrates how AI-driven cybersecurity tools cannot succeed without cultural alignment, ethical governance, and leadership accountability. This insight carries immediate relevance for organizations considering investments in advanced analytics but underestimating implementation risk.

IMPORTANCE OF CONTEXTUALIZED EVIDENCE OVER ABSTRACT GENERALIZATION

While abstract studies contribute to foundational knowledge, they often prioritize internal validity at the expense of external relevance. Case studies invert this tradeoff by emphasizing contextual richness and practical significance. In domains such as cybersecurity, organizational behavior, and AI governance, where threats evolve rapidly and human judgment plays a central role, context matters as much as, if not more than, statistical generalization.

Case-based research captures the influence of industry-specific regulations, organizational history, workforce composition, and leadership style. These factors shape outcomes in ways that abstract models cannot easily replicate. As a result, case studies produce insights that are transferable rather than universally generalizable, allowing practitioners to draw analogies, identify patterns, and adapt lessons to their own organizational settings.

CONTRIBUTION TO EVIDENCE-BASED DECISION-MAKING

One of the most compelling advantages of case studies is their ability to support evidence-based decision-making. Organizations rarely make strategic choices based on theoretical elegance alone; they rely on precedent, narrative coherence, and demonstrated outcomes. Case studies provide credible evidence of what worked, what failed, and why. They also expose unintended consequences, such as reputational damage resulting from delayed breach notification or the erosion of employee trust caused by poorly governed monitoring technologies.

For policymakers and regulators, case studies offer empirical grounding for standards, guidance, and oversight mechanisms. For educators, they serve as pedagogical tools that cultivate critical thinking, ethical reasoning, and systems-level analysis. For researchers, they surface new questions that can later be examined through quantitative or experimental methods.

WHY THIS RESEARCH MATTERS IN THE REAL WORLD

In an era defined by rapid technological change, rising systemic risk, and increasing dependence on AI-enabled systems, organizations need research that reflects the complexity of their operating environments. Case studies respond to this need by producing knowledge that is actionable, ethically informed, and context-sensitive. They do not replace abstract research; rather, they complement it by ensuring that theory remains grounded in reality.

The HomeTown Bank case exemplifies why this form of research is indispensable. It demonstrates that cybersecurity is not merely a technical discipline but an organizational capability shaped by human behavior, leadership decisions, and cultural norms. By revealing how these elements interact in practice, case studies enable scholars and practitioners alike to move beyond simplistic solutions and toward more resilient, human-centered approaches to managing risk.

In this sense, case-based research is not a lesser form of scholarship; it is a critical mechanism for ensuring that academic inquiry remains relevant, responsible, and responsive to the real-world challenges organizations face.

CYBERSECURITY RISK ASSESSMENT AND BUSINESS INTEGRATION

Cybersecurity risk assessment in banking involves systematically identifying, analyzing, and prioritizing cyber threats that may compromise the confidentiality, integrity, and availability of information systems and customer data (Dawodu et al., 2023). As banks expand digital services and online platforms, the scope and complexity of cyber risk increase accordingly. Effective risk assessment enables institutions to allocate resources strategically, deploy appropriate controls, and maintain compliance with regulatory standards (Dawodu et al., 2023).

From a business application perspective, AI-enhanced risk assessment tools allow banks to move from static, compliance-driven assessments to dynamic, predictive models. These systems can integrate technical signals with human behavioral data to identify emerging risks in real time. For example, AI can correlate unusual login behavior with changes in employee sentiment or workload, providing early warning indicators of insider risk. This approach transforms cybersecurity from a reactive cost center into a proactive risk intelligence function that supports enterprise decision-making.

SIGNIFICANCE OF HUMAN-CENTERED CYBER RISK MANAGEMENT

The contemporary cybersecurity threat landscape remains highly challenging, particularly as digital transformation expands organizational attack surfaces. Evidence suggests that a majority of data breaches are linked to human error, misconfiguration, or manipulation rather than purely technical exploits. During periods of disruption, such as the COVID-19 pandemic, these vulnerabilities were amplified as employees adapted to remote work and unfamiliar technologies.

Cyber adversaries increasingly rely on cognitive and psychological manipulation to bypass technical controls. Cognitive hacking, which seeks to alter users' perceptions and behaviors, can be either covert, disguised as legitimate activity, or overt, such as persistent nuisance-based attacks. Research defines cognitive hacking as attacks that succeed by influencing human decision-making rather than directly compromising systems.

The HomeTown Bank case illustrates three interconnected risk categories: human factors risk, human error risk, and reputational risk. These risks align with broader operational and performance risks identified by Decker and Galer (2013), including poorly defined processes, inconsistent adherence to established procedures, insufficient performance metrics, and failure to meet regulatory requirements. When these weaknesses converge, they degrade operational efficiency and increase the cost of doing business.

Reputational risk further amplifies the impact of cybersecurity incidents. According to Decker and Galer (2013), reputational damage can disrupt an organization's ability to operate by eroding public trust and triggering revenue loss, negative publicity, litigation, client attrition, employee turnover, and challenges in talent acquisition. HomeTown Bank's delayed breach notification and ineffective communication strategy exemplify how poor crisis management can transform a security incident into a long-term strategic setback.

IMPLICATIONS FOR ORGANIZATIONAL CULTURE AND LEADERSHIP

Ultimately, the effective use of AI in cybersecurity depends on organizational culture and leadership commitment. Institutions that frame cybersecurity as a shared responsibility, supported by transparent policies, ethical AI deployment, and continuous learning, are better positioned to reduce human-centered risk. Leaders play a critical role in shaping norms around accountability, psychological safety, and ethical technology use.

For HomeTown Bank, rebuilding trust will require more than technological upgrades. It will necessitate cultural change, reinforced by leadership messaging, employee engagement, and governance structures that balance security, privacy, and operational efficiency. When aligned effectively, AI technologies can enhance, not replace, human judgment, enabling organizations to manage cyber risk in a manner that supports both security objectives and sustainable business performance.

CYBER RISK IN THE CONTEMPORARY DIGITAL ECONOMY

The scale and economic impact of cyberattacks have escalated dramatically, transforming cybersecurity from a technical concern into a core business risk. In 2023 alone, more than 2,300 documented cyberattacks affected over 343 million victims worldwide, marking a 72 percent increase in data breaches compared to 2021 (St. John, 2024). The financial consequences are equally alarming. The average global cost of a data breach reached $4.88 million in 2024, with incidents in the United States proving the most expensive at approximately $9.36 million per breach (St. John, 2024). These figures highlight the growing financial exposure organizations face when cybersecurity controls fail.

Email-based attacks remain one of the most persistent and effective threat vectors, accounting for roughly 35 percent of malware delivery in 2023 (St. John, 2024). Business email compromise schemes alone generated losses exceeding $2.9 billion during the same period (St. John, 2024). Projections estimating cybercrime costs to reach $10.5 trillion by 2025 underscore the systemic nature of the problem and its implications for organizational resilience, investor confidence, and long-term economic stability (St. John, 2024). Beyond immediate financial losses, cyber incidents impose indirect costs, including regulatory penalties, legal exposure, intellectual property theft, operational disruption, and reputational erosion (St. John, 2024).

CYBERSECURITY AS A BUSINESS AND HUMAN-CENTERED DISCIPLINE

Cybersecurity is commonly defined as the protection of internet-connected systems, software, devices, and data from malicious activity. While this definition captures the technical scope of cybersecurity, it understates the central role of human behavior in shaping cyber risk outcomes. As organizations become increasingly digitalized, employees interact with information systems continuously, making human judgment, awareness, and decision-making integral components of security effectiveness.

Cybercrime is driven by diverse motivations, with financial gain cited most frequently due to its relatively low barriers and high potential returns (Gomes et al., 2022). Other motivations include revenge, extortion, and ideological or political objectives (Gomes et al., 2022). Law enforcement agencies attribute the growth of cybercrime to rapid technological advancement and the ease with which sensitive information can be accessed or exploited (Gomes et al., 2022). These dynamics illustrate that cybersecurity threats evolve alongside organizational processes and workforce behaviors, reinforcing the need for adaptive, human-aware risk management strategies.

CYBERSECURITY RISK IN THE FINANCIAL SECTOR

The financial sector occupies a uniquely sensitive position within the global economy, serving as the infrastructure through which economic activity, payments, and wealth management occur (Familoni & Shoetan, 2024). Consequently, financial institutions face heightened cybersecurity expectations from regulators, customers, and markets alike. Recent surveys of bank executives and directors identify cybersecurity as the most significant risk concern, surpassing interest rate, compliance, liquidity, and credit risks (Alix, 2024).

For community and regional banks, cybersecurity and data privacy risks carry particularly severe implications. These institutions rely heavily on trust-based relationships with local customers, who are often long-standing members of the communities the banks serve (Servidio & Taylor, 2015). A major cyber incident can therefore produce cascading effects, damaging not only the bank's financial position but also community confidence and local economic stability. Moreover, banks frequently bear indirect costs when cyber incidents affect third parties, such as reimbursing customers for fraudulent transactions following retail data breaches (Servidio & Taylor, 2015).

THREAT LANDSCAPE

Among the most prevalent threats facing financial institutions are malware attacks, which encompass a broad category of malicious software designed to infiltrate systems, disrupt operations, or exfiltrate sensitive information (Familoni & Shoetan, 2024). Phishing campaigns, compromised websites, and infected software updates remain common delivery mechanisms. Once deployed, malware can enable unauthorized access to banking platforms, facilitate fraudulent transactions, and undermine customer trust (Familoni & Shoetan, 2024). Banking-specific malware is often engineered to harvest authentication credentials, enabling attackers to bypass traditional security controls (Kazi et al., 2022).

Insider threats present a distinct and particularly complex challenge. These threats originate from individuals with legitimate access to systems, including employees, contractors, or third-party vendors (Familoni & Shoetan, 2024). Insiders may act maliciously, seeking personal gain or retaliation, or negligently, through poor security hygiene or lack of awareness (Thakur, 2024). The difficulty in detecting insider threats lies in the fact that perpetrators operate within authorized boundaries, often blending harmful actions with legitimate workflows.

Research outlines a typical progression of malicious insider activity, beginning with unrestricted access, followed by reconnaissance and decision-making regarding targets, and culminating in data theft or privilege escalation (Rauf et al., 2023). These stages often go unnoticed in organizations that lack behavioral monitoring or contextual risk analysis. Real-world cases involving financial institutions have demonstrated that insider-driven breaches frequently persist longer and cause greater damage than external attacks due to delayed detection.

SYSTEMIC RISK AND INTERCONNECTED FINANCIAL INFRASTRUCTURE

As financial institutions increasingly rely on interconnected digital platforms, cyber risk has evolved into a form of systemic risk that extends beyond individual organizations (Uddin et al., 2020). A successful attack on one institution can disrupt interconnected payment systems, delay interbank transfers, and compromise shared service providers. Such disruptions can cascade across the financial ecosystem, amplifying operational and reputational damage (Uddin et al., 2020).

The expansion of digital banking, mobile payments, and cloud-based services has significantly increased the attack surface available to cyber adversaries (Familoni & Shoetan, 2024). While regulatory frameworks in the United States mandate robust cybersecurity controls, compliance alone has proven insufficient to address evolving threats, particularly those rooted in human behavior and insider activity (Familoni & Shoetan, 2024).

PRACTICAL APPLICATIONS OF ARTIFICIAL INTELLIGENCE IN CYBER RISK MANAGEMENT

Artificial intelligence has emerged as a critical enabler in modern cybersecurity strategies, particularly in addressing scale, speed, and complexity. Survey data indicate strong interest among bank leaders in deploying AI to combat fraud and cyber threats, with 90 percent expressing openness to such applications (Alix, 2024). However, adoption remains uneven, as many institutions await regulatory clarity or struggle to align AI initiatives with broader business objectives (Alix, 2024).

In practical terms, AI enhances cybersecurity by enabling real-time threat detection, behavioral analytics, and predictive risk modeling. Machine learning algorithms can analyze vast volumes of user activity to identify anomalies indicative of insider misuse or compromised credentials—capabilities that exceed traditional rule-based systems (Zhang et al., 2022). For example, several large financial institutions have deployed AI-driven user and entity behavior analytics (UEBA) platforms to detect subtle deviations in employee behavior, reducing detection time for insider threats while minimizing false positives.

Importantly, the effectiveness of AI in cybersecurity depends on thoughtful implementation. AI systems must be calibrated to organizational workflows and supported by transparent governance structures to maintain employee trust. Overly intrusive monitoring can undermine morale and foster resistance, while insufficient oversight can allow bias or errors to persist. As such, AI should be viewed not as a replacement for human judgment but as a decision-support tool that augments risk awareness and supports informed managerial action (Zhang et al., 2022).

ORGANIZATIONAL CULTURE, BEHAVIOR, AND AI INTEGRATION

The integration of AI into cybersecurity operations has profound implications for organizational culture and behavior. Successful adoption requires cultivating a culture that values shared responsibility for security, continuous learning, and ethical technology use. Employees must understand not only how AI tools function, but why they are deployed and how they contribute to organizational resilience.

Organizations that align AI-enabled cybersecurity with leadership accountability, clear communication, and ongoing training are better positioned to manage human-centered risks. Real-world examples from the financial sector demonstrate that institutions investing in both advanced analytics and cultural reinforcement experience lower breach frequency and faster recovery times. In contrast, organizations that treat cybersecurity as a purely technical function often struggle to realize the full value of AI investments.

THEORETICAL FOUNDATIONS FOR UNDERSTANDING HUMAN-CENTERED CYBER RISK

The cybersecurity failures experienced by HomeTown Bank are rooted in two distinct but interrelated human-driven events: a deliberate insider data breach motivated by employee dissatisfaction and an inadvertent system compromise caused by an employee's interaction with a malicious email. Together, these incidents illustrate that cyber risk is not merely a technological problem but a behavioral and organizational one. Addressing such risks requires a theoretical lens capable of explaining why individuals act in ways that undermine security and how organizational structures, culture, and controls either constrain or enable those actions.

Pollini et al. (2022) argue that cybersecurity challenges involving human factors are best understood through a socio-technical framework that integrates four dimensions: individual behavior, organizational context, technological systems, and ethical considerations. This perspective is particularly relevant for financial institutions, where employees operate at the intersection of sensitive data, strict regulatory expectations, and performance pressures.

GENERAL STRAIN THEORY AND MALICIOUS INSIDER BEHAVIOR

General Strain Theory (GST) posits that individuals experience strain when they encounter conditions they perceive as unjust, threatening, or obstructive to valued goals. These strains may include unmet financial expectations, perceived loss of status, or adverse workplace experiences. While GST has traditionally been applied to street crime, its explanatory power extends to white-collar and corporate misconduct, particularly when individuals believe legitimate avenues for resolving grievances are unavailable.

Applied to HomeTown Bank, GST provides a useful framework for understanding the behavior of the disgruntled employee who sold customer data. Although the case does not explicitly identify the employee's motivation, empirical research suggests that insider misconduct is frequently associated with financial stress, perceived organizational injustice, or declining career prospects. In organizational settings, such strains can silently accumulate, creating latent risk that remains invisible until a triggering event occurs.

From a business and risk management perspective, the relevance of GST lies in its implications for prevention. AI technologies can be leveraged not to punish employees, but to identify early warning signals associated with insider risk. For example, AI-driven user and entity behavior analytics (UEBA) can detect unusual access patterns, excessive data downloads, or deviations from normal work behavior that may indicate elevated risk. When combined with non-punitive HR interventions, such as confidential grievance reporting mechanisms or employee assistance programs, these tools allow organizations to address strain before it escalates into malicious action.

To mitigate future occurrences, HomeTown Bank should adopt a multi-layered insider risk strategy that includes periodic human-centered risk assessments, role-based access controls aligned with job responsibilities, AI-enabled behavioral monitoring, and formal mechanisms for employees to voice concerns anonymously. Importantly, these controls must be framed within a culture of fairness and transparency to avoid reinforcing the very strains they are designed to detect.

HUMAN ERROR THEORY AND UNINTENTIONAL SECURITY FAILURES

While malicious insiders pose a significant threat, unintentional human error remains one of the most common causes of cybersecurity incidents. Human Error Theory (HET) provides a structured way to analyze these failures by examining how predictable limitations in attention, perception, and decision-making interact with system design (Read et al., 2021). Read et al. (2020) identify four perspectives within HET, mechanistic, individual, interactionist, and systems, each reflecting an evolution in safety and risk management thinking.

The mechanistic perspective is particularly relevant to the phishing-related breach at HomeTown Bank. This perspective treats human error as a foreseeable outcome of system interactions, emphasizing that errors arise not solely from individual negligence but from environments that fail to accommodate human limitations (Read et al., 2021). In this context, the employee's decision to click a malicious link reflects a breakdown in defensive layers rather than an isolated lapse in judgment.

From a practical standpoint, HET supports the integration of AI into both prevention and response. AI-enhanced email filtering systems, for instance, can reduce the volume of malicious content reaching employees, while adaptive learning platforms can personalize cybersecurity training based on individual risk profiles. Many financial institutions now deploy AI-driven phishing simulations that adjust difficulty based on employee performance, reinforcing learning without stigmatization.

Equally important is the organizational response to error. HomeTown Bank would benefit from adopting a "just culture" approach, where employees are encouraged to report mistakes promptly without fear of punitive consequences. AI can support this model by enabling rapid containment and root-cause analysis, allowing organizations to learn from incidents and continuously improve system design. This approach shifts the narrative from individual blame to collective resilience.

SCHEIN'S THEORY OF ORGANIZATIONAL CULTURE AND CYBERSECURITY BEHAVIOR

Edgar Schein's Theory of Organizational Culture offers a critical lens for understanding how shared assumptions, values, and visible practices shape employee behavior over time (Akpa et al., 2021). Schein conceptualizes culture as operating at three levels: observable artifacts, espoused values, and deeply held underlying assumptions. Together, these elements influence how employees interpret rules, respond to risk, and make decisions under uncertainty.

At HomeTown Bank, the cybersecurity incidents suggest misalignment across these cultural levels. While formal policies may have emphasized data protection, the underlying assumption that "cybersecurity is primarily an IT responsibility" likely weakened individual accountability. In such environments, employees may underestimate the consequences of their actions or fail to recognize their role in risk mitigation.

Applying Schein's model requires intentional cultural redesign. At the artifact level, the bank could introduce visible indicators of security commitment, such as AI-powered insider risk dashboards, phishing awareness certifications, and regular communication of security metrics. At the level of espoused values, leadership must consistently articulate that trust, ethical behavior, and cybersecurity vigilance are core organizational priorities; not compliance obligations.

Most critically, cultural change must reach the level of underlying assumptions. The belief that "breaches are inevitable" should be replaced with the assumption that cyber risk is manageable through shared responsibility and continuous learning. AI technologies can reinforce this shift by providing actionable insights that empower employees rather than surveil them. For example, real-time risk alerts can help employees make safer decisions without requiring deep technical expertise.

Aligning HR practices with these cultural goals is essential. Performance evaluations, promotion criteria, and leadership development programs should incorporate adherence to cybersecurity protocols and ethical behavior. In doing so, HomeTown Bank can embed cybersecurity into everyday organizational life rather than treating it as a specialized or peripheral function.

INTEGRATIVE IMPLICATIONS FOR PRACTICE

Together, these theories underscore that effective cybersecurity risk management requires more than advanced tools, it demands alignment between technology, human behavior, and organizational culture. AI offers powerful capabilities for detecting anomalies, predicting risk, and supporting decision-making, but its effectiveness depends on thoughtful integration into social and organizational systems.

For HomeTown Bank, the practical implication is clear: cybersecurity strategy must be designed as a socio-technical system in which AI augments human judgment, leadership reinforces ethical norms, and employees are treated as active participants in risk mitigation. When theory informs practice in this way, organizations are better positioned to reduce insider threats, manage human error, and build durable cyber resilience.

RESEARCH AND INTERVENTION DESIGN

This study employed a qualitative, practice-oriented management consulting methodology designed to diagnose and address cybersecurity vulnerabilities within a mid-sized financial institution (HomeTown Bank). The intervention was structured as a diagnostic and change-oriented engagement rather than a purely observational study. The primary objective was to identify the underlying causes of repeated cybersecurity breaches and to design actionable recommendations aligned with business strategy, organizational culture, and human behavior.

A root cause analysis (RCA) framework was selected as the guiding methodological approach because of its suitability for examining complex, multi-factor organizational failures. RCA is particularly effective in socio-technical environments where outcomes emerge from interactions among people, processes, technology, and governance structures. The intervention unfolded across six sequential phases, each combining qualitative data collection with iterative analysis to ensure both analytical rigor and practical relevance.

PHASE 1: SCOPING AND STAKEHOLDER ALIGNMENT

The engagement began with a formal scoping phase to clarify objectives, constraints, and success criteria. Senior executives, risk managers, IT leaders, and human resources representatives participated in structured alignment sessions. These discussions established a shared understanding of the breach history, regulatory expectations, and business priorities, including customer trust, operational continuity, and reputational protection.

During this phase, the consulting team articulated a working hypothesis that cybersecurity incidents were unlikely to be driven solely by technical deficiencies. This hypothesis informed the design of subsequent data collection activities, ensuring equal emphasis on human behavior, organizational culture, and leadership practices alongside technical controls.

PHASE 2: INCIDENT RECONSTRUCTION AND PROCESS MAPPING

The second phase focused on reconstructing the two major cybersecurity incidents using detailed process mapping. Incident timelines were developed through document review, system logs, and interviews with personnel involved in breach detection, response, and remediation. This reconstruction traced each incident from initial trigger to organizational response, highlighting decision points, control failures, and communication breakdowns.

Process mapping revealed that both breaches followed predictable patterns associated with human-centered risk. In the insider data exfiltration incident, excessive access privileges and the absence of behavioral monitoring enabled prolonged unauthorized activity. In the phishing-related breach, insufficient email filtering and inconsistent security awareness practices allowed a routine human error to escalate into a system-wide compromise.

PHASE 3: QUALITATIVE DATA COLLECTION AND BEHAVIORAL ANALYSIS

To uncover underlying behavioral and cultural drivers, the consulting team conducted semi-structured interviews and focus groups across organizational levels, including frontline employees, middle managers, and executives. Interview protocols explored perceptions of cybersecurity responsibility, training effectiveness, reporting norms, leadership messaging, and psychological safety.

Data were analyzed using thematic coding to identify recurring patterns. A dominant theme emerged: employees generally viewed cybersecurity as a technical or compliance function rather than a shared organizational responsibility. Many participants expressed uncertainty about reporting mistakes or suspicious activity, citing fear of blame or disciplinary action. These findings indicated that human error was not merely an individual failure but a predictable outcome of cultural norms and incentive structures.

PHASE 4: ROOT CAUSE ANALYSIS AND SYSTEMS-LEVEL SYNTHESIS

Using RCA tools such as the "Five Whys" technique and cause-and-effect (fishbone) diagrams, the consulting team synthesized findings across incidents, behaviors, and organizational structures. This analysis revealed that the most significant contributors to cybersecurity breaches were not isolated technical gaps, but systemic human and cultural factors.

The root causes were identified as:

1. A lack of continuous, role-specific cybersecurity awareness and reinforcement.
2. Cultural assumptions that cybersecurity accountability resided primarily with IT.
3. Inadequate mechanisms for detecting early indicators of insider risk.
4. Leadership messaging that emphasized compliance over learning and shared responsibility.

These factors collectively created conditions in which both malicious insider behavior and unintentional human error could occur with minimal resistance.

PHASE 5: VALIDATION THROUGH CROSS-FUNCTIONAL REVIEW

To ensure credibility and organizational buy-in, preliminary findings were validated through cross-functional workshops involving leadership, risk, IT, and HR stakeholders. Participants reviewed RCA outputs and confirmed that the identified root causes aligned with their lived experiences and operational realities. This collaborative validation process reduced defensiveness and reframed cybersecurity failures as organizational learning opportunities rather than individual shortcomings.

PHASE 6: INTERVENTION DESIGN AND CULTURAL REORIENTATION

The final phase translated diagnostic insights into actionable interventions. Recommendations emphasized a shift toward a culture of shared cybersecurity ownership, supported by AI-enabled tools and human-centered governance. Proposed interventions included AI-driven user behavior analytics to detect anomalous activity, adaptive training programs tailored to employee risk profiles, and leadership-led communication strategies reinforcing psychological safety and ethical accountability.

Importantly, the intervention design prioritized cultural alignment. AI technologies were positioned as enablers of awareness and early intervention rather than surveillance mechanisms. Performance management and training systems were reoriented to reward secure behaviors and transparent reporting, reinforcing the cultural shift identified as necessary through the RCA.

METHODOLOGICAL CONTRIBUTION

This methods approach demonstrates how management consulting interventions can generate rigorous, actionable insights by integrating root cause analysis with organizational behavior and cultural assessment. By uncovering human error and cultural misalignment as primary drivers of cybersecurity breaches, the intervention illustrates the value of socio-technical diagnostic methods over narrowly technical assessments. The methodology provides a replicable framework for organizations seeking to address complex, human-centered cybersecurity risks through evidence-based, culturally informed change.

Below are 30 practical, prioritized recommendations designed to reduce human error and human-centered cyber risk in organizations similar to HomeTown Bank.

The recommendations were developed by a team of management consultants after the engagement in a comprehensive diagnostic intervention. They include the following:

1. **Establish cybersecurity as a shared organizational responsibility** Formally redefine cybersecurity from an IT-only function to a collective obligation embedded in leadership messaging, job roles, and performance expectations.
2. **Deploy AI-driven User and Entity Behavior Analytics (UEBA)** Use AI to detect anomalous employee behavior (e.g., unusual data access, privilege misuse) that may indicate insider threats or compromised accounts.
3. **Implement a blame-free, psychologically safe incident reporting culture** Encourage rapid reporting of mistakes or suspicious activity without fear of punishment to reduce dwell time and limit breach impact.
4. **Adopt adaptive, AI-personalized security awareness training** Replace static training with AI-driven programs that tailor content and frequency based on employee behavior, role, and risk exposure.
5. **Align leadership incentives with cybersecurity outcomes** Incorporate cybersecurity accountability into executive and managerial performance evaluations to reinforce tone at the top.
6. **Apply role-based and just-in-time access controls** Limit employee access strictly to what is required for their role and duration, reducing insider risk exposure.
7. **Integrate AI-enhanced phishing detection and email filtering** Use machine learning to continuously improve detection of phishing and business email compromise attempts before they reach employees.
8. **Conduct continuous human-centered risk assessments** Regularly evaluate employee workflows, stress points, and cognitive load to identify conditions that increase error likelihood.
9. **Use AI-supported incident triage and response orchestration** Automate initial incident classification, prioritization, and containment actions to accelerate response while reducing human decision fatigue.
10. **Embed cybersecurity expectations into onboarding and offboarding processes** Ensure employees understand security responsibilities from entry through exit, including data access revocation and monitoring during transitions.
11. **Implement AI-based insider risk scoring models** Combine behavioral signals, access patterns, and contextual data to generate dynamic insider risk profiles.
12. **Standardize secure-by-design workflows** Redesign business processes to make secure behavior the default, reducing reliance on constant vigilance.
13. **Introduce regular phishing simulations with targeted remediation** Conduct simulations that adapt in sophistication over time and trigger focused coaching rather than punitive responses.

14. **Create cross-functional cyber risk governance committees** Include IT, HR, legal, compliance, and business leaders to ensure human risks are addressed holistically.
15. **Leverage AI to analyze post-incident root causes** Use machine learning to identify recurring human and process failures across incidents and near-misses.
16. **Establish confidential grievance and whistleblower channels** Provide employees with safe avenues to report concerns that could otherwise manifest as malicious insider behavior.
17. **Train managers to recognize behavioral indicators of strain** Equip leaders to identify burnout, disengagement, or resentment that may elevate insider risk.
18. **Apply AI-assisted access recertification reviews** Use analytics to flag unnecessary or risky access privileges during periodic reviews.
19. **Formalize decision-making playbooks for cyber incidents** Reduce uncertainty during crises by defining clear roles, escalation paths, and communication protocols.
20. **Regularly test organizational response through tabletop exercises** Simulate human-centered cyber scenarios (e.g., insider theft, phishing cascades) to reinforce learning.
21. **Use AI to monitor security training effectiveness** Analyze completion rates, retention, and behavioral change to continuously refine training programs.
22. **Publish internal metrics on human risk trends** Share anonymized insights on phishing susceptibility or reporting rates to normalize learning and improvement.
23. **Rotate employees in high-risk roles periodically** Reduce prolonged access exposure and insider risk through job rotation or mandatory vacations.
24. **Incorporate cybersecurity behavior into performance feedback** Reinforce expectations through routine feedback rather than annual compliance checks.
25. **Deploy AI-enabled chatbots for real-time security guidance** Provide employees with immediate, contextual advice when they encounter suspicious situations.
26. **Clarify ethical expectations through scenario-based training** Use realistic dilemmas to reinforce norms around data protection and responsible access.
27. **Align vendor and third-party access policies with internal standards** Extend human risk controls beyond employees to contractors and partners.
28. **Conduct periodic culture assessments related to security** Measure perceptions of accountability, trust, and ownership to track cultural progress.
29. **Establish post-incident learning reviews rather than fault-finding reviews** Focus on systemic improvement rather than individual blame.
30. **Maintain visible executive sponsorship of cybersecurity initiatives** Reinforce long-term commitment through consistent leadership engagement, even outside crisis periods.

Collectively, these recommendations emphasize that human error is not a failure to be eliminated, but a risk to be managed. AI technologies significantly enhance detection, prediction, and response capabilities, but their effectiveness depends on organizational culture, leadership alignment, and trust. The most resilient organizations treat cybersecurity as a socio-technical system, where people, processes, and intelligent technologies reinforce one another to reduce risk sustainably.

CONCLUSION

This analysis demonstrates that cybersecurity breaches within complex organizations are rarely the result of isolated technical failures. Instead, they emerge from the interaction of human behavior, organizational culture, leadership decisions, and technological systems. Across the examined cases and interventions, human error and insider behavior consistently surfaced as the most significant contributors to cyber risk, often amplified by cultural norms that framed cybersecurity as a technical or compliance issue rather than a shared organizational responsibility.

The findings reinforce the necessity of adopting a socio-technical approach to cybersecurity, one that integrates artificial intelligence with human-centered risk management and cultural transformation. AI technologies offer substantial value in detecting anomalies, predicting risk, and accelerating incident response. However, their effectiveness is contingent on ethical deployment, transparency, and alignment with organizational values. When implemented without cultural readiness or trust, AI tools risk reinforcing resistance and undermining their intended benefits.

Ultimately, sustainable cyber resilience requires organizations to move beyond reactive, control-focused strategies toward adaptive systems that recognize human behavior as both a vulnerability and a critical asset. Organizations that successfully align leadership, culture, and intelligent technologies are better positioned to manage cyber risk, preserve trust, and sustain long-term performance in an increasingly digital threat landscape.

MANAGERIAL IMPLICATIONS

For managers, these findings underscore that cybersecurity leadership extends far beyond technical oversight. Managers at all levels play a pivotal role in shaping how employees perceive, prioritize, and respond to cyber risk. Leadership behaviors, such as how mistakes are handled, how incidents are communicated, and how accountability is distributed, directly influence employee willingness to report issues and adhere to security practices.

Managers must therefore shift from enforcement-oriented approaches toward enablement and learning. This includes fostering psychological safety, reinforcing shared responsibility, and modeling secure behaviors. AI-enabled tools, such as behavioral analytics and adaptive training platforms, should be framed as decision-support mechanisms that help managers identify risk early and intervene constructively rather than punitively.

Additionally, managers are responsible for aligning cybersecurity objectives with broader business goals. This requires integrating cyber risk considerations into performance management, resource allocation, and strategic planning. Managers who treat cybersecurity as a core operational risk, comparable to financial, legal, or reputational risk, are more likely to drive meaningful behavioral change and sustain organizational resilience.

EMPLOYEE IMPLICATIONS

From an employee perspective, the findings highlight the evolving nature of individual responsibility in digital workplaces. Employees are no longer passive users of technology but active participants in organizational security ecosystems. Everyday decisions—such as responding to emails, handling sensitive data, or reporting anomalies—carry significant risk implications.

However, expecting flawless behavior is neither realistic nor effective. Employees are more likely to engage in secure practices when organizations provide clear expectations, supportive training, and non-punitive reporting mechanisms. AI-enabled tools can assist employees by reducing cognitive burden, offering real-time guidance, and filtering threats before they require human judgment. When designed transparently, these tools enhance employee confidence and competence rather than eroding trust.

Importantly, employees benefit from cultures that recognize human fallibility and prioritize learning over blame. Such environments encourage proactive risk identification, ethical behavior, and collective ownership of security outcomes. In this sense, employees become a frontline defense rather than a persistent point of failure.

ORGANIZATIONAL IMPLICATIONS

At the organizational level, the findings point to the necessity of reframing cybersecurity as an enterprise-wide capability rather than a specialized technical function. Organizations that compartmentalize cybersecurity within IT departments fail to address the human and cultural dimensions that drive most breaches. In contrast, organizations that embed cybersecurity into governance structures, cultural norms, and operational processes are better equipped to manage both current and emerging threats.

The integration of AI into cybersecurity operations offers significant strategic advantages, including scalability, speed, and predictive insight. Yet these advantages are only realized when AI adoption is accompanied by robust governance, ethical oversight, and cultural alignment. Organizations must invest not only in technology but also in leadership development, workforce engagement, and continuous cultural assessment.

Ultimately, the organizational implication is clear; which is that cyber resilience is a dynamic capability that must be cultivated over time. It requires sustained leadership commitment, cross-functional collaboration, and a willingness to treat security incidents as opportunities for systemic improvement. Organizations that embrace this perspective are more likely to protect critical assets, maintain stakeholder trust, and remain competitive in an increasingly interconnected digital economy.

THEORETICAL IMPLICATIONS

This study contributes to the theoretical understanding of cybersecurity by reinforcing and extending socio-technical systems theory within contemporary organizational contexts. The findings challenge dominant techno-centric models of cybersecurity that conceptualize breaches primarily as failures of infrastructure, controls, or technical safeguards. Instead, the evidence supports a socio-technical perspective in which cybersecurity outcomes emerge from the dynamic interaction among human behavior, organizational culture, leadership practices, and intelligent technologies. By empirically demonstrating that human error and cultural misalignment are primary drivers of cyber risk, this research underscores the inadequacy of theories that isolate technical systems from their social environments.

The study also advances organizational culture theory by positioning cybersecurity culture as a distinct yet integrated dimension of organizational culture. Rather than treating security awareness as a compliance artifact or training outcome, the findings suggest that cybersecurity culture reflects deeper assumptions about accountability, trust, psychological safety, and shared responsibility. This reframing aligns with and extends Schein's cultural model by illustrating how espoused values (e.g., "security is everyone's responsibility") must be reinforced through enacted practices, leadership incentives, and governance structures to meaningfully influence behavior. Theoretical models of culture that fail to account for digital risk environments may therefore underestimate the role of cyber-related norms in shaping organizational resilience.

Additionally, the research contributes to human error and organizational behavior theory by conceptualizing human error not as an anomaly or deviation, but as a predictable and manageable condition shaped by system design, cognitive load, role expectations, and cultural responses to failure. The findings support a shift away from individual blame models toward systems-oriented interpretations of error, consistent with high-reliability organization (HRO) theory. By demonstrating how blame-free reporting, learning-oriented incident reviews, and secure-by-design workflows reduce cyber risk, the study provides empirical grounding for theories that emphasize learning, adaptation, and psychological safety as mechanisms of organizational reliability.

From a technology and organization theory perspective, this study extends emerging scholarship on artificial intelligence by highlighting the contingent nature of AI effectiveness in cybersecurity. While AI-enhanced tools significantly improve detection, prediction, and response capabilities, the findings indicate that their value is mediated by organizational culture, leadership alignment, and employee trust. This supports socio-material and affordance-based theories suggesting that technology does not independently determine outcomes; rather, its impact is shaped by how organizational actors interpret, adopt, and integrate it into daily practice. The study thus cautions against deterministic views of AI and contributes to theory by framing AI as an enabling component within a broader socio-technical system rather than a standalone solution.

Methodologically, the study contributes to theory-building by demonstrating how management consulting interventions, when structured around rigorous diagnostic frameworks, can serve as legitimate sources of theoretical insight. The integration of root cause analysis, organizational behavior assessment, and cultural diagnostics provides a replicable approach for studying complex, human-centered phenomena that are difficult to capture through purely quantitative or technical methods. This supports practice-based and engaged scholarship traditions, suggesting that theory development can be meaningfully advanced through applied, intervention-based research in real organizational settings.

Collectively, these theoretical implications suggest the need for more integrative cybersecurity theories that bridge organizational behavior, culture, leadership, and intelligent technologies. Cyber resilience emerges not as a static capability or control maturity level, but as a dynamic organizational capability continuously shaped by learning, trust, and adaptation. Future theory development should therefore move beyond linear models of prevention and control toward frameworks that conceptualize cybersecurity as an evolving socio-technical system in which human behavior is both a source of vulnerability and a critical driver of resilience.

REFERENCES

Akpa, V. O., Asikhia, O. U., & Nneji, N. E. (2021). Organizational culture and organizational performance: A review of literature. *International Journal of Advances in Engineering and Management, 3*(1), 361–372. https://www.researchgate.net/profile/Professor-Asikhia/publication/356105838_Organizational_Culture_and_Organizational_Performance_A_Review_of_Literature/links/618bed3907be5f31b762d272/Organizational-Culture-and-Organizational-Performance-A-Review-of-Literature.pdf

Alix, L. (2024). Regulators intensify the pressure on banks: Bank director's 2024 risk survey finds heightened concern among bank leaders around regulation, liquidity management and cybersecurity threats. *Bank Director, 34*(2), 42-46. https://www.bankdirector.com/magazine/2nd-quarter-2024/regulators-intensify-the-pressure-on-banks/

Dawodu, S. O., Omotosho, A., Akindote, O. J., Adegbite, A. O., & Ewuga, S. K. (2023). Cybersecurity risk assessment in banking: methodologies and best practices. *Computer Science & IT Research Journal, 4*(3), 220-243. https://fepbl.com/index.php/csitrj/article/view/659

Decker, A., & Galer, D. (2013). *Enterprise risk management straight to the point: An implementation guide function by function*. ERMSTTP, LLC. https://www.amazon.com/Enterprise-Risk-Management-Implementation-Viewpoints/dp/1481287788

Familoni, B. T., & Shoetan, P. O. (2024). Cybersecurity in the financial sector: a comparative analysis of the USA and Nigeria. *Computer Science & IT Research Journal, 5*(4), 850-877. https://www.scirp.org/reference/referencespapers?referenceid=3828230

Gomes, L., Deshmukh, A., & Anute, N. (2022). Cyber security and internet banking: Issues and preventive measures. *Journal of Information Technology and Sciences, 8*(2), 31–42. https://www.researchgate.net/publication/362013259_Cyber_Security_and_Internet_Banking_Issues_and_Preventive_Measures. DOI: 10.46610/JOITS.2022.v08i02.005

Kazi, M. A., Woodhead, S., & Gan, D. (2022). An investigation to detect banking malware network communication traffic using machine learning techniques. *Journal of Cybersecurity and Privacy, 3*(1), 1–23. https://www.mdpi.com/2624-800X/3/1/1. DOI: 10.3390/jcp3010001

Pollini, A., Callari, T. C., Tedeschi, A., Ruscio, D., Save, L., Chiarugi, F., & Guerri, D. (2022). Leveraging human factors in cybersecurity: An integrated methodological approach. *Cognition Technology and Work*, *24*(2), 371–390. https://link.springer.com/article/10.1007/s10111-021-00683-y. DOI: 10.1007/s10111-021-00683-y PMID: 34149309

Rauf, U., Mohsen, F., & Wei, Z. (2023). A Taxonomic Classification of Insider Threats: Existing Techniques, Future Directions & Recommendations. *Journal of Cyber Security and Mobility*, 221-252. https://ieeexplore.ieee.org/abstract/document/10963763

Read, G. J., Shorrock, S., Walker, G. H., & Salmon, P. M. (2021). State of science: Evolving perspectives on 'human error'. *Ergonomics*, *64*(9), 1091–1114. https://www.tandfonline.com/action/showCopyRight?scroll=top&doi=10.1080%2F00140139.2021.1953615. DOI: 10.1080/00140139.2021.1953615 PMID: 34243698

Servidio, J. S., & Taylor, R. D. (2015). Safe and Sound: Cybersecurity for Community Banks. *Journal of Taxation & Regulation of Financial Institutions*, *28*(4). https://www.civicresearchinstitute.com/online/PDF/Cybersecurity%20for%20Community%20Banks.pdf

St. John, M. (2024, August 28). *Cybersecurity stats: facts and figures you should know*. Forbes https://www.forbes.com/sites/chuckbrooks/2024/06/05/alarming-cybersecurity-stats-what-you-need-to-know-in-2024/

Thakur, M. (2024). Cyber security threats and countermeasures in digital age. [JASE]. *Journal of Applied Science and Education*, *4*(1), 1–20. https://jase.a2zjournals.com/index.php/ase/article/view/42

Uddin, M. H., Ali, M. H., & Hassan, M. K. (2020). Cybersecurity hazards and financial system vulnerability: A synthesis of literature. *Risk Management*, *22*(4), 239–309. https://ideas.repec.org/a/pal/risman/v22y2020i4d10.1057_s41283-020-00063-2.html. DOI: 10.1057/s41283-020-00063-2

Zhang, Z., Ning, H., Shi, F., Farha, F., Xu, Y., Xu, J., Zhang, F., & Choo, K.-K. R. (2022). Artificial intelligence in cyber security: Research advances, challenges, and opportunities. *Artificial Intelligence Review*, *55*(2), 1029–1053. https://link.springer.com/article/10.1007/S10462-021-09976-0. DOI: 10.1007/s10462-021-09976-0

Chapter 7
Healthcare Cybersecurity: A Qualitative Analysis on the Vulnerability of Medical Devices

Oladele Stephen Olawoye
http://orcid.org/0009-0003-1117-1374
Capitol Technology University, USA

Eugene J. Lewis
http://orcid.org/0000-0002-2956-0760
Capitol Technology University, USA

ABSTRACT

The medical field has experienced a transformation through connected devices which include infusion pumps and patient monitoring systems. It also includes embedded systems such sensors, processors, and firmware. Yet these advancements introduce critical cybersecurity vulnerabilities. The research uses three qualitative case studies to analyze main security problems which include Risk Management Theory for studying authentication protocol weaknesses and Change Management Theory for studying weak encryption standards and Cybersecurity Resilience Theory for studying software update and patch implementation delays. Materials used include industry standards like NIST, HIPAA, GDPR, CISA, ISO/IEC 27001, peer-reviewed journals and articles, authors from medical journals and related sources. The research used qualitative evidence synthesis, that is, findings from other credible researchers. Robust cybersecurity and cooperation between healthcare, tech, and regulators are vital to secure medical devices, protect patients and ensure reliable care.

DOI: 10.4018/979-8-2600-1021-1.ch007

INTRODUCTION

Healthcare delivery has experienced significant improvement through digital transformation, which brought better patient care and operational efficiency during the last ten years. The healthcare industry made significant progress through the adoption of Electronic Health Records (EHRs) and Internet of Medical Things (IoMT) and IoT device integration. Medical devices that use IoT and IoMT technology contain embedded systems which function as dedicated medical computers to perform monitoring tasks and diagnostic and therapeutic operations. The systems contain processing units and sensors together with firmware memory and power sources and communication capabilities that include Bluetooth and Wi-Fi and HL7 (Vantage Medtech, n.d.). Healthcare providers now use these technological developments to optimize their workflows and deliver better patient interactions, instant data exchange and distant patient tracking which was previously unattainable. The advancement of technology brought network-connected devices including connected wearable sensors for managing conditions such as Parkinson's disease, ventilators and infusion pumps, pacemakers, dialysis machines, MRI and CT scanners which enable continuous patient monitoring and responsive care through IoT communication standards like ZigBee and ANT+ and OneM2M (Ozturk et al., 2020).

The emergence of new technologies has revealed multiple security weaknesses in the system. The first researchers and practitioners identified weak encryption and authentication systems in IoT protocols which recent studies by Alexander (2022) and Ozturk et al. (2020) and IBM (2023) and Arctic Wolf (2024) confirm still exist in medical devices. The combination of security weaknesses with delayed software updates and patches has made critical care devices vulnerable to cyber threats which threatens to cause severe patient care problems. The digital environment expansion enabled cybercriminals to find and exploit newly discovered system vulnerabilities that are not yet known to the owners of such hardware or software assets. This is also known as zero-day vulnerability. Healthcare organizations faced a rising number of malwares cyberattacks which targeted medical device security vulnerabilities through ransomware and trojans and spyware attacks against outdated operating systems and delayed patch implementations (Verizon, 2023; Ponemon Institute, 2022; Arctic Wolf, 2024). Furthermore, cybersecurity data breaches can have a significant mental and emotional impact on patients, with studies indicating effects such as increased anxiety and diminished trust in their providers (Orsini et al., 2022).

Ransomware-as-a-Service (RaaS) and Malware-as-a-service entered the threat environment as a new threat which enabled untrained users to perform sophisticated attacks through pre-developed ransomware tools (Deskin, 2025). As law enforcement increased its efforts, some decline in attacks was noted, yet the market continued to evolve. Artificial intelligence tools adopted by new attackers enabled them to create complex attacks which security systems struggled to detect, and these attacks achieved higher success rates according to research which indicates AI-based ransomware attacks made up 80% of total ransomware attacks in 2023 (Parker, 2023). Healthcare organizations needed to establish multiple security layers because these threats required them to use encryption alongside authentication improvement, software update timeliness, network segmentation, intrusion detection, multi-factor authentication, threat intelligence and incident response planning for proactive security measures (Ponemon Institute, 2022; Arctic Wolf, 2024).

Healthcare sector cybersecurity challenges led to major changes in regulatory frameworks which now address modern threats through expanded definitions of personal data and risk assessment requirements and increased penalty structures (Smith Law, 2025). The NIST Cybersecurity Framework 2.0 and ISO/IEC 27001:2022 received updates that added adaptive risk-based controls and enhanced supply chain security measures to fight against the cyber risks (NATIONAL INSTITUTE OF STANDARDS AND TECHNOLOGY, 2024). Organizations must now dedicate more resources to supply chain risk management and incident response planning and software patch deployment under new regulatory requirements (Smith Law, 2025). The combination of multiple regulatory frameworks with fast technological progress makes essential systems vulnerable to emerging security threats (Arctic Wolf, 2024).

Research studies have found that healthcare organizations face three main security risks because of insufficient authentication systems and weak encryption methods and delayed software update deployments. The healthcare sector faces multiple systemic problems because of its fragmented incident reporting systems and inconsistent third-party vendor oversight and extended security patch deployment times. The combined security weaknesses of network-connected medical devices require a unified standardized cybersecurity framework for healthcare organizations to protect their systems effectively (Arctic Wolf, 2024).

The consequences of these cybersecurity failures extend past financial losses and regulatory penalties because they impact both personal privacy and business operational continuity. The unauthorized access to healthcare systems through breaches results in compromised sensitive information and creates direct threats to patient safety and medical service disruptions and increased anxiety among patients who need immediate care. The combination of human errors with weak encryption and inadequate authentication and unprepared systems made these attacks more dangerous according to Ponemon Institute (2022) and Arctic Wolf (2024). Healthcare leaders learned this lesson which led them to establish patient-centered practices that focus on continuous staff education about phishing threats and insider attacks and safe device practices (Verizon, 2023), and zero-trust architecture deployment for ongoing device and user and connection authentication (NATIONAL INSTITUTE OF STANDARDS AND TECHNOLOGY, 2024).

The process of enhancing healthcare cybersecurity needed both technical solutions and standardized regulations and effective vendor management practices according to policymakers and practitioners. International standards for unified regulation gained increasing support because they would create uniform patient data protection systems which would simplify regulatory compliance and establish global data protection standards (Office for Civil Rights, 2022). The healthcare supply chain required technology suppliers to meet three essential security standards which included ISO/IEC 27001:2022 and NIST CSF 2.0 and regular audits and immediate device patching (NATIONAL INSTITUTE OF STANDARDS AND TECHNOLOGY, 2024; Craig & Corey, 2021). The concept of creating a single incident reporting system became more popular because it would enable quick exchange of information and coordinated responses and efficient trend monitoring (NATIONAL INSTITUTE OF STANDARDS AND TECHNOLOGY, 2024).

PROBLEM STATEMENT

Health from 2023 indicates ransomware attacks resulted in 30% of healthcare data breaches throughout that year. Medical devices stay vulnerable to security threats because they use outdated operating systems and weak authentication methods, and healthcare organizations face increasing cybersecurity threats because cybercriminals exploit vulnerabilities in their medical devices. The Verizon report does not receive adequate software updates (Craig & Corey, 2021). The TransLogic Pneumatic Tube Systems (PTS) contain security vulnerabilities which Ben and Barak (2021) state will compromise 80% of North American hospitals. Medical device breaches create more than data theft risks because they disrupt healthcare operations while eroding patient trust and resulting in financial penalties and regulatory sanctions (Ponemon Institute, 2022). The current execution gaps in HIPAA and GDPR regulations prevent these laws from protecting essential infrastructure (Office for Civil Rights, 2022).

SIGNIFICANCE OF THE STUDY

The research investigates medical device vulnerabilities in healthcare cybersecurity through an in-depth analysis of authentication protocol weaknesses and encryption standard vulnerabilities and delayed software update implementations. The research identifies multiple IoT-enabled and embedded medical devices including infusion pumps and ventilators and pacemakers as having persistent critical technical vulnerabilities (Alexander, 2022; Ponemon Institute, 2022). The research demonstrates how security vulnerabilities together with human mistakes and insufficient organizational readiness threaten patient welfare and combines knowledge from computer science with healthcare management and behavioral studies to demonstrate the necessity of a comprehensive approach for solving these cybersecurity problems.

The research provides quantitative evidence about how malware attacks weak authentication and encryption systems through ransomware-as-a-service and malware-as-a-service platforms operated by emerging cybersecurity actors. The attacks which range from sophisticated operations of advanced persistent threat groups and nation-state actors to organized operations exploit unpatched software vulnerabilities to compromise medical devices which threatens patient safety (Verizon, 2023; Ponemon Institute, 2022). The research investigates how technical vulnerabilities link to organizational culture because cybercriminals frequently exploit these weaknesses to create operational difficulties and elevate patient safety risks (Verizon, 2023). Healthcare organizations must establish authentication security and encryption protection and software update systems as fundamental elements of their security framework.

Research activities produce essential information which helps governments create new policies. The current security standards of HIPAA and GDPR and NIST fail to protect IoT and embedded medical devices from security threats because they lack sufficient measures for authentication and encryption and patch management (NATIONAL INSTITUTE OF STANDARDS AND TECHNOLOGY, 2024). The fast pace of technological development creates security gaps in device protection and supply chain security and vendor protection because regulatory updates cannot keep up (Arctic Wolf, 2024). The study supports new data protection rules that should enforce advanced authentication systems and enhanced encryption methods and immediate software update and patch deployment (Office for Civil Rights, 2022). The research supports the implementation of real-time monitoring systems together with strict vendor compliance rules to enhance patient information security and national healthcare system stability (NIST 2024; Arctic Wolf 2024).

The research provides healthcare administrators and IT specialists and medical staff with functional operational methods to enhance their organizations' cybersecurity defenses against cyber threats. The study demonstrates that cybersecurity protection through authentication improvement and encryption enhancement and prompt software updates needs to become an integral part of organizational culture and clinical operations instead of existing as a standalone technical issue (Verizon, 2023; NATIONAL INSTITUTE OF STANDARDS AND TECHNOLOGY, 2024). Staff members need to receive ongoing training about phishing detection and insider threat awareness and secure device practices to stop breaches caused by these vulnerabilities (Verizon, 2023). The research supports implementing multiple security layers which include strong encryption and intrusion detection systems and multi-factor authentication and incident response planning and third-party vendor audits and immediate software and device updates (Ponemon Institute, 2022; Arctic Wolf, 2024). The complete security plan enables both medical staff and leadership to establish ongoing defensive actions against cyber threats which leads to an improvement-focused security culture (Office for Civil Rights, 2022).

METHODOLOGY

The research uses three qualitative case studies to analyze main security problems which include Risk Management Theory for studying authentication protocol weaknesses and Change Management Theory for studying weak encryption standards and Cybersecurity Resilience Theory for studying software update and patch implementation delays. The research used qualitative evidence synthesis, that is, findings from other credible researchers. The research also used thematic analysis to find security weaknesses that result from insufficient authentication systems and weak encryption methods and delayed software updates. The study used multiple data sources to validate its findings which included HIPAA, GDPR regulations, NIST technical standards, peer-reviewed author contributions, IBM expert insights, Ponemon Institute reports and Verizon's Cybersecurity Incident Report. The research examined how healthcare facilities remain vulnerable to technical threats because of authentication protocol weaknesses and insufficient encryption standards and delayed software update implementations.

The healthcare industry encounters three distinct cybersecurity problems which researchers analyze through detailed case studies that reveal how inadequate authentication systems and insufficient encryption and delayed software updates lead to security vulnerabilities. The chosen attack vectors demonstrate critical security vulnerabilities which research proves allow ransomware attacks to persistently endanger healthcare organizations. The selected cases present distinct risk domains which align with core principles of cybersecurity theory. Risk Management Theory demonstrates the necessity of robust authentication systems because they stop unauthorized system access. The need for security practice development against emerging threats links weak encryption standards to Change Management Theory. Organizations that successfully manage their identified vulnerabilities at a fast pace demonstrate Cybersecurity Resilience Theory which aligns with the problem of delayed software updates or patches. The three attack vectors function as fundamental components because they establish the basis for ransomware attacks. Healthcare organizations face two primary risks from ransomware attacks which simultaneously threaten patient safety and disrupt vital medical operations while exposing protected patient information to unauthorized access. Healthcare organizations became the target of more than 80% of cyber-attacks during the previous year which demonstrates an urgent requirement for enhanced security measures (Cybersecurity Help, 2022).

The healthcare sector needs multiple security measures to handle the rising number of ransomware attacks that occur within its systems. The research uses particular case studies to demonstrate how these security weaknesses create a chain reaction that affects medical treatment quality and protects patient information. The research findings will establish a detailed relationship between healthcare cybersecurity practices and patient results which support the need for enhanced security protocols in medical facilities. The research supports current theories while providing healthcare administrators and policymakers with operational guidance to protect digital patient information in modern healthcare systems.

THEORIES FROM THE LITERATURE

The healthcare sector faces new cybersecurity threats because of technological progress which makes IoT embedded devices and medical equipment more susceptible to cyberattacks. The development of generative and agentic AI systems has enabled attackers to create more sophisticated and fast-moving cyber threats. The fast adoption of Electronic Health Records (EHRs), Internet of Medical Things (IoMT) and Internet of Things (IoT), and medical device connectivity has revealed weaknesses in authentication systems and encryption methods and software update procedures (Smith, 2023; NATIONAL INSTITUTE OF STANDARDS AND TECHNOLOGY, 2024). The speed of technological advancement continues to outpace regulatory development which maintains ongoing security weaknesses in device protection and supply chain management and vendor responsibility. Researchers support complete regulatory framework updates which should include improved authentication systems and better encryption methods and rapid software update implementation (Office for Civil Rights, 2022).

Early efforts to secure IoT embedded medical devices centered on building a strong governance framework and fostering a culture of cybersecurity awareness (KPMG, 2025; Syner-G BioPharma Group, 2025). Gaining the support of executive leadership proved essential, as did adopting recognized security frameworks recommended by agencies such as the Administration for Strategic Preparedness and Response (ASPR, 2023). As the landscape evolved, the need to address human-related risks became apparent. Tailored training programs were developed to combat user interface errors like alarm fatigue, while also promoting secure practices such as password hygiene (Crothall Healthcare, 2025). At the same time, organizations faced ongoing regulatory challenges, particularly as the Food and Drug Administration

(FDA) began requiring that security be integrated throughout a medical device's entire lifecycle, rather than as an afterthought (FDA, 2025; Wirth, et al., 2020).

Against this backdrop, the methodology of the research took on a qualitative multiple-case study approach, analyzing regulatory reports, write-ups from medical experts, and peer-reviewed articles to understand healthcare cyber incidents. The focus was on uncovering issues such as insufficient authentication protocols, weak encryption standards, and delays in deploying software updates or patches. The research employed thematic analysis to pinpoint vulnerabilities arising from poor authentication, inadequate encryption, and untimely patch management while also examining attack methods and proposed mitigation strategies. Validity was ensured by triangulating data from regulations like HIPAA and GDPR, technical standards set by NIST, and organizational practices around staff training and change management.

In exploring the literature, the research synthesized Risk Management Theory, Change Management Theory, and Cybersecurity Resilience Theory to build a holistic understanding of the persistent vulnerabilities facing IoT medical devices.

Risk Management Theory

Risk Management Theory serves as a foundational framework for understanding the persistent challenges associated with authentication protocol weaknesses in networked medical devices, particularly those connected through the Internet of Medical Things (IoMT). This theory emphasizes the systematic identification of assets, evaluation of threats, and implementation of controls to mitigate cyber risks within healthcare environments. Despite the adoption of security frameworks such as those recommended by NIST, empirical evidence demonstrates that authentication vulnerabilities remain widespread and largely unresolved (NATIONAL INSTITUTE OF STANDARDS AND TECHNOLOGY, 2024; Arctic Wolf, 2024).

Risk Management Theory investigates the following questions about authentication methods: What level of protection do multi-factor authentication and biometrics, and zero-trust frameworks provide for IoMT devices in healthcare and how do new AI-based cyber threats require healthcare organizations to develop improved security measures?

The research shows that default passwords and poor password security and insufficient MFA implementation and absent biometric authentication systems are widespread issues in IoMT devices. Security risks become severe because attackers exploit outdated systems and weak passwords through phishing emails and insecure networks and compromised downloads (Microsoft, n.d; NATIONAL INSTITUTE OF STANDARDS AND TECHNOLOGY, 2024). The rapid deployment of IoT devices in healthcare facilities has increased security risks because it established numerous unsecured access points that organizations fail to detect during their asset tracking operations (Craig & Corey, 2021).

The threat environment has become more complex because new developments in generative and agentic AI systems allow attackers to create complex attacks which target authentication vulnerabilities. The current literature shows an essential knowledge gap because although technical standards and best practices exist for authentication controls of IoMT devices there is no comprehensive multi-site evaluation process. The current research on authentication practices in healthcare organizations consists mainly of theoretical models and single-case studies which fail to provide a complete evidence-based assessment of authentication methods across different healthcare facilities (AuditBoard, 2024; Zach 2025).

Several knowledge gaps continue to exist in different domains. Healthcare organizations face two main challenges because they do not have real-time access to their device inventory which makes it difficult to detect authentication failures in a timely manner. The current state of research lacks sufficient empirical evidence to demonstrate how zero-trust frameworks and adaptive authentication systems protect against IoMT-related security threats. The implementation of strong authentication protocols faces challenges because organizations struggle with insufficient resources and divided cybersecurity responsibilities and inconsistent staff training (Kamalanathan et al., 2025)

The 2021 Scripps Health ransomware attack exemplifies these unresolved challenges. Attackers exploited weak authentication mechanisms to access electronic health records and IoT-connected devices, forcing a regression to paper-based operations and severely disrupting patient care. This incident highlights the operational and security risks posed by insufficient authentication controls and demonstrates the urgent need for comprehensive device-level audits and advanced identity management solutions (Health IT Security, 2021; NATIONAL INSTITUTE OF STANDARDS AND TECHNOLOGY, 2024).

Change Management Theory

Change Management Theory is increasingly recognized as a vital framework for advancing cybersecurity in healthcare organizations, particularly as these entities grapple with complex network environments, evolving threat landscapes, and regulatory demands. The theory's application to cybersecurity focuses on systematic oversight of network and device activities, structured approval processes, and the integration of executive leadership to ensure resilient and secure digital infrastructures within healthcare settings.

The research field of Change Management Theory focuses on developing methods for organizations to track network and device activities across their networks.

The healthcare industry lacks sufficient research about change management for cybersecurity incident management although many studies have investigated this topic. Organizations need complete visibility to control their shadow IT operations to some degree. Organizations need to establish a change management model to achieve control over their network activities. The change request process must evaluate all network-bound hardware and software assets before granting approval through proper vetting procedures. The Change Management Control Board must evaluate software before the cybersecurity department provides final approval. The cybersecurity department grants a certificate of net-worthiness to authorized software and hardware which allows them to stay on the network for two to three years based on organizational standard operating procedures (SOP) (Olawoye, 2025). The assets receive ongoing monitoring to detect any upcoming Common Vulnerabilities and Exposures (CVE) alerts.

This change management model is practiced by the Department of Defense (DoD), now the Department of War (DoW). This practice is one reason why cyberattacks are rare within the DoW spectrum. While healthcare organizations might not have the same budget as the DoW, they can still improve their cybersecurity by ensuring that proper requests, approvals, and disposals of end-of-life assets are conducted to strengthen their defense layers (Olawoye, 2025). A recent real-world case that further underscores the importance of not just change management, but also robust encryption and active executive leadership, is the 2023 HCA Healthcare data breach.

Change management models ask this question: How do change management models such as executive leadership involvement, the change request and approval process, and strong encryption affect visibility, control, and cybersecurity of network hardware and software in healthcare organizations?

The 2023 HCA Healthcare data breach demonstrates the critical role of encryption in data protection while showing that executive leaders need to join forces with healthcare cybersecurity teams and implement successful change management approaches. In July 2023, a cyberattack on HCA Healthcare resulted in the exposure of personal data of about 11 million patients. This breach compromised their personal identifiable information (PII), and Personal Health Information (PHI), contact information and appointment scheduling details. The incident revealed significant vulnerabilities in the organization's data protection systems, highlighting the need for robust encryption solutions and ongoing cybersecurity training, as well as effective change management programs (Bracken, 2023).

As the healthcare-cybersecurity arena continues to evolve, an expanding body of scholars repeatedly underscores the necessity of a grasp of network assets, shadow-IT activities and software deployments. Olawoye (2025) research study drives the point home, formal change-management procedures are essential, demanding evaluation and approval, by teams that include dedicated cybersecurity experts. A slew of models often highlighted by agencies such as the Department of Defense, now the Department of War (DoW) rests on a disciplined tactic which states that each asset receives a certificate of net-worthiness granting such hardware or software asset permission to interact with other devices or software on the same network. The change management model also suggests continuous monitoring of these assets in case there is a common vulnerability exposure (CVE) alerts of any zero-day vulnerability that is announced by the vendor. Moreover, while healthcare providers do not have the budget and manpower of the DoW, they can still practice change management models such that will include executive leadership involvement to drive the change request and approval process, and strong encryption that affect visibility, control, and cybersecurity of network hardware and software in healthcare organizations (Olawoye, 2025).

Several notable gaps persist in the current body of research. Majorly, existing studies often fail to address how visibility and control over network assets directly correlate with reductions in security incidents. Moreover, the interplay between executive leadership involvement in cybersecurity decision-making and measurable improvements in organizational resilience remains insufficiently explored. Research seldom investigates the integration of change management with robust encryption practices and ongoing staff training, leaving questions about the optimal combination of interventions for effective threat mitigation (Olawoye, 2025).

The 2023 HCA Healthcare data breach demonstrates how weak change management practices combined with unencrypted data and demonstrated major weaknesses in data protection systems which requires immediate implementation of strong change management systems and ongoing cybersecurity training inadequate executive supervision create major security risks for personal health information. The breach of 11 million patient records and leadership participation. The actual impact of poor change management practices demonstrates the necessity for research-based solutions which address healthcare cybersecurity challenges (Bracken, 2023).

The organization implemented new encryption systems and access control procedures following the attack. The organization conducted extensive training sessions which taught information assurance principles to all staff members and their vendor partners. The training sessions received direct supervision from executive leaders and senior organizational members to guarantee proper implementation. The organization enhanced its cybersecurity protection through these fundamental measures which Bracken (2023) recognized as fundamental for enhancing its security posture.

The Cybersecurity Resilience Theory

The Cybersecurity Resilience Theory delivers superior strategic protection because it recognizes that complete prevention of cyber incidents becomes unattainable (Palo Alto Networks, 2025; World Economic Forum, 2024). The theory helps organizations develop readiness against cyber threats through preparedness and response and recovery operations which protect their core business operations (World Economic Forum, 2024). The healthcare industry is being exposed to cyber threats because of artificial intelligence advancements in generative and agentic AI systems, yet previous studies demonstrate IoT devices experience ongoing network attacks. Organizations can develop adaptable incident response systems and security event learning platforms through this approach which enhances their overall security position (Palo Alto Networks, 2025). The approach strengthens organizational security through adaptable incident response and proactive measures and ongoing security event learning (Palo Alto Networks, 2025). The Cybersecurity Resilience Theory now emphasizes AI-based attack prevention alongside network breaches and exploitation because software updates and patches have become critical security weaknesses that require immediate attention. The security weaknesses in systems attract cybercriminals who use them to execute major healthcare data breaches (AuditBoard, 2024; Arctic Wolf, 2024).

The Cybersecurity Resilience Theory asks this question: How can healthcare organizations integrate AI-driven technologies and effective third-party risk management practices, while also leveraging leadership involvement and continuous staff training, to anticipate, mitigate, and recover from advanced cybersecurity threats and supply chain-related breaches?

Existing research has shown that delayed software updates or patches allow attackers to exploit known flaws in healthcare networks and IoT-connected devices, compromising sensitive patient data and disrupting essential operations (AuditBoard, 2024). The deployment of updates became more efficient through IBM BigFix and ManageEngine Patch Manager Plus automated systems, while Darktrace and SentinelOne Singularity used AI to monitor networks in real time, detect anomalies, and trigger automated incident responses. The combination of security tools with Sophos Intercept X anti-ransomware protection successfully handled RaaS and MaaS attacks, which AuditBoard (2024) and Arctic Wolf (2024) identified as evolving threats.

Research findings show that healthcare organizations face multiple security risks because of the growing number of Internet of Things (IoT) and Internet of Medical Things (IoMT) devices, the increasing use of artificial intelligence (AI) in medical and administrative operations. Research shows that medical devices connected to IoT and IoMT networks experience regular network attacks because cybercriminals take advantage of delayed software updates and insufficient patch management (AuditBoard, 2024; Arctic Wolf, 2024). However, the combination of IBM BigFix and ManageEngine Patch Manager Plus with AI-powered security platforms like Darktrace and SentinelOne Singularity provides real-time threat detection and automated response capabilities which boost organizational security (Palo Alto Networks, 2025). Healthcare organizations need to implement incident response systems and security event learning platforms to build a stronger security position. It is hopeful that products such as Sophos Intercept X had demonstrated its ability to stop Ransomware-as-a-Service (RaaS) and Malware-as-a-Service (MaaS) attacks through its advanced anti-ransomware tool deployment (Palo Alto Networks, 2025).

The threat environment continues to evolve because organizations now face new security risks from generative and agentic AI systems which create complex challenges for established defensive systems. The ALPHV BlackCat attack on Change Healthcare demonstrates how unpatched systems and weak authentication protocols and insufficient third-party risk governance create single-point failures that result in disastrous consequences for patient care and financial stability.

One of the prominent cases that show system vulnerability resulting in the attack of the ALPHV BlackCat group which launched a cyberattack on Change Healthcare through an unsecured remote access portal which lacked multi-factor authentication to steal more than 6 terabytes of data in February 2024. The incident demonstrates Cybersecurity Resilience Theory because it shows how one security weakness can damage a national system while demonstrating the importance of preparedness for breaches that stem from vendor system vulnerabilities. The attack interrupted essential healthcare operations including prescription handling and claims payment processing which resulted in major financial problems for healthcare providers while demonstrating the necessity for effective recovery plans and third-party risk assessment. The American Hospital Association declared that this incident proves healthcare organizations and the entire healthcare sector need to develop immediate cyber preparedness measures.

The combination of theoretical perspectives resulted in a unified system for healthcare cybersecurity protection. The evaluation process shows that organizations face ongoing challenges to understand how authentication weaknesses and poor encryption and delayed software updates create security risks that endanger patient safety (Arctic Wolf, 2024; Ponemon Institute, 2022). Organizations need to conduct device-level authentication audits while investing in scenario-based encryption training and implementing automated patch management systems with real-time dashboards to protect their operations. The combination of standardized authentication and encryption and patching regulations with continuous education and robust controls and technological solutions enables healthcare leaders to build a secure digital environment (NATIONAL INSTITUTE OF STANDARDS AND TECHNOLOGY, 2023; Picus Security, 2025; Hoxhunt, 2025). The path to resilience emerges through human dedication to protect patient information and life safety in addition to technological advancements.

RESEARCH DESIGN

The research examined IoT medical device security threats in healthcare facilities through an analysis of three specific cases. The case study method involves examining individual cases in their natural context to better understand complex issues and events Creswell and Poth (2023). The research used non-human qualitative methods to integrate findings from previous studies. The study examined US healthcare organizations to identify three primary security concerns which included authentication protocol vulnerabilities based on Risk Management Theory and weak encryption standards based on Change Management Theory and software update and patch delays based on Cybersecurity Resilience Theory. The research incorporated NIST and HIPAA and GDPR and CISA and ISO/IEC 27001 standards together with peer-reviewed articles and medical publications and relevant resources. The case study approach allowed researchers to implement various data collection methods which delivered detailed knowledge about medical device malware effects on healthcare infrastructure (KPMG, 2025; Syner-G BioPharma Group, 2025).

The selection of qualitative research methods occurred because quantitative metrics fail to address the complex nature of healthcare cybersecurity problems stemming from organizational and regulatory and behavioral elements. The case study method allowed researchers to perform an extensive analysis of IoT device malware incidents that included RaaS and MaaS developments and organizational threat handling and identification of authentication problems and encryption weaknesses and delayed software updates. The literature review demonstrated that authentication weaknesses and encryption problems and delayed software updates represent major risk factors which align with Risk Management Theory and Change Management Theory and Cybersecurity Resilience Theory. The three theoretical frameworks together create a complete understanding of how IoT medical devices face ongoing security threats (Health IT Security, 2021; Arctic Wolf, 2024; Ponemon Institute, 2022).

CASE SELECTION

The research design used case triangulation to study multiple attack vectors because it prevented the analysis from focusing on one specific entry point while showing the wide range of system vulnerabilities (Bracken, 2023). The chosen cases examined different types of attacks which included authentication protocol breakdowns and weak encryption and delayed software updates (Health IT Security, 2021).

The first case study based on Risk Management Theory examined authentication protocols as it relates to the main subject. The 2021 Scripps Health ransomware attack along with other hospital operational disruptions showed how attackers use weak authentication to gain access to essential healthcare systems including electronic health records and IoT-connected devices which compromised the data of approximately 1.2 million people (Health IT Security, 2021). The security breaches demonstrate that weak authentication systems create system instability which triggers multiple security breakdowns.

Organizations need to run authentication audits on a regular basis while maintaining uniform security standards for all third-party vendors who need system access. Automated monitoring systems help organizations detect authentication activities which deviate from standard user behavior patterns. Organizations should implement multi-factor authentication for their essential systems that include EHRs and IoT devices while providing complete training to staff members and vendors about secure access methods. The implementation of these risk management strategies through a framework will decrease operational interruptions and data breaches that stem from authentication system vulnerabilities (Arctic Wolf, 2024; Health IT Security, 2021; Ponemon Institute, 2022).

The second case based on Change Management Theory demonstrates that organizations need to establish strong encryption standards and demonstrate their dedication to cybersecurity practices. The initial step of effective change management requires executive leadership support together with clear communication and the implementation of established frameworks such as ASPR (2023). Security procedures need to be enforced by leadership who will also take responsibility for their implementation. The 2023 HCA Healthcare data breach exposed 11 million patient records to risk because of insufficient encryption and inadequate change management practices. The organization implemented better encryption and access controls and staff training through executive oversight and continuous feedback which proved the need for continuous leader-driven cybersecurity enhancements (ASPR, 2023).

The prevention of human errors in medical devices needs specific training programs which teach secure practices and strong password management techniques (Crothall Healthcare, 2025). The process of change management enables these initiatives through regular communication and feedback systems. The deployment of enhanced encryption protocols requires change management to handle both stakeholder involvement and outcome assessment and technical vulnerability mitigation through strong encryption implementation. Organizations need to stay updated with regulatory changes implementation of a change management framework enables sustained compliance through leadership support and continuous process improvement (Crothall Healthcare, 2025).

The third case study examined Cybersecurity Resilience Theory by studying how delayed software update and patch deployment create security risks. Organizations need to apply software updates and patches as soon as possible because unsecured systems become direct targets for cybercriminals. Healthcare organizations should adopt complete patch management systems as part of their resilience plans to stop cyberattacks from happening. Automated patch management systems with real-time monitoring dashboards under vendor supervision enable organizations to maintain consistent security across their managed systems which include external partner-operated systems. Organizations can keep their essential operations running during security breaches caused by delayed updates through implementing multiple security layers and dependable backup systems. The protection of these measures needs continuous vendor patch audits together with strict encryption standards for verification. The implemented resilience principles help organizations achieve quick recovery of secure operations after incidents that stem from delayed patch implementations (Ozturk et al., 2020; Vidals, 2025).

The February 2024 cyberattacks on Change Healthcare by the ALPHV BlackCat group, which capitalized on an unsecured remote access portal and insufficient encryption and authentication controls, provides a salient illustration (American Hospital Association, 2024). Attackers used an unsecured remote access portal which included the ConnectWise ScreenConnect tool. ConnectWise released security patches for two critical remote code execution (RCE) vulnerabilities in ScreenConnect software during mid-February 2024, however, Change Healthcare delayed the implementation on their patches to these vulnerabilities which had led to the attack (NIST National Vulnerability Database (NVD), 2024; ConnectWise, 2024).

The attack resulted in the theft of more than six terabytes of confidential information while causing major operational problems which demonstrated how one security weakness can create extensive damage (Bracken, 2023). The theory of resilience demonstrates that organizations need strong systems which can handle disruptions while keeping operations running and allowing for fast recovery (KPMG, 2025). The American Hospital Association stresses that these incidents demonstrate why healthcare organizations need to develop complete preparedness plans and strong recovery systems and perform thorough assessments of third-party risks (American Hospital Association, 2024). Nonetheless, healthcare IT professionals can protect their systems from breaches by requiring vendors to implement strong encryption and build resilience into their systems (Syner-G BioPharma Group, 2025; ASPR, 2023).

Data Sources

The research depends on multiple official sources to evaluate security weaknesses that exist in healthcare organizations. The research incorporated NIST and HIPAA and GDPR and CISA and ISO/IEC 27001 standards together with peer-reviewed articles and medical publications and relevant resources. The research uses breach reports from the U.S. Department of Health and Human Services (HHS) and Cybersecurity and Infrastructure Security Agency (CISA) to analyze current security incidents and identify emerging threats. The analysis benefits from white papers and detailed case studies and annual threat assessments such as IBM and Verizon Data Breach Investigations Reports which deliver statistical evidence about cyber threat occurrence and effects. The research incorporates peer-reviewed academic studies about medical device weaknesses and malware attacks to support its findings through both experimental evidence and theoretical frameworks. The study unites various sources to present a complete understanding of healthcare institution cybersecurity challenges through regulatory requirements and practical applications and academic research.

Ethical Assurances

The study received Institutional Review Board (IRB) approval for secondary data analysis although it did not involve human participants to follow ethical guidelines. The research used public data sources which contained no personal information that exceeded what was available through public channels. The research followed ethical standards through correct source referencing and non-judgmental analysis of institutional decisions and complete disclosure of source materials. The research followed all data usage guidelines by treating unclassified government and healthcare information with proper ethical standards (Bhandari, 2024).

RESULTS, RECOMMENDATIONS, CONCLUSIONS, AND SOLUTIONS

Results

The research findings based on case triangulation demonstrate that healthcare facilities continue to face security risks because of their use of outdated medical equipment and their implementation of weak authentication systems and insufficient encryption methods and delayed software update deployment. The analysis uses multiple attack vectors and theoretical frameworks to demonstrate how outdated authentication and encryption methods and delayed software updates create substantial operational risks that expose sensitive healthcare information to ongoing threats.

Risk Management Theory serves as the foundation for the first case study which analyzed authentication vulnerabilities through the examination of Scripps Health data breach. The security incidents showed how weak authentication systems combined with disorganized access rules allowed attackers to penetrate vital system infrastructure which compromised the data of approximately 1.2 million people. The Scripps Health breach occurred because of poor authentication security yet the

CaptureRx incident revealed the dangers of depending on vendors who maintain insufficient security measures. This case proved that outdated authentication systems together with inconsistent security protocols for third-party vendors led to patient data breaches and operational interruptions. The analysis shows that healthcare organizations need to implement strong multi-factor authentication systems for all critical systems including EHRs and IoT devices while performing continuous vendor security audits to establish standardized protection protocols (Health IT Security, 2021).

The HCA Healthcare breach served as a second case study which demonstrated Change Management Theory through its examination of encryption standards and organizational governance practices. The incident demonstrated that organizations which lack proper encryption and change management systems will experience major data breaches because weak encryption and poor oversight led to the exposure of 11 million patient records. The case showed that executive leadership combined with clear communication within organizational governance structures enables the successful implementation of advanced encryption technologies and access control systems and complete staff training programs. The implementation of security practice improvements followed change management principles which established a structured process for leadership-driven accountability and continuous adaptation and improvement. The case proves that organizations need to fix encryption weaknesses at the same time, build a security culture which supports continuous change and maintains stakeholder involvement and regulatory compliance (Ponemon Institute, 2022; ASPR, 2023).

The third case study applied Cybersecurity Resilience Theory explored how delayed software update and patch deployment create security risks. This theory centers on February 2024 Change Healthcare cyberattack by the ALPHV BlackCat group. This attack exploited an unsecured remote access portal and inadequate encryption and authentication controls, resulting in the exfiltration of over 6 terabytes of sensitive data and significant operational disruption. The incident exemplified how a single vulnerability resulting from unpatched software has had cascading effects across critical healthcare operations. Resilience theory advocates for layered defenses, redundancy, and rapid recovery strategies, such as robust incident response plans and thorough third-party risk assessments. Embedding resilience principles enable healthcare organizations to absorb shocks, maintain essential services during attacks, and restore secure operations promptly (Health IT Security, 2021; Arctic Wolf, 2024; Ponemon Institute, 2022).

The evidence from these three case studies shows that healthcare organizations face ongoing security risks because of fragmented security controls and outdated infrastructure and inadequate staff cybersecurity training and dependence on vendor services. The combination of human mistakes during operations and phishing attacks along with insider threats that take advantage of system weaknesses continues to cause security breaches. The healthcare sector faces increased exposure risks because organizations depend on third-party vendors for their operations. Healthcare IT professionals need to implement strong authentication systems and advanced encryption methods and effective change management protocols and resilience measures to protect against diverse security threats. A complete security framework that addresses all vulnerabilities becomes necessary to defend patient safety and maintain operational stability against advancing cyber threats.

Solutions & Recommendations

Layered Defense Strategy

Healthcare organizations need to build a defense-in-depth system that combines endpoint detection and response (EDR) with zero-trust architecture and network segmentation to achieve complete security protection. Organizations should implement AI-based defense systems through Extended Detection and Response (XDR) because this technology gives complete network threat and incident visibility according to IBM (2021). Security measures remain ineffective unless organizations resolve ongoing security issues that stem from system entry and weak encryption protocols enable data interception and delayed software updates leave systems vulnerable to known security threats, insufficient authentication systems and poor encryption practices and delayed software updates. The lack of modern authentication protocols enables unauthorized.

The defense strategy needs to focus on implementing multi-factor authentication and complete data encryption and immediate software update deployment. Zero-trust models need continuous authentication verification while EDR systems and network segmentation work together to stop threats and defend essential assets when one security barrier fails. Organizations can achieve better protection against malware and ransomware attacks through combined security controls that reduce the impact of authentication and encryption vulnerabilities and patching delays (Health IT Security, 2021 and Arctic Wolf 2024 and Ponemon Institute 2022).

Staff Training and Culture

Healthcare data breaches primarily stem from human errors which become worse because of inadequate authentication systems and insufficient encryption methods and delayed software update implementations. Staff training programs according to Vidals (2025) should evolve from standard annual compliance sessions to include practical simulations which teach employees to detect phishing attacks and protect against insider threats and device misuse when authentication and encryption systems are weak or outdated. A cybersecurity culture requires leadership support through regular drills and performance evaluations which check employee compliance with security protocols including immediate software updates. A security-oriented organizational culture emerges when all personnel, including non-IT staff members grasp their responsibilities for protecting patient information while recognizing the necessity of strong authentication and encryption and regular software updates to fight external and internal security threats (Kamalanathan et al., 2025).

Device Hardening

Medical device manufacturers need to collaborate with hospitals to develop robust security-by-design principles for their products which will fix authentication problems and weak encryption and delayed update issues. Organizations must implement device hardening using secure default configurations and immediate software and firmware updates and complete data transmission encryption and multi-factor authentication for device interface access (Ozturk et al., 2020). The expanding Internet of Things medical device market attracts cybercriminals because most of these devices operate with uncatchable outdated operating systems. Hospitals need to establish vendor accountability systems which force manufacturers to support ongoing product updates and patches while internal IT teams maintain complete asset records and perform security audits and deactivate unused features to protect against authentication and encryption vulnerabilities (Ozturk et al., 2020).

Regulatory Alignment

Healthcare organizations need to establish authentication protocols and encryption standards and perform timely patch management as core security measures to achieve regulatory compliance between federal and international and state laws. Organizations must follow HIPAA federal regulations to protect electronic protected health information (ePHI) and personally identifiable information (PII) through strong access controls and encryption as technical safeguard requirements. The European Union requires organizations to use appropriate technical and organizational measures for GDPR compliance which includes strong authentication systems and encryption to protect personal data confidentiality and integrity. The United States has multiple state laws including the California Consumer Privacy Act (CCPA) and New York's SHIELD Act which require organizations to protect data and notify about breaches through specified encryption standards and immediate system update and patching procedures.

Healthcare organizations need to create a single system for regulatory compliance through three essential steps: (1) vendor certification programs must verify all partners follow authentication and encryption standards; (2) healthcare organizations need to establish uniform breach reporting systems which meet both federal and state notification deadlines and GDPR's immediate disclosure requirements; and (3) organizations should receive financial support through grants and tax benefits and subsidies to help them implement security updates and patches in a timely manner. Organizations must face substantial financial consequences for non-compliance to ensure they properly implement authentication and encryption and update protocols. Healthcare providers can achieve regulatory compliance and equal security standards through unified requirements which protect patient data throughout all jurisdictions.

Incident Response Readiness

Healthcare organizations need to develop readiness plans to manage security breaches that occur because of authentication protocol weaknesses and poor encryption standards and delayed software update schedules. The Department of Defense cybersecurity practice-based incident response playbooks from CISA (2021) help organizations achieve quick incident containment and operational recovery through established ransomware isolation procedures and patient and staff notification protocols and backup care strategies. Organizations should conduct red team/blue team vulnerability exercises regularly. Organizations that train for incident response procedures in advance will reduce system downtime duration and enhance damage mitigation and tabletop simulations on a regular basis to evaluate their authentication systems and encryption controls and their unsecured system and speed up operational recovery times when breaches occur from these common vulnerabilities (CISA, 2021).

Conclusions

Healthcare organizations face worsening cyber threats because they lack adequate risk management systems and change management protocols and cybersecurity resilience measures. Risk management theory requires organizations to develop strong authentication systems because weak controls allow unauthorized access threaten patient safety and break down healthcare provider-patient trust. Organizations need to implement change management theory to protect patient data because their current encryption standards remain weak and their delayed encryption updates and insufficient oversight create patient data exposure. Healthcare organizations become vulnerable to security threats when they postpone software system updates because outdated systems give attackers simple access to disrupt operations. The healthcare sector faces increasing security risks because it depends on IoT and embedded medical devices yet many organizations do not implement standardized protection protocols. Healthcare organizations need to establish cybersecurity as their top priority for patient safety through dual strategies which combine technological solutions with human-centered initiatives that include full staff education and defined roles to create a safer and more resilient system.

RECOMMENDATIONS FOR FUTURE RESEARCH

Future research needs to concentrate on healthcare and cybersecurity because these fields encounter new technologies including generative and agentic AI systems. The cybersecurity environment experiences daily occurrences of advanced persistent threats (APTs) and nation-state attacks and Ransomware-as-a-Service and Malware-as-a-Service and autonomous AI-driven attacks because of sophisticated cyber threats that emerge from these new technologies. Organizations fight this problem through the implementation of agentic systems which operate autonomously while monitoring their surroundings and taking decisions without extensive human supervision (Rippling, 2025; Parker, 2023). Security solutions that function based on predictable behaviors lose their effectiveness when agents obtain autonomy because compromised agents can execute security-threatening actions that deviate from human-established goals (SecurityInfoWatch, 2025). Agentic AI systems provide essential benefits to users, but organizations must create particular security protocols to address their unique protection needs (Parker, 2023; SecurityInfoWatch, 2025; Rippling, 2025).

Risk management needs multi-factor authentication systems and strong identity verification protocols and periodic control evaluations to combat AI-based intrusion techniques made by attackers; organizations need to perform ongoing monitoring of software and hardware assets from development to retirement and all stages in between to address authentication vulnerabilities (SecurityInfoWatch, 2025).

Organizations require change management theory to deploy modern defense systems and enhance their encryption protocols. The combination of AI-assisted cryptanalysis and agentic malware produces an environment which makes outdated encryption systems vulnerable to quick and intelligent attacks. Organizations need advanced change management to deploy new encryption technologies because it supports methodical planning and approval procedures and technology integration and training and communication to reduce resistance and enhance adoption speed. The deployment of encryption schemes that defend against AI and agentic threats becomes possible through structured change management which safeguards sensitive health data from evolving automated attacks on cryptographic defenses (SecurityInfoWatch, 2025; Rippling, 2025).

Cybersecurity resilience theory is important because AI-powered threats and autonomous agents now exploit zero-day vulnerabilities to attack systems when software updates or patches experience delays. Organizations must create robust incident response plans and establish zero-trust architectures and perform continuous vulnerability assessments to achieve resilience. Organizations should perform simulated attacks with AI-powered adversaries and autonomous intrusions to build their threat containment abilities and quick recovery from breaches that outpace traditional attack speeds. Healthcare organizations can protect themselves from RaaS and MaaS and AI and agentic-based threats by embedding resilience principles into their organizational culture and technical infrastructure (SecurityInfoWatch, 2025; Rippling, 2025).

Healthcare organizations can protect their systems from vulnerabilities in authentication and encryption and patching by using risk management and change management and resilience theory while monitoring new AI and agentic attack methods. The combination of these three approaches creates an essential framework for protecting patient data and system operations during the current period of increasing traditional and intelligent automated threats (SecurityInfoWatch, 2025; Rippling, 2025).

REFERENCES

Administration for Strategic Preparedness and Response. (2023). *Healthcare sector cybersecurity framework implementation guide.* U.S. Department of Health and Human Services. https://aspr.hhs.gov/cip/hph-cybersecurity-framework-implementation-guide/Documents/HPH-Sector-CSF-Implementation-Guide-508.pdf

Alexander, S. G. (2022). *What is the internet of things (IoT)?* Retrieved from https://www.techtarget.com/iotagenda/definition/Internet-of-Things-IoT

American Hospital Association. (2024). *Change Healthcare Cyberattack: Network Connectivity Issues, Indicators of Compromise.* https://www.connectwise.com/company/trust/security-bulletins/connectwise-screenconnect-23.9.8

American Hospital Association. (2024). *AHA survey: Change Healthcare cyberattack significantly disrupts patient care, hospitals' finances.* https://www.aha.org/2024-03-15-aha-survey-change-healthcare-cyberattack-significantly-disrupts-patient-care-hospitals-finances

American Hospital Association. (2024). *A look at 2024's health care cybersecurity challenges.* https://www.aha.org/news/aha-cyber-intel/2024-10-07-look-2024s-health-care-cybersecurity-challenges

Arctic Wolf. (2024). Breaking down ransomware-as-a-service. https://arcticwolf.com/resources/blog/breaking-down-ransomware-as-a-service

AuditBoard. (2024). SEC cybersecurity rules update: The complete guide. https://auditboard.com/blog/sec-cybersecurity-rules

Ben, S., & Barak, H. (2021). *Security flaws affect hospital pneumatic tube systems.* Retrieved from https://www.armis.com/research/pwnedpiper

Bhandari, P. (2024, October 1). Ethical considerations in research: Types & examples. Scribbr. https://www.scribbr.com/methodology/research-ethics/

Bracken, B. (2023). *11M HCA Healthcare patients impacted by data breach. Dark Reading.* https://www.darkreading.com/cyberattacks-data-breaches/11m-hca-healthcare-patients-impacted-data-breach

ConnectWise. (2024). *ConnectWise ScreenConnect 23.9.8 security fix.* ConnectWise Trust Center. Retrieved October 18, 2025, from https://www.connectwise.com/company/trust/security-bulletins/connectwise-screenconnect-23.9.8

Corporation, I. B. M. (2021). *IBM launches QRadar XDR, a comprehensive open XDR solution*. IBM TechXchange Community. https://community.ibm.com/community/user/discussion/ibm-launches-qradar-xdr-a-comprehensive-open-xdr-solution?hlmlt=VT

Craig, R., & Corey, D. (2021). Cyber threats in healthcare: A comprehensive review. *Journal of Healthcare Information Management*, *35*(2), 112–119.

Creswell, J. W., & Poth, C. N. (2023). *Qualitative inquiry and research design: Choosing among five approaches* (5th ed.). SAGE Publication.

Crothall Healthcare. (2025). *Five building blocks to a resilient healthcare cybersecurity culture*. https://www.crothall.com/blog/five-building-blocks-to-a-resilient-healthcare-cybersecurity-culture/

Cybersecurity Help. (2022). *Zero-Day vulnerability statistics*. Retrieved from https://www.zero-day.cz/research/

Deskin, G. (2025). *Law enforcement pressure is reshaping the global ransomware threat landscape. Security Boulevard*. https://securityboulevard.com/2025/10/law-enforcement-pressure-is-reshaping-the-global-ransomware-threat-landscape/

Food and Drug Administration. (2025). *Cybersecurity in medical devices: Quality system considerations and content of premarket submissions. Federal Register*. https://www.federalregister.gov/documents/2025/06/27/2025-11669/cybersecurity-in-medical-devices-quality-system-considerations-and-content-of-premarket-submissions

Health, I. T. Security. (2021). *Scripps Health ransomware attack disrupts care*. HealthITSecurity.com. https://healthitsecurity.com

Healthcare, H. C. A. (2023). *HCA Healthcare reports data security incident*. https://investor.hcahealthcare.com/news/news-details/2023/HCA-Healthcare-Reports-Data-Security-Incident/default.aspx

Hoxhunt. (2025). *Does gamified security training actually work?* https://hoxhunt.com/blog/gamified-cyber-security-training

IBM. (2023). *Cost of a data breach report 2023*. IBM Security. https://www.stickleyonsecurity.com/news.jspx?articleid=%200F34F898A5586B334B4C8FACC8B02008&v5=1&playerid=407315631#:~:text=Every%20year%2C%20%22IBM's%20Cost%20of%20a%20Data,breaches%20and%20other%20key%20findings%20from%202023

Kamalanathan, S., Rajan, S. M., & Schell, S. (2025). *Implementing zero trust in healthcare. Cognizant.* https://www.cognizant.com/en_us/industries/documents/cognizant-implementing-zero-trust-in-healthcare.pdf

KPMG. (2025). *Healthcare – Cybersecurity considerations 2025.* https://kpmg.com/xx/en/our-insights/ai-and-technology/cybersecurity-considerations-2025/healthcare.html

Microsoft. (n.d.). *US healthcare at risk: Strengthening resiliency against ransomware attacks.* https://www.microsoft.com/en-us/security/security-insider/emerging-threats/us-

National Institute of Standards and Technology. (2024). *NVD - CVE-2024-1708 detail.* Retrieved October 18, 2025, from https://nvd.nist.gov/vuln/detail/cve-2024-1708

Olawoye, S. (2025). *Malware threats and resilience in healthcare IT systems* [Doctoral dissertation, Capitol Technology University]. ProQuest Dissertations Publishing.

Orsini, N. F., Hassoon, A., De La Garza, R., Torres, R., Brenner, L. A., Palmisano, J., & Heller, M. (2022). *A systems approach to preparing for cybersecurity incidents in healthcare: A conceptual framework.* https://pmc.ncbi.nlm.nih.gov/articles/PMC9403058/

Osama, O. F., Rahman, M. M., & Kshetri, N. (2025). healthMLsec: Machine learning-based vulnerability assessment in health systems: A framework for enhancing cybersecurity and patient data [Preprint]. *Preprints.org.* DOI: 10.20944/preprints202502.2165.v1

Ozturk, S., Ayanoğlu, F. B., Parmaksiz, M., Elçin, A. E., & Elçin, Y. M. (2020). Clinical and surgical aspects of medical materials' biocompatibility. *Handbook of Biomaterials Biocompatibility, 219–250.* DOI: 10.1016/B978-0-08-102967-1.00012-8

Palo Alto Networks. (2025). *Unit 42 Global Incident Response Report.* https://www.paloaltonetworks.com/resources/research/unit-42-incident-response-report

Parker, J. (2023). *80% of ransomware attacks now use artificial intelligence. MIT Sloan School of Management.* https://mitsloan.mit.edu/ideas-made-to-matter/80-ransomware-attacks-now-use-artificial-intelligence

Picus Security. (2025). *What is attack path visualization (APV) in cybersecurity? Picus Security.* https://www.picussecurity.com/resource/glossary/what-is-attack-path-visualization

Ponemon Institute. (2022). *Cost of a data breach report.* IBM Security. https://www.ibm.com/reports/data-breach

PuppyGraph. (2025). *Visualizing cyber threats: An introduction to attack graphs. PuppyGraph.* https://www.puppygraph.com/blog/attack-graph

Rippling. (2025). *Agentic AI security: A guide to threats, risks & best practices. Rippling Blog.* https://www.rippling.com/blog/agentic-ai-security

SecurityInfoWatch. (2025). *Autonomous and unchecked: The mounting risks of agentic AI. SecurityInfoWatch.* https://www.securityinfowatch.com/ai/article/55316293/autonomous-and-unchecked-the-mounting-risks-of-agentic-ai

Smith Law. (2025). *Healthcare cyberattacks are on the rise: Steps to safeguard your organization.* Smith Law. https://www.smithlaw.com/newsroom/publications/healthcare-cyberattacks-are-on-the-rise-steps-to-safeguard-your-organization

Syner-G BioPharma Group. (2025). *Why human factors dictate the safety of medical devices.* https://synergbiopharma.com/human-factors-medical-devices/

The HIPAA Guide. (2025). *New HIPAA regulations 2024-2025.* https://www.hipaaguide.net/new-hipaa-regulations/

United States, Department of Health and Human Services, Office for Civil Rights. (2022). *OCR cybersecurity newsletters.* HHS.gov. https://www.hhs.gov/hipaa/for-professionals/security/guidance/cybersecurity-newsletter-october-2022/index.html

U.S. Department of Homeland Security, Cybersecurity and Infrastructure Security Agency. (2021). *Federal government cybersecurity incident and vulnerability response playbooks.* https://www.cisa.gov/resources-tools/resources/federal-government-cybersecurity-incident-and-vulnerability-response-playbooks

Vantage Medtech. (n.d.). *Understanding embedded medical device software.* Retrieved October 19, 2025, from https://vantagemedtech.com/embedded-medical-device-software/

Verizon. (2020). *2023 Data breach investigations report (DBIR).* Verizon Enterprise Solutions. https://www.verizon.com/business/resources/reports/dbir/

Vidals, G. (2025). *Zero trust security for healthcare: Why your HIPAA compliance strategy needs an upgrade. Medium.* https://hipaavault.medium.com/zero-trust-security-for-healthcare-why-your-hipaa-compliance-strategy-needs-an-upgrade-fba4541fbd00

Wirth, A., Gates, C., & Smith, J. (2020). *Medical device cybersecurity for engineers and manufacturers.* https://www.goodreads.com/book/show/54494363-medical-device-cybersecurity-for-engineers-and-manufacturers

World Economic Forum. (2024). *Unpacking cyber resilience.* https://www.weforum.org/publications/unpacking-cyber-resilience/

Zach, C. (2025). *80% of ransomware attacks now use artificial intelligence.* https://mitsloan.mit.edu/ideas-made-to-matter/80-ransomware-attacks-now-use-artificial-intelligence

Chapter 8
Healthcare Cybersecurity: Third-Party Vendor Risks

Oladele Stephen Olawoye
http://orcid.org/0009-0003-1117-1374
Capitol Technology University, USA

Eugene J. Lewis
http://orcid.org/0000-0002-2956-0760
Capitol Technology University, USA

ABSTRACT

The partnerships between companies bring operational improvements and innovation but they create major cybersecurity threats. With the advent of technologies like Internet-of-Things (IoT) and Internet of Medical Things (IoMT), healthcare organizations need third-party vendors to access essential services which include cloud storage, electronic health records and embedded devices. Organizations move their operations to outside vendors lose their ability to control vendor security which makes them vulnerable to supply chain attacks and regulatory violations The combination of complex vendor networks with insufficient subcontractor operation monitoring creates security risks which threaten patient data privacy while causing financial damage and damaging organizational reputation. The evaluation examines Risk Management Theory which evaluates common attack vectors; Change Management Theory which examines regulatory challenges, and Risk Resilience Theory which examines ways to limit the attack surface on healthcare IT infrastructure.

INTRODUCTION

Healthcare organizations use various third-party vendors who operate electronic health record (HER) platforms, cloud services and billing solutions, Internet-of-

DOI: 10.4018/979-8-2600-1021-1.ch008

Things (IoT) and Internet of Medical Things (IoMT) devices. The third-party entities handle sensitive data containing personal health information (PHI) and personal identifiable information (PII) which makes them susceptible to cyber-attacks. The complex network structure of healthcare operations creates challenges for monitoring and controlling systems which increases the risk of security vulnerabilities that cyber attackers can use for exploitation. The 2024 data breach statistics reveal that third-party medical device connections resulted in 48% of all security incidents according to KELA Cyber Threat Intelligence (2025).

Healthcare facilities implement (IoMT) and Things (IoT) devices with embedded sensors and processors to track patients continuously through distant data transmission. These devices function through dedicated batteries containing lithium-ion cells which implement firmware programs from memory to support reliable operation of wearable heart monitors and hospital asset tracking systems (Keystride, 2024; Mark & Spark Solutions, 2024). The healthcare sector connects these devices through wireless communication systems which use Bluetooth for local connections and Wi-Fi for hospital network data transfers. The healthcare industry uses these components to achieve continuous data collection and remote patient tracking and predictive analytics which supports the development of personalized and proactive healthcare systems. The development of network-capable medical equipment such as ventilators, infusion pumps, pacemakers, dialysis machines, MRI scanners, and CT scanners enabled continuous patient monitoring and immediate medical care through ZigBee and ANT+ and OneM2M standards - ZigBee, ANT+, and OneM2M are all standards used in wireless communication, particularly in the context of the IoT and IoMT (Symmetry Electronics, 2023).

The healthcare industry depends on third-party vendors to achieve better clinical results and improved patient care, but these vendors introduce significant cybersecurity risks. The protection of patient information together with healthcare organization-client trust has emerged as the primary security concern. Research indicates that cybercriminals use third-party vendor supply chain attacks to execute their cyberattacks. The insertion of harmful code into software or hardware at any point during product development or distribution enables cybercriminals to penetrate hospital network systems (Basu et al., 2019; Sun et al., 2018). The trust vendors receive from their business partners enables attackers to spread malicious content which evades endpoint protection systems and reveals sensitive information (Radware, 2022).

High-profile breaches show the major security threats that healthcare organizations face at present. The CaptureRx ransomware attack exposed personal information of 1.2 million patients who received care at hundreds of hospitals. The MedNetworx system encountered an autonomous security breach which compromised their medical software and electronic health record (EHR) platform, EHR is a digital versions of a patient's medical history, stored and accessed electronically) (Kolbasuk, 2022). The combination of insufficient risk assessments with old facilities and weak vendor monitoring systems creates security weaknesses in healthcare facilities according to these reported incidents. The connected nature of IoT-enabled medical devices introduces new security risks because it expands the attack surface and makes security protection more difficult (Craig & Corey, 2021). In addition, since the advent of Large Model Language Which Artificial Intelligence is built on, new entrant of challenges has plagued the healthcare environment. Ransomware-as-a-Service (RaaS) and Malware-as-a-service (MaaS) attacks which operate as a business model where cybercriminals sell malicious software access and supporting infrastructure to customers are now prevalent in most of the new attacks (Kaspersky, n.d).

The research used non-human qualitative methods to integrate findings from previous studies. It will examine Risk Management Theory regarding attack vectors involving healthcare third parties; Change Management Theory will examine regulatory challenges in these relationships; and Cybersecurity Resilience Theory by identifying technical and non-technical measures to strengthen connections between healthcare organizations and vendors relative to hardening of attack surface.

DEFINITION OF KEY TERMS

Attack Surfaces: The complete set of system weaknesses which attackers can use to launch successful attacks (Kaspersky, n.d).

Change Management Theory: The method provides organizations with a systematic way to execute changes while handling employee reactions during the process (Kaspersky, n.d).

Cybersecurity Resilience: Organizations that prepare for cyber incidents and respond effectively will achieve minimal damage during recovery operations (Kaspersky, n.d).

Continuous Monitoring Frameworks: Organizations use these frameworks to maintain continuous security oversight which enables them to identify and handle security incidents quickly (Kaspersky, n.d).

Electronic Health Records (EHRs): A digital versions of a patient's medical history, stored and accessed electronically.

Deep Packet Inspection (DPI): A technique that analyzes packet contents to identify specific protocols and enhance security (Kaspersky, n.d).

Intrusion Detection Systems (IDS): A system that monitors malicious activities and alerts threats but does not take action (Kaspersky, n.d).

Intrusion Prevention Systems (IPS): A proactive system that blocks and prevents detected threats in real-time (Kaspersky, n.d).

Passkeys: The authentication system known as passkeys operates through cryptographic keys which function as a replacement for conventional password authentication (Kaspersky, n.d).

Third-party Vendor Risks: External vendors create operational risks for businesses through their security and compliance vulnerabilities (Kaspersky, n.d).

Ransomware-as-a-Service (RaaS): Cybercriminals operate a business model which lets others use their ransomware tools to execute attacks (Kaspersky, n.d).

Risk Management Theory: The framework helps organizations detect their most critical risks before they occur while using resources to reduce their impact (Kaspersky, n.d).

Supply Chain Attacks: Cyber attackers use supply chain weaknesses to launch attacks which result in system compromises through indirect means (Kaspersky, n.d).

Zero-trust Architectures: The security model demands authentication for all access requests because it treats all users and devices as potential security threats (Kaspersky, n.d).

Zero-trust Frameworks: The frameworks establish step-by-step guidelines to deploy zero-trust security through identity authentication and restricted access permissions (Kaspersky, n.d).

Zero-Day exploit: This term is used to describe exploit code that has been written to take advantage of a vulnerability before the software vendor knows about it and has had the chance to publish a patch for it (Kaspersky, n.d).

Vendor Risk Management: Organizations use this process to evaluate and manage security and compliance threats from their third-party vendors (Kaspersky, n.d).

Vendor Risk Assessments: Organizations conduct these evaluations to determine the security and compliance risks that third-party vendors present to their operations (Kaspersky, n.d).

PROBLEM STATEMENT

Healthcare organizations experience rising cyber threats because their third-party vendor connections establish security weaknesses. Attackers launch supply chain attacks against healthcare organizations by embedding dangerous software or hardware through external vendors into hospital network systems. The security threats evade endpoint protection systems because organizations trust their vendors to such an extent (Radware, 2022; Sun et al., 2018). Healthcare organizations face security threats when third-party vendors experience system breaches because their systems reveal multiple healthcare organizations to potential security risks. The security vulnerabilities of third-party vendors create multiple threats to healthcare organizations which were demonstrated by the CaptureRx ransomware attack and the MedNetworx breach of hosted electronic health record systems (Kolbasuk, 2022).

The incidents demonstrate major weaknesses in vendor risk assessments and outdated infrastructure and untrained staff which create expanded opportunities for cybercriminals to attack (Craig & Corey, 2021). Healthcare organizations fail to properly enforce vendor oversight and verify software and hardware authenticity even though the NIST Cybersecurity Framework exists (NIST, 2020; Basu et al., 2019). Pondurance (2025) recommends healthcare organizations to add cybersecurity requirements to their contracts and perform vendor risk management through criticality-based vendor prioritization and continuous performance monitoring to defend against third-party service risks.

SIGNIFICANCE OF THE STUDY

The research investigates Risk Management Theory to understand third-party healthcare attack vectors and Change Management Theory will examine regulatory challenges in these relationships and Cybersecurity Resilience Theory to determine technical and non-technical methods for enhancing healthcare organization-vendor connections. The research adds to academic understanding about how supply chain attacks and insufficient vendor oversight and insufficient compliance practices create essential security vulnerabilities. Research indicates malware creates major threats to healthcare systems yet there is limited study on how third-party vendors elevate these risks through their platform links and outdated technology and non-standard security protocols (Craig & Corey, 2021; Radware, 2022).

The research proves that governments require standardized policies which target third-party vendor risk management through regulatory frameworks. The current legal framework includes HIPAA and GDPR, but these regulations fail to establish clear requirements for vendor responsibility and supply chain security protocols. The research also explores most regulations face the challenges of standardization of privacy and security laws of local and international laws or regulations. The research demonstrates that healthcare organizations experience multiple security incidents because their vendor risk evaluations omit essential elements and their agreements fail to enforce adequate cybersecurity standards (Basu et al., 2019; NIST, 2020). The research exposes these vulnerabilities to help policymakers understand the need for updated data protection laws which must include vendor management and supply chain security requirements.

The research provides operational recommendations for healthcare administrators and IT security experts and medical staff. The inadequate vendor controls at CaptureRx and MedNetworx resulted in massive patient data exposure and operational disruptions of clinical services (Kolbasuk, 2022). The prevention of these risks requires organizations to use preventive measures including vendor network monitoring and zero-trust security frameworks and software and hardware component verification through multi-factor authentication. The protection of patient data and operational continuity and institutional trust in healthcare systems depends on effective vendor oversight.

METHODOLOGY

The research employed a qualitative multiple-case study design to investigate third-party vendor cybersecurity threats which affect healthcare organizations. The research used non-human qualitative methods to integrate findings from previous studies. It will examine Risk Management Theory regarding attack vectors involving healthcare third parties. Change Management Theory examines regulatory challenges in these relationships. Cybersecurity Resilience Theory will identify technical and non-technical measures to strengthen connections between healthcare organizations and vendors in relation to hardening of attack surface.

The research required a qualitative method because vendor systems present socio-technical complexity which includes regulatory elements and technological aspects and organizational factors that quantitative methods cannot fully capture. The case study method analyzed particular security incidents to show how vendor vulnerabilities caused major breaches which researchers used to identify recurring risk patterns.

For data sources, the research used secondary data as its primary source of information. The research used HIPAA and GDPR and NIST guidelines and Verizon Data Breach Investigations Report and CISA advisories and academic studies about supply chain attacks. The study analyzed third-party vendor breaches on healthcare organizations in the U.S through simulated attacks and actual security incidents which affected CaptureRx and MedNetworx systems. The research used different vendor-related risks to study ransomware transmission through service providers and hardware supply chain attacks and electronic health record hosting service vulnerabilities. The cases demonstrate how healthcare system third-party vulnerabilities create major patient data exposure and operational failures.

The case study investigates Risk Management Theory through an analysis of third-party healthcare attack paths. The research examines the CaptureRx ransomware attack. The 2021 CaptureRx ransomware attack revealed more than 1.2 million patient records and medical information from over 100 healthcare organizations to unauthorized entities (Kolbasuk, 2022). The system breakdown occurred because pharmacy benefit management services were outsourced to a third-party company which demonstrated the dangers of outsourcing essential business operations.

The second case research Change Management Theory through the MedNetworx breach, analyzing regulatory problems as an example. The security weaknesses in EHR systems used by small and medium healthcare facilities became apparent when their intrusion detection systems failed to function properly and patient information became accessible to unauthorized users. The attackers successfully interrupted operational activities which resulted in delayed patient care while service contracts failed to specify security protocols (Kolbasuk, 2022). As evident in the incident, proper change management proposes proper oversight on IT infrastructure in term of timely patches and security updates.

The Change Healthcare cyberattack serves as an example which Kapko (2024) documented during 2024. The author explained that Change Healthcare faced remote access portal attacks through Citrix because it did not implement multi-factor authentication. The attackers gained access to sensitive financial information and medical records which resulted in the exposure of more than 100 million U.S. citizen records. The complete shutdown of claims processing operations led to delayed payments for multiple hospitals and pharmacies. The incident demonstrated that poor vendor authentication systems combined with insufficient endpoint security protocols (Kapko, 2024).

The third case study is on Cybersecurity Resilience Theory which examines technical and non-technical strategies to improve collaboration between healthcare organizations and vendors, in relation to hardening of attack surface. The 2015 Anthem Inc. data breach exposed 78.8 million patient records due to vulnerabilities in a vendor's database and poor risk management. This led to a $16 million HIPAA settlement, the largest at that time, highlighting how weak vendor compliance can result in severe financial and reputational damage. The case demonstrated the need for third-party vendors to harden their security layer through measures like deployment of cryptographic and encryption, VPN, and Two-factor authentication (2FA).

The cases show that third-party vendors help improve healthcare operations, yet they introduce security risks to medical organizations.

THEORIES FROM THE LITERATURE

Healthcare organizations need to follow a systematic method to assess third-party vendor security risks in their cybersecurity operations. The evaluation of third-party vendor risks in healthcare cybersecurity uses three separate frameworks which include Risk Management Theory and Change Management Theory and Cybersecurity Resilience Theory. Multiple frameworks exist to help organizations detect security weaknesses while creating protective measures that enhance their healthcare cybersecurity position.

The healthcare sector faces multiple third-party attack paths which include supply chain threats and access management problems, device security weaknesses and social engineering attacks and non-compliance issues. It also faces compliance challenges from unaligned local and international regulations and laws that guide healthcare and third-party vendors. Healthcare organizations need to perform complete vendor assessment procedures and maintain ongoing surveillance and implement secure access systems and create specific plans for handling incidents to achieve effective risk management.

Risk Management Theory

Risk Management Theory identifies the security threats which third-party vendors in healthcare create through their attack paths. Healthcare organizations use third-party services for EHRs and cloud storage and medical device integration of IoT and IoMT which improves operational efficiency yet creates multiple entry points for cyber threats. The framework evaluates vendor risks through the CaptureRx ransomware attack which demonstrates how inadequate vendor oversight creates security weaknesses. Organizations can develop better risk management strategies through incident analysis of these types of attacks. Third-party vendors in healthcare create security risks through supply chain attacks, weak authentication systems, and zero-day exploit vulnerabilities (Radware, 2022).

Risk Management Theory investigates the following questions about authentication methods: What level of protection do multi-factor authentication and biometrics, and zero-trust frameworks provide for IoMT devices in healthcare and how do new AI-based cyber threats require healthcare organizations to develop improved security measures?

Supply Chain Attacks

Cyber attackers use supply chain weaknesses to launch attacks which result in system compromises through indirect means (Kaspersky, n.d). Research shows that supply chain attacks represent a prevalent hacking method which targets vulnerabilities in third-party suppliers (Radware, 2022). Attackers use external vendor exploitation to spread malicious content while evading standard security protocols.

The software supply chain faces attacks through development and distribution phases (Sun et al., 2018) while hardware supply chain attacks occur when manufacturers insert malicious components (Basu et al., 2019). Research findings show third-party vendor breaches in healthcare organizations result in massive data breaches that affect millions of people. The ransomware attack on CaptureRx exposed 1.2 million patient records to unauthorized access (Kolbasuk, 2022). Healthcare organizations face these security risks because they lack proper risk evaluation and use outdated systems and insufficient cybersecurity training for their medical device networks.

Healthcare organizations need to perform complete vendor risk evaluations and follow secure software development standards (NIST, 2020) and train their staff members of staff about cybersecurity practices (Craig & Corey, 2021).

The Target.com data breach serves as an example of third-party vendor risks because it started with a vendor attack which led to an $18.5 million settlement and exposed 70 million customer records (Corrin, 2021). The incident demonstrates that healthcare organizations must establish strong vendor management systems and authentication protocols.

Weak Credential

Emphatical findings show that security systems face ongoing difficulties because of weak password vulnerabilities (Shacklett, 2021). The security of organizational assets becomes at risk when unauthorized access occurs because of weak authentication methods that hackers can easily discover or break (Verizon, 2020). The solution to this problem requires knowledge about the methods hackers use to exploit system weaknesses. The hacking technique of brute force attack functions through a trial-and-error process to break passwords and login credentials and encryption keys (Fortinet, 2022). The basic method of brute force attacks allows hackers to access both personal accounts and business networks through successful password guessing attempts (Fortinet, 2022). The technique focuses on systems with poor password security which operate both through the internet and offline networks thus requiring strong authentication systems (WIZ, 2025).

The Fortinet (2022) research demonstrates that attackers perform brute force attacks on IT systems through AirCrack-ng and John the Ripper tool exploitation of system vulnerabilities. Users continue to use weak passwords multiple times which makes their accounts vulnerable to dictionary attacks that use popular words and personal information (Shacklett, 2021). The combination of brute force and dictionary attack methods in hybrid attacks makes systems more exposed to security threats. The healthcare industry faces elevated security risks because its systems remain unpatched despite growing awareness about malware threats. The attackers use CrackStation and Password Cracker and Brutus tools to perform password guessing attacks which combine standard patterns with complete algorithmic methods (Fortinet, 2022).

The security weakness exposed Change Healthcare to a major data breach which demonstrated the actual consequences of such system vulnerabilities. The attackers gained access to Change Healthcare systems through an unsecured Citrix portal which did not require multi-factor authentication. The security incident exposed sensitive information from more than 100 million American citizens which demonstrates why organizations need to establish robust password protocols and enable multi-factor authentication to protect their systems (Kapko, 2024).

The healthcare sector faces major security risks because of zero-day exploit attacks which create complex challenges for cybersecurity defense systems.

Zero Day Exploit

This term is used to describe exploit code that has been written to take advantage of vulnerability before the software vendor knows about it and has had the chance to publish a patch for it (Kaspersky, n.d). The IT sector faces zero-day exploits as its primary security threat. The period from 2006 to 2016 saw attackers exploit 334 zero-day vulnerabilities with Microsoft accounting for 46% and Adobe responsible for 18% of these incidents (Cybersecurity Help, 2022). The healthcare sector continues to experience cybersecurity threats because "PwnedPiper" vulnerabilities in hospital pneumatic tube controls endanger both system stability and patient information protection (Torrence, 2021).

Healthcare technology requires enhanced security monitoring systems to protect against new security threats. The healthcare sector faces ongoing cybersecurity challenges because pneumatic transport systems remain vulnerable to attacks which could impact 80% of North American hospitals (Cybersecurity Help, 2022). The number of zero-day exploits continues to rise because researchers discover more than half of these vulnerabilities before vendors can create patches which require an average of 30 days for implementation (Chen et al., 2014). The Zero Day Initiative along with other initiatives serve as vulnerability detection programs which reward researchers for finding software and hardware flaws before malicious users can access them (Kaspersky, 2021). Against this backdrop, the vulnerability reward program at Google has paid more than $35.5 million to 2,640 bug hunters worldwide who received an average of $12,888 each while the largest reward reached $161,337 in December 2019. The Microsoft Security Response Centre paid $2.4 million to researchers through its program by July 2022 while awarding $13.6 million to 340 researchers from 58 countries including a $200,000 Hyper-V Bounty (Microsoft Security Response Centre, 2021).

The Stuxnet attack from 2010 serves as a well-known example of zero-day exploitation because it used four unidentified Windows vulnerabilities to attack Iran's nuclear facilities and destroy centrifuges while remaining undetectable. The incident which occurred in 2010 demonstrated how zero-day threats can endanger vital infrastructure systems worldwide (Mohn, 2023).

Change Management Theory

The theory examines how change management systems affect vendor accountability operations in healthcare organizations. A centralized system for tracking third-party change requests and approvals creates an essential audit trail which helps regulators and internal auditors verify proactive oversight (Olawoye, 2025). Healthcare organizations need to develop improved vendor management systems because cybersecurity regulations keep changing. A properly designed change management system improves accountability through its ability to educate all stakeholders about how new regulations affect their work activities. Organizations that follow strict documentation procedures establish an unambiguous record of vendor modifications which serve as evidence for regulatory compliance and internal auditor verification (ResilientX, n.d.). The process of managing changes through transparent methods leads vendors to fulfill their responsibilities better while increasing their level of accountability.

Third-party vendors need to receive consistent and open communication from organizations to develop accountability. Organizations can match vendor expectations with their own needs through ongoing dialogues about compliance requirements and regulatory changes (Gartner, n.d.). Vendors who receive proper information about established guidelines will follow these standards more effectively. The change management process requires organizations to create a structured plan for ending essential vendor partnerships. The exit strategy provides vendors with detailed instructions to end their partnership when they fail to fulfill regulatory standards or performance targets (RMA, 2025; Venminder, n.d.). The organization's readiness to terminate vendor relationships when necessary, serves two purposes: it protects business operations from disruptions, and it strengthens vendor accountability through performance-based partnership requirements.

Healthcare organizations can achieve better vendor accountability through effective change management which helps them handle regulatory issues and maintain secure practices. The principles of Change Management Theory demonstrate how regulatory challenges affect vendor accountability when they need to follow GDPR and HIPAA and other privacy and security regulations that protect Protected Health Information (PHI) and Personally Identifiable Information (PII).

Change management models ask this question: How do change management models such as executive leadership involvement, the change request and approval process, and strong encryption affect visibility, control, and cybersecurity of network hardware and software in healthcare organizations?

General Data Protection Regulation (GDPR)

The General Data Protection Regulation (GDPR) operates as a legally binding European Union law which entered effect on May 25, 2018 to demonstrate its worldwide importance. The GDPR enables people to manage their personal information better while creating a unified system for international businesses to follow including their third-party healthcare service providers. The GDPR extends its jurisdiction to all EU nations and all organizations which handle EU resident personal information regardless of their location.

The GDPR defines personal data as any information which enables the identification of a specific person or allows someone to identify them through additional details such as names and email addresses and IP addresses. The GDPR establishes seven core principles which organizations must follow when handling personal data. The seven fundamental principles of the GDPR have drawn criticism because they could create difficulties that make it harder for third-party vendors to maintain accountability (Wolford, 2024).

Moreover, research shows that fifteen states, among them California, Virginia, Connecticut, Colorado and Utah have enacted data-privacy statutes. Those state laws generally cover a mix of organizations. They specifically target third-party health-care vendors that handle sensitive medical information. The regulations add layers of accountability obliging vendors to prove they're compliant, in the ways they collect, use and disclose data. Consumers now hold rights, over their data a fact that sharply underscores the need, for health-care vendors to uphold data-protection practices (Bloomberg Law, 2024; Wolford, 2024).After the strides the GDPR framework has covered, there is still notable gaps among these laws which shows uneven way its guiding principles are enforced across local and international jurisdictions, which produces protections that range from robust, to flimsy. Equally unsettling is the lack of a set of standards among both international and domestic statutes that govern the privacy and security of PHI and PII.

Health Insurance Portability and Accountability Act of 1996 (HIPAA)

HIPAA protects sensitive information, but its protection extends only to specific areas. The regulations apply to three types of entities which include health plans, healthcare clearinghouses and healthcare providers who perform specific electronic transactions. The different ways local authorities interpret HIPAA regulations create inconsistent protective measures that resemble GDPR's inconsistencies (Alder, 2025; Wolford, 2024). The privacy standard established by HIPAA does not provide enough detail about breach notification procedures and encryption methods and data deletion rights which GDPR includes as essential features. Organizations would achieve better malware threat resistance through a unified framework that merges HIPAA rules with GDPR principles (Alder, 2025; Wolford, 2024).

In furtherance, Cybersecurity Resilience Theory framework helps healthcare organizations develop vendor connection strength through both technological and non-technological security measures.

Cybersecurity Resilience Theory

Cybersecurity Resilience Theory maps out both non-technical levers for tightening the relationship, between health-care organizations and their vendors in relations to hardening attack surface of healthcare IT infrastructure. It probes the capacity of health-care systems to resist cyber-attacks recognizing that total breach avoidance is a pipe-dream (Linkov et al., 2019). In response organizations are urged to spin up systems that cut across vendor networks to install fast-acting alert mechanisms and to codify recovery procedures that keep care flowing when disruptions strike.

Healthcare organizations should use three main technical security measures which include better encryption methods, strong access management systems and scheduled security vulnerability assessments. Organizations should train their staff in cybersecurity best practices while maintaining open communication with vendors to establish a shared commitment for cybersecurity protection. Healthcare organizations that implement a complete system which combines technical and non-technical elements will achieve better cyber defense capabilities and vendor security compliance (Alder, 2025; Wolford, 2024).

In healthcare, where sensitive patient data is both highly valuable and vulnerable, robust technical solutions are imperative to mitigate such risks. Implementing advanced tools like firewalls, encryption, and intrusion detection systems ensures comprehensive protection of critical information systems, aligning with the stringent requirements of modern cybersecurity frameworks. To identify technical and non-technical measures to strengthen connections between healthcare organizations and vendors there should be technical solutions that include deployment of data encryption, antivirus software, Virtual Private Networks (VPNs), Secure Sockets Layer/Transport Layer Security (SSL/TLS), Two-factor authentication (2FA), Endpoint detection and response (EDR), and Security Information and Event Management (SIEM) (NIST, n.d.; Verizon, 2020).

The Cybersecurity Resilience Theory asks this question: How can healthcare organizations integrate AI-driven technologies and effective third-party risk management practices, while also leveraging leadership involvement and continuous staff training, to anticipate, mitigate, and recover from advanced cybersecurity threats and supply chain-related breaches?

Non-Technical Solutions

The training of all staff members represents a non-technical measure for cybersecurity defense. Staff members can practice offensive and defensive strategies through red-team versus blue-team simulated attack exercises that take place in a controlled environment. The combination of incident response drills and playbook simulations enables personnel to develop expertise in executing correct responses during cybersecurity incidents (Ponemon Institute, 2019; Verizon, 2020).

The Importance of Staff Training in Cybersecurity

Healthcare sectors need to ensure that all staff members need to undergo training as an essential non-technical method to defend against cyber threats. Enforcement with incentives or penalty normally works. Technological security measures remain crucial but human conduct frequently turns out to be the most vulnerable point. The training program teaches staff members to detect security threats and execute proper responses (Ponemon Institute, 2019; Verizon, 2020).

Red-Team vs. Blue-Team Simulations

The training method of red-team versus blue-team simulations delivers exceptional results. The red team functions as attackers who attempt to penetrate security systems while the blue team defends against these attacks. The simulated environment enables blue team members to develop incident response abilities through real-world scenarios. The combination of simulation training with incident response drills and playbook exercises creates an optimal training program. The security playbooks contain incident response procedures which employees learn through simulated role-playing activities to build their confidence in executing these procedures. The organization should perform scheduled security drills against different types of attacks to detect vulnerabilities and improve their response capabilities (NIST, n.d; Ponemon Institute, 2019; Verizon, 2020).

Security Awareness

The organization needs to develop security awareness throughout all its staff members. The organization should promote open cybersecurity communication because staff members who report suspicious activities without facing consequences will create a safer workplace. The organization should conduct educational sessions about social engineering and phishing defense and data protection to help staff members understand their security responsibilities (NIST, n.d.; Verizon, 2020).

The Role of Leadership in Cybersecurity

Leadership teams must take charge of developing security awareness throughout their organizations. Leaders who demonstrate cybersecurity best practices through their actions create an organizational standard that all staff members must follow. The organization should implement three essential security-focused initiatives which include developing clear policies and offering ongoing training resources and providing recognition to staff members who show security vigilance (Ponemon Institute, 2019; Verizon, 2020).

Technical Solutions

Network protection requires the implementation of firewalls and antivirus software and encryption as fundamental technical solutions. The security system includes virtual private networks (VPNs) and Secure Sockets Layer/Transport Layer Security (SSL/TLS) and two-factor authentication (2FA) and behavioral analysis and machine learning-based security and endpoint detection and response (EDR) and security information and event management (SIEM) (NIST, n.d.; Verizon, 2020).

Antivirus Software and Firewalls

Firewalls operate as traffic controllers for network entry and exit points while antivirus software identifies and eliminates malicious software. The protection of sensitive information depends on encryption while intrusion detection systems notify administrators about security threats. The combination of technical security measures establishes an effective defense system which safeguards essential information systems (CISOMAG, 2020; Ponemon Institute, 2019; Verizon, 2020).

Next-generation antivirus (NGAV). The cybersecurity field has received a major upgrade through the development of Next-generation antivirus (NGAV) which enhances the capabilities of conventional antivirus software. The system protects users from Ransomware-as-a-Service (RaaS) and Malware-as-a-service (MaaS) attacks which operate as a business model where cybercriminals sell malicious software access and supporting infrastructure to customers (Kaspersky, n.d). The system updates its database daily through public vulnerability information which traditional antivirus systems do not have. The system uses threat intelligence and behavior analysis to detect and stop zero-day threats. The system includes real-time threat feeds and malware similarity analysis and machine learning file evaluation and behavior monitoring capabilities which provide effective protection against contemporary cyber threats. In addition, NGFWs extend capabilities by incorporating advanced features such as deep packet inspection (DPI), intrusion detection systems (IDS), and intrusion prevention systems (IPS) (Cynet, 2022; Forrest et al., n.d.; Kaspersky, n.d).

The system protects against zero-day vulnerabilities through its analysis of dangerous files and its ability to stop malicious data transmissions which minimizes ransomware attack risks (Cynet, 2022). The system provides network segmentation and encrypted traffic inspection capabilities which enhance network visibility and control to enable faster breach response times.

Windows Defender Exploit Guard (WDEG). The security system of Windows Defender Exploit Guard (WDEG) protects against dangerous content by reducing network vulnerabilities and enabling fast incident response. The system tracks all network traffic to detect security threats and blocks unauthorized file modifications. The system now detects and fights advanced AI-based threats including AI-generated Ransomware-as-a-Service (RaaS) and Malware-as-a-Service (MaaS) which evade standard network security measures (Cynet, 2022; Forrest et al., n.d.; Kaspersky, n.d.).

Data Encryption

Research evidence shows that encryption technology makes unauthorized users unable to access unprotected Protected Health Information (PHI) or Personally Identifiable Information (PII) (HHS, n.d.). The HIPAA security rules require electronic PHI to receive encryption protection while keeping encryption and decryption keys in separate storage locations from the main data. The Department of Health and Human Services (HHS) follows National Institute of Standards and Technology (NIST) security standards which are detailed in NIST Special Publication 800-series (NIST, n.d.). Special Publication 800-53 provides healthcare organizations with security and privacy controls for their information systems and operations (Hyperproof, 2025).

Survey results show that 62% of organizations discovered their existing security weaknesses only after their systems experienced breaches. The healthcare sector faces an essential challenge to stop malware attacks because of its insufficient capabilities. Healthcare organizations need to implement proactive security measures which include encryption and software updates and antivirus protection and vulnerability scanning and advanced threat detection systems and employee-specific training programs. Healthcare organizations that close their security gaps will achieve better protection against malware attacks which helps them prevent data breaches that endanger patient safety and operational stability (Ponemon Institute, 2019).

Research conducted earlier showed healthcare facilities face rising cyberattack risks because patient information holds value and operations need to run continuously. The 2017 WannaCry ransomware attack on healthcare systems worldwide demonstrates why organizations need to implement mitigation strategies and best practices because it affected the United Kingdom's National Health Service (NHS) and other global healthcare systems (CISOMAG, 2020).

The ransomware attack used unsecured software flaws to gain access to systems which then encrypted essential data while asking for payment in exchange for decryption keys. The attack triggered major system disruptions which forced hospitals to postpone surgeries and delayed medical care and redirected emergency patients thus threatening patient security (CISOMAG, 2020).

Virtual Private Networks (VPNs)

Virtual Private Networks (VPNs) function as vital security measures which protect user privacy during online activities. The system encrypts internet data before it travels through protected servers which defend confidential information from potential interception (CISOMAG, 2020). Healthcare organizations implement VPNs to defend protected health information (PHI) while fulfilling their regulatory obligations (Kaspersky, n.d).

Secure Sockets Layer/Transport Layer Security (SSL/TLS)

The Secure Sockets Layer/Transport Layer Security (SSL/TLS) protocols enable secure encrypted data transfer while protecting network data from unauthorized access. Healthcare organizations depend on these protocols to protect patient data privacy while following regulatory requirements (Sullivan, 2022).

Two-factor authentication (2FA)

Two-factor authentication (2FA) functions as a vital security system which protects online accounts through dual verification requirements before allowing system access. The security method protects systems from unauthorized access because it operates in environments that handle confidential data (CISOMAG, 2020).

Passkeys

The authentication system known as passkeys operates through cryptographic keys which function as a replacement for conventional password authentication. The authentication system uses a public key which servers store while users maintain their private keys within their devices. The system provides better security because it eliminates password requirements and protects users from phishing attacks since their private keys remain confined to their devices. Passkeys enable users to access different platforms through a secure and effortless authentication process (Kaspersky, n.d).

Endpoint detection and response (EDR)

EDR systems function as essential cybersecurity tools because they deliver complete monitoring of all endpoint system operations. The tools help organizations detect threats in real-time while enabling them to analyze and respond to incidents which healthcare organizations need for their sensitive information management (Klinghofer, 2022).

Security Information and Event Management (SIEM)

Security Information and Event Management (SIEM) systems monitor security data in real-time through their ability to collect logs from all digital infrastructure devices and applications and networks. The system provides complete security management through its ability to collect logs from servers and firewalls and endpoints. The system uses advanced algorithms to link different data points for threat detection while its continuous monitoring system detects unusual system behavior. SIEM systems provide fast incident response through alert-based insights and automated compliance monitoring which streamlines regulatory compliance. The healthcare sector depends on SIEM to achieve better data protection through its ability to detect system weaknesses and defend against new cyber threats (CISOMAG, 2020; Kaspersky, n.d.).

RESEARCH DESIGN

The research used qualitative multiple-case study methods to analyze how third-party vendors create security threats for healthcare organizations. The research used non-human qualitative methods to integrate findings from previous studies. Qualitative research design became necessary because vendor vulnerabilities emerge from social-technical elements which include regulatory systems and human conduct and organizational systems that quantitative methods cannot measure properly (Yin, 2018). The case research method allowed researchers to study multiple vendor-related security breaches which revealed common patterns that stem from supply chain attacks and vendor management difficulties and insufficient regulatory oversight (Kolbasuk, 2022).

The research framework combined three connected models which included Risk Management Theory for third-party healthcare attack paths and Change Management Theory for regulatory complexities in partnerships and Cybersecurity Resilience Theory for identifying technical and non-technical methods to improve vendor-organization relationships.

The research analyzed four cases to demonstrate third-party vendor security risks through the CaptureRx ransomware attack, the MedNetworx hosted EHR data breach, the Change Healthcare cyberattack, and the Anthem Inc. data breach. The cases demonstrated how different vendor security weaknesses create cybersecurity threats which result in financial damage and compromise organizational integrity (Kapko, 2024; Kolbasuk, 2022).

The research used secondary data from peer-reviewed journals and government reports which included NIST and HIPAA enforcement actions and industry analyses from Verizon and Ponemon Data Breach Report and forensic breach incident summaries. The study achieved higher validity through source triangulation which combined different information types from NIST and CISA and technical assessments and regulatory frameworks and organizational governance body evaluations.

The analysis of data revealed that vendor risk assessments conducted by Gupta et al. (2024) exposed major security problems which included authentication weaknesses and difficulties in vendor oversight and non-compliance with regulatory standards. The research established that risk reduction depends on continuous surveillance and binding contractual terms. The research used thematic analysis to organize different risks while applying triangulation and iterative coding methods to boost credibility and demonstrate the intricate nature of vendor-related problems.

The research design achieved both extensive case study analysis and strong theoretical foundation through its combination of multiple case studies which produced detailed findings about third-party vendor risks to healthcare cybersecurity and patient safety and organizational resilience.

CASE SELECTION

Healthcare organizations need to implement vendor risk management strategies which protect technical systems while following regulations and building resilience capabilities. The analysis of major vendor security incidents uses Risk Management Theory to evaluate attack vectors followed by Change Management Theory to handle regulatory issues and Cybersecurity Resilience Theory to implement protective measures. The combined framework enables healthcare staff and researchers to create an extensive system for protecting confidential patient data while preserving system stability.

Risk Management Theory - Case Analysis of Attack Vectors

Risk Management Theory explains how healthcare systems become vulnerable to attacks because third-party vendors bring vulnerable entry points into their systems.

The 2021 CaptureRx ransomware attack demonstrated how attackers used supply chain weaknesses together with poor password security and unsecured system vulnerabilities to gain access to healthcare data. The pharmacy benefit management vendor's inadequate system infrastructure allowed hackers to steal more than 1.2 million patient records from over 100 healthcare facilities (Bracken, 2023; Kolbasuk, 2022). The security breach demonstrates that healthcare organizations need to implement strict vendor monitoring and maintain strict system update protocols to prevent major system failures. The 2024 Change Healthcare portal breach occurred because Citrix system lacked multi-factor authentication which exposed 100 million patient records and caused medical claims processing disruptions across the entire country (Kapko, 2024). The two incidents demonstrate that ongoing vendor system weaknesses create security threats which spread across healthcare networks that depend on interconnected systems thus requiring ongoing risk evaluations and strict monitoring systems.

Change Management Theory: Case Analysis of Regulatory Challenges

The regulatory compliance problems that vendor partnerships create can be understood through the framework of Change Management Theory. The MedNetworx EHR breach showed how vendor-run electronic health record systems create protected medical information risks because of weak monitoring systems and inadequate contractual security requirements (Kolbasuk, 2022). The 2015 Anthem Inc. data breach demonstrated how weak vendor monitoring and non-compliance with regulations result in major security incidents. The Office for Civil Rights (OCR) found that Anthem's insufficient vendor evaluation process resulted in 78.8 million patient data exposure which led to a $16 million HIPAA settlement that became the largest ever recorded. The incidents prove that vendor management systems need to adopt new regulatory standards through strict contract enforcement and active monitoring to prevent financial losses and damage to reputation.

Cybersecurity Resilience Theory: Analysis of Technical and Non-Technical Protective Methodologies

The Cybersecurity Resilience Theory supports a complete system which unites technological security measures with business operations to defend healthcare organizations from vendor-based threats. The Change Healthcare portal breach demonstrates why healthcare organizations need to implement strong authentication systems and sophisticated monitoring systems (Kapko, 2024). Healthcare organizations need to implement technical security measures including system monitoring and zero-trust models and regular system updates while implementing non-technical strategies for supply chain oversight and employee training programs. Organizations also need strong leadership support to make training and compliance effective and result oriented (Bracken, 2023).

Summary: Integrated Approach to Vendor Risk Management

The analyzed cases demonstrate that healthcare organizations need to implement vendor risk management through strategic combinations of risk management and regulatory compliance and resilience frameworks. Organizations need to monitor their systems continuously while following all regulatory requirements and implementing both sophisticated technical defenses and organizational security protocols. The complete security system protects patient data while ensuring business operations continue and develops enduring defense capabilities against evolving cyber threats (Bracken, 2023; Kolbasuk, 2022; Kapko, 2024; Cybersierra, 2025).

Ethical Assurances

The research team obtained IRB approval for analyzing secondary data because the study did not involve human participants to maintain ethical standards. The research used publicly accessible non-personal data while adhering to all data usage guidelines through proper source documentation and ethical practices (Bhandari, 2024).

RESULTS, RECOMMENDATIONS, CONCLUSIONS, AND SOLUTIONS

Results

The research demonstrates that vendor-related breaches occur through supply chain weaknesses and research demonstrates that third-party vendors create major security threats which endanger healthcare organizations through their ability to compromise both insufficient authentication methods and weak oversight and non-compliance with regulations. The Risk Management Theory shows that system vulnerabilities in vendor systems combined with inadequate monitoring practices lead to security incidents such as the 2021 CaptureRx ransomware attack. The pharmacy benefit management vendor system vulnerability allowed attackers to access more than 1.2 million patient records from over 100 healthcare facilities. The breach occurred because the vendor failed to maintain proper patch updates and lacked ongoing monitoring of their systems (Kolbasuk, 2022).

The MedNetworx EHR breach demonstrates that vendor-operated electronic health record systems create substantial security risks which threaten to expose protected medical information. The attackers successfully infiltrated the vendor's systems which resulted in system breakdowns and unauthorized disclosure of sensitive information. The incident exposed that the organization operated without proper monitoring systems and failed to enforce essential cybersecurity standards through their contractual agreements (Kolbasuk, 2022).

The 2024 Change Healthcare portal breach demonstrates how insecure authentication systems combined with missing multi-factor authentication create security risks which Risk Management Theory identifies as attack vectors. The breach exposed more than 100 million patient records while disrupting claims processing operations throughout the national healthcare system (Kapko, 2024).

The 2015 Anthem Inc. breach demonstrated regulatory difficulties which Change Management Theory explains. The breach of 78.8 million patient records occurred because Anthem failed to properly assess its vendors and did not follow necessary regulatory standards. The Office for Civil Rights (OCR) imposed a $16 million settlement on Anthem because their security failures led to the biggest HIPAA breach which became the largest at that time.

The vendor-related security breaches in these cases show that both technical and organizational systems have fundamental weaknesses which lead to these incidents. The research shows healthcare organizations stay exposed because their contracts fail to include strong security measures, and they lack proper authentication systems and weak oversight systems and inconsistent regulatory enforcement and alignment. The research supports Cybersecurity Resilience Theory by demonstrating that healthcare organizations need to implement protective measures which unite technological defenses with organizational strategies for supply chain responsibility and employee training.

The research demonstrates that healthcare organizations need to implement vendor risk management through continuous monitoring and strict regulatory adherence and advanced technical and non-technical security measures and organizational policies that promote resilience. Healthcare organizations that implement this integrated security frameworks will achieve better protection of patient information while sustaining operational stability and developing sustainable defenses against future cyber-attacks.

Recommendations

Taking the study's results into account a handful of concrete suggestions surface that could reduce cyber-security threats posed by third-party vendors, in the health-care sector.

On-Boarding

For instance, before onboarding any third-party vendor healthcare organizations must carry out a risk assessment. Keep repeating that evaluation for the entire term of the contract. A risk-driven review should scrutinize authentication mechanisms while also examining incident-response capabilities and data-management practices. Studies have shown that insufficient due-diligence, in healthcare settings creates security gaps that adversaries exploit to launch supply-chain attacks (Basu et al., 2019; NIST, 2020).

Zero-Trust Model implementation

Healthcare organizations need to establish Zero-Trust Model implementation to minimize their malware attack frequency. The network requires authentication and verification of all entities that want to connect before establishing any network relationship. Healthcare organizations now need to treat all devices and third-party connections as untrusted because perimeter defense no longer provides sufficient protection. Organizations that implement continuous authentication and identity checks and access policies will experience substantial reduction in vendor-related breach risks (Gupta et al. 2024).

Regulatory Enhancement

The healthcare sector can enhance its security through regulatory enhancement which involves strengthening existing rules and guidelines. All software and hardware assets seeking network connection must undergo formal approval through change management processes. The change management board needs to assess these assets before the cybersecurity assessment and authorization team conducts their evaluation for network access permission. This method helps organizations decrease their number of unmonitored and unauthorized assets (Olawoye, 2025). Organizations must include specific security protocols in their vendor agreements which demand immediate breach alerts and password verification systems and encrypted data protection and adherence to HIPAA and GDPR and NIST standards. The enforcement of regulations requires innovative methods to monitor vendor performance because recent security incidents like Anthem have revealed system weaknesses.

Continuous Monitoring and Threat Intelligence

Healthcare organizations need to monitor their systems continuously while sharing threat intelligence data to stay secure. Healthcare organizations should purchase Security Information and Event Management (SIEM) systems and anomaly detection tools to monitor vendor activities continuously while detecting new AI-based threats including RaaS and MaaS. Healthcare providers who share threat intelligence data with vendors will enhance their ability to detect security threats which leads to better protection against ransomware and phishing attacks that target supply chain operations (Kapko, 2024; Radware, 2022). The implementation of change management frameworks according to Olawoye (2025) enables organizations to execute new vendor oversight policies and security updates and regulatory requirements through systematic implementation and maintenance. Leaders must participate in the process to get stakeholder support for security as a fundamental company value which will decrease opposition and meet regulatory needs (Olawoye, 2025).

Training of Staff

Healthcare organizations need to provide cyber threat defense training to all staff members because performance-based rewards and penalties show effectiveness.Staff members learn to identify security threats and take appropriate actions through training programs according to the Ponemon Institute (2019) and Verizon (2020). The red-team versus blue-team simulation approach enables organizations to develop incident response competencies through realistic attack scenarios where the red team plays the role of attackers and the blue team defends against them. Organizations should create an effective training system through the combination of simulation training with response drills and playbook exercises.

Conclusions

The research findings show that third-party vendors create a significant ongoing security risk for healthcare cybersecurity infrastructure. Healthcare organizations that use outside providers for EHR hosting and pharmacy benefit management and revenue cycle processing and connected medical devices have established security vulnerabilities which exceed the capabilities of internal controls. The healthcare industry has experienced major data breaches through vendors CaptureRx and MedNetworx and Change Healthcare and Anthem because weak vendor oversight and authentication systems and insufficient regulatory enforcement lead to substantial data breaches and financial damage and treatment interruptions (Kapko, 2024; Kolbasuk, 2022;.

The research demonstrates that vendor risks exist as a network of interconnected problems which need unified solutions between technical and organizational and regulatory domains. Risk Management Theory demands organizations to identify and reduce vulnerabilities before attackers can exploit them (Olawoye, 2025). The Change Management Theory explains why healthcare organizations must establish vendor oversight and security practices as core organizational values to achieve lasting policy success (Olawoye, 2025). The Cybersecurity Resilience Theory indicates that certain breaches cannot be prevented so organizations should focus on vendor risk management through redundancy and attack surface hardening (Linkov et al. 2019).

Multiple strategies need to be implemented for vendor risk management through complete risk assessments and zero-trust network architecture and vendor contracts and continuous system monitoring and enhanced regulatory supervision. Healthcare organizations can protect their systems and maintain patient trust through these security practices which defend against complex supply chain attacks.

Solutions

Technical Safeguards and Advanced Security Systems

Healthcare organizations need to implement sophisticated technical security systems because third-party vendor threats continue to increase. The implementation of zero-trust architecture by healthcare organizations will protect their systems from vendor account breaches because it requires continuous user and device authentication (Gupta et al., 2024). Healthcare organizations need to protect vendor data through complete encryption during all communication exchanges while demanding vendors to use multi-factor authentication for security enhancement. The implementation of Security Information and Event Management (SIEM) systems with AI-powered anomaly detection tools allows healthcare organizations to track vendor activities in real-time for immediate identification of security threats (Amazon Web Services, 2025).

Vendor Governance and Organizational Oversight

Healthcare organizations need to establish strong governance systems for their vendor management operations. The establishment of vendor risk management committees under Chief Information Security Officers (CISOs) enables organizations to conduct complete vendor compliance evaluations and maintain continuous monitoring and scheduled audits. Security-by-design principles need to be included in vendor agreements which should require vendors to fix security vulnerabilities right away and to alert the organization about security incidents promptly.

Regulatory Alignment and Enforcement

The current healthcare frameworks including HIPAA and GDPR and local standards need unified policy development to establish specific security requirements for third-party vendor operations. Healthcare organizations need standardized vendor relationship regulations which must include PHI and PII protection protocols. The implementation of vendor accountability through regulatory oversight and standardized breach reporting and mandatory compliance certification will help solve ongoing security weaknesses. The government should establish severe financial penalties for organizations that fail to meet compliance standards while providing security funding to small businesses to enhance their defensive capabilities.

Collaborative Threat Intelligence Sharing

Healthcare organizations need to share threat intelligence actively because this practice strengthens their collective cybersecurity defenses. Organizations can develop shared defense systems through their strategic alliances with vendors and government agencies and cybersecurity companies. The collaborative work between organizations helps them detect and handle active supply chain attacks which leads to fast and unified security responses. The healthcare sector achieves better cybersecurity defense and develops stronger system-wide resistance through these strategic alliances (Radware, 2022).

Resilience Planning and Incident Response Preparedness

Healthcare organizations need to establish resilience as their core organizational value because security breaches will inevitably occur. Organizations should include backup system redundancy and secure data storage and proven disaster recovery protocols in their vendor agreements to maintain patient care operations during cyber-attacks. Organizations need to conduct simulation-based exercises including red-team/blue-team scenarios and tabletop drills with vendors to improve their breach readiness and speed up recovery operations (Linkov et al., 2019).

RECOMMENDATIONS FOR FUTURE RESEARCH

The research identifies multiple research domains which need additional study to improve healthcare cybersecurity defenses against third-party vendor threats. Future research should concentrate on using Large Language Model that generative and agentic AI is built on. Artificial Intelligence (AI) and Machine Learning (ML) systems to detect vendor-related risks before they become threats. The development of methods should focus on teaching AI and ML systems to identify third-party vendor system weaknesses before attackers can exploit them. The system uses predictive analytics to track vendor activities through ongoing security compliance assessments which help identify supply chain risks (Gupta et al., 2024; Amazon Web Services, 2025).

Healthcare organizations need to maintain their research focus on cybersecurity because they now use new technologies including generative and agentic AI systems. The cybersecurity environment faces ongoing faces multiple complex threats which include advanced persistent threats (APTs) and nation-state intrusions and Ransomware-as-a-Service and Malware-as-a-Service and autonomous AI-driven attacks from sophisticated cyber threats that emerge from new technological developments. Organizations solve their security problems through the implementation of agentic systems which operate independently while monitoring their environment and making decisions without human supervision (Rippling, 2025; Parker, 2023). Security solutions that operate based on predictable behaviors will lose their effectiveness when agents gain autonomy because compromised agents can perform actions that contradict human-established goals (SecurityInfoWatch, 2025).

Organizations need to create customized security protocols which address their specific protection needs because agentic AI systems provide users with substantial advantages (Parker, 2023; SecurityInfoWatch, 2025; Rippling, 2025).

Research needs to be conducted across multiple nations to determine how GDPR in the EU and APRA in the US affect third-party vendor accountability through international privacy regulations. The research would show how standardized security protocols for medical equipment and vendors improve their regulatory compliance in the U.S. and reveal present shortcomings in current U.S. standards (Smith, 2024).

Research should evaluate the effectiveness of current change management frameworks when used to enhance vendor oversight systems within healthcare facilities. The change management approach of Kotter's model which Olawoye (2025) describes guides the implementation and ongoing maintenance of vendor security policies across various healthcare facilities.

The research should concentrate on RaaS and MaaS attacks which target third-party vendors in healthcare supply chains because these attacks have become more common. The evaluation of its economic and operational structure enables researchers to develop defensive strategies and economic policies which will stop its expansion. Research must develop and validate open supply chain management systems which unite vendor certification programs with blockchain-based vendor auditing and collaborative threat intelligence sharing capabilities. (Forrest & Lindemulder, n.d.).

Third-party vendor dependence on healthcare creates major cybersecurity threats which organizations can handle through cyber insurance and risk assessment methods. Organizations can use cyber insurance to protect their financial assets during data breaches and cyber-attacks while they implement improved cybersecurity measures. The presence of insurance coverage makes vendors more attractive to their potential clients. Healthcare organizations can make better cybersecurity investment choices through risk quantification methods like the FAIR model which helps them evaluate cyber threat financial impacts. Healthcare organizations that implement these strategies will achieve improved security protection for their patients and business operations through their third-party relationship management (Miller, 2021).

REFERENCES

Alder, S. (2025). *HIPAA training requirements - updated for 2025. HIPPA Training Requirements.* https://www.hipaajournal.com/hipaa-training-requirements/

Amazon Web Services. (2025). *Predictive analytics and machine learning in cybersecurity: Enhancing reliability and security.* AWS White Paper. https://aws.amazon.com/whitepapers

Basu, S., Liu, F., & Wang, C. (2019). Hardware supply chain security risks in healthcare systems. *Journal of Cybersecurity*, *5*(3), 1–14. DOI: 10.1093/cybsec/tyz012

Bloomberg Law. (2024). *Which states have consumer data privacy laws?* https://pro.bloomberglaw.com/insights/privacy/state-privacy-legislation-tracker/#:~:text=Currently%2C%20there%20are%2015%20states,data%20privacy%20laws%20in%20place

Bracken, B. (2023). *11M HCA Healthcare patients impacted by data breach. Dark Reading.* https://www.darkreading.com/cyberattacks-data-breaches/11m-hca-healthcare-patients-impacted-data-breach

Chen, C.-K., Zhang, Z.-K., Cho, M. C., Wang, C.-W., Hsu, C.-W., & Shieh, S. (2014). *IOT security: Ongoing challenges and research opportunities. 2014 IEEE 7th International Conference on Service-Oriented Computing and Applications.* DOI: 10.1109/SOCA.2014.58

CISA. (n.d.). *Incident response plan (IRP) basics.* Retrieved from https://www.cisa.gov/sites/default/files/publications/Incident-Response-Plan-Basics_508c.pdf

Craig, R., & Corey, D. (2021). Cyber threats in healthcare: A comprehensive review. *Journal of Healthcare Information Management, 35*(2), 112–119.

Cyber Threat Intelligence, K. E. L. A. (2025*). Third-party risk in healthcare demands immediate attention.* https://www.kelacyber.com/blog/why-third-party-risk-in-healthcare-demands-immediate-attention/

Cybersecurity *Help. (2022). Zero-Day vulnerability statistics.* Retrieved from https://www.zero-day.cz/research/

Cynet. (2022). *Cynet Next-Gen Antivirus (NGAV).* Retrieved from https://www.cynet.com/platform/next-gen-antivirus/

Forrest, A., & Lindemulder, G. (n.d.). *What is a next-generation antivirus (NGAV)? IBM.* Retrieved from https://www.ibm.com/think/topics/next-generation-antivirus/#:~:text=Authors,IBM%20Think

Fortinet (2022). *Brute Force Attack Definition.* Retrieved from https://www.fortinet.com/resources/cyberglossary/brute-force-attack

Gartner. (n.d.). *Third-party risk management (TPRM): A complete guide.* Retrieved from https://www.gartner.com/en/legal-compliance/topics/third-party-risk-management-tprm

Gupta, D., Elluri, L., Jain, A., Moni, S. S., & Aslan, O. (2024). *Blockchain-enhanced framework for secure third-party vendor risk management and vigilant security controls.* arXiv preprint. https://arxiv.org/abs/2411.13447 DOI: 10.1109/BigData62323.2024.10825025

Hyperproof. (2025). NIST 800-53: *Security and privacy controls for information systems and organizations.* https://hyperproof.io/nist-800-53/

Kapko, M. (2024, March 1). *Change Healthcare cyberattack: What we know, what's next. CSO Online.* https://www.csoonline.com/article/652749/change-healthcare-cyberattack-what-we-know-whats-next.html

Kaspersky (n.d.). *Malware-as-a-service (MaaS).* Retrieved from https://encyclopedia.kaspersky.com/glossary/malware-as-a-service-maas/

Kaspersky (n.d.). *Malware-as-a-service (MaaS).* Retrieved from https://encyclopedia.kaspersky.com/glossary/

Keystride. (2024). *Transforming healthcare through IoMT firmware development. Keystride.* https://www.keystride.com/blog/transforming-healthcare-through-iomt-firmware-development/

Klinghofer, B. (2022). *Introducing Microsoft Defender for Endpoint plan 1.* Retrieved from https://techcommunity.microsoft.com/t5/microsoft-defender-for-endpoint/introducing-microsoft-defender-for-endpoint-plan-1/ba-p/2636641

Kolbasuk, M. (2022). Healthcare data breaches: CaptureRx and MedNetworx case studies. *Healthcare IT Security Journal, 28*(4), 55–63.

Linkov, I., Trump, B. D., Poinsatte-Jones, K., & Florin, M.-V. (2019). Governance strategies for a sustainable digital world. *Sustainability, 11*(3), 705. DOI: 10.3390/su11030705

Mark & Spark Solutions. (2024). *Medical batteries market to reach USD 3,539M by 2030.* https://marksparksolutions.com/reports/medical-batteries-market-2024-2030

Microsoft Security Response Center. (2021). *Microsoft bug bounty programs year in review: $13.6M in rewards.* Retrieved from https://msrc-blog.microsoft.com/2021/07/08/microsoft-bug-bounty-programs-year-in-review-13-6m-in-rewards/

Miller, R. (2021). 2021 *Cyberrisk landscape. Risk Management Magazine.* Retrieved from https://www.rmmagazine.com/articles/article/2021/02/01/-2021-Cyberrisk-Landscape-#:~:text=Unfortunately%2C%20this%20appears%20unlikely%20to,data%20exposure%20or%20system%20disruption

Mohn, E. (2023). Stuxnet: *A brief history of the cyber weapon.* EBSCO. https://www.ebsco.com/research-starters/computer-science/stuxnet

National Institute of Standards and Technology. (2020). *Framework for improving critical infrastructure cybersecurity* (Version 1.1). U.S. Department of Commerce. DOI: 10.6028/NIST.CSWP.04162018

NIST. (n.d.). *Guide for conducting risk assessments.* [PDF file]. https://nvlpubs.nist.gov/nistpubs/Legacy/SP/nistspecialpublication800-30r1.pdf

Olawoye, S. (2025). Malware threats and resilience in healthcare IT systems [Doctoral dissertation, Capitol Technology University]. ProQuest Dissertations Publishing.

Parker, J. (2023). *80% of ransomware attacks now use artificial intelligence. MIT Sloan School of Management.* https://mitsloan.mit.edu/ideas-made-to-matter/80-ransomware-attacks-now-use-artificial-intelligence

Pondurance. (2025, June 25). *Practical strategies for vendor risk management in healthcare. Pondurance.com.* https://www.pondurance.com/blog/practical-strategies-for-vendor-risk-management-in-healthcare

Radware. (2022). *Supply chain attack trends and mitigation strategies in healthcare.* Radware Security Reports.

Resilient, X. (n.d.). *Common third-party risk management challenges and solutions.* Retrieved from https://www.resilientx.com/blog/common-third-party-risk-management-challenges

Rippling. (2025). Agentic AI security: *A guide to threats, risks & best practices.* Rippling Blog. https://www.rippling.com/blog/agentic-ai-security

Risk Management Association (RMA). (2025). *A playbook for third-party exits.* Retrieved from https://www.rmahq.org/blogs/2025/a-playbook-for-third-party-exits/

SecurityInfoWatch. (2025). *Autonomous and unchecked: The mounting risks of agentic AI.* SecurityInfoWatch. https://www.securityinfowatch.com/ai/article/55316293/autonomous-and-unchecked-the-mounting-risks-of-agentic-ai

Shacklett, M. (2021). *What is an attack vector?* Retrieved from https://www.techtarget.com/searchsecurity/definition/attack-vector

Smith, M. L. (2024, July 5). *Developing a conceptual framework: A step-by-step guide for researchers*. Blainy. https://blainy.com/conceptual-framework/

Splunk. (n.d.). *The Internet of Medical Things (IoMT): A brief introduction. Splunk.* Retrieved from https://www.splunk.com/en_us/blog/learn/the-internet-of-medical-things-iomt.html

Sullivan, J. (2022*). Is TLS enough for HIPAA? HIPAA Vault.* https://www.hipaavault.com/resources/is-tls-enough-for-hipaa/

Sun, Y., Zhang, R., & Yu, H. (2018). Software supply chain attacks: Emerging threats and security measures. *ACM Computing Surveys, 50*(6), 1–31. DOI: 10.1145/3106741

Torrence, R. (2021). *HHS warns of increasing zero-day attacks in healthcare.* Retrieved from https://www.fiercehealthcare.com/tech/hhs-warns-increasing-zero-day-attacks-healthcare

Venminder. (n.d.*). 4 exit strategies for offboarding a vendor.* Retrieved from https://www.venminder.com/podcast/offboarding-vendor-exit-strategies

Verizon. (2020). *2020 Data breach investigations report (DBIR).* Verizon Enterprise Solutions. https://www.verizon.com/business/resources/reports/dbir/

WIZ. (2025). *What is a brute force attack? Types and countermeasures. wiz.io.* https://www.wiz.io/academy/brute-force-attacks

Wolford, B. (2024). *What is GDPR, the EU's new data protection law?* Retrieved from https://commission.europa.eu/law/law-topic/data-protection/data-protection-eu_en

Yin, R. K. (2018). *Case study research and applications: Design and methods* (6th ed.). SAGE Publications.

Chapter 9
Exploring the Organizational Psychological Perspectives of Management Consulting Interventions in Healthcare Cybersecurity

Darrell Norman Burrell
http://orcid.org/0000-0002-4675-9544
Marymount University, USA

Adina Lundy
http://orcid.org/0000-0001-7564-2110
University of Rhode Island, USA

Sharon L. Burton
http://orcid.org/0000-0003-1653-9783
EmbryRiddle Aeronautical University, USA

Calvin Nobles
http://orcid.org/0000-0003-4002-1108
University of Maryland Global Campus, USA

Maurice Dawson
http://orcid.org/0000-0003-4609-3444
Illinois Institute of Technology, USA

Kim L. Brown Jackson
http://orcid.org/0000-0001-9231-2076
Claremont Lincoln University, USA

Philip Reed
http://orcid.org/0009-0000-1266-0151
Marymount University, USA

Jessica Parker
http://orcid.org/0009-0008-9574-3275
Marymount University, USA

DOI: 10.4018/979-8-2600-1021-1.ch009

Gregory Karl Smith
http://orcid.org/0009-0000-5122-2250
Marymount University, USA

Julia DeFrance
http://orcid.org/0009-0005-8105-2594
Marymount University, USA

Kylei L. Conti
http://orcid.org/0009-0009-0495-6601
Marymount University, USA

ABSTRACT

This article examines cybersecurity breaches in healthcare through an organizational psychology and leadership performance lens, arguing that human factors and cultural dynamics are central drivers of cyber risk. Using an action research–based management consulting framework, the study integrates incident analysis, policy and training reviews, and interviews with cybersecurity professionals and healthcare employees to diagnose misalignment between technology, workflows, and leadership behavior. The research applies organizational culture, human factors, and change management theories to identify how cognitive load, normalization of deviance, psychological safety, and leadership signaling shape cybersecurity outcomes. A set of leadership performance indicators is proposed to operationalize accountability for human-error risk reduction, learning, and resilience. Findings demonstrate that cybersecurity effectiveness improves when leadership designs error-tolerant systems, embeds security into clinical workflows, and institutionalizes effective organizational culture practices.

INTRODUCTION

Digital transformation in healthcare extends well beyond the adoption of advanced technologies; it constitutes a fundamental organizational and psychological reconfiguration of how care is delivered, decisions are made, and risk is perceived. The rapid integration of electronic health records, telehealth platforms, mobile health applications, wearable and implantable devices, artificial intelligence systems, blockchain-enabled data management, and interconnected medical devices has significantly altered clinical workflows and expanded the cognitive demands placed on healthcare professionals (Turuk, 2020; Hermes et al., 2020; Yogev et al., 2023). Clinicians operating in modern healthcare systems must now navigate multiple digital interfaces simultaneously while providing time-sensitive and high-stakes patient care. Although these innovations enhance efficiency, scalability, and value delivery (Kelly et al., 2020), they also introduce new behavioral vulnerabilities that traditional cybersecurity models are ill-equipped to address.

From an organizational psychology perspective, cybersecurity breaches in healthcare are rarely the result of isolated technical failures (Nobles, 2018; Muller & Burrell, 2022). Rather, they emerge from predictable patterns of human behavior embedded within complex organizational systems (Nobles et al., 2025; Nobles, 2022). As healthcare work becomes increasingly digitized, employees are required to make rapid judgments under cognitive load, time pressure, and emotional stress, conditions known to amplify reliance on heuristics, weaken attention, and increase susceptibility to error (Wright & Burrell, 2023; Huff et al., 2023; Burton et al., 2023; Burrell, 2024). Phishing attacks, for example, succeed not because users lack knowledge, but because they exploit authority cues, urgency framing, and familiar organizational scripts that align with everyday work expectations (Burrell, 2024). Similarly, repeated exposure to low-signal security warnings fosters habituation, leading staff to disregard alerts even when they signal genuine threats (Burton et al., 2023; Nobles, 2022; Nobles, 2018).

Organizational culture further shapes whether secure behavior is reinforced or undermined in daily practice (Burton et al., 2023; Nobles, 2022; Nobles, 2018). In healthcare environments where productivity, speed, and uninterrupted access to systems are implicitly rewarded, employees often learn that bypassing security controls is an acceptable means of meeting clinical demands. Informal norms, such as credential sharing or the use of unapproved applications, frequently override formal security policies, especially when compliance is perceived as incompatible with patient care (Burrell, 2024). The presence or absence of psychological safety also plays a critical role: when staff fear blame or punishment, they are less likely to report suspicious activity, near-misses, or mistakes, allowing small vulnerabilities to escalate into major breaches.

Leadership behavior and organizational power dynamics further influence cybersecurity outcomes (Jones & Burrell, 2025). Executives and senior clinicians who request exceptions to security protocols signal that rules are flexible, normalizing risk-taking throughout the organization (Burrell, 2024). Hierarchical structures common in healthcare amplify susceptibility to impersonation and authority-based social engineering attacks, particularly when cybersecurity is framed narrowly as an information technology responsibility rather than a shared organizational concern (Wright & Burrell, 2023). In such contexts, employees disengage from security-related decision-making, perceiving it as peripheral to their professional role and ethical obligations (Nobles, 2018; Nobles, 2022).

Breaches also reflect misalignment between job design, workload, and security expectations. When security tasks are added without redesigning workflows, they become discretionary behaviors that are quickly abandoned under stress (Burton,

2021; Burton, 2024). Poorly designed or unusable security systems further exacerbate noncompliance, creating a person–environment misfit in which secure behavior is cognitively costly and operationally impractical (Burrell, 2024). Traditional training approaches compound this problem by emphasizing information transmission over behavior change, resulting in limited transfer to real-world decision-making (Burton, 2024).

Finally, the psychological dimensions of cybersecurity extend into incident response and post-breach learning (Nobles, 2018; Brown-Jackson et al., 2024). Blame-oriented reactions, role ambiguity, and stress during incidents impair judgment and discourage transparency, while organizations that foster psychologically safe postmortems are better positioned to learn, adapt, and build resilience. Taken together, these dynamics underscore a central premise: cybersecurity in healthcare is not merely a technical challenge but an organizational psychology problem (Nobles, 2018; Nobles, 2022; Nobles et al., 2025). Understanding how cognition, culture, leadership, and system design interact under conditions of digital complexity is essential for explaining why breaches occur and for designing interventions capable of meaningfully reducing risk in healthcare environments (Burrell et al., 2023; Burrell, 2023; Burrell, 2024).

PROBLEM STATEMENT

As healthcare organizations expand their digital ecosystems, they simultaneously increase their exposure to cybersecurity breaches driven by predictable human and organizational factors. Each new system, remote access capability, or connected device enlarges the attack surface while intensifying cognitive load and decision fatigue among healthcare workers (Cartwright, 2023). This dynamic is evident in ransomware incidents that originate from phishing emails opened during high-stress clinical shifts, where urgency and divided attention impair threat recognition (Burrell, 2024). Healthcare's dependence on uninterrupted data access further encourages workarounds that weaken security controls, such as credential sharing or delayed software updates. Organizational psychology suggests that these behaviors are not individual failings but consequences of misaligned incentives, workflow design, and cultural norms (Nobles, 2018; Nobles, 2022; Nobles et al., 2025). As a result, healthcare organizations experience disproportionate breach rates and escalating financial and operational damages compared to other industries (Coventry et al., 2020; Palatty, 2022; Tin et al., 2023)."

PURPOSE STATEMENT FOR MANAGEMENT CONSULTING AND ACTION RESEARCH INTERVENTION

The purpose of this inquiry is to examine how organizational psychology principles can inform management consulting and action research interventions aimed at reducing cybersecurity breaches within healthcare organizations. Specifically, this effort seeks to identify how leadership behaviors, cultural norms, role design, and psychological safety influence secure decision-making in digitally intensive healthcare environments. By integrating behavioral insights into cybersecurity strategy, healthcare organizations can move beyond compliance-based training toward interventions that align security practices with real-world clinical workflows (Burrell, 2023; Burrell, 2024). For instance, action research initiatives may involve redesigning authentication processes to reduce cognitive friction, implementing psychologically safe reporting mechanisms for near-miss incidents, or coaching leaders to model secure behaviors consistently. Through iterative diagnosis, intervention, and evaluation, this approach positions cybersecurity as a shared organizational responsibility embedded within daily operations rather than a peripheral technical function.

SIGNIFICANCE OF THE INQUIRY

This inquiry is significant because cybersecurity breaches in healthcare generate consequences that extend far beyond financial loss, directly affecting patient safety, organizational trust, and workforce well-being. Between 2016 and 2021, ransomware attacks on healthcare organizations increased steadily, compromising tens of millions of patient records and disrupting care delivery across hospitals, clinics, and emergency services (Neprash et al., 2022). Documented incidents have resulted in ambulance diversions, delayed surgeries, and prolonged system outages, illustrating how cyber events translate into tangible clinical harm. The psychological aftermath of such breaches, including heightened stress, moral distress, and burnout among healthcare workers, further undermines organizational resilience (Okafor et al., 2023). By centering organizational psychology in cybersecurity strategy, this inquiry contributes actionable insight into how healthcare systems can protect sensitive data while sustaining safe, reliable, and ethical patient care in an increasingly digital landscape.

IMPACT ON HEALTHCARE EMPLOYEES AND CYBERSECURITY EXPOSURE

Modern healthcare work requires employees to operate well beyond traditional organizational and digital boundaries. Clinicians, administrators, and support staff must interact continuously with electronic health records, patient portals, telehealth platforms, cloud-based systems, and third-party vendors to deliver coordinated care. Boundary theory helps explain how this constant permeability between organizational systems and external actors increases cognitive strain and role ambiguity, which in turn elevates susceptibility to cyber threats. Human-factor attacks such as phishing and social engineering remain the most effective attack vectors in healthcare, accounting for the vast majority of successful breaches (Klimburg-Witjes & Wentland, 2021; Barlow et al., 2020; Kioskli et al., 2023). In practice, many hospital ransomware incidents originate when employees respond to deceptive emails that mimic routine communications from laboratories, suppliers, or IT departments during high-pressure clinical shifts. From an organizational psychology perspective, healthcare employees are labeled simultaneously as the weakest link and the most critical defense asset because their security-relevant decisions are shaped by workload, attentional limits, and professional identity rather than by intent or technical competence (Alahmari et al., 2023; Prasad et al., 2023; Reeves et al., 2021).

PSYCHOLOGICAL AND ORGANIZATIONAL BARRIERS TO CYBERSECURITY COMPLIANCE

Healthcare employees operate in environments characterized by chronic workload demands, emotional labor, and high accountability, leaving limited psychological capacity for additional compliance tasks. Job demands–resources theory provides a useful lens for understanding why cybersecurity procedures are often deprioritized: when job demands exceed available resources, employees conserve energy by minimizing behaviors perceived as nonessential (Javaid et al., 2023). Cybersecurity requirements are frequently viewed as administrative burdens rather than integral components of care delivery, particularly within strong patient-first cultures where speed and accessibility are implicitly rewarded (Jalali & Kaiser, 2018). For example, clinicians may reuse passwords, delay system updates, or bypass authentication controls to avoid disrupting patient interactions. These behaviors reflect adaptive responses to competing organizational demands rather than negligence. Organizational psychology highlights that when performance metrics and cultural signals prioritize productivity over security, employees internalize those priorities, resulting in systematic noncompliance despite formal policies.

EMPLOYEE MOTIVATION, RISK PERCEPTION, AND CYBERSECURITY BEHAVIOR

Employee adoption of cybersecurity behaviors is fundamentally shaped by motivational and cognitive appraisals of risk. Traditional technology adoption models, such as the Technology Acceptance Model, emphasize perceived usefulness and ease of use as drivers of adoption; however, these constructs are insufficient for explaining cybersecurity behavior because security technologies are designed to prevent negative outcomes rather than produce immediate functional benefits (Reeves et al., 2021). Protection Motivation Theory offers a more robust explanatory framework by emphasizing self-efficacy, perceived severity, perceived vulnerability, response efficacy, and response cost as determinants of protective behavior (Ng et al., 2021; Almansoori et al., 2020). In healthcare settings, employees who lack confidence in their ability to recognize cyber threats or who perceive reporting mechanisms as ineffective are less likely to engage in secure behaviors. For instance, a nurse who doubts that reporting a suspicious email will lead to timely action may choose inaction instead. Organizational psychology underscores that cybersecurity compliance improves when employees believe they are capable, supported, and meaningfully contributing to risk reduction.

PROCESS BURDEN, KNOWLEDGE MANAGEMENT, AND RISK NORMALIZATION

Healthcare organizations continue to experience tension between legacy knowledge management practices and post-digital cybersecurity requirements. Prior to widespread electronic health record adoption driven by the Health Information Technology for Economic and Clinical Health Act, many workflows were locally optimized to prioritize efficiency and patient care, often relying on informal processes (Adler-Milstein & Jha, 2017; Coventry et al., 2020). From the perspective of normalization of deviance theory, behaviors such as credential sharing, unattended workstations, and use of personal devices became acceptable because they solved immediate operational problems without producing immediate negative consequences. Investigations of healthcare breaches frequently identify these normalized practices as contributing factors, not due to lack of awareness but because they are embedded in everyday work routines (Coventry et al., 2020). Cognitive load theory further explains how the introduction of security controls without corresponding workflow redesign increases mental effort, leading to shortcuts and errors under stress (Fauzi et al., 2021). Organizational psychology highlights that sustainable cybersecurity requires aligning security practices with how work is actually performed rather than how it is ideally prescribed.

TRAINING FATIGUE, BURNOUT, AND RESISTANCE TO CYBERSECURITY INITIATIVES

Employee responses to cybersecurity training are strongly influenced by fatigue, burnout, and perceived misalignment with core job responsibilities. As healthcare organizations expand security education, training, and awareness programs, employees often experience these initiatives as encroachments on limited time and attention, exacerbating stress rather than improving performance (Coventry et al., 2020). Conservation of resources theory explains this resistance by suggesting that employees seek to protect remaining cognitive and emotional resources when they feel depleted. Attitudinal fatigue, characterized by cynicism and disengagement, and cognitive fatigue, resulting from sustained mental effort and decision overload, both impair secure decision-making (Reeves et al., 2021). Under these conditions, employees are more likely to rely on intuitive or habitual responses, such as clicking familiar-looking emails or postponing security-related decisions altogether. Organizational psychology emphasizes that cybersecurity initiatives perceived as overly burdensome, misaligned with patient care priorities, or easily circumvented will be resisted, whereas interventions that reduce cognitive friction and support professional identity are more likely to succeed.

ORGANIZATIONAL IMPACT OF CYBERSECURITY BREACHES IN HEALTHCARE

Cybersecurity breaches in healthcare organizations create cascading organizational consequences that extend far beyond technical disruption. Between 2014 and 2019, healthcare data breaches averaged approximately four million dollars per incident and accounted for nearly one-quarter of all breaches across industries (Kotte et al., 2020; Dhawan et al., 2023). From an organizational psychology perspective, breaches destabilize healthcare systems by introducing uncertainty, fear, and role ambiguity across clinical and administrative teams. For example, when a regional hospital network experiences a ransomware attack, leadership often shifts into crisis-response mode while frontline clinicians struggle with unclear procedures, temporary documentation methods, and concerns about patient safety. These psychological disruptions undermine coordination, slow decision-making, and erode confidence in organizational leadership, magnifying the overall impact of the breach (Wasserman & Wasserman, 2022).

FINANCIAL CONSEQUENCES AND ORGANIZATIONAL STRESS RESPONSES

Although ransom payments receive the most public attention, the true financial burden of healthcare cyberattacks is distributed across numerous operational and human costs. Organizations incur expenses related to activating emergency operations, repairing or replacing compromised systems, restoring data, engaging legal counsel and public relations firms, increasing cybersecurity insurance premiums, and paying regulatory fines (Wasserman & Wasserman, 2022). Operational downtime frequently leads to canceled procedures and delayed diagnostic services, directly affecting revenue and patient outcomes. Organizational stress theory explains how these compounding pressures trigger reactive decision-making and resource depletion. For instance, hospitals facing prolonged electronic health record outages have been forced to divert ambulances and postpone elective surgeries, creating moral distress among clinicians and accelerating burnout. These stress responses often persist long after systems are restored, shaping organizational behavior and risk tolerance in lasting ways.

DATA LOSS, IRREVERSIBILITY, AND ORGANIZATIONAL VULNERABILITY

Data loss represents one of the most psychologically consequential outcomes of healthcare cyber breaches because compromised information can rarely be considered fully recoverable. From 2010 to 2019, data theft and loss accounted for more than one-third of reported breaches, and between 2016 and 2021 only a minority of healthcare organizations were able to restore lost data from backups following attacks (Seh et al., 2020; Neprash et al., 2022). Even when data is technically recovered, uncertainty remains regarding whether records were altered, copied, or sold for future exploitation (Wasserman & Wasserman, 2022). In practice, this uncertainty forces organizations to treat all affected data as permanently compromised. From an organizational psychology standpoint, this creates persistent anxiety, heightened risk aversion, and a loss of perceived control among leadership and staff. Smaller healthcare organizations without robust backup infrastructures have, in some cases, faced closure or acquisition following attacks, illustrating how data dependency and insufficient preparedness can threaten organizational survival.

REPUTATION, TRUST EROSION, AND PATIENT BEHAVIOR

Cybersecurity breaches fundamentally undermine the relational foundation of healthcare organizations by eroding patient trust and institutional credibility. Following a breach, patients often report feelings of anger, betrayal, and fear due to the long-term implications of exposed personal and medical data (Wasserman & Wasserman, 2022). Trust theory helps explain how these emotional reactions translate into behavioral changes, such as reluctance to disclose sensitive health information or avoidance of specific healthcare providers. For example, patients affected by large-scale breaches have been shown to withhold mental health histories, substance use information, or financial details during intake processes, increasing the risk of misdiagnosis or incomplete care (Playing with Lives, 2021). Internally, reputational damage also affects employees, diminishing organizational pride and increasing turnover intentions. These trust-based consequences illustrate how cybersecurity breaches weaken healthcare organizations from both external and internal psychological dimensions.

CYBERSECURITY STRATEGY AS A SOCIO-TECHNICAL SYSTEM

Healthcare cybersecurity strategies are often conceptualized as technical solutions, yet their effectiveness depends on how well they align with human behavior and organizational structure. The principles of confidentiality, integrity, and availability emphasize protecting data privacy, accuracy, and system access; each of which directly intersects with clinical workflows and professional judgment (Abdelghani, 2019). When availability is compromised during a ransomware attack, clinicians frequently revert to paper documentation, personal devices, or informal communication channels, increasing the likelihood of errors and future vulnerabilities. Organizational psychology frames cybersecurity as a socio-technical system in which people, processes, and technology must be designed together. When strategies fail to account for how work is actually performed under pressure, employees develop workarounds that unintentionally weaken security.

DEFENSE-IN-DEPTH AND LAYERED RESPONSIBILITY IN PRACTICE

Defense-in-depth strategies reflect recognition that no single safeguard can compensate for human error or system complexity. By combining physical, technical, and administrative controls, healthcare organizations attempt to distribute responsibility across multiple layers (Abdelghani, 2019; Keshta & Odeh, 2021). However, organizational psychology highlights that the effectiveness of these layers depends on employee understanding, perceived legitimacy, and cultural reinforcement. For instance, badge-controlled access systems are undermined when staff prop doors open to save time during shift changes, and password policies fail when clinicians share credentials to maintain workflow continuity. These examples demonstrate how informal norms can override formal safeguards. Defense-in-depth succeeds only when organizational culture reinforces collective accountability and aligns security behaviors with clinical realities.

SYSTEM SECURITY LAYERS, ALERT FATIGUE, AND COGNITIVE LOAD

Data-, device-, and network-centric security systems are designed to monitor, detect, and respond to threats across complex healthcare environments (Akbaş, 2023; Ramadan et al., 2021). However, these systems also introduce additional alerts, authentication steps, and decision points that increase cognitive load. Cognitive load theory explains how excessive notifications and poorly integrated systems contribute to alert fatigue, reducing the likelihood that genuine threats will be recognized. In real-world breach investigations, early warning signs were often present but ignored because staff were overwhelmed by routine alerts. Organizational psychology emphasizes the importance of usability and prioritization in security system design to ensure that technology supports, rather than overwhelms, human judgment.

MAPPING ORGANIZATIONAL PSYCHOLOGY CONSTRUCTS TO ZERO TRUST IMPLEMENTATION CHALLENGES

Zero Trust cybersecurity strategies represent a fundamental shift toward continuous verification in response to distributed healthcare environments (Yeoh et al., 2023). While technically robust, Zero Trust implementations frequently encounter resistance rooted in organizational psychology rather than technical feasibility. Psychological contract theory explains why employees may perceive constant verification as a signal of mistrust, particularly in professions grounded in autonomy and ethical responsibility. Without clear framing, clinicians may interpret Zero Trust controls as surveillance rather than protection, leading to disengagement or circumvention.

Self-determination theory further highlights the importance of autonomy, competence, and relatedness in Zero Trust adoption. When access restrictions are introduced without adequate explanation or support, employees experience reduced autonomy and competence, increasing frustration and noncompliance. Conversely, organizations that frame Zero Trust controls as mechanisms that protect patients and support professional judgment see higher acceptance and adherence.

Social identity theory also plays a critical role. Contractors, temporary staff, and third-party vendors may feel less identification with the organization and therefore less intrinsic motivation to comply with strict access controls. Zero Trust strategies that fail to address these identity gaps risk increased insider threats. Finally, sensemaking theory explains how employees interpret and respond to security changes during implementation. Clear communication, leadership modeling, and psychologically safe feedback mechanisms help employees construct coherent narratives about why Zero Trust matters, reducing uncertainty and resistance. By explicitly aligning Zero Trust architectures with organizational psychology principles, healthcare organizations can transform security from a perceived obstacle into a shared, value-driven responsibility that enhances both patient safety and organizational resilience.

APPLYING LEVELS OF CULTURE TO CYBERSECURITY BEHAVIOR

Schein's model of organizational culture offers healthcare executives a diagnostic framework for understanding why cybersecurity vulnerabilities persist despite investments in technology, policy, and training (Braathe, 2021). At the artifact level, visible behaviors such as unattended workstations, shared credentials, or clinicians using personal devices to access clinical systems are often treated as compliance failures. From an executive perspective, however, these behaviors signal deeper systemic tensions between strategic priorities and operational realities. For example, when staffing shortages or throughput pressures are not addressed at the leadership level, frontline employees adapt by informally bypassing controls to maintain patient flow. These adaptations, while well intentioned, create predictable entry points for cyberattacks and expose the organization to ethical, legal, and operational risk (Burrell et al., 2023).

At the level of espoused values, healthcare executives routinely emphasize patient safety, data privacy, and regulatory compliance. Yet employees infer true priorities not from mission statements but from leadership responses to tradeoffs. When leaders tolerate insecure practices in the name of efficiency or implicitly reward speed over compliance, cybersecurity becomes culturally framed as negotiable. Organizational psychology highlights that this misalignment weakens normative control and reinforces the belief that security is secondary to clinical productivity. Executives who fail to reconcile these competing values unintentionally institutionalize risk by allowing cybersecurity to exist outside the organization's core identity (Burrell, 2023).

At the level of underlying assumptions, executives face the greatest challenge and the greatest leverage. Deeply embedded beliefs, such as the assumption that cyber incidents are unlikely, that responsibility rests with IT, or that professional judgment should override system safeguards, shape organizational behavior far more powerfully than formal controls. These assumptions persist when leaders have not personally experienced or meaningfully engaged with the consequences of cyber incidents. From a governance perspective, failing to surface and challenge these assumptions leaves organizations structurally vulnerable, regardless of technological maturity (Burrell, 2024).

LEADERSHIP ENGAGEMENT, POWER DYNAMICS, AND CULTURAL DIAGNOSIS

Executive leadership plays a decisive role in shaping how cybersecurity is interpreted and enacted across healthcare organizations. Cultural authority in healthcare is often distributed unevenly, with senior clinicians exerting influence that rivals or exceeds formal leadership roles. When executives grant informal exceptions to influential physicians or administrators, they unintentionally redefine acceptable behavior across the organization. Organizational psychology underscores that power asymmetries amplify modeling effects: what leaders do matters far more than what they say (Burton, 2021).

Effective cultural diagnosis requires executives to engage directly with frontline realities rather than relying solely on dashboards or audit reports. Structured observation, cross-functional listening sessions, and psychologically safe inquiry allow leaders to understand how employees rationalize cybersecurity-related decisions within the constraints of care delivery. Challenging the assumption that cybersecurity competes with patient care requires reframing security as a clinical risk management function; one that protects continuity of care, diagnostic integrity, and patient trust. Leaders who consistently align their decisions, messaging, and resource allocation with this framing create the conditions for sustainable behavioral change (Burrell et al., 2023).

DRIVING CYBERSECURITY CULTURE CHANGE THROUGH STRUCTURED ORGANIZATIONAL CHANGE

From an executive standpoint, cybersecurity culture change is not an operational initiative but a strategic transformation challenge. Kotter's change framework provides healthcare leaders with a structured approach to mobilizing organizational commitment while managing resistance and uncertainty (Ovington, 2018; Burton, 2024). Establishing urgency requires executives to connect cybersecurity risk to outcomes that resonate with clinical identity and fiduciary responsibility, such as patient harm, service disruption, reputational damage, and board-level accountability.

Building coalitions across executive leadership, clinical leadership, compliance, and IT reduces siloed ownership and reinforces shared accountability. Executives must articulate a clear vision that positions cybersecurity as integral to ethical care and organizational resilience rather than as a regulatory obligation. Removing obstacles often requires executive sponsorship of workflow redesign, investment in usable security technologies, and alignment of performance metrics to discourage risky shortcuts. Recognizing early wins, such as reductions in phishing susceptibility or faster incident escalation, signals that leadership values behavioral progress, not just policy adherence. Anchoring these changes in governance structures, leadership evaluations, and talent development ensures that cybersecurity becomes part of how the organization defines excellence (Burrell, 2023; Burton, 2024).

INTEGRATING CULTURAL CHANGE TO STRENGTHEN ORGANIZATIONAL RESILIENCE

Healthcare organizations face cybersecurity threats from both external adversaries and internal cultural misalignment. Executives who focus exclusively on perimeter defense or compliance controls overlook the behavioral dynamics that attackers routinely exploit. Organizational psychology makes clear that resilience emerges when cultural assumptions, leadership behavior, and system design reinforce one another. Organizations that successfully integrate cybersecurity into patient safety narratives and professional identity demonstrate higher engagement, faster adaptation during incidents, and more effective recovery. Conversely, organizations that treat cybersecurity as a technical add-on experience repeated breaches despite escalating investment (Burrell et al., 2023; Burrell, 2024).

THEORY-TO-PRACTICE SYNTHESIS FOR HEALTHCARE EXECUTIVES

Taken together, Schein's cultural framework and Kotter's change model translate into a practical leadership agenda for healthcare cybersecurity. Schein's model helps executives diagnose where misalignment exists between visible behavior, stated priorities, and deeply held beliefs, while Kotter's framework provides a roadmap for deliberately shifting those beliefs through structured action. When integrated with strategic models such as the 7-S framework, executives can ensure that cybersecurity is aligned across strategy, structure, systems, skills, staff, style, and shared values (Burrell, 2023).

In practice, this synthesis means that executives must treat cybersecurity culture as a leadership competency rather than a technical outcome. It requires visible engagement, ethical framing, investment in human capital, and sustained reinforcement through governance and incentives. Organizational psychology underscores that lasting cybersecurity improvement is achieved not by perfect controls, but by coherent leadership action that aligns how people think, decide, and behave with the realities of digital healthcare delivery (Burton, 2021; Burrell, 2024).

RESEARCH DESIGN AND METHODOLOGICAL APPROACH

This study employs an action research methodology to examine and improve cybersecurity resilience within a healthcare organization through an organizational psychology lens. Action research is particularly appropriate for this inquiry because it enables simultaneous diagnosis and intervention within complex, socio-technical systems while actively engaging organizational stakeholders in the change process. The approach emphasizes iterative cycles of data collection, reflection, intervention, and evaluation, allowing leadership to address cybersecurity not as a static compliance requirement but as an evolving cultural and behavioral challenge.

Consistent with organizational psychology and management consulting practice, this research integrates qualitative and document-based methods to capture how cybersecurity policies, training programs, leadership behaviors, and employee perceptions interact to shape real-world security outcomes. The methodology is designed to surface misalignment between formal cybersecurity strategy and everyday operational behavior, a dynamic repeatedly implicated in healthcare breaches.

DATA SOURCES AND COLLECTION METHODS

Review of Cybersecurity Incident Reports

The first data source consists of a systematic review of internal cybersecurity incident reports over a defined retrospective period. These reports include documented phishing attempts, ransomware events, unauthorized access incidents, near-misses, and system outages. Incident reports are analyzed to identify recurring behavioral patterns, decision points, and contextual conditions associated with successful or attempted breaches.

From an organizational psychology perspective, incident reports are treated not merely as technical records but as behavioral artifacts that reveal how employees respond under cognitive load, time pressure, and ambiguity. Particular attention is paid to indicators of normalization of deviance, delayed reporting, workarounds, and role confusion during incident response. This analysis informs subsequent interview protocols and highlights areas where cultural assumptions may be undermining cybersecurity controls.

Analysis of Organizational Policies and Governance Documents

A comprehensive review of cybersecurity-related organizational policies, procedures, and governance documents is conducted to assess alignment between formal expectations and operational realities. Documents reviewed include acceptable use policies, access control standards, incident response plans, onboarding requirements, and leadership communications related to cybersecurity.

This document analysis evaluates how cybersecurity is framed institutionally, whether as a technical obligation, regulatory mandate, or patient safety imperative, and how responsibilities are distributed across roles. Using Schein's cultural framework, policies are analyzed as expressions of espoused values, which are then compared against observed behaviors and employee narratives. Gaps between policy intent and practical applicability are documented as potential drivers of noncompliance and resistance.

Evaluation of Cybersecurity Training and Awareness Processes

Cybersecurity education, training, and awareness (SETA) programs are reviewed to assess content relevance, delivery methods, frequency, and alignment with adult learning principles. Training materials, participation records, and assessment tools are examined to determine whether training emphasizes information transmission or behavior change.

This analysis incorporates organizational psychology constructs such as cognitive load, self-efficacy, and fatigue to evaluate whether training approaches inadvertently contribute to disengagement or superficial compliance. For example, repeated generic modules without contextual relevance may increase attitudinal fatigue, while overly complex content may overwhelm cognitive capacity. Findings from this review guide the design of targeted interventions focused on skill-building, behavioral rehearsal, and contextual learning.

SEMI-STRUCTURED INTERVIEWS WITH CYBERSECURITY PROFESSIONALS

Semi-structured interviews are conducted with internal cybersecurity professionals, including information security leaders, incident response personnel, and IT administrators. These interviews explore perceptions of organizational culture, leadership support, resource constraints, and recurring behavioral challenges encountered during prevention and response efforts.

Cybersecurity professionals provide critical insight into where technical controls fail due to human behavior, informal norms, or leadership decisions. Interview questions probe how often security recommendations are overridden, how incident lessons are communicated, and how leadership engagement influences compliance. These perspectives help contextualize incident data and illuminate systemic barriers to effective cybersecurity implementation.

SEMI-STRUCTURED INTERVIEWS WITH HEALTHCARE EMPLOYEES

Additional interviews are conducted with a cross-section of healthcare employees, including clinicians, administrators, and support staff. These interviews focus on employees' lived experiences with cybersecurity requirements, perceived barriers to compliance, trust in leadership, and beliefs about the relationship between cybersecurity and patient care.

Using an organizational psychology lens, interview protocols are designed to surface underlying assumptions, value conflicts, and identity-based motivations. Employees are asked to describe how they make security-related decisions under pressure, how they interpret leadership messaging, and how training influences real-time behavior. These narratives provide direct insight into cultural dynamics that cannot be captured through incident reports or policy reviews alone.

INTENT, GOALS, AND STRATEGY OF THE REVIEW AND DATA COLLECTION PHASE

The review and data collection phase is intentionally designed to move beyond surface-level compliance assessment and instead uncover the behavioral, cultural, and leadership dynamics that shape cybersecurity outcomes in healthcare organizations. Each data source serves a distinct analytical purpose while contributing to a triangulated understanding of how cybersecurity risk is produced, normalized, and sustained within the organization.

REVIEW OF CYBERSECURITY INCIDENT REPORTS

Intent

The intent of reviewing cybersecurity incident reports is to identify recurring behavioral and organizational patterns that precede, enable, or exacerbate security incidents. Rather than treating incidents as isolated technical failures, this review positions them as outcomes of decision-making under pressure within complex systems.

Goals

The primary goals are to:

- Identify common human and organizational factors associated with incidents and near-misses
- Detect patterns of delayed reporting, workarounds, or misinterpretation of threats
- Understand how incidents are framed, escalated, and resolved across organizational levels

Strategy

Incident reports are analyzed longitudinally to detect trends rather than one-off events. Particular attention is paid to contextual variables such as time of day, staffing levels, role involvement, and decision points. Reports are examined for evidence of normalization of deviance, cognitive overload, unclear accountability, and leadership response patterns. Findings are used to inform interview protocols and target intervention design.

REVIEW OF ORGANIZATIONAL POLICIES AND GOVERNANCE DOCUMENTS

Intent

The intent of the policy and governance review is to assess how cybersecurity expectations are formally articulated and whether these expectations are realistically aligned with operational and clinical realities.

Goals

The goals of this review include:

- Evaluating consistency between cybersecurity policies and daily work practices
- Identifying ambiguity, redundancy, or unrealistic requirements within policies
- Assessing how responsibility for cybersecurity is distributed and enforced

Strategy

Policies are analyzed as expressions of espoused organizational values and compared against observed behaviors and incident data. Language framing is evaluated to determine whether cybersecurity is positioned as a technical requirement, regulatory obligation, or patient safety imperative. Governance structures are examined to understand escalation paths, accountability mechanisms, and leadership ownership of cybersecurity risk.

EVALUATION OF CYBERSECURITY TRAINING AND AWARENESS PROCESSES

Intent

The intent of evaluating cybersecurity training and awareness processes is to determine whether existing programs meaningfully influence behavior or merely satisfy compliance requirements.

Goals

This evaluation seeks to:

- Assess whether training builds self-efficacy and practical decision-making skills
- Identify sources of cognitive and attitudinal fatigue
- Evaluate relevance of training content to specific healthcare roles

Strategy

Training materials, participation records, and assessment tools are reviewed through an organizational psychology lens. Emphasis is placed on identifying gaps between knowledge acquisition and real-world application. Training frequency, modality, and contextual relevance are analyzed to determine whether programs reduce risk or inadvertently contribute to disengagement and resistance.

INTERVIEWS WITH CYBERSECURITY PROFESSIONALS

Intent

The intent of interviewing cybersecurity professionals is to capture expert insight into where technical controls intersect, and often fail, due to human behavior, leadership decisions, and cultural constraints.

Goals

The goals include:

- Understanding perceived organizational barriers to effective cybersecurity

- Identifying patterns of leadership override or inconsistent enforcement
- Gaining insight into incident response challenges and learning practices

Strategy

Semi-structured interviews allow cybersecurity professionals to reflect on recurring challenges, organizational blind spots, and unmet resource needs. These interviews contextualize technical data within organizational dynamics and help identify leverage points for leadership intervention.

INTERVIEWS WITH HEALTHCARE EMPLOYEES

Intent

The intent of interviewing healthcare employees is to understand how cybersecurity is experienced, interpreted, and enacted at the frontline level under real-world constraints.

Goals

The goals are to:

- Surface underlying assumptions and value conflicts related to cybersecurity
- Understand how employees make security-related decisions under pressure
- Assess perceptions of leadership credibility, support, and fairness

Strategy

Interviews are designed to foster psychological safety and elicit candid reflection rather than socially desirable responses. Questions are open-ended and scenario-based to reveal how employees reconcile cybersecurity expectations with patient care priorities.

EMPLOYEE INTERVIEW PROTOCOL (SAMPLE QUESTIONS)

Section 1: Role Context and Work Environment

1. Can you describe your role and the systems or technologies you interact with most frequently during a typical shift?
2. At what points in your workday do technology or security requirements feel most disruptive or stressful?

Section 2: Decision-Making Under Pressure

3. Can you walk me through a situation where you had to make a quick decision involving patient care and system access?
4. How do you decide when it is acceptable to bypass or delay a security step, if at all?

Section 3: Perceptions of Cybersecurity

5. What does "cybersecurity" mean to you in the context of your role?
6. Do you see cybersecurity as supporting patient care, interfering with it, or something separate altogether? Why?

Section 4: Leadership and Culture

7. How do leaders in your department talk about cybersecurity, if at all?
8. What behaviors do you see being rewarded or tolerated when it comes to security and efficiency?

Section 5: Training and Support

9. How useful do you find the cybersecurity training you receive in helping you make real-time decisions?
10. Can you recall a time when training helped—or failed to help—you avoid a potential security issue?

Section 6: Reporting and Psychological Safety

11. If you noticed a suspicious email or made a security-related mistake, how comfortable would you feel reporting it?
12. What concerns, if any, would prevent you from reporting a near-miss or error?

Section 7: Reflection and Improvement

13. In your view, what would make it easier to follow cybersecurity practices without compromising patient care?
14. If you could change one thing about how cybersecurity is handled here, what would it be?

INTEGRATION INTO THE ACTION RESEARCH CYCLE

The intent, goals, and strategies outlined above ensure that data collection serves not only diagnostic purposes but also intervention readiness. Insights from each data source are synthesized to inform leadership engagement, workflow redesign, training reform, and cultural reframing. This deliberate alignment between data collection and action reflects the core principle of action research: generating knowledge that directly enables organizational change.

ACTION RESEARCH INTERVENTION AND ITERATIVE CYCLES

Triangulation across data sources enhances credibility by validating themes that emerge consistently across documents, incidents, and participant narratives. Discrepancies between leadership intent and employee experience are treated as analytically significant rather than anomalous, highlighting leverage points for intervention.

Findings from the diagnostic phase inform the design of targeted interventions co-developed with organizational leadership. Interventions may include leadership workshops, workflow redesign, revised training approaches, and cultural reframing initiatives that position cybersecurity as integral to patient safety and professional ethics.

The action research process proceeds through iterative cycles of implementation, observation, reflection, and adjustment. Outcome measures include changes in incident reporting behavior, phishing susceptibility, training engagement, and employee perceptions of cybersecurity relevance. This cyclical approach ensures that interventions remain adaptive and responsive to organizational feedback rather than prescriptive or static (Burton, 2024).

RECOMMENDATIONS

1. Engineer Cybersecurity Systems to Anticipate and Absorb Human Error

Organizational leadership must ensure that cybersecurity systems are intentionally designed with the expectation that human error will occur, especially in healthcare environments marked by fatigue, time pressure, emotional labor, and cognitive overload. Leaders have a duty to move the organization away from models that depend on perfect user behavior and toward error-tolerant system design. This includes adaptive authentication, automated session timeouts, anomaly detection, least-privilege defaults, and safeguards that prevent single errors from cascading into major breaches. From an organizational psychology standpoint, this reflects a mature leadership posture that treats error as a predictable system condition rather than an individual failure.

Leadership should evaluate effectiveness by tracking reductions in incidents linked to misclicks, credential misuse, configuration errors, and delayed responses, as well as by measuring how often automated controls successfully contain threats before escalation. Metrics should be reviewed longitudinally to assess resilience under stress, not just during normal operations.

After evaluation, leaders should sponsor structured root-cause analyses that explicitly ask whether system design, workload, or environmental conditions contributed to the error. Continuous improvement efforts should prioritize redesigning systems that repeatedly rely on vigilance alone.

2. Normalize Human Error Reporting Through a Just Culture Cybersecurity Model

Senior leadership has a responsibility to establish and model a just culture for cybersecurity; one that distinguishes between unintentional human error, at-risk behavior, and reckless misconduct. Leaders must ensure that employees can report mistakes, near-misses, and suspicious activity without fear of retaliation, while maintaining clear accountability for intentional violations. Organizational psychology research consistently shows that fear-based cultures suppress reporting and allow small issues to evolve into catastrophic breaches.

Effectiveness should be measured by increases in near-miss and early-warning reports, reductions in mean time to detect incidents, and improvements in employee perceptions of psychological safety and fairness. These indicators should be treated as leading measures of cybersecurity maturity.

Following evaluation, leadership should visibly close the feedback loop by communicating what was learned from reports, what changes were made, and how reporting contributed to organizational protection. Continuous improvement should focus on refining reporting channels, clarifying accountability boundaries, and reinforcing trust through consistent leadership behavior.

3. Redesign Cybersecurity Training Around Human Factors and Real Decision-Making

Organizational leaders must ensure that cybersecurity training reflects how employees actually make decisions in clinical and administrative settings. Training should move beyond policy awareness and focus on decision-making under pressure, addressing cognitive biases, interruptions, urgency, and competing priorities. Leadership has a duty to fund and support scenario-based, role-specific training that builds practical competence and confidence rather than relying on compliance-driven modules.

Effectiveness should be evaluated using behavioral indicators such as simulated phishing outcomes, voluntary reporting behavior, real-world incident trends, and post-training confidence assessments. Training completion alone should never be considered sufficient evidence of effectiveness.

After evaluation, leaders should mandate regular updates to training scenarios based on recent incidents, audit findings, and emerging threats. Continuous improvement should emphasize relevance, brevity, and reinforcement over frequency, reducing fatigue while increasing transfer to practice.

4. Reduce Cognitive Load at High-Risk Clinical Decision Points

Leadership must take responsibility for identifying and mitigating moments of peak cognitive demand where cybersecurity errors are most likely, such as shift changes, emergency admissions, patient surges, and cross-coverage situations. Security controls should be redesigned to reduce cognitive burden during these periods through simplified authentication, prioritized alerts, and automation where possible.

Effectiveness should be measured by changes in alert override rates, phishing susceptibility during peak hours, response times to critical alerts, and incident frequency correlated with workload intensity.

Process improvement should involve regular review of alerting logic, elimination of low-value notifications, and direct feedback from clinicians about usability. Leadership should ensure that security design decisions explicitly consider cognitive load as a risk factor.

5. Embed Cybersecurity Directly into Clinical Workflows to Eliminate Workarounds

Organizational leadership must ensure that cybersecurity is integrated into clinical workflows rather than imposed as a parallel set of tasks. When security requirements conflict with care delivery, employees rationally adopt informal workarounds such as credential sharing. Leaders have a duty to resolve these conflicts through workflow redesign rather than enforcement alone.

Effectiveness should be evaluated by declines in convenience-based policy violations, reductions in shared credentials, audit findings related to unauthorized access, and qualitative feedback from staff regarding workflow fit.

After evaluation, leaders should sponsor cross-functional redesign initiatives involving clinicians, IT, compliance, and operations to eliminate friction points. Continuous improvement should be treated as an ongoing operational responsibility, not a one-time fix.

6. Increase Employee Self-Efficacy to Drive Voluntary Secure Behavior

Leadership should prioritize building employee self-efficacy in cybersecurity; employees' belief that they can recognize threats and take effective action. This requires investment in feedback-rich simulations, just-in-time guidance, and role-specific scenarios. From an organizational psychology perspective, self-efficacy is a stronger predictor of secure behavior than fear or policy awareness.

Effectiveness should be measured by improvements in threat recognition accuracy, sustained voluntary reporting, and reductions in repeat errors. Self-reported confidence should be triangulated with behavioral data.

Process improvement should focus on tailoring interventions to different roles, updating content as threat patterns evolve, and identifying populations that may need additional support due to workload or exposure.

7. Address Normalization of Deviance by Redesigning Unsafe Informal Practices

Leadership must actively identify informal practices that violate cybersecurity policy but persist because they solve operational problems. Rather than responding with punitive controls, leaders should treat these practices as signals of system misalignment and redesign workflows to offer secure alternatives.

Effectiveness should be evaluated through reductions in repeated policy exceptions, decreases in unsecured endpoints, and increased adoption of approved alternatives.

After evaluation, leaders should require root-cause analyses that focus on why the practice emerged and what organizational conditions sustained it. Continuous improvement should emphasize co-design with frontline staff to prevent recurrence.

8. Align Zero Trust Implementation with Trust, Autonomy, and Professional Identity

Organizational leadership has a duty to ensure that Zero Trust cybersecurity strategies are implemented in a way that preserves trust and professional identity. Continuous verification must be framed as protecting patients, clinical integrity, and organizational continuity; not as surveillance of employees. Leaders must communicate intent clearly and involve clinicians in access governance decisions.

Effectiveness should be measured by adherence to least-privilege access, reductions in access-related complaints, and lower rates of intentional circumvention.

Process improvement should involve refining communication strategies, adjusting access rules as roles evolve, and maintaining transparency around access decisions.

9. Increase Autonomy and Ownership Through Participatory Security Design

Leadership should create structures that allow employees to participate meaningfully in cybersecurity design and governance. Peer security champions, feedback mechanisms, and role-based access justification increase autonomy, competence, and ownership; key drivers of intrinsic motivation.

Effectiveness should be evaluated by participation rates in voluntary initiatives, growth in peer-led reporting, and sustained secure behavior beyond mandatory requirements.

After evaluation, leaders should scale successful participatory practices and ensure they are equitably distributed across departments and roles.

10. Strengthen Social Identity and Inclusion to Reduce Insider Risk

Organizational leaders must ensure that contractors, vendors, and temporary staff are fully integrated into the cybersecurity culture. Weak organizational identification increases insider risk. Leadership has a responsibility to enforce consistent onboarding, expectations, and access lifecycle management across all worker categories.

Effectiveness should be measured by reductions in incidents involving peripheral staff, improved compliance metrics, and fewer access misuse events.

Process improvement should focus on tightening onboarding processes, improving role clarity, and reinforcing shared responsibility messaging.

11. Institutionalize Sensemaking Through Structured Post-Incident Learning

Leadership should require psychologically safe, structured post-incident reviews that focus on decision-making, communication, and system constraints rather than blame. These reviews are essential for organizational learning and adaptive capacity.

Effectiveness should be evaluated by improvements in response coordination, reductions in decision errors, and higher-quality corrective action plans. After evaluation, leaders must ensure that lessons learned are translated into concrete changes in policy, training, system design, and governance; and that follow-through is tracked.

12. Explicitly Manage Human Error as a Core Enterprise Risk

Organizational leadership must formally recognize human error as a distinct and measurable enterprise risk within ERM frameworks. Fatigue, workload, cognitive overload, and training decay should be tracked alongside technical and compliance risks.

Effectiveness should be evaluated through trend analysis of incident root causes, reductions in human-factor-related events, and correlations between staffing levels and security outcomes.

Process improvement should include leadership action on staffing models, workload distribution, and system redesign to mitigate identified risks.

SUMMARY

Across all recommendations, organizational leadership carries a duty of care to protect patients, employees, and institutional integrity by recognizing cybersecurity as a human and organizational challenge, not solely a technical one. Leaders are responsible for aligning strategy, systems, culture, and incentives so that secure behavior is the natural outcome of everyday work. Measuring effectiveness, acting on findings, and sustaining improvement are not optional activities; they are core leadership responsibilities within HIPAA-compliant, ERM-aligned healthcare organizations.

Leadership Performance Indicators (LPIs) for Cybersecurity and Human Factors

Leadership performance indicators translate cybersecurity culture and human-factor risk into observable, measurable leadership behaviors and outcomes. These indicators shift accountability from frontline employees to those with authority over systems, priorities, and resources.

1. Human-Error Risk Reduction Index

Leadership accountability: System design, staffing decisions, and workflow integration

Indicator definition: The proportion of cybersecurity incidents and near-misses attributable to human error relative to total incidents, adjusted for workload intensity.

Measurement approach:

- Incident root-cause categorization (human error vs. system design vs. external attack)
- Correlation analysis with staffing levels, shift length, and peak workload periods

Performance expectation: A downward trend over time, demonstrating leadership success in reducing reliance on perfect human behavior.

2. Psychological Safety and Reporting Effectiveness Score

Leadership accountability: Culture, trust, and just culture enforcement

Indicator definition: A composite score reflecting employee willingness to report near-misses, mistakes, and suspicious activity.

Measurement approach:

- Volume and quality of near-miss reports
- Mean time to detect incidents (MTTD)
- Employee survey items measuring fear of blame and trust in leadership

Performance expectation: Increased reporting volume with reduced incident severity and faster detection.

3. Training-to-Behavior Transfer Ratio

Leadership accountability: Training design, relevance, and reinforcement
Indicator definition: The degree to which cybersecurity training results in measurable behavior change rather than mere completion.
Measurement approach:

- Pre- and post-training phishing simulation performance
- Voluntary reporting rates following training cycles
- Decline in repeat errors by trained populations

Performance expectation: Sustained behavioral improvement across quarters, not short-term gains only.

4. Workflow–Security Alignment Index

Leadership accountability: Operational design and clinical integration
Indicator definition: The extent to which cybersecurity controls are embedded into clinical workflows without generating workarounds.
Measurement approach:

- Audit findings related to convenience-based violations
- Employee feedback on workflow friction
- Frequency of credential sharing or unauthorized access

Performance expectation: Declining workaround rates with stable or improved clinical efficiency metrics.

5. Zero Trust Cultural Acceptance Indicator

Leadership accountability: Communication, transparency, and professional identity alignment
Indicator definition: Employee acceptance and adherence to Zero Trust access principles without resistance or circumvention.
Measurement approach:

- Access exception requests
- Complaints related to access controls
- Intentional policy circumvention rates

Performance expectation: High adherence with low resistance and minimal exception escalation.

6. Post-Incident Learning and Adaptation Score

Leadership accountability: Learning culture and follow-through
Indicator definition: The organization's ability to convert incidents into systemic improvement.
Measurement approach:

- Completion rate of corrective actions
- Time from incident review to implementation
- Reduction in recurrence of similar incidents

Performance expectation: Demonstrated organizational learning rather than repeated failure patterns.

7. Human Factors ERM Integration Metric

Leadership accountability: Risk governance and strategic oversight
Indicator definition: The degree to which human factors are explicitly identified, tracked, and mitigated within the enterprise risk register.
Measurement approach:

- Presence of fatigue, workload, and cognitive load risks in ERM
- Trend analysis of human-factor risk scores
- Executive action taken in response to identified risks

Performance expectation: Human error treated as a first-order enterprise risk with active mitigation.

Formal Action Research Intervention Plan

(Management Consulting and Organizational Change)

Phase 1: Diagnostic Inquiry (Plan)

Objective: To identify misalignment between cybersecurity policy, system design, leadership behavior, and employee decision-making.
Key activities:

- Review cybersecurity incident and near-miss reports
- Analyze policies, governance documents, and training materials
- Conduct interviews with cybersecurity professionals and healthcare employees
- Assess ERM documentation for human-factor risk inclusion

Outputs:

- Cultural and behavioral risk profile
- Leadership accountability gaps
- Baseline leadership performance indicators

Phase 2: Collaborative Sensemaking (Observe & Reflect)

Objective: To surface underlying assumptions, normalize shared understanding, and build leadership ownership of risk.

Key activities:

- Leadership workshops to review diagnostic findings
- Facilitated discussions linking human error to system and leadership decisions
- Validation of findings with frontline and technical staff

Outputs:

- Shared problem definition
- Leadership commitment to targeted interventions
- Prioritized intervention areas

Phase 3: Targeted Intervention Design (Act)

Objective: To implement interventions that address human factors, workflow misalignment, and cultural barriers.

Key interventions may include:

- Error-tolerant system redesign
- Just culture reporting mechanisms
- Scenario-based training reforms
- Workflow-integrated security controls
- Zero Trust communication and governance alignment

Outputs:

- Implemented changes with clear ownership
- Updated policies, training, and workflows

Phase 4: Measurement and Evaluation (Observe)

Objective: To determine whether leadership actions produce measurable behavioral and risk reduction outcomes.

Key activities:

- Monitor leadership performance indicators
- Conduct follow-up surveys and simulations
- Compare pre- and post-intervention incident data

Outputs:

- Evidence of improvement or stagnation
- Identification of unintended consequences

Phase 5: Adaptive Improvement and Institutionalization (Reflect & Act)

Objective: To embed successful practices into organizational governance and leadership expectations.

Key activities:

- Refine interventions based on evaluation results
- Update ERM risk registers and leadership scorecards
- Integrate cybersecurity leadership indicators into performance reviews

Outputs:

- Sustained cultural and behavioral change
- Institutionalized learning mechanisms
- Reduced breach likelihood and impact

REFERENCES

Abdelghani, T. (2019). Implementation of defense in depth strategy to secure industrial control system in critical infrastructures. *American Journal of Artificial Intelligence*, *3*(2), 17. DOI: 10.11648/j.ajai.20190302.11

Adler-Milstein, J., & Jha, A. K. (2017). HITECH Act Drove Large Gains In Hospital Electronic Health Record Adoption. *Health Affairs*, *36*(8), 1416–1422. https://www.healthaffairs.org/doi/abs/10.1377/hlthaff.2016.1651. DOI: 10.1377/hlthaff.2016.1651 PMID: 28784734

Akbaş, E. (2023). *The importance of real-time detection and correlation in SIEM/UEBA solutions and criticality for SOAR*. Unpublished. DOI: 10.13140/RG.2.2.12607.69285

Alahmari, S., Renaud, K., & Omoronyia, I. (2023). Moving beyond cyber security awareness and training to engendering security knowledge sharing. *Information Systems and e-Business Management*, *21*(1), 123–158. DOI: 10.1007/s10257-022-00575-2

Almansoori, A., AlShamsi, M., Salloum, S. A., & Shaalan, K. (2020). Critical Review of Knowledge Management in Healthcare. *Studies in Systems, Decision and Control*, 99–119. DOI: 10.1007/978-3-030-47411-9_6

Barlow, L., Bendiab, G., Shiaeles, S., & Savage, N. (2020). A novel approach to detect phishing attacks using binary visualisation and machine learning. *2020 IEEE World Congress on Services (SERVICES)*. https://ieeexplore.ieee.org/abstract/document/9284172?casa_token=9pQ68r3RPtwAAAAA:hvpoXRjjooVcrnMGfP2qhVZdENYDNDJlY47BijC3tDRCkWuGK0W9Zu9j9bYwFDl-cFQHlRnkFns

Braathe, R. (2021, January 23). *The Schein model of organization culture: Three levels of a robust organization culture*. Robert Braathe's HR & Albany Jobs Blog. https://www.albany.com/hr/2021/01/the-schein-model-of-organization-culture-three-levels-of-a-robust-organization-culture/

Brown-Jackson, K. L., Burton, S. L., & Burrell, D. N. (2024). Cybersecurity's Shaping of Wearable Healthcare Devices and Digital Marketing: What Leaders Need to Know. In Saeed, S., Azizi, N., Tahir, S., Ahmad, M., & Almuhaideb, A. (Eds.), *Strengthening Industrial Cybersecurity to Protect Business Intelligence* (pp. 294–319). IGI Global Scientific Publishing., DOI: 10.4018/979-8-3693-0839-4.ch013

Burrell, D. N. (2023). Cybersecurity in healthcare through the 7-S model strategy. *Scientific Bulletin-Nicolae Balcescu Land Forces Academy, 28*(1), 26-35. https://reference-global.com/download/article/10.2478/bsaft-2023-0003.pdf

Burrell, D. N. (2024). Understanding Cognitive and Behavioral Psychological Factors that Lead to Cybersecurity Breaches in Healthcare. *RAIS Journal for Social Sciences, 8*(2), 43-53. https://ideas.repec.org/a/smo/jornl1/v8y2024i2p43-53.html

Burrell, D. N., Burton, S. L., Nobles, C., Springs, D., Huff, A. J., Brown-Jackson, K. L., Richardson, K., Wright, J. B., Muller, S. R., & Jones, A. J. (2023). The Managerial Ethical and Operational Challenges of Hospital Cybersecurity. In Burrell, D. (Ed.), *Transformational Interventions for Business, Technology, and Healthcare* (pp. 444–458). IGI Global Scientific Publishing., DOI: 10.4018/979-8-3693-1634-4.ch026

Burton, S. L. (2021). Cybersecurity leaders: Knowledge driving human capital development. *Science Bulletin, 26*(2), 109–120. https://reference-global.com/download/article/10.2478/bsaft-2021-0013.pdf

Burton, S. L. (2024). Securing tomorrow: Synergizing change management and cybersecurity in the digital era. *Holistica, 15*(1), 1. https://reference-global.com/download/article/10.2478/hjbpa-2024-0001.pdf

Burton, S. L., Burrell, D. N., Nobles, C., & Jones, L. A. (2023). Exploring the nexus of cybersecurity leadership, human factors, emotional intelligence, innovative work behavior, and critical leadership traits. *Scientific Bulletin-Nicolae Balcescu Land Forces Academy, 28*(2), 162-175. https://reference-global.com/download/article/10.2478/bsaft-2023-0016.pdf

Cartwright, A. J. (2023). The elephant in the room: Cybersecurity in healthcare. *Journal of Clinical Monitoring and Computing, 37*(5), 1123–1132. DOI: 10.1007/s10877-023-01013-5 PMID: 37088852

Coventry, L., Branley-Bell, D., Sillence, E., Magalini, S., Mari, P., Magkanaraki, A., & Anastasopoulou, K. (2020). Cyber-Risk in Healthcare: Exploring Facilitators and Barriers to Secure Behaviour. *HCI for Cybersecurity, Privacy and Trust,* 105–122. DOI: 10.1007/978-3-030-50309-3_8

Dhawan, M., Purohit, L., & Gupta, Dr. N. (2023). A comprehensive study on the latest trends of cyber security in the medical management. *SSRN Electronic Journal.* DOI: 10.2139/ssrn.4361044

Fauzi, M. A., Yeng, P., Yang, B., & Rachmayani, D. (2021). Examining the Link Between Stress Level and Cybersecurity Practices of Hospital Staff in Indonesia. *The 16th International Conference on Availability, Reliability and Security.* DOI: 10.1145/3465481.3470094

Hermes, S., Riasanow, T., Clemons, E. K., Böhm, M., & Krcmar, H. (2020). The digital transformation of the healthcare industry: Exploring the rise of emerging platform ecosystems and their influence on the role of patients. *Business Research, 13*(3), 1033–1069. DOI: 10.1007/s40685-020-00125-x

Huff, A. J., Burrell, D. N., Nobles, C., Richardson, K., Wright, J. B., Burton, S. L., Jones, A. J., Springs, D., Omar, M., & Brown-Jackson, K. L. (2023). Management practices for mitigating cybersecurity threats to biotechnology companies, laboratories, and healthcare research organizations. In *Applied Research Approaches to Technology, Healthcare, and Business* (pp. 1-12). IGI Global. https://www.igi-global.com/chapter/management-practices-for-mitigating-cybersecurity-threats-to-biotechnology-companies-laboratories-and-healthcare-research-organizations/331637

Jalali, M. S., & Kaiser, J. P. (2018). Cybersecurity in Hospitals: A Systematic, Organizational Perspective. *Journal of Medical Internet Research, 20*(5), e10059. DOI: 10.2196/10059 PMID: 29807882

Javaid, M., Haleem, A., Singh, R. P., & Suman, R. (2023). Towards insighting cybersecurity for healthcare domains: A comprehensive review of recent practices and trends. *Cyber Security and Applications, 1*(100016), 100016. DOI: 10.1016/j.csa.2023.100016

Jones, L. A., & Burrell, D. N. (2025). Illegal Cybersecurity Threats Created by Organizational Arsonists in Healthcare Organizations. *Law. Economics and Society, 1*(1), 93–p93. https://j.ideasspread.org/index.php/les/article/view/1427

Kelly, J. T., Campbell, K. L., Gong, E., & Scuffham, P. (2020). The internet of things: Impact and implications for healthcare delivery. *Journal of Medical Internet Research, 22*(11), e20135. Advance online publication. DOI: 10.2196/20135 PMID: 33170132

Keshta, I., & Odeh, A. (2021). Security and privacy of electronic health records: Concerns and challenges. *Egyptian Informatics Journal, 22*(2), 177–183. DOI: 10.1016/j.eij.2020.07.003

Kioskli, K., Fotis, T., Nifakos, S., & Mouratidis, H. (2023). The importance of conceptualising the human-centric approach in maintaining and promoting cybersecurity-hygiene in healthcare 4.0. *Applied Sciences (Basel, Switzerland), 13*(6), 3410. DOI: 10.3390/app13063410

Klimburg-Witjes, N., & Wentland, A. (2021). Hacking humans? Social engineering and the construction of the "deficient user" in cybersecurity discourses. *Science, Technology & Human Values, 46*(6), 1316–1339. DOI: 10.1177/0162243921992844

Kotte, D., Venkatesh, R., Satish Kumar, B., Rao, U., & Kshatra, P. (2020). Analysis of data breaches and its impact on organizations. *International Journal of Emerging Trends in Engineering Research, 8*(10), 6989–6994. DOI: 10.30534/ijeter/2020/588102020

Muller, S. R., & Burrell, D. N. (2022). Social Cybersecurity and Human Behavior. [IJHIoT]. *International Journal of Hyperconnectivity and the Internet of Things, 6*(1), 1–13. DOI: 10.4018/IJHIoT.305228

Neprash, H. T., McGlave, C. C., Cross, D. A., Virnig, B. A., Puskarich, M. A., Huling, J. D., Rozenshtein, A. Z., & Nikpay, S. S. (2022). Trends in Ransomware Attacks on US Hospitals, Clinics, and Other Health Care Delivery Organizations, 2016-2021. *JAMA Health Forum, 3*(12), e224873. DOI: 10.1001/jamahealthforum.2022.4873 PMID: 36580326

Ng, K. C., Zhang, X., Thong, J. Y. L., & Tam, K. Y. (2021). Protecting against threats to information security: An attitudinal ambivalence perspective. *Journal of Management Information Systems, 38*(3), 732–764. DOI: 10.1080/07421222.2021.1962601

Nobles, C. (2018). Botching human factors in cybersecurity in business organizations. *HOLISTICA Journal of Business and Public Administration, 9*(3), 71-88. https://holisticajournal.ro/docs/1589fb80c59c854cabe168f3b7b8c1d7.pdf

Nobles, C. (2022). Stress, burnout, and security fatigue in cybersecurity: A human factors problem. *Holistica Journal of Business and Public Administration, 13*(1), 49-72. https://reference-global.com/download/article/10.2478/hjbpa-2022-0003.pdf

Nobles, C., Rangarajan, A., & Burrell, D. N. (2025). Human Factors Engineering-as-a-Service in Cybersecurity. In *New Horizons in Leadership: Inclusive Explorations in Health, Technology, and Education* (pp. 315-342). IGI Global Scientific Publishing. https://www.igi-global.com/chapter/human-factors-engineering-as-a-service-in-cybersecurity/371041

Okafor, C., Kolade, A., Onunka, T., Daraojimba, C., Eyo-Udo, N., & Omotosho, A. (2023). Mitigating Cybersecurity Risks in the U.S. Healthcare Sector [Review of Mitigating Cybersecurity Risks in the U.S. Healthcare Sector]. *International Journal of Innovation and Scientific Research, 10*(9), 177–194. DOI: 10.51244/IJRSI

Ovington, T. (2018, December 16). *How to use Kotter's 8-step model: The key to change success.* The Change Management Blog; Change Management. https://change.walkme.com/kotters-8-step-change-model/

Palatty, N. J. (2022, December 6). 80+ Healthcare data breach statistics 2023. *Astra Security Blog*. https://www.getastra.com/blog/security-audit/healthcare-data-breach-statistics/

Prasad, G., Gujjar, P., Naveen Kumar, H. N., Anand Kumar, M., & Chandrappa, S. (2023). Advances of cyber security in the healthcare domain for analyzing data. In *Advances in Information Security, Privacy, and Ethics* (pp. 1–14). IGI Global.

Ramadan, R. A., Aboshosha, B. W., Alshudukhi, J. S., Alzahrani, A. J., El-Sayed, A., & Dessouky, M. M. (2021). Cybersecurity and countermeasures at the time of pandemic. *Journal of Advanced Transportation, 2021*, 1–19. DOI: 10.1155/2021/6627264

Reeves, A., Delfabbro, P., & Calic, D. (2021). Encouraging Employee Engagement With Cybersecurity: How to Tackle Cyber Fatigue. *SAGE Open, 11*(1), 215824402110000. DOI: 10.1177/21582440211000049

Seh, A. H., Zarour, M., Alenezi, M., Sarkar, A. K., Agrawal, A., Kumar, R., & Khan, R. A. (2020). Healthcare data breaches: Insights and implications. *Healthcare, 8*(2), 133. NCBI. DOI: 10.3390/healthcare8020133

Tin, D., Hata, R., Granholm, F., Ciottone, R. G., Staynings, R., & Ciottone, G. R. (2023). Cyberthreats: A primer for healthcare professionals. *The American Journal of Emergency Medicine, 68*, 179–185. Advance online publication. DOI: 10.1016/j.ajem.2023.04.001 PMID: 37061434

Turuk, M. (2020). Digital strategy. *International Journal of Contemporary Business and Entrepreneurship, 1*(1), 62–76. DOI: 10.47954/ijcbe.1.1.5

Wasserman, L., & Wasserman, Y. (2022). Hospital cybersecurity risks and gaps: Review (for the non-cyber professional). *Frontiers in Digital Health, 4*, 862221. Advance online publication. DOI: 10.3389/fdgth.2022.862221 PMID: 36033634

Wright, J., & Burrell, D. N. (2023). Telemedicine cybersecurity protection in reproductive healthcare. *HOLISTICA Journal of Business and Public Administration, 14*(2), 1-14. https://reference-global.com/download/article/10.2478/hjbpa-2023-0012.pdf

Yeoh, W., Liu, M., Shore, M., & Jiang, F. (2023). Zero trust cybersecurity: Critical success factors and A maturity assessment framework. *Computers & Security, 133*(103412), 103412. DOI: 10.1016/j.cose.2023.103412

Yogev, D., Goldberg, T., Arami, A., Tejman-Yarden, S., Winkler, T. E., & Maoz, B. M. (2023). Current state of the art and future directions for implantable sensors in medical technology: Clinical needs and engineering challenges. *APL Bioengineering, 7*(3), 031506. Advance online publication. DOI: 10.1063/5.0152290 PMID: 37781727

Chapter 10

Building Data Agility to Combat Human Trafficking:

Overcoming Fragmentation Through Technology-Driven Collaboration

Annamaria Szakonyi
http://orcid.org/0000-0002-1958-2042
Embry-Riddle Aeronautical University, USA

ABSTRACT

Human trafficking remains a data-deficient and rapidly evolving global crisis. While technology such as AI and geospatial analytics hold promise for detection and prevention, anti-trafficking efforts are limited by fragmented data, inconsistent reporting, and weak collaboration. This chapter introduces the Platform of Freedom, a conceptual framework that integrates data and technology, collaboration, and policy to cultivate organizational and national agility in the anti-trafficking context. Grounded in Socio-Technical Systems Theory, Actor-Network Theory, and Critical Data Studies, the model reframes anti-trafficking work as a socio-technical challenge requiring ethical governance, interoperability, and adaptive data ecosystems. It argues that technology alone cannot disrupt trafficking without coordinated networks that enable secure information exchange. The Platform of Freedom offers a guide for transforming fragmented systems into cohesive, ethically governed infrastructures that strengthen prevention, protection, and policy innovation in the fight against human trafficking.

DOI: 10.4018/979-8-2600-1021-1.ch010

INTRODUCTION

Human trafficking (one of the world's fastest-growing and most lucrative criminal industries) continues to evolve in complexity and scale. The International Labour Organization (ILO, 2022) estimates that roughly one out of every 150 people globally are trapped in modern slavery worldwide. Many of these victims are children (Cole & Sprang, 2015; ILO, 2022; United Nations Office on Drugs and Crime [UNODC], 2024). Trafficking is no longer confined to shadow economies: it is embedded within global digital systems, exploiting vulnerabilities created by technology and inequality. As traffickers adapt to online environments, using cryptocurrencies, encrypted apps, and social media to conceal activity, anti-trafficking organizations face the urgent challenge of keeping pace with this technological transformation (Foley et al., 2019; Keller & Dance, 2019).

While technological innovation offers new opportunities for detection (through artificial intelligence, blockchain, and geospatial analytics), these advances are constrained by fragmented, inconsistent, and inaccessible data systems (Cho, 2015a; City of Milwaukee, 2020; Cockbain & Wallis, 2019; Gardner et al., 2017; Ibanez & Suthers, 2014; Smith, 2018; Voloshin et al., 2016). No centralized framework exists to unify data across law enforcement, NGOs, and international agencies, leaving critical intelligence siloed and underutilized. The result is a widening gap between technological capacity and organizational readiness, a socio-technical failure that weakens coordination, transparency, and policy response. Despite significant research on trafficking prevention and rescue operations, few studies address how organizations can establish adaptive, technology-enabled collaboration.

This chapter fills that gap by introducing the Platform of Freedom, a model for organizations to adaptively cultivate data in the anti-trafficking context. The chapter argues that the central failure is not a lack of technology but a lack of data agility: the organizational capacity to assemble, interpret, and act on diverse data streams within ethically governed, interoperable systems. By applying Socio-Technical Systems Theory, Actor-Network Theory, and Critical Data Studies, the chapter reframes anti-trafficking work as a challenge of organizational and data agility rather than technological insufficiency. It argues that technology alone cannot disrupt trafficking networks unless embedded in agile, networked, and ethically grounded systems that unite data, collaboration, and policy. The Platform of Freedom is a conceptual model that links interoperable data, adaptive collaboration mechanisms, and dynamic policy levers to enable coordinated, evidence-driven action. By reframing anti-trafficking as a socio-technical challenge, the Platform bridges the divide between innovation and governance, offering a guide for more responsive, evidence-based, and humane approaches to ending human trafficking in the digital age.

PROBLEM STATEMENT

The central problem this chapter addresses is the absence of a coherent, ethically grounded, and interoperable framework that enables organizations to convert emerging technologies into coordinated, data-driven action; without such an approach, innovation will continue to outpace the governance, organizational capacity, and cross-sector coordination needed to combat trafficking effectively.

Despite decades of global anti-trafficking initiatives, human trafficking persists as a rapidly evolving, data-deficient crime. Various estimates on its volume exist, but the true scale of the problem remains unknown due to the absence of consistent, reliable, and comprehensive data sources (Albanese, 2007; Daniel-Wrabetz & Penedo, 2015; Smith, 2018). The lack of data interoperability and coordinated governance has significant implications for both policy and practice.

Despite the increased availability of digital tools and AI-driven analytics, anti-trafficking organizations continue to operate with highly fragmented, non-interoperable data systems. Agencies, NGOs, and private-sector entities collect critical information, but incompatible taxonomies, privacy requirements, and reporting structures prevent this data from functioning as a cohesive intelligence ecosystem (Farrell & De Vries, 2020; UNODC, 2024). A U.S. Government Accountability Office review similarly found that federal agencies rely on systems lacking standardization, coordination, and cross-agency data sharing, resulting in duplicated efforts and significant intelligence blind spots (U.S. Government Accountability Office, 2020). This fragmentation limits early detection, delays victim identification, and hinders multi-jurisdictional responses.

Trafficking information is often collected through disparate systems, each using different definitions, collection methods, and privacy standards (Cho, 2015a; Cho, 2015b). These silos obstruct efforts to identify cross-border routes and gender-based exploitation patterns (Szakonyi et al., 2021). Likewise, while advanced technologies (such as machine learning, blockchain, and geospatial analytics) show potential to improve detection and situational awareness (City of Milwaukee, 2020; Cockbain & Wallis, 2019; Fleury, 2019; Gardner et al., 2017; Ibanez & Suthers, 2014; Stylianou et al., 2019; Szakonyi et al., 2021; Voloshin et al., 2016), their effectiveness is constrained by the absence of shared frameworks for ethical data exchange and collaboration.

This fragmented data landscape reveals a deeper socio-technical and organizational problem: institutions lack the agility to adapt and integrate information systems across human, technological, and policy domains. Without interoperable data governance and cross-sector collaboration, anti-trafficking systems remain reactive, duplicating efforts while leaving major data gaps unaddressed. Solving this problem requires cultivating data agility: the capacity to co-design social and technological systems that can adaptively collect, analyze, and act on data through ethical, collaborative, and networked governance (Gallagher, 2010; Hernandez & Rudolph, 2015).

Although recent scholarship and policy reviews acknowledge the importance of ethical data governance, cross-sector coordination, and responsible technology design, relatively few studies provide an integrated socio-technical framework that combines these elements into an operational model for practice. Systematic reviews of analytics and operations research in the anti-trafficking domain highlight a fragmented evidence landscape in which tools, methods, and datasets are developed in silos and rarely translated into coherent, multi-actor systems for detection or response (Dimas et al., 2022). Empirical reviews focused on sex-trafficking similarly find that digital technologies are often studied and deployed in isolation (with limited attention to interoperability, governance, or survivor-centered safeguards), creating practical and ethical blind spots (Gezinski & Gonzalez-Pons, 2022). Multi-state policy reviews document pervasive gaps in cross-border coordination, inconsistent reporting standards, and weak mechanisms for responsible data sharing across governments, NGOs, and the private sector (Council of Europe, 2022). Together, these sources demonstrate a persistent absence of an integrated, operationally realistic socio-technical model that practitioners can use to convert technological capability into scalable, ethically grounded counter-trafficking strategies.

This chapter seeks to fill this critical gap by proposing a data agility and management framework, the Platform of Freedom, that integrates technology, collaboration, and policy into a cohesive socio-technical system. By applying the lenses of Socio-Technical Systems Theory, Actor-Network Theory, and Critical Data Studies, this work addresses how fragmented and ethically constrained data environments can be transformed into adaptive, networked ecosystems. In doing so, the study contributes a conceptual and practical framework for creating interoperable, ethically governed data infrastructures that enhance coordination, improve intelligence sharing, and strengthen both organizational agility and the global response to human trafficking.

SIGNIFICANCE

Human trafficking remains deeply under-documented, and policy responses are often undermined by lack of reliable, comparable, and shareable data. Without standardized, high-quality data, efforts to prevent trafficking, identify victims, and prosecute perpetrators remain reactive, fragmented, and inefficient. A recent publication of the International Organization for Migration (IOM) and the United Nations Office on Drugs and Crime (UNODC) in 2023 recognized this gap, acknowledging that existing data sources are "diverse, mostly disconnected and limited in scope" and incapable of supporting evidence-based, coordinated interventions (IOM & UNODOC, 2023).

Yet, reliable data is critical for policy formulation, resource allocation, and cross-agency coordination. Incompatible data systems, incomplete reporting, and inconsistent cross-agency collaboration significantly impair national efforts to estimate prevalence, evaluate program effectiveness, and coordinate responses (U.S. Government Accountability Office, 2020). Without integrated data systems, policymakers operate with limited situational awareness, reducing the effectiveness of funding decisions, program interventions, and accountability mechanisms. This highlights the broader significance of establishing socio-technical approaches capable of improving data alignment across diverse stakeholders.

In response to these deficiencies, the Platform of Freedom offers a unified socio-technical model that integrates data governance, interoperability, ethical principles, and cross-sector collaboration. This aligns with international recommendations emphasizing the need for comprehensive frameworks to address technology-facilitated trafficking, including coordinated data-sharing, survivor-centered protections, and multi-stakeholder governance (Council of Europe, 2022). By proposing a scalable and ethically grounded structure for data agility, this chapter contributes a needed conceptual foundation that can guide policymakers, practitioners, and researchers seeking to transform fragmented data practices into coherent, adaptive, and actionable systems.

This chapter is significant because it reframes the persistent data fragmentation in anti-trafficking work as a socio-technical organizational challenge, rather than solely a technical or policy gap. It demonstrates that the ability to combat human trafficking effectively depends on cultivating data agility: the capacity of organizations to adapt, share, and act on information in real time through integrated technologies and collaborative governance. By applying Socio-Technical Systems Theory, Actor-Network Theory, and Critical Data Studies, the chapter emphasizes that human trafficking data systems are not neutral infrastructures but dynamic, co-created ecosystems that reflect human, technological, and ethical interdependencies.

The significance of this work lies in its practical and theoretical contribution: it offers a conceptual framework, the Platform of Freedom, for transforming fragmented data practices into adaptive, ethical, and interoperable frameworks that can enhance prevention, protection, and policy development. In doing so, it bridges the gap between data innovation and social responsibility, providing a model for how technology adoption, organizational agility, and ethical governance can jointly strengthen the global response to human trafficking.

For policymakers, it highlights the need to establish cross-sector data-sharing standards, regulatory frameworks, and funding models that promote responsible innovation. By embedding socio-technical design, networked collaboration, and digital ethics into both operational and legislative processes, this work supports the creation of agile anti-trafficking organizations and systems that can adapt to emerging trafficking trends while safeguarding human rights and promoting transparency.

METHODOLOGY

This chapter uses a perspective-style methodology, often used by authors seeking to synthesize existing research, highlight emerging gaps, analyze cross-sector challenges, and propose forward-looking frameworks or conceptual models for evolving phenomena, especially in areas where empirical research remains limited or fragmented (Narula, 2024).

The chapter draws from the author's doctoral dissertation, Trafficking Policy Analysis Using a Multidisciplinary Approach: Recommendations for U.S. Anti-Trafficking Policy (Szakonyi, 2022). That broader study integrated several lines of inquiry (including computational modeling, geospatial mapping, and policy analysis) to examine human trafficking as a global socio-technical phenomenon. Within that larger research program, data emerged not only as an analytical tool but as a critical policy challenge in itself.

The present chapter expands specifically on that data systems dimension, translating the dissertation's empirical insights into a conceptual model (the Platform of Freedom) that articulates how data, technology, and collaboration can be aligned through agile organizational design. This paper represents a conceptual continuation and theoretical refinement of the original study's findings, focusing on how adaptive data infrastructures can enhance technological and organizational responsiveness in anti-trafficking work.

The analysis builds on patterns and relationships identified in the dissertation's computational and spatial analyses of global trafficking data (Szakonyi et al., 2021), reframing those results through the lenses of Socio-Technical Systems Theory, Actor-Network Theory, and Critical Data Studies. These frameworks inform the interpretation of data as a living, co-produced system of human and technological interactions, and they provide the theoretical foundation for the Platform of Freedom as a model for cultivating data agility.

The chapter synthesizes peer-reviewed academic literature, government reports, and international policy documents reflecting on the period of rapid innovation in AI, data governance, and technology-facilitated trafficking. An integrative, interdisciplinary synthesis is methodologically valuable for complex, socio-technical problems like human trafficking where multi-sector collaboration is required; as the collective insights from technology studies, criminology, public policy, and social science can reveal system-level dynamics and propose actionable frameworks.

Although this chapter does not include empirical testing, its methodological aim is to consolidate existing evidence, identify systemic gaps, and propose a theoretically grounded, operationally relevant model to guide future research and implementation. This perspective is further strengthened by the author's professional expertise and ongoing work in the anti-trafficking field, including advising service providers, law enforcement agencies, policymakers, NGOs, and other stakeholders engaged in prevention, intervention, and data-driven decision-making. These insights are informed by real-world experiences observing the same systemic challenges across jurisdictions, reinforcing the consistency of these issues in both practice and scholarship.

Theoretical Foundations

This chapter's methodological approach is guided by three interrelated theoretical frameworks: Socio-Technical Systems (STS) Theory, Actor-Network Theory (ANT), and Critical Data Studies (CDS), each offering a distinct yet complementary lens for understanding how human, technological, and institutional systems interact within the global anti-trafficking ecosystem. Together, these perspectives highlight the intertwined dynamics of data, technology, and the social context, forming the conceptual foundation for the analysis and for the development of the Platform of Freedom model.

Socio-Technical Systems (STS) Theory

Socio-Technical Systems Theory provides the foundational framework for examining how technological infrastructures and human actors (traffickers, victims, law enforcement, and NGOs) co-evolve within the trafficking ecosystem. Originally developed by Eric Trist, Ken Bamforth and Fred Emery in the 1950s, STS emphasizes joint optimization, or the principle that social and technical systems must be designed in tandem to function effectively (Bostrom & Heinen, 1977; Cherns, 1976, 1987; Cooper & Foster, 1971; Kaminski, 2022; Mumford, 2006; Trist & Bamforth, 1951).

Applied to this study, STS theory frames human trafficking as a socio-technical phenomenon, shaped by the reciprocal interactions between digital infrastructures (e.g., social media platforms, encrypted communication channels, and machine learning systems for detection) and social actors (traffickers, victims, investigators, and community organizations). The theory highlights that neither technology nor human behavior alone determines outcomes; rather, it is their interdependence that drives both exploitation and intervention.

Actor-Network Theory (ANT)

Actor-Network Theory complements STS by extending analysis to the networks of relationships among human and non-human actors that constitute the trafficking ecosystem. Rooted in the works of Callon (1986), Latour (1987, 1996), and Walsham (1997), ANT conceptualizes technology, people, policies, and organizations as interlinked "actors" that continuously negotiate and redefine their roles through interaction.

In the context of this study, ANT provides a methodological lens for tracing relationships between traffickers, digital platforms, law enforcement systems, algorithms, and data infrastructures. It allows for understanding how online technologies facilitate recruitment, how law enforcement relies on digital evidence, and how NGOs and data intermediaries reshape these systems through advocacy and innovation.

By applying ANT principles, this analysis identifies intervention points within these networks, moments where data-sharing protocols, ethical standards, or cross-sector partnerships can realign the relationships between human and technical agents toward prevention and accountability. ANT therefore supports the Platform of Freedom's emphasis on collaboration and adaptability as essential to building organizational agility across a distributed, multi-actor system.

Critical Data Studies and Digital Ethics

While STS and ANT explore how systems operate and interconnect, Critical Data Studies (CDS) and Digital Ethics provide the normative framework for assessing the social, ethical, and political implications of data use in anti-trafficking efforts. CDS critically examines the production, governance, and impact of big data within societal power structures (Boyd & Crawford, 2012; Crawford et al., 2014; Dalton & Thatcher, 2014; Ekbia et al., 2015; Iliadis & Russo, 2016).

This approach emphasizes that data are not neutral artifacts; they are shaped by the biases, values, and power dynamics of the institutions that collect and interpret them. Applying CDS to this research allows for a critical interrogation of how algorithms, AI, and machine learning systems used in trafficking detection may reproduce inequalities, generate false positives, or compromise privacy and consent.

In this context, CDS ensures that the integration of advanced computational tools is balanced with human rights safeguards and ethical reflexivity. It informs the chapter's argument that data-driven agility must coexist with digital responsibility, ensuring that innovation in detection and prevention does not come at the expense of vulnerable populations.

Integration of Theoretical Frameworks

Together, STS, ANT, and CDS create a comprehensive theoretical foundation that bridges technical analysis, social interaction, and ethical governance:

- STS grounds the methodology in the network of social and technological systems.
- ANT traces the evolving networks that connect human and non-human actors across data ecosystems.
- CDS ensures critical reflection on the consequences and ethics of data practices.

These theories collectively support the development of the Platform of Freedom, framing it as both a theoretical and practical model for aligning technological innovation with adaptive, ethical, and collaborative data and systems design. These theoretical foundations directly inform the Platform of Freedom by illustrating why anti-trafficking systems require both socio-technical integration and critical governance. STS highlights the need for aligned human-technical workflows; ANT explains the importance of multi-stakeholder coordination and distributed agency; and CDS reinforces the centrality of ethical, transparent, and equitable data practices. Integrating these insights clarifies how the Platform of Freedom can serve as a bridge between conceptual understanding and practical implementation in complex anti-trafficking environments.

LITERATURE REVIEW

Understanding the Human Trafficking Landscape

Human trafficking, often described as modern-day slavery, remains one of the world's most pressing human rights and public health crises. Defined by the Palermo Protocol, trafficking involves the use of force, fraud, or coercion for the purpose of labor or commercial sexual exploitation (United Nations General Assembly Resolution 55/25, 2000; U.S. Department of Homeland Security, 2025). Globally, the International Labour Organization estimates the number of victims of trafficking at around 50 million (ILO, 2022). Despite these staggering estimates, reliable data remain difficult to collect. Detected victim statistics show a bleak picture: between

2020-2023, UN member states reported only 202,478 victims, showcasing a significant gap between estimates and results (UNODC, 2024).

Trafficking has profound physical, psychological, and economic consequences. Victims frequently suffer trauma, chronic illness, and post-traumatic stress (Baldwin et al., 2011; Coverdale et al., 2020; Dovydaitis, 2010; Lederer & Wetzel, 2014; Oram et al., 2016; Zimmerman et al., 2011). Economically, trafficking constitutes a multi-billion-dollar illicit industry, generating an estimated $236 billion in profits annually, with an average of over $10,000 per victim per year (ILO, 2024). These figures highlight both the scope of the problem and the global incentive structures that sustain it.

Technology as a Double-Edged Sword

The rise of digital platforms has radically transformed the landscape of human trafficking. On one hand, technology has facilitated trafficking by providing new venues for recruitment, advertisement, and financial transactions. The internet enables traffickers to obscure identities, communicate anonymously, and exploit victims at scale through online classifieds, social media, and encrypted applications (Dank et al., 2014; Gezinski & Gonzalez-Pons, 2022; Keller & Dance, 2019; Lazarus et al., 2025; Mishra, 2015; Moyo et al., 2025). Cryptocurrency has also become a preferred medium for illicit payments, with an estimated $76 billion of illegal transactions annually financed through Bitcoin and related digital currencies (Foley et al., 2019).

However, these same technologies also offer new tools for detection, prevention, and response. Emerging applications of machine learning, natural language processing, image recognition, and blockchain have opened pathways for innovative anti-trafficking interventions (Fleury, 2019; Katta et al., 2025; Masud et al., 2025; Stylianou et al., 2019). For example, research teams have developed algorithms to analyze online advertisements and identify probable trafficking cases (Stylianou et al., 2019; Tong et al., 2017). Blockchain technologies have also been explored to improve supply chain transparency and trace labor exploitation (Bryans, 2014; Wolfson, 2018).

Yet, despite these advances, technological potential is limited by fragmented data ecosystems and insufficient organizational coordination. The absence of standardized reporting and secure information-sharing frameworks means that even powerful analytic tools operate within narrow data silos, reducing their collective effectiveness.

The Data Deficit in Anti-Trafficking Efforts

Recent research consistently demonstrates that anti-trafficking data systems suffer from fragmentation, inconsistent definitions, and limited interoperability.

Across the literature, one of the most persistent challenges identified is the lack of comprehensive, reliable, and interoperable data (Cho, 2015a, 2015b; Smith, 2018). Because trafficking is a hidden crime, much of the available information comes from victim self-reports, law enforcement cases, or NGO service data, each collected through different definitions and protocols. Farrell and de Vries (2020) note that national and organizational data sets are often built on divergent conceptualizations of trafficking, making cross-comparison and coordinated responses difficult. The UNODC Global Report on Trafficking in Persons similarly emphasizes gaps between administrative data sources, limited coverage of hidden populations, and persistent underreporting (United Nations Office on Drugs and Crime, 2024).

Currently, there is no central body that consolidates comprehensive data from the many anti-trafficking organizations worldwide, integrating information from rescue operations, law enforcement, and other sources into a single comprehensive repository. Consequently, researchers, policymakers and providers struggle to form an accurate, unified picture of trafficking dynamics. Some attempts exist to consolidate data across agencies, such as the Counter-Trafficking Data Collaborative (CTDC), but this still remains limited by voluntary reporting and access restrictions (Counter Trafficking Data Collaborative, n.d.). These findings confirm what earlier scholars have suggested: data gaps impede the identification of trafficking routes, victim vulnerabilities, and the evaluation of policy outcomes (Albanese, 2007; Hernandez & Rudolph, 2015). This reinforces the need for governance frameworks that support consistency, alignment, and cross-sector data integration.

The Role of Collaboration

Data gaps are not purely technical, they reflect deeper issues of organizational fragmentation and lack of agile coordination. Anti-trafficking efforts are carried out by a constellation of actors (law enforcement agencies, international organizations, NGOs, private technology firms, and researchers) often working in isolation. Each organization collects and stores data differently, guided by its own mandates, privacy policies, and funding constraints. As a result, collaboration across these entities is sporadic and reactive rather than systematic (Gallagher & Holmes, 2008; Newton et al., 2008; Wilson & Dalton, 2008).

In my work in the St. Louis metro region, I have witnessed how law enforcement and child advocacy centers must rely on manual, ad hoc coordination when a child is identified as a potential trafficking victim. Rather than using integrated digital systems to share information or mobilize multidisciplinary responses, officers often have to place individual phone calls to the local Child Advocacy Center to determine whether a forensic interviewer is available, whether immediate services can be provided, and how the child should be supported. The same fragmented process occurs when identifying emergency shelter or safe placement: survivor advocates must often contact shelters individually, one by one, to determine whether they have an available bed for a survivor. Every call is made one by one, agency to agency, because our systems do not communicate with each other. This reliance on personal contacts and informal communication channels (even during critical moments of victim identification) creates delays, increases the risk of miscommunication, and highlights the absence of interoperable systems that could streamline care and protect victims more effectively.

Despite the strong collaborative spirit among providers in the region, the lack of shared, real-time data infrastructure makes sustained collaboration extraordinarily difficult, forcing partners to depend on relationships rather than the reliable systems victims deserve. Successful data-driven responses require both technological interoperability and organizational agility to adapt structures, policies, and partnerships as trafficking methods evolve. Data cannot achieve their full potential unless institutions can share, interpret, and act on insights collectively.

Technology, Ethics, and Responsible Data Use

While data innovation promises to strengthen anti-trafficking responses, it also introduces significant ethical considerations. Scholars warn that algorithms can perpetuate bias, misclassify vulnerable populations, and compromise privacy (Boyd & Crawford, 2012; Crawford et al., 2014). In contexts involving survivors of exploitation, mishandled or de-identified data may still reveal personal details, exposing victims to further harm. The literature therefore highlights the need for critical data governance, balancing technological capability with human rights protections (Barney, 2018; Gallagher, 2010, 2017).

This ethical tension reinforces the importance of designing systems that are socio-technical and collaborative by nature, integrating human oversight, transparent algorithms, and participatory policy development. In doing so, technology becomes not only a detection mechanism but also a platform for trust, accountability, and empowerment.

Synthesis of Literature

The literature demonstrates that while technology has amplified both the risks and opportunities within the human trafficking ecosystem, its effectiveness hinges on data quality and collaboration. The absence of standardized, shared, and ethically governed data infrastructures undermines even the most advanced analytic approaches. At the same time, it reveals how data-driven insights, when supported by cross-sector collaboration and agile governance, can transform fragmented responses into cohesive, proactive systems.

Currently, no existing framework fully integrates socio-technical design, governance structures, and cross-sector coordination, and therefore analytical and technological innovations remain disconnected from operational decision-making, resulting in limited scalability and inconsistent implementation. This gap highlights the need for a unified, operationally grounded socio-technical model, precisely the contribution this chapter seeks to provide. This literature synthesis provides the intellectual foundation for the Platform of Freedom framework, which reimagines how technology adoption and data governance, paired with collaboration and policy can be harmonized to strengthen the global response to human trafficking.

RESULTS AND RECOMMENDATIONS

The synthesis of literature combined with field experience consistently demonstrate that the lack of interoperable data systems is one of the central barriers to coordinated anti-trafficking responses. Research shows that inconsistent data standards, limited information sharing, and unaligned digital infrastructures significantly reduce the effectiveness of detection, referral, and prosecution efforts (United Nations Office on Drugs and Crime, 2024; U.S. Government Accountability Office, 2020). These findings reinforce that data agility, rather than technology alone, is the key determinant of operational effectiveness.

Therefore, anti-trafficking organizations must prioritize the development of interoperable data infrastructures supported by shared taxonomies, cross-agency protocols, and survivor-centered governance frameworks. Recent systematic reviews identify that technological tools are only effective when embedded within coordinated workflows and ethically grounded governance structures (Dimas at al., 2022; Gezinski & Gonzalez-Pons, 2022). As a result, improving collaboration and data mechanisms is essential for measurable impact.

The Platform of Freedom: A Model for Data Agility in Anti-Trafficking Systems

Based on these findings, we developed a conceptual framework titled The Platform of Freedom, depicted in Figure 1. This data management framework represents an integrated model for building organizational capability to adaptively collect, analyze, and share information across complex, multidisciplinary networks engaged in anti-human-trafficking efforts. At its core, the Platform of Freedom demonstrates that the global fight against human trafficking cannot be advanced through technology alone; it requires a synchronized ecosystem where data, collaboration, and policy dynamically reinforce one another. Each element of the platform represents a critical enabler of organizational agility and effective technology implementation.

Figure 1.The Platform of Freedom

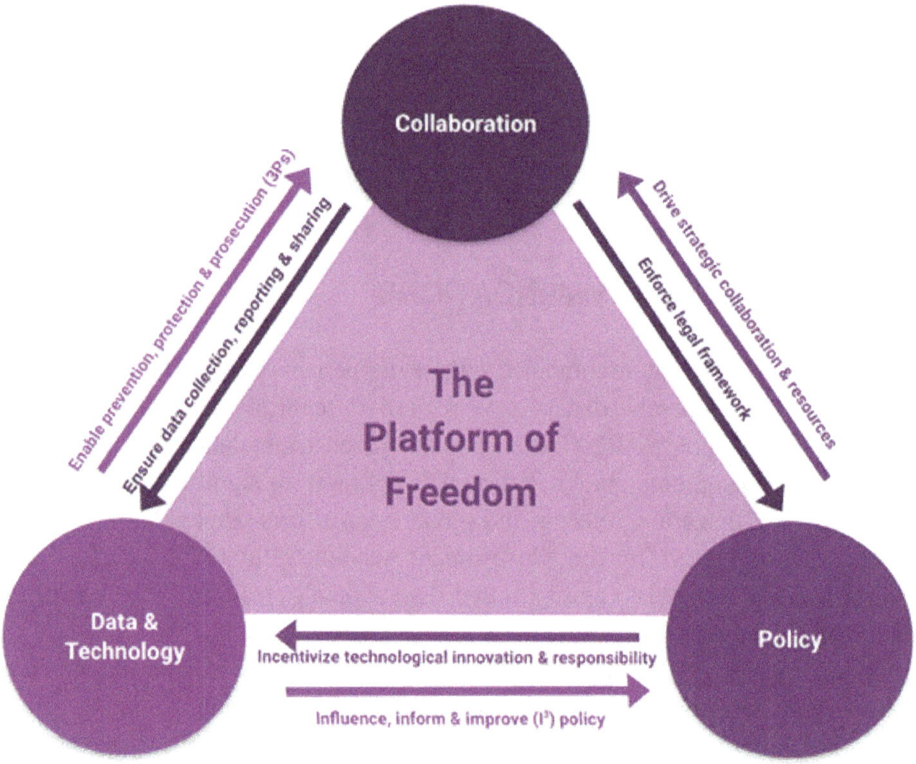

Data and Technology: Foundations for Adaptive Insight

The first pillar, data and technology, reflects the need for advanced, interoperable digital systems that can collect, manage, and interpret trafficking-related information from multiple sources. Current anti-trafficking efforts are constrained by inconsistent, siloed datasets and limited analytical capacity. Fragmented data structures prevent a holistic understanding of trafficking trends, obscuring connections between actors.

The model identifies that organizations must invest in technological agility, the ability to rapidly integrate, upgrade, and align data systems to evolving threats. Machine learning, blockchain, and geospatial analytics were identified as transformative tools capable of enhancing predictive capacity and situational awareness

(City of Milwaukee, 2020; Cockbain & Wallis, 2019; Gardner et al., 2017; Szakonyi et al., 2021; Stylianou et al., 2019). However, these technologies can only be effective when supported by shared data standards, ethical governance, and secure infrastructures for information exchange. Thus, the Platform of Freedom calls for an interoperable data architecture that bridges humanitarian, law enforcement, and private-sector systems, enabling data to flow safely and meaningfully across the anti-trafficking ecosystem.

The data and technology pillar embodies the intersection of the three guiding theories (Socio-Technical Systems, Actor-Network Theory, and Critical Data Studies) by framing data infrastructures as living, adaptive systems shaped by both human and technological actors. From the STS lens, data systems must be co-designed with the social contexts that sustain them, ensuring technical innovation aligns with organizational and human needs. ANT reinforces this by viewing databases, algorithms, and institutions as interconnected nodes within a constantly shifting network that must reconfigure relationships to remain responsive. CDS adds an ethical dimension, emphasizing that data practices must be transparent, equitable, and protective of vulnerable populations. Together, these perspectives position data and technology not simply as tools for detection, but as collaborative, socio-ethical systems through which anti-trafficking organizations can cultivate true agility and trust.

Collaboration: The Engine of Organizational Agility

The second pillar, collaboration, is the mechanism that transforms data into actionable intelligence. No single organization (governmental, nonprofit, or private) can independently manage the complexity of global trafficking networks. Sustainable progress requires organizational agility at the ecosystem level, where diverse actors can co-create, share insights, and adapt strategies in real time. The Platform of Freedom envisions an agile collaborative infrastructure characterized by:

- Cross-sector partnerships between technologists, policymakers, law enforcement, and social service providers;
- Shared governance mechanisms for data access, ethics, and accountability;
- Continuous feedback loops that translate local operational insights into global intelligence.

This adaptive collaboration reflects the principles of socio-technical and actor-network systems, where human and technological actors continuously co-evolve and reconfigure their relationships to meet emerging challenges. Within anti-trafficking ecosystems, this interplay allows organizations to sense changes through data flows, adapt tools and partnerships in real time, and redistribute resources as networks shift.

Such agility, rooted in the constant negotiation between people, technologies, and institutions, enables more rapid detection of trafficking trends, faster dissemination of intelligence, and more synchronized interventions across jurisdictions.

Policy: The Governance Framework for Ethical Agility

The third pillar, policy, provides the regulatory and ethical structure that sustains the entire system. Inadequate policy coherence and inconsistent reporting requirements across jurisdictions are major barriers to effective data sharing and technology use. The Platform of Freedom proposes that agile policy frameworks must:

- Incentivize inter-organizational collaboration through standardized reporting and open-data protocols;
- Establish data protection and privacy standards for sensitive victim information;
- Support funding mechanisms that reward innovation and responsible AI adoption;
- Mandate accountability across government, civil society, and industry actors.

In this configuration, policy is not static regulation, it functions as a dynamic feedback mechanism, continuously informed by real-time data and collaborative learning. Through iterative policymaking, organizations can respond to emerging trafficking patterns and adapt governance mechanisms without stifling innovation.

The policy component of the Platform of Freedom also aligns closely with STS, ANT, and CDS. From an STS perspective, policy serves as the social structure that guides how technical systems are designed and implemented, ensuring that governance evolves alongside innovation. Through the ANT lens, policy acts as a mediator connecting diverse human and non-human actors (governments, databases, algorithms, and advocacy networks) into coordinated action. Informed by CDS, it embeds ethical reflexivity into regulation, mandating transparency, data protection, and accountability so that technological progress advances justice rather than exploitation.

The Interaction of Data, Collaboration, and Policy

The most significant insight of the Platform of Freedom is the interdependence of these three pillars. The platform is not a linear process but a cyclical, reflexive system in which data informs policy, policy enables collaboration, and collaboration enhances data quality.

- Data drives collaboration by revealing trends that guide targeted interventions and resource allocation, contributing to the 3Ps (i.e. the main objectives) of the Palermo Protocol: prevention, protection and prosecution (United Nations General Assembly Resolution 55/25, 2000). In reverse, collaboration ensures data collection, reporting and sharing, therefore increasing data outputs and technology's positive impact.
- Technological and data tools can influence, inform and improve (I3) policy: they can inform policy about trafficking factors, and provide valuable metrics on the effectiveness of policy frameworks. Policy, on the other hand, can foster a favorable environment for technological innovation, experimentation and development, while also ensuring accountability and ethical responsibility within the broader technological ecosystem.
- Policy can mobilize strategic collaboration and resource alignment by establishing national and international standards that mandate coordination and secure data-sharing among stakeholders. Conversely, collaboration among diverse anti-trafficking stakeholders is essential to effectively implement and uphold the broader policy framework.

When these elements operate in synergy, organizations and nations can develop a capacity to learn, respond, and evolve dynamically in the face of the emerging trafficking landscape. By synthesizing the technological, collaborative, and policy dimensions of anti-trafficking efforts, the Platform of Freedom demonstrates how organizations and nations can build agility and resilience to support these efforts. The Platform of Freedom thus provides a model for how technology and data adoption, when embedded in agile organizational systems, can transform fragmented data landscapes into coordinated, intelligence-driven anti-trafficking operations.

The Platform of Freedom framework integrates these insights by outlining how data governance, socio-technical integration, and cross-sector collaboration can operate as a unified system. Conceptually, the model demonstrates that anti-trafficking outcomes improve when data flows are structured, ethical safeguards are built into system design, and multi-agency coordination is supported by shared digital tools. This provides a practical pathway for translating socio-technical theory into actionable system architecture.

Overall, the analysis concludes that anti-trafficking systems cannot rely on isolated technological innovations. Instead, improvements in data standards, coordinated governance, and collaborative infrastructures are necessary to reduce fragmentation and strengthen protection and justice. These results align with international findings that emphasize the importance of integrated approaches to technology-facilitated trafficking (Council of Europe, 2022).

CONCLUSIONS

Human trafficking continues to evolve as a data-driven and technology-enabled crime, outpacing the systems designed to counter it. The most significant barrier to effective intervention is not the absence of technology but the absence of data and the ability of organizations to integrate, interpret, and act on information collectively. Fragmented databases, incompatible reporting systems, and limited coordination between agencies prevent a full understanding of trafficking patterns and weaken the global response.

The analysis across literature, field practice, and cross-sector evidence demonstrates that technology alone cannot resolve the systemic fragmentation that characterizes many anti-trafficking responses. Instead, the central insight emerging from this study is that data agility (defined by interoperable systems, shared governance, and coordinated workflows) is the key foundation enabling meaningful prevention, protection, and prosecution outcomes.

The Platform of Freedom model offers a strategic framework to address these gaps by linking data and technology, collaboration, and policy as mutually reinforcing pillars of organizational and global solutions for trafficking. To translate this framework into practice, anti-trafficking systems must prioritize:

- Developing interoperable data standards across governments, NGOs, and private partners to enable secure information exchange;
- Creating national and international data-sharing agreements that incentivize collaboration while safeguarding privacy;
- Investing in capacity building so frontline agencies can adopt and sustain advanced analytic and visualization tools;
- Embedding ethical and human-rights safeguards into all data-collection and AI-driven detection systems;
- Aligning policy frameworks to reward innovation and adaptive governance in technology use.

In essence, combating human trafficking in the digital age requires more than new tools; it demands adaptive systems, agile leadership, and responsible data stewardship. When organizations coordinate through interoperable technologies and ethical collaboration, they can transform fragmented information into actionable intelligence, accelerating prevention, protection, and justice for victims worldwide.

The Platform of Freedom contributes to the field by offering a unified socio-technical framework that integrates ethical data governance, collaborative infrastructures, and system-level coordination. Unlike existing approaches that isolate technology, policy, or organizational behavior, this model demonstrates how these elements must function together to reduce fragmentation and improve decision-making in real-world contexts. This integrated perspective responds directly to gaps identified in recent analyses of technology-facilitated trafficking.

Effective anti-trafficking policy must begin with the establishment of standardized data protocols and interoperable information systems across law enforcement, social services, NGOs, and state agencies. Policymakers should require the adoption of shared taxonomies, mandatory reporting structures, and secure data-governance frameworks to ensure that critical information flows seamlessly across jurisdictions. To support this, governments should invest in regional or statewide digital infrastructures that enable real-time data exchange, reducing the fragmented coordination that currently delays victim support and hampers investigative outcomes. Policies should also require cross-sector training focused on ethical data practices, survivor-centered approaches, and coordinated response procedures to ensure that technology is deployed safely and equitably.

In addition, governments should establish multi-agency oversight bodies responsible for ensuring consistent data-sharing practices, evaluating system performance, and coordinating interagency collaboration. Funding mechanisms must prioritize capacity-building for frontline NGOs, survivor advocacy groups, and shelters so they can fully participate in digital coordination systems rather than operate in isolation. Finally, policies should support ongoing evaluation and research to assess the effectiveness of these integrated data systems, ensuring continuous improvement and accountability across the anti-trafficking ecosystem.

In summary, the Platform of Freedom framework informs and guides practitioners and policymakers on the necessity of building standardized data protocols, shared taxonomies, interoperable information-sharing systems, and cross-agency governance structures that reduce fragmentation and enable real-time coordination across law enforcement, service providers, NGOs, and policy agencies. Strengthening infrastructure and collaboration is therefore the most practical pathway to improving outcomes for survivors.

While the Platform of Freedom provides a theoretically grounded and practice-oriented model, its application and validation require further empirical testing. This chapter is limited by its reliance on a conceptual and perspective-based methodology. Although such approaches are recognized as valuable for theory-building and identifying research gaps, the Platform of Freedom has not yet been validated through field trials, quantitative evaluation, or implementation studies. The analysis also draws on existing administrative data and secondary literature, which are themselves constrained by inconsistent definitions, underreporting, and fragmented data systems. As a result, the framework proposed here should be viewed as a foundation for future empirical research rather than a fully tested operational model.

Finally, as with all perspective-based and experience-informed analyses, there is also a potential for researcher bias, as interpretations may be influenced by the author's professional background and direct engagement with practitioners. Although this expertise strengthens the practical relevance of the framework, it may shape the emphasis placed on certain themes or system challenges (Bertero, 2016).

RECOMMENDATIONS FOR FUTURE RESEARCH

Future research should expand on this study by empirically validating the Platform of Freedom framework across diverse organizational and regional contexts to assess its feasibility, scalability, and impact on victim identification, service coordination, and investigative outcomes. Testing how its three pillars (data and technology, collaboration, and policy) function together in practice would provide evidence of its effectiveness in strengthening agility, improving data governance, and accelerating coordinated responses. Mixed-methods studies, combining qualitative insights from practitioners with quantitative analyses of data-sharing patterns, would provide critical evidence on how socio-technical integration affects real-world anti-trafficking responses. Comparative studies across sectors and regions, including NGOs, law enforcement, and private technology partners, could illuminate how variations in policy, infrastructure, organizational design, culture and funding influence data-sharing behaviors and outcomes.

Further research should also explore the development of interoperable data standards and ethical, survivor-centered data governance models that balance innovation with human rights protections. As advanced analytics and artificial intelligence become more integrated into anti-trafficking strategies, there is a pressing need to evaluate algorithmic fairness, privacy preservation, and consent management. Investigating how cross-border data regulations and privacy laws affect global collaboration will be essential for operationalizing responsible technology use.

Finally, future inquiry should examine the social and behavioral dimensions of data collaboration: how trust, leadership, and institutional incentives shape participation in shared data ecosystems. Longitudinal research tracking how agile data infrastructures evolve over time could provide valuable insights into sustaining technological innovation amid shifting geopolitical and economic conditions. Collectively, these lines of research would deepen understanding of how to build adaptive, ethically governed, and globally coordinated data systems capable of transforming anti-trafficking work of organizations in the digital era.

REFERENCES

Albanese, J. (2007). A criminal network approach to understanding & measuring trafficking in human beings. In Savona, E., & Stefanizzi, S. (Eds.), *Measuring human trafficking: Complexities and pitfalls* (pp. 55–71). Springer., DOI: 10.1007/0-387-68044-6_7

Baldwin, S. B., Eisenman, D. P., Sayles, J. N., Ryan, G., & Chuang, K. S. (2011). Identification of human trafficking victims in health care settings. *Health and Human Rights*, *13*, 36–49. https://heinonline-org.ezp.slu.edu/HOL/Page?collection=journals&handle=hein.journals/harhrj13&id=40&men_tab=srchresults PMID: 22772961

Barney, D. (2018). Trafficking technology: A look at different approaches to ending technology-facilitated human trafficking. *Pepperdine Law Review*, *45*(4), 747–784. https://heinonline.org/HOL/LandingPage?handle=hein.journals/pepplr45&div=25&id=&page=

Bertero, C. (2016). Guidelines for writing a commentary. *International Journal of Qualitative Studies on Health and Well-being*, *11*(1), 31390. Advance online publication. DOI: 10.3402/qhw.v11.31390 PMID: 26976608

Bostrom, R. P., & Heinen, J. S. (1977). MIS problems and failures: A socio-technical perspective, Part I: The causes. *Management Information Systems Quarterly*, *1*(3), 17–32. DOI: 10.2307/248710

Boyd, D., & Crawford, K. (2012). Critical questions for Big Data: Provocations for a cultural, technological, and scholarly phenomenon. *Information Communication and Society*, *15*(5), 662–679. DOI: 10.1080/1369118X.2012.678878

Bryans, D. (2014). Bitcoin and money laundering: Mining for an effective solution. *Industrial Law Journal*, *89*(1), 441–472. https://heinonline-org.ezp.slu.edu/HOL/Page?handle=hein.journals/indana89&div=16

Callon, M. (1986). The sociology of an actor-network: The case of the electric vehicle. In Callon, M., Law, J., & Rip, A. (Eds.), *Mapping the dynamics of science and technology* (pp. 19–34). The Macmillan Press., DOI: 10.1007/978-1-349-07408-2_2

Cherns, A. (1976). The principles of sociotechnical design. *Human Relations*, *29*(8), 783–792. DOI: 10.1177/001872677602900806

Cherns, A. (1987). Principles of sociotechnical design revisited. *Human Relations*, *40*(3), 153–161. DOI: 10.1177/001872678704000303

Cho, S. Y. (2015a). Human trafficking, a shadow of migration - Evidence from Germany. *The Journal of Development Studies*, *51*(7), 905–921. DOI: 10.1080/00220388.2015.1010158

Cho, S. Y. (2015b). Modelling for determinants of human trafficking. *Social Inclusion (Lisboa)*, *3*(1), 2–21. http://dx.doi.org.ezp.slu.edu/10.17645/si.v3i1.125. DOI: 10.17645/si.v3i1.125

City of Milwaukee. (2020). *Geospatial characteristics of sex trafficking of juveniles and young adults in Milwaukee.* https://www.mcw.edu/-/media/MCW/Departments/Epidemiology/MHRC/2020-Milwaukee-Juveniles-and-Young-Adults-Sex-Trafficking-Report.pdf?la=en

Cockbain, E., & Wallis, A. (2019, April 17). *The social, spatial and temporal systems behind human trafficking.* Delta 8.7. https://delta87.org/2019/04/social-spatial-temporal-systems-human-trafficking/

Cole, J., & Sprang, G. (2015). Sex trafficking of minors in metropolitan, micropolitan, and rural communities. *Child Abuse & Neglect*, *40*, 113–123. https://doi-org.ezp.slu.edu/10.1016/j.chiabu.2014.07.015. DOI: 10.1016/j.chiabu.2014.07.015 PMID: 25151302

Cooper, R., & Foster, M. (1971). Sociotechnical systems. *The American Psychologist*, *26*(5), 467–474. DOI: 10.1037/h0031539

Council of Europe. (2022). *Online and technology-facilitated trafficking in human beings.* https://rm.coe.int/online-and-technology-facilitated-trafficking-in-human-beings-summary-/1680a5e10c

Counter Trafficking Data Collaborative. (n.d.). *The Counter Trafficking Data Collaborative.* https://www.ctdatacollaborative.org/

Coverdale, J. H., Gordon, M. R., & Nguyen, P. T. (Eds.). (2020). *Human trafficking: A treatment guide for mental health professionals*. American Psychiatric Association Publishing. DOI: 10.1176/appi.books.9781615379439

Crawford, K., Miltner, K., & Gray, M. L. (2014). Critiquing Big Data: Politics, ethics, epistemology. *International Journal of Communication*, *8*, 1663–1672. https://ijoc.org/index.php/ijoc/article/view/2167/1164

Dalton, C., & Thatcher, J. (2014). What does a Critical Data Studies look like, and why do we care? Seven points for a critical approach to 'big data.' *Environment and Planning D: Society and Space. Online journal companion.* https://societyandspace.com/material/commentaries/craig-dalton-and-jim-thatcher-what-does-a-critical-data-studies-look-like-and-why-do-we-care-seven-points-for-a-critical-approach-to-big-data/

Daniel-Wrabetz, J., & Penedo, R. (2015). Trafficking in human beings in time and space. A socioecological perspective. In Guia, M. (Ed.), *The illegal business of human trafficking* (pp. 1–19). Springer., DOI: 10.1007/978-3-319-09441-0_1

Dank, M., Khan, B., Downey, P. M., Kotonias, C., Mayer, D., Owens, C., Pacifici, L., & Yu, L. (2014). *Estimating the size and structure of the underground commercial sex economy in eight major US cities.* The Urban Institute (Award No. 2010-IJ-CX-1674, U.S. Department of Justice, Office of Justice Programs, National Institute of Justice). https://www.urban.org/sites/default/files/alfresco/publication-pdfs/413047-Estimating-the-Size-and-Structure-of-the-Underground-Commercial-Sex-Economy-in-Eight-Major-US-Cities.PDF

Dimas, G. L., Konrad, R. A., Maass, K. L., & Trapp, A. C. (2022). Operations research and analytics to combat human trafficking: A systematic review of academic literature. *PLoS One, 17*(8), e0273708. Advance online publication. DOI: 10.1371/journal.pone.0273708 PMID: 36037198

Dovydaitis, T. (2010). Human trafficking: The role of the health care provider. *Journal of Midwifery & Women's Health, 55*(5), 462–467. DOI: 10.1016/j.jmwh.2009.12.017 PMID: 20732668

Ekbia, H., Mattioli, M., Kouper, I., Arave, G., Ghazinejad, A., Bowman, T., Suri, V.R., Tsou, A., Weingart, S. & Sugimoto, C.R. (2015), Big data, bigger dilemmas: A critical review. *Journal of The Association for Information Science & Technology, 66*(8), 1523-1545. (First published in 2014)DOI: 10.1002/asi.23294

Farrell, A., & De Vries, I. (2020). Measuring the nature and prevalence of human trafficking. In Winterdyk, J., & Jones, J. (Eds.), *The Palgrave International Handbook of Human Trafficking* (pp. 147–162). Palgrave Macmillan. DOI: 10.1007/978-3-319-63058-8_6

Fleury, D. (2019, July 8). *A Rescue Mission: 3 Ways Deep Learning Could Combat Human Tracking.* Towards Data Science. https://towardsdatascience.com/a-rescue-mission-3-ways-deep-learning-could-combat-human-trafficking-85700eb62be5

Foley, S., Karlsen, J. R., & Putniņš, T. J. (2019). Sex, drugs, and bitcoin: How much illegal activity is financed through cryptocurrencies? *Review of Financial Studies*, *32*(5), 1798–1853. DOI: 10.1093/rfs/hhz015

Gallagher, A., & Holmes, P. (2008). Developing an effective criminal justice response to human trafficking: Lessons from the front line. *International Criminal Justice Review*, *18*(3), 318–343. DOI: 10.1177/1057567708320746

Gallagher, A. T. (2010). *The international law of human trafficking*. Cambridge University Press. DOI: 10.1017/CBO9780511761065

Gallagher, A. T. (2017). What's wrong with the Global Slavery Index? *Anti-Trafficking Review*, (8), 90–112. DOI: 10.14197/atr.20121786

Gardner, W. L., Panaou, T., Watterson, K., Alao, S., & Jacob, B. G. (2017). Predicting potential human trafficking recruiting geolocations using eigendecomposed non-zero spatial autocorrelation coefficients and Poissonian heterogeneous gamma distributed variables. *International Journal of Geographical Information Systems*, *4*(2), 1–23. https://www.researchgate.net/publication/320044978_Predicting_potential_human_trafficking_recruiting_geolocations_using_Eigendecomposed_non-zero_spatial_autocorrelation_coefficients_and_Poissonian_heterogeneous_gamma_distributed_variables

Gezinski, L. B., & Gonzalez-Pons, K. M. (2022). Sex trafficking and technology: A systematic review of recruitment and exploitation. *Journal of Human Trafficking*, *10*(3), 497–511. DOI: 10.1080/23322705.2022.2034378

Hernandez, D., & Rudolph, A. (2015). Modern day slavery: What drives human trafficking in Europe? *European Journal of Political Economy*, *38*, 118–139. DOI: 10.1016/j.ejpoleco.2015.02.002

Ibanez, M., & Suthers, D. D. (2014). Detection of domestic human trafficking indicators and movement trends using content available on open internet sources. In *2014 47th Hawaii international conference on system sciences* (pp. 1556-1565). IEEE. DOI DOI: 10.1109/HICSS.2014.200

Iliadis, A., & Russo, F. (2016). Critical data studies: An introduction. *Big Data & Society*, *3*(2). (Original work published 2016)DOI: 10.1177/2053951716674238

International Labour Office. (2022). *Global estimates of modern slavery: Forced labour and forced marriage.* https://www.ilo.org/publications/major-publications/global-estimates-modern-slavery-forced-labour-and-forced-marriage

International Labour Office. (2024). *Profits and poverty: The economics of forced labour.* DOI: 10.54394/JJJE9035

International Organization for Migration & United Nations Office on Drugs and Crime. (2023). *International classification standard for administrative data on trafficking in persons.* https://www.unodc.org/documents/data-and-analysis/tip/2023/ICS-TIP_2023-v4.pdf

Kaminski, J. (2022). Editorial. Theory applied to informatics: Socio-Technical Theory. *Canadian Journal of Nursing Informatics, 17*(3-4). https://cjni.net/journal/?p=10442

Katta, J. V., Pagadavarapu, U. C., Selvi, G. A., & Subapriya, V. (2025). A comprehensive human trafficking identification and prediction system using machine learning techniques. In *Proceedings of the International Conference On Cognitive Computing And Artificial Intelligence, 3257*(1), Article 020036. DOI: 10.1063/5.0265865

Keller, M. H., & Dance, G. J. X. (2019, September 29). *The internet is overrun with images of child sexual abuse. What went wrong?* The New York Times. https://www.nytimes.com/interactive/2019/09/28/us/child-sex-abuse.html

Latour, B. (1987). *Science in action: How to follow scientists and engineers through society.* Harvard University Press.

Latour, B. (1996). On actor-network theory: A few clarifications. *Soziale Welt, 47*(4), 369–381. https://www.jstor.org/stable/40878163

Lazarus, S., Chiang, M., & Button, M. (2025). Assessing Human Trafficking and Cybercrime Intersections Through Survivor Narratives. *Deviant Behavior*, •••, 1–18. DOI: 10.1080/01639625.2025.2470402

Lederer, L. J., & Wetzel, C. A. (2014). The health consequences of sex trafficking and their implications for identifying victims in healthcare facilities. *Annals of Health Law, 23*, 61–91. https://heinonline-org.ezp.slu.edu/HOL/Page?collection=journals&handle=hein.journals/anohl23&id=68&men_tab=srchresults

Masud, N., Bassam, A. A., Sobhan, A., & Sourav, M. T. I. (2025). Data-driven solutions for human trafficking: Detection and impact analysis using machine learning. In *2025 International Conference on Electrical, Computer and Communication Engineering (ECCE)* (pp. 1-6). IEEE. DOI: 10.1109/ECCE64574.2025.11014018

Mishra, V. (2015). *Combating human trafficking: Gaps in policy and law.* SAGE Publications India. DOI: 10.4135/9789354797965

Moyo, T. J., Gunes, O., & Jirotka, M. D. (2025). Investigating human trafficking recruitment online: A study of fraudulent job offers on social media platforms. *Proceedings of the ACM on Human-Computer Interaction, 9*(2), 1–31. DOI: 10.1145/3711016

Mumford, E. (2006). The story of socio-technical design: Reflections on its successes, failures and potential. *Information Systems Journal, 16*(4), 317–342. DOI: 10.1111/j.1365-2575.2006.00221.x

Narula, R. (2024). From the editor: On writing a perspectives article — what they are, what they are not (and what they should be). *Journal of International Business Policy, 7*(2), 253–259. DOI: 10.1057/s42214-024-00191-6

Newton, P. J., Mulcahy, T. M., & Martin, S. E. (2008). *Finding victims of human trafficking*. National Opinion Research Center (NORC) at the University of Chicago (Grant No. 2007VTBX0001, U.S. Department of Justice, Office of Justice Programs, National Institute of Justice). https://citeseerx.ist.psu.edu/viewdoc/download?doi=10.1.1.218.2468&rep=rep1&type=pdf

Oram, S., Abas, M., Bick, D., Boyle, A., French, R., Jakobowitz, S., Khondoker, M., Stanley, N., Trevillion, K., Howard, L., & Zimmerman, C. (2016). Human trafficking and health: A survey of male and female survivors in England. *American Journal of Public Health, 106*(6), 1073–1078. DOI: 10.2105/AJPH.2016.303095 PMID: 27077341

Smith, D. P. (2018). Population geography I: Human trafficking. *Progress in Human Geography, 42*(2), 297–308. https://doi-org.ezp.slu.edu/10.1177/0309132516685196. DOI: 10.1177/0309132516685196

Stylianou, A., Xuan, H., Shende, M., Brandt, J., Souvenir, R., & Pless, R. (2019, January 26). *Hotels-50K: A Global Hotel Recognition Dataset.* ArXiv.org https://arxiv.org/abs/1901.11397

Szakonyi, A. (2022). *Trafficking policy analysis using a multidisciplinary approach: Recommendations for US anti-trafficking policies* (29210298). [Doctoral dissertation, Saint Louis University]. ProQuest Dissertations & Theses Global. https://www.proquest.com/pqdtglobal/docview/2681205947

Szakonyi, A., Chellasamy, H., Vassilakos, A., & Dawson, M. (2021). Using technologies to uncover patterns in human trafficking. In S. Latifi (Ed.), *ITNG 2021 18th international conference on information technology - New generations: Advances in intelligent systems and computing, 1346* (pp. 497-502). Springer. DOI: 10.1007/978-3-030-70416-2_64

Tong, E., Zadeh, A., Jones, C., & Morency, L. (2017). Combating Human Trafficking with Deep Multimodal Models. *Proceedings of the 55th Annual Meeting of the Association for Computational Linguistics, 1.*, 1547–1556. DOI: 10.18653/v1/P17-1142

Trist, E. L., & Bamforth, K. W. (1951). Some social and psychological consequences of thc Longwall Method of coal-getting: An examination of the psychological situation and defences of a work group in relation to the social structure and technological content of the work system. *Human Relations, 4*(1), 3-38. (Original work published 1951)DOI: 10.1177/001872675100400101

United Nations General Assembly Resolution 55/25, (2000), Article 3, Protocol to Prevent, Suppress and Punish Trafficking in Persons, Especially Women and Children, Supplementing the United Nations Convention against Transnational Organized Crime (November 15, 2000). https://treaties.un.org/doc/Treaties/2000/11/20001115%2011-38%20AM/Ch_XVIII_12_ap.pdf

United Nations Office on Drugs and Crime. (2024). *Global report on trafficking in persons 2024.* https://www.unodc.org/documents/data-and-analysis/glotip/2024/GLOTIP2024_BOOK.pdf

U.S. Department of Homeland Security. (2025). *What Is Human Trafficking?* https://www.dhs.gov/blue-campaign/what-human-trafficking

U.S. Government Accountability Office. (2020). *Forced labor imports: DHS increased resources and enforcement efforts, but needs to improve workforce planning and monitoring.* https://www.gao.gov/products/gao-21-106

Voloshin, D., Derevitskiy, I., Mukhina, K., & Karbovskii, V. (2016). Identifying venues for female commercial sex work using spatial analysis of geocoded advertisements. *Procedia Computer Science, 80,* 345–355. DOI: 10.1016/j.procs.2016.05.349

Walsham, G. (1997). Actor-Network Theory and IS research: Current status and future prospects. In A.S. Lee, J. Liebenau, & J.I. DeGross (Eds.), *Information systems and qualitative research: Proceedings of the IFIP (The International Federation for Information Processing) TC8 WG 8.2 International Conference on Information Systems and Qualitative Research* (pp. 466–480). Springer. DOI: 10.1007/978-0-387-35309-8_23

Wilson, J. M., & Dalton, E. (2008). Human trafficking in the heartland: Variation in law enforcement awareness and response. *Journal of Contemporary Criminal Justice, 24*(3), 296–313. https://heinonline-org.ezp.slu.edu/HOL/Page?collection=journals&handle=hein.journals/jccj24&id=284&men_tab=srchresults. DOI: 10.1177/1043986208318227

Wolfson, R. (2018). *Tracing illegal activity through the Bitcoin blockchain to combat cryptocurrency-related crimes.* Forbes. https://www.forbes.com/sites/rachelwolfson/2018/11/26/tracing-illegal-activity-through-the-bitcoin-blockchain-to-combat-cryptocurrency-related-crimes/?sh=2622b55133a9

Zimmerman, C., Hossain, M., & Watts, C. (2011). Human trafficking and health: A conceptual model to inform policy, intervention and research. *Social Science & Medicine*, *73*(2), 327–335. DOI: 10.1016/j.socscimed.2011.05.028 PMID: 21723653

Chapter 11
Putting Safety First:
Technology Adaptation, Employing AI, VR, and AR to Enhance Construction Professionals' Safety

Thomas C. Gibbs
http://orcid.org/0009-0003-8340-3306
Capitol Technology University, USA

ABSTRACT

This study found that applying technological innovation can influence the behavior of construction professionals and enhance organizational safety. The Bureau of Labor Statistics (BLS) report on construction safety issues revealed that falls, slips, and trips caused 35.3 percent of construction and extraction worker deaths in 2020 (BLS, 2020). This study argues that the construction industry can enhance safety by aligning its practices with the concerns of employees and supervisors. This chapter is a call for collaboration to change industry safety and protection protocols. The study's findings suggest that reducing preventable injuries can improve safety (Akinlolu & Haupt, 2019). Additionally, the study enhances industry knowledge by examining the intersection of technology and construction safety training. As a result, this research integrates academic concepts and real-world applications, incorporating technology and managerial innovation, and producing academically sound and practical content that draws on empirical studies, practitioner insights, and conceptual frameworks.

DOI: 10.4018/979-8-2600-1021-1.ch011

INTRODUCTION

By utilizing AI, VR, and AR, the construction industry can establish a safer, healthier, and more efficient workplace for its workforce, thereby enhancing project outcomes and fostering a culture that prioritizes safety. This study examines the current landscape of innovative training strategies for wellness, health, and safety in the construction sector (Sacks et al.,2013; Shringi et al., 2022). This chapter examines agile project management methodologies and ecosystem-based innovation strategies, highlighting their scholarly significance and practical applicability, recent developments, and dominant trends. The chapters' themes converge on the understanding that agility encompasses not only technical and procedural aspects but is also essential for technological adaptation and cultural innovation (Akinlolu & Haupt, 2019; Sorlini et al., 2023). This research study explores why organizational safety culture is integral to future forecasting, risk management, stakeholder engagement, and the development of resilient infrastructures for innovation. This chapter, informed by contributions from researchers, technologists, public sector leaders, and change agents, serves as a roadmap and reflective tool for individuals seeking to enhance wellness, health, and safety standards within the construction industry while responsibly leveraging effective technology with clarity and courage.

PROBLEM STATEMENT

Current data from the Bureau of Labor Statistics (BLS) indicates a safety problem in the construction industry. Falls, slips, and trips constituted 35.3 percent of workplace fatalities in construction and extraction occupations in 2020 (BLS, 2020). In construction and extraction occupations, 21,400 nonfatal workplace injuries and illnesses were recorded, primarily attributed to falls, slips, and trips. Consequently, out of 345 fatalities in the construction industry due to falls, 96 involved construction laborers (BLS, 2020). Falls facilitate dangerous injuries. While falls represent the primary cause of mortality among construction workers, individuals in this field face additional hazards that lead to injuries and fatalities. Safety can be improved by reducing the number of falls (Purushothaman et al., 2025). Consequently, this study aims to investigate the present fundamental issue in the construction environment: What are the effective methods for deploying technology in the construction industry to reduce hazards related to falls, slips, and trips?

BACKGROUND OF STUDY

Reducing the number of falls, slips, and trips is significant because they pose a major threat to physical safety in the construction industry. As a result, reducing the number of falls, slips, and trips will enhance safety and create an environment that prioritizes safety for construction professionals (Sacks et al., 2013; Shringi et al., 2022). However, when CPs are not adequately prepared to recognize hazards that result in falls, slips, and trips, they will likely succumb to current data, which reflects significant fatalities and a deteriorating trend in industry growth (BLS, 2020).

Significance of Research

This chapter critiques traditional training models and redefines agile leadership, highlighting the importance of technological innovation and resilience (Purushothaman et al., 2025). It advocates for collaboration with innovative stakeholders, allies, researchers, and managers. In an era marked by rapid technological disruption, construction professionals must adapt and evolve with purpose, foresight, and flexibility (Verschueren, 2021).

This research study is designed to align with the central theme of cultivating organizational agility through the adoption and implementation of technology. The study examines recent artificial intelligence (AI) tools and trends in virtual reality (VR) and augmented reality (AR) that relate to innovative educational methods for training professionals in wellness, health, safety, and construction within a virtual environment (Akinlolu & Haupt, 2019; Rivas, 2020; Sorlini et al., 2023).

The chapter examines the organizational mindsets and evidence-based strategies essential for cultivating a culture of health and safety with sustained agility in the construction industry. In an era characterized by rapid technological disruption, organizations must not only adapt but also evolve with deliberate intention, a clear vision, and agility (Rivas, 2020). This chapter explores how contemporary organizations and professionals, particularly in the construction sector, can leverage emerging technologies such as AI, VR, and AR to enhance wellness and improve health and safety (Dodoo et al., 2024). The construction industry is recognized as one of the most hazardous fields. As a result, safety is particularly relevant in the context of compliance with OSHA regulations within the construction industry (Thach et al., 2024).

Relevance of the Study

This chapter consolidates topical resolutions into evidence-based models and innovative insights derived from research and practice regarding the adoption of artificial intelligence frameworks, as well as training built through virtual and augmented reality. The findings of this chapter suggest that construction professionals (CP) should incorporate practical technology adaptations to improve training in wellness, health, and safety (Dodoo et al., 2024). To do this, CPs must integrate organizational and industry policies and procedures into effective platforms, enabling the digital transformation of health and safety training. This chapter shows the potential to improve industry wellness and safety through the integration of innovative AI technology, VR change management strategies, and AR technology for training and testing OSHA health and safety policies (Sorlini et al., 2023).

METHODOLOGY

This study employed the following methodology techniques, strategies, and article types.

Rapid Literature Review: Synthesizing existing research, literature reviews play a vital role in identifying gaps, controversies, and future research directions, establishing a cohesive understanding of the subject matter (Smela et al., 2023). As a result, this study's rapid review explored a variety of literature on community and consulting interventions. The existing literature from stakeholder engagement addresses global challenges, making the literature valuable for scholars interested in applied research that fosters social and organizational change. Additionally, the rapid review examined perspective and commentary literature. The article encourages scholars to reflect critically on current trends, propose forward-looking policy recommendations, and foster scholarly debate on key issues (Smela et al., 2023).

Lastly, this research employs a content analysis review methodology. This method is a recognized approach for reviewing and synthesizing literature that rationalizes outcomes, and it has been widely applied in the fields of engineering and construction management. Scopus and Academia, recognized abstract and citation databases for peer-reviewed literature, were utilized to identify several first-tier articles pertinent to VR/AR from reputable scholarly journals in specific fields, including engineering/construction management, science, technology, safety, and human factors (Shankar et al., 2023). The criteria for selection are outlined as follows: The chosen journals must be sourced from the Science Citation Index (SCI)-Expanded database or the Engineering Index (EI) Compendex database, as these databases index over 6000 prominent journals across more than 150 disciplines. The chosen journals demonstrated substantial influence in the relevant fields, as indicated by their citation indexes.

Additionally, book reviews and editorials were excluded from the analysis. This strategy requires that all retrieved documents be examined through a uniform analytical framework that aligns with research objectives and methodologies. A two-stage review method is proposed to conduct a targeted and structured literature review covering the period from 2017 to 2025 (Shankar et al., 2023). Stage One involved a comprehensive search utilizing Scopus, Academia, Google Scholar, and various scientific search engines. A variety of terms, including VR, AR, mixed reality, gaming technology, immersive, interactive, construction, and safety, were employed to guarantee a comprehensive search across related fields (Shankar et al., 2023). A total of 243 articles were identified as most relevant to the topic during this search. In the second stage, publications lacking the specified keywords in their titles or abstracts were excluded. Subsequently, a brief visual examination of the article content led to the elimination of less relevant and irrelevant papers, resulting in a total of 103 publications for further analysis.

FRAMEWORKS, THEORIES, AND APPLICABLE MODELS

This study presents a viable framework for examining the construction industry through organizational safety culture. This research examines the impact of technology on the health and safety of construction professionals. As a result, this research investigates injuries experienced by CPs in construction and building service downturns, which diminished industry morale and exacerbated isolation due to CP safety concerns during the COVID-19 pandemic (Meza, 2022).

RELEVANT THEORIES

Mindful Communication

According to Burgoon et al. (Burgoon et al., 2000; Khukhlaev et al., 2022), mindful communication is characterized as planful, effortfully processed, creative, strategic, flexible, and/or reason-based. Consequently, mindful communication can foster outcomes that include thoughts, opinions, and ideas of marginalized voices. The lived experiences of CPs offer valuable insights into how to engage with CPs and potential future construction professionals. As a result, when mindful communication is practiced, it is responsive rather than reactive. The sender must be flexible in their delivery and not rigid (Burgoon et al., 2000; Khukhlaev et al., 2022). Furthermore, flexible training modalities increase the opportunity to serve a larger demographic of CPs. Therefore, mindful communication requires bold organizational leadership and a committed, courageous organizational safety culture that invests in the power of working collectively towards mutually agreed-upon health and safety goals (Burgoon et al., 2000; Khukhlaev et al., 2022).

Mutually Beneficial Partnerships and Allyships

Another great way to promote CP health and safety culture is by creating a community concerned with CP safety. Building community requires focus on the needs and desires of others, and being inclusive of diverse needs and expectations is fundamental in developing a safe community and organizational culture (Warren & Warren, 2023). The inclusion necessary to establish community is achieved by facilitating partnerships and allyships. Creating educational opportunities to discuss and demonstrate the power and significance of allyship can strengthen an organization's culture. Allyships are vehicles that can bring diverse groups together (Warren & Warren, 2023). As a result, allyships can be employed to support and advocate for employees who feel marginalized. When all employees are appropriately educated, they can foster a positive organizational culture by becoming allies with one another, especially when they are adequately equipped and prepared to focus on listening, supporting, and advocating for their safety and that of their coworkers (Warren & Warren, 2023). As a result, allies galvanized by sincerity can play a critical role in promoting CP safety.

Credible Feedback Loops

To be effective, each organization needs to identify its significant barriers to an organizational culture focused on health and safety. To establish an organizational safety culture, ardent listening must occur. Listening ardently is an essential principle of a credible feedback loop (Sethi & Seth, 2009; Abed et al., 2023). This principle must be utilized to discover organizational safety needs and must use plain language understood by the audience the communication is directed towards. This must be accomplished by placing oneself in the sender's position and understanding what they are trying to express (Sethi & Seth, 2009; Tang et al., 2022). As a result, this principle can uncover the needs of the community and audience.

This study found that to ensure that health and safety training is practical and effective, the administrator of the training must be credible. Additionally, the administrator must maintain a credible feedback loop. Accordingly, a feedback loop must be explored to account for successes and failures in communication and training implementation. Moreover, this must be accomplished by the receiver sending out a confirmation symbol to the sender (Sethi & Seth, 2009; Abed et al., 2023). As a result, this principle can help establish a process of addressing a communicated need in a self-sustainable manner.

According to Sethi and Seth, feedback symbolizes confirmation (Sethi & Seth, 2009; Tang et al., 2022). The outcome is confirmation from the receiver to the sender that the receiver acknowledges the message. As a result, the receiver in the feedback loop can use the information in real-time. The information can be used to refine and improve the design (Sethi & Seth, 2009; Abed et al., 2023). Furthermore, the chances of CPs avoiding injuries from detectable hazards increase the more information and experience they receive. As a result, this study encourages the use of strategic communication principles to support VR training (Shringi et al., 2022).

Strategic Communication

When communication focuses on the importance of bringing about actual change and action, it is classified as constitutive communication (Holtzhausen et al., 2015; Holtzhausen et al., 2021). This concept frames the desired outcome of training as practicing safety and protecting people. Furthermore, this study suggests that the desired outcome of CP safety training is educating construction professionals on industry hazards (Holtzhausen et al., 2021). As a result, by practicing constitutive communication, organizations have an opportunity to enhance CP safety. Additionally, CPs have an opportunity to learn from dangerous situations without risking physical injury (Petosa et al., 2022). Therefore, the strategic communication model of constitutive communication aligns with the findings of this study and the desired outcome of construction safety training.

Sustainable Organizational Culture

Before an employee or public servant demonstrates organizational safety culture buy-in, trust, and credibility within the organization, these elements need to be established. A credible feedback loop can help facilitate building trust. Once trust is established, a feedback loop can be considered credible (Sethi & Seth, 2009; Parincu, 2022). As a result, this can only occur through sincere efforts to connect to the personal motivation of CPs, gain trust, and add value to the organizational culture. Trust must be cultivated over time and verified by actions. Establishing trust that supports a credible feedback loop is a challenging task. For a feedback loop to be credible, it must be tested (Sethi & Seth, 2009; Parincu, 2022). Moreover, a sincere spirit of cooperation must be present, along with dedicated and diligent efforts, to facilitate change. There must be a committed effort to promote accuracy over speed (Holtzhausen et al., 2015; Holtzhausen et al., 2021). Time delays can be fixed as the process is fine-tuned. However, a learning curve will initially require patience, empathy, and a clear understanding of agreed-upon desired outcomes.

Additionally, the adjustments need to be made in real-time through feedback. During an injury, trust is put to the test. Consequently, establishing a level of trust and connectivity with staff requires building an internal community and establishing a credible organizational culture (Holtzhausen et al., 2021). Building an organizational safety culture requires time, effort, and sincere effort to build trust. Building trust is paramount to developing a positive organizational culture.

After trust is established, it must still be maintained. Furthermore, a feedback loop must be in place before an injury, and it is not a solution (Petosa et al., 2022). It is a vehicle that can transport you to a solution collectively. That makes it work; it is a series of collective decisions, each moving the collective one step closer toward a mutually shared long-term goal (Sethi & Seth, 2009; Parincu, 2022). As a result, if a feedback loop is not in place before an injury, response credibility may be questioned. Unfortunately, trust relationships must be established and tested before a credible feedback loop can exist. Therefore, when a feedback loop is in place, it can provide an effective injury response, although this may occur with a delay (Holtzhausen et al., 2021). It will be the most effective because it received community buy-in and has been vetted by community champions and stakeholders.

LITERATURE REVIEW

This literature review primarily operates as a narrative literature review with some characteristics reminiscent of a rapid literature review. A narrative or traditional literature review is a comprehensive, critical, and objective analysis of the current knowledge on a topic (Sukhera, 2022). It is an essential part of the research process, helping to establish a theoretical framework and focus or context for this research study. Consequently, characteristics from a rapid literature review (RLR) were also employed in this study. An RLR is an alternative to a systematic literature review (SLR) and can speed up the analysis of newly published data topics (Sukhera, 2022). The objective of utilizing these strategies was to identify and summarize available information regarding different approaches to defining the central research question of this study and the methodology applied to conduct reviews of applicable literature (Smela et al., 2023). As a result, this literature review focused on reviewing relevant literature that explored how technology and organizational culture can influence CP health and safety. The selected methodological framework provides a blueprint for readers and future researchers about how sources were selected, evaluated, and synthesized.

Furthermore, this literature review provided a theoretical framework for safety management (Salvi, 2021). According to the findings of this study, the construction sector has a high rate of fatalities and protracted injuries. In modern culture, this is unacceptable, and it also renders the sector inefficient, as days are frequently missed due to injury (Goel & Garg, n.d.). Construction sites represent complex environments with particular characteristics and high baseline levels of risk, in which accidents are a primary point of analysis in much of the industry's safety literature (Forteza et al., 2020).

Therefore, this literature reviews provide a theoretical background about safety management (SAEED, 2017; Salvi, 2021). Additionally, health and safety (H&S) are significant concerns in the construction industry. Training is a key strategy to reduce H&S risks in the construction industry. As a result, serious games for health and safety training in construction, which serve as a complement to traditional training methods, have garnered significant interest in recent years (João Patacas et al., 2014; Anireddy, 2024). Furthermore, computer-mediated learning is becoming an increasingly common form of education in institutions of higher learning (IHL) (IJCT Editor, 2016; Addison & Dawood, 2025). In alignment with current CP safety trends, this study examines the reduction of workplace injuries through OSHA inspections, focusing on the types of injuries that decline following inspections and the issuance of citations for specific standards (Haviland et al., 2010; Forteza et al., 2020).

Foundation of the OSH Act

The OSH Act emphasizes each employer's responsibility to recognize, correct, and reduce potential hazards (Kotelchuck, 1994; Salvi, 2021). The Occupational Safety and Health Act of 1970 (OSH Act) is one of the most important statutes found in federal, state and international law protecting people at work—but it is only one of the laws that create a web of employer obligations to fashion and demonstrate the validity of health and safety protections in their workplace (Kotelchuck, 1994; Michaels & Barab et al., 2020; Anireddy, 2024). With an annual budget of about $400 million, OSHA is about 5 percent the size of the Environmental Protection Agency, another federal agency created by President Richard M. Nixon in 1970, the "Year of the Environment." (Leeth, 2000). Accordingly, the philosophy that work-related illnesses are an avoidable aspect of industrialization is a fundamental tenet of all (Kotelchuck, 1994; Anireddy, 2024). Thirty years after its inception, OSHA was responsible for protecting over 100 million workers at approximately 6 million worksites with the help of only 2,000 workplace health and safety inspectors (Leeth, 2000; OSHA, 2023).

Consequently, the lingering, catastrophic impact of COVID-19 has refocused attention on health and safety. As a result, Occupational safety and health (OSH) has evolved in recent years (OSHA, 2023). The construction industry has a poor safety record when compared to many other industries. Therefore, this rapid literature review aimed to provide an overview of future challenges in occupational safety and health. A search within the Scopus database returned 103 peer-reviewed journal articles published since 2017 on new and emerging OSH risks and challenges of the future (Lindholm et al., 2020).

Technological Innovations in Safety

Virtual Reality (VR) is poised to become a technology used by millions of people. As a result, VR technology must be employed to onboard new CPs and train veteran CPs about daily hazards on the job site in the construction environment (Seo et al.,2021). It will expand into a broad spectrum of our current world. VR is a technology that enables the creation of computer-generated virtual worlds, allowing users to interact and become immersed (Velev & Zlateva, 2017; Seo et al.,2021). Because students often become fatigued when learning new information, CP safety trainers need to utilize virtual reality to help CPs become safety experts. Additional technology, such as GIS mapping, could also contribute to the accumulation of real-time hazards that CPs encounter and must navigate around to stay safe at work (Zhou et al., 2013; Shaikh et al., 2020).

Future of Safety Management

Safety management is crucial for ensuring a safe construction site. This research identifies and evaluates the use of safety management in construction projects to minimize and control health and safety risks for construction workers (Zhou et al., 2013; Shaikh et al., 2020). The study reviewed relevant literature on H&S as the first step in obtaining information from previously conducted studies (SAEED, 2017; Salvi, 2021). Corresponding analysis was performed using the collected data. The data was employed to analyze the trends in technology application for construction safety and the evolution of research topics (Zhou et al., 2013; Verma, 2023). Studies on the application of virtual reality in the classroom have demonstrated positive effects on students' academic performance, as well as their levels of interest and overall learning experiences (Velev & Zlateva, 2017; Verma, 2023).

Additionally, this study examined literature on occupational health and safety (OHS). This study's findings revealed a contemporary argument that the growth in the number of specialists in OHS has led to an emphasis on policy and practice, shifting away from more scholastic concerns previously addrcssed by academics in the disciplines of psychology and sociology (Zanko & Dawson, 2011; Tang et al., 2022).

Consequently, most construction health and safety research has focused on the potential benefits of cmploying virtual reality in educational settings (Verma, 2023). This study found that high accident rates are attributed to several common factors, including poor construction planning, inadequate safety design, insufficient safety training, worker behavior, inherent safety risks, health and safety risks in construction, and a lack of knowledge of site rules (SAEED, 2017; Salvi, 2021). Analyzing data from previous studies facilitates a learning process that fosters effective adjustments to enhance the health and safety of Construction professionals.

Using Technology to Overcome Foreseeable Risk

The existence of avoidable hazards, such as slips, trips, and falls, is a preventable risk. Preventable risks are unacceptable in modern society (Akinlolu & Haupt, 2019; Petosa et al., 2022). Accordingly, this research found that the construction industry has a high number of fatalities and long-term injuries that can be reduced or eliminated. Foreseeable and preventable risks can render the construction sector inefficient, resulting in days being lost due to injuries (Seo et al.,2021). Consequently, the recommendations of this study can significantly decrease the gap between health and safety needs and the availability of effective mitigation technology (Petosa et al., 2022). Utilizing appropriate technologies responsibly, such as VR training, AR inspections, and GIS hazard site mapping, enhances industry sustainability by improving CP health and safety.

Current Pedagogy

One of the reasons construction Health and Safety education is not effective is that current pedagogy is weak (A., 2019; Addison & Dawood, 2025). Since current standard training modalities do not effectively incorporate modern technology, a disconnect exists between the methods used to teach safety practices and the technology available to keep CPs safe (Zhou et al., 2013; Olugbemiga et al., 2023). As a result, current training trends are less effective because the pedagogy used is ineffective. Therefore, the lack of technology integration and a hazardous learning environment leads to low learning performance and poor safety procedures (A., 2019; Addison & Dawood, 2025). Subsequently, a safe environment that educates CPs on job-site hazards before they are allowed on the job site is a necessary investment. Safety is a key component of industry workforce sustainability. Furthermore, investment in health and safety can preserve lives and demonstrate commitment to CP health and safety (Zvirtualhou et al., 2013; Olugbemiga et al., 2023). Virtual reality technologies play a vital role in enhancing safety in the construction industry. Accordingly, research suggests that virtual reality technologies offer greater safety benefits when compared to physical reality (Avhad, 2007; Faruk et al., 2023).

Available Technological Tools

Construction safety education plays a vital role in equipping students with concrete safety knowledge and promoting safe practices before they enter construction sites. An example of safety assisting technology that promotes CP safety is exoskeleton suits. The FORTIS Exoskeleton is a wearable robotics tool that enhances users' strength and endurance (Frane, 2016; Li & Ng, 2017; Verma, 2023). These exoskeletons are available in both power-assist and unpowered forms. Power-assist exoskeletons are designed to transfer energy through the wearer's skeletal structure. The unpowered form provides a feeling of weightlessness, redistributes weight, and improves the wearer's posture when carrying heavy objects (Dude, 2014; Verma, 2023).

Another technological innovation that facilitates CP safety is the Virtual Field Trip System (VIFITS). VIFITS is a mobile construction safety education modality that utilizes a 360-degree panoramic virtual reality (Dao, 2018; Faruk et al., 2023). The VIFITS prototype is developed and validated with virtual scenarios derived from real construction sites. The results reveal that VIFITS is a powerful pedagogical method for effectively providing students with practical experience and safety knowledge (Dao, 2018; Faruk et al., 2023). Unfortunately, even with technological advances like VIFITS, the available literature on Construction Safety is not very optimistic about the chances of evidence-based safety in the construction industry exerting a positive influence (M. Demichela et al., 2013; Anireddy, 2024). Furthermore, current studies suggest that safety has been given a bad connotation. Additionally, safety has been labeled as a detractor from the primary construction production process and is seen as a bureaucratic burden (M. Demichela et al., 2013; Anireddy, 2024). Consequently, safety has critical limitations. The safety issues this study exposes reveal that the most critical causes of accidents are inadequate training, drugs and alcohol, horseplay by workers, excessive working hours resulting in mental fatigue, and communication issues (Eze et al., 2020). This suggests the training environment impacts training effectiveness; this also implies that behavior is demonstrative of the constructed organizational culture. As a result, strategic communication is paramount (Eze et al., 2020).

Strategic Communication, Articulation, and Innovation

Strategic communication is a process of cultural articulation. Construction professionals develop articulation, as Balkin (Balkin, 1998; Parincu, 2022; Khukhlaev et al., 2022) describes it, from exposure to and use of the cultural tools available to them. However, one of the barriers to greater articulation is that CPs may only use cultural tools that are familiar to them. Thus, the metaphor of the tool-making process unites culture, defined as learned behavior in this study, and articulation, which is defined as expressed behavior in this study (Balkin, 1998; Parincu, 2022). Consequently, the study also explores the examination of ideology as the tools of human understanding that are produced by and through human culture. It is the study of the cumulative creation of these tools using previously existing tools of understanding, and the study of the consequences of this recursive manufacturing that promote organizational clarity (Balkin, 1998; Khukhlaev et al., 2022). Therefore, to understand organizational culture and safety ideology, CPs and stakeholders must comprehend the tools of human understanding, including both their advantages and deficiencies, their intended and unintended consequences, their capacity to empower CPs, and their potential to exercise power over them (Silbey, 1999; Eze et al., 2020).

Construction Industry Perils and Consequences

Additionally, the construction sector is inherently high-risk due to its production processes and labor-intensive characteristics (Forteza et al., 2020). To improve safety, technological intervention is necessary. The New Normal Set-up on Safety and Health Standards in Government Construction Projects during the COVID-19 pandemic is a new guideline or protocol for construction sites (Florencondia et al., 2021). Consequently, the construction sector incurs significant financial losses due to a high number of occupational accidents. Also, occupational accidents cause important social and economic problems, including loss of life and physical injuries (Fatih Yılmaz, 2015; Forteza et al., 2020). As a result, the construction sector is one of the most important sectors. The construction industry makes a significant contribution to economic development through its employment capacity and by adding value to the economy (Fatih Yılmaz, 2015; Forteza et al., 2020). This study's findings align with previous studies and verify the effectiveness of the New Normal Set-up in implementing safety and health protocols to prevent the spread of the virus during a pandemic (Florencondia et al., 2021). Therefore, this study provides an assessment, evaluation, and recommendations on the current mandated rules of government agencies regarding safety and health guidelines.

RESULTS: QUESTION, THEMES, RECOMMENDATIONS

Question: How can modern technology be utilized responsibly to educate construction professionals and address health and safety issues in the construction industry?

Themes From the Research Study

1. Use artificial intelligence (AI) to improve and modernize OSHA standards.
2. Utilize AR to test and inspect health and safety techniques effectively.
3. Employ VR to train CPs on hazardous conditions and job site safety.
4. Utilize GIS mapping technology to familiarize CPs with job site hazards.
5. Use technology to attract, retain, and protect the future workforce.

Recommendations

Five practical or actionable recommendations

1. Create an augmented reality simulation teaching and testing OSHA safety standards.
2. Use the collective impact model to research the most effective methods, models available to deploy educational virtual reality and augmented reality, and simulation to overcome the most prevalent injuries to construction professionals' safety, falls, slips, and trips.
3. Incorporate virtual reality training for veteran staff and during onboarding for new hires.
4. Empower a diverse council of construction professionals to develop a credible feedback loop capable of identifying efficiency and effectiveness errors in real-time and disseminating community-driven solutions.
5. Utilize technology to develop a sustainable health and safety program that enhances awareness and training experiences for current and future CPs, as well as interns.

Practical solutions

This study identifies five practical solutions for addressing construction, health, and safety issues.

1. One actionable solution to current issues related to the use of technology to promote job site safety is to utilize existing mobile app solutions to support VR training. An audit of the most common injuries for an organization will

reveal which area of safety training needs the most attention. Issues ranging from slips and falls to effective communication can be resolved or mitigated by using technology.

2. An additional actionable solution creates a credible community to overcome training and adaptation to technological challenges. Empower a diverse council of construction professionals to develop a credible feedback loop capable of identifying efficiency and effectiveness errors in real-time and disseminating health and safety community-driven solutions.
3. Another actionable solution is to allocate funding for the development of an augmented reality (AR) simulation module that can teach and test OSHA safety standards.
4. Accordingly, another actionable solution requires utilizing technology to develop a sustainable health and safety program that enhances awareness and training experiences for current and future CPs and interns.
5. Lastly, another practical solution is to adapt and fully integrate technology into the organizational culture. Incorporate VR training during onboarding for new hires, interns, and veteran staff.

RECOMMENDATIONS FOR FUTURE RESEARCH

Based on the findings of this research, the following recommendations are made for future studies.

1. This study should be utilized to build partnerships at the federal, state, and local municipality levels to perform research on safety adaptation technology feasibility.
2. This study should be employed to catalyze collaborative research across the disciplines of construction and computer science on occupational health and safety. This research warrants a private-public partnership. As a result, research involving AI programmers and OSHA professionals should be conducted in collaboration with the Department of Occupational Safety and Health Administration.
3. Additionally, collaborative research should be conducted with video game theorists and virtual reality designers to develop a course on safety and hazardous environments for construction professionals. The primary strategy should be to prioritize safety. Currently, OSHA compliance is incentivized by a desire to avoid penalties and fines for safety violations.
4. Accordingly, qualitative research into the effectiveness of virtual reality health and safety training is necessary and should be conducted by engaging active CPs and managerial staff.

5. Lastly, this study recommends that further research into the reliability of augmented reality inspections must be conducted to foster industry safety and reduce injuries caused by recognizable hazards.

CONCLUSIONS

The findings of this study demonstrate that there is an opportunity to improve the safety, health, and well-being of construction professionals. The health and safety of CPs can be enhanced by incorporating current appropriate technologies and techniques. Modern teaching strategies and distance learning modalities must be utilized in construction education (Zhou et al., 2013; Olugbemiga et al., 2023). Distance learning can improve the probability of a CP surviving an encounter with known hazards. Furthermore, exposure to hazards through a virtual reality experience can facilitate an experience that helps reduce safety injuries. As a result, integrating VR training technology can help mitigate hazards and prevent safety injuries (Sacks et al., 2013; Shringi et al., 2022). Additionally, employing distance learning training for CPs provides an opportunity for CPs to become more exposed to hazardous situations without the risk of physical harm. Furthermore, safety training that employs virtual reality and augmented reality inspection technologies can prevent injuries and save lives (Dao, 2018; Faruk et al., 2023). Therefore, employing appropriate technology in construction safety training and inspections strengthens the sustainability of the construction industry by enhancing construction professionals' awareness and exposure to hazards.

LIMITATIONS

Although rapid literature reviews are a valuable tool for quickly synthesizing evidence to inform timely decision-making, it is crucial to recognize and acknowledge their inherent limitations when focusing on rapidly evolving fields like construction safety technology (Smela et al., 2023). This study is not without limitations. The two-stage search may not ensure thorough coverage of relevant documents for review. This approach effectively provides a substantial body of significant state-of-the-art research, enabling the study to generalize its findings and suggest directions for future research. However, time constraints and available material confine the study.

REFERENCES

. A, T. B. (2019). Effectiveness of Construction Safety Hazards Identification in Virtual Reality Learning Environment. *Environment-Behaviour Proceedings Journal, 4*(12). DOI: 10.21834/e-bpj.v4i12.1901

Abed, L. G., Abed, M. G., & Shackelford, T. K. (2023). Interpersonal communication style and personal and professional growth among saudi arabian employees. *International Journal of Environmental Research and Public Health, 20*(2), 910. DOI: 10.3390/ijerph20020910

Addison, A., & Dawood, N. (2025). *THE IMPORTANCE OF ENGAGING ENGINEERING AND CONSTRUCTION LEARNERS IN VIRTUAL WORLDS AND SERIOUS GAMES.* Academia.edu. https://www.academia.edu/7044694/THE_IMPORTANCE_OF_ENGAGING_ENGINEERING_AND_CONSTRUCTION_LEARNERS_IN_VIRTUAL_WORLDS_AND_SERIOUS_GAMES

Akinlolu, M. T., & Haupt, T. (2019). *Emerging Technologies in Construction Safety and Health Management.* International Conference on Innovation, Technology, Enterprise and Entrepreneurship. https://www.academia.edu/44018807/Emerging_Technologies_in_Construction_Safety_and_Health_Management

Anireddy, A. R. (2024). Construction Safety Management: Analyzing the Effectiveness of Safety Training Programs on Job Sites. *INTERANTIONAL JOURNAL of SCIENTIFIC RESEARCH in ENGINEERING and MANAGEMENT, 08*(11), 1–7. DOI: 10.55041/IJSREM16079

Avhad, A. (2007). Certified Organization) Website: www. *International Journal of Innovative Research in Science, Engineering and Technology (an ISO, 3297.* https://doi.org/DOI: 10.15680/IJIRSET.2017.0606276

Balkin, J. M. (1998). *Cultural Software : A Theory of Ideology.* Yale University Press. Print

Burgoon, J. K., Berger, C. R., & Waldron, V. R. (2000). Mindfulness and Interpersonal Communication. *The Journal of Social Issues, 56*(1), 105–127. DOI: 10.1111/0022-4537.00154

Dao, N.-N. (2018). Virtual Field Trip for Mobile Construction Safety Education using 360-degree Panoramic Virtual Reality. International Journal of Engineering Education. https://www.academia.edu/37063856/Virtual_Field_Trip_for_Mobile_Construction_Safety_Education_using_360_degree_Panoramic_Virtual_Reality

. Demichela M., Baldissone G., & Luzzi, R. (2013). Advances tools for occupational accidents data analysis for prevention purposes. *CRC Press EBooks*, 1595–1600. DOI: 10.1201/b15938-239

Dodoo, J. E., Al-Samarraie, H., Alzahrani, A. I., Lonsdale, M., & Alalwan, N. (2024). Digital Innovations for Occupational Safety: Empowering Workers in Hazardous Environments. *Workplace Health & Safety*, *72*(3), 84–95. Advance online publication. DOI: 10.1177/21650799231215811

Dude: Fortis Exoskeleton (2014). http://www.dudeiwantthat.com/fitness/equipment/fortisexoskeleton. asp. Accessed 22Mar 2019.

. Eze, E., Sofolahan, O., & Siunoje, L. (2020). Health and Safety Management on Construction Projects: The View of Construction Tradespeople. *CSID Journal of Infrastructure Development, 3*(2), 152. researchgate. DOI: 10.32783/csid-jid.v3i2.165

Faruk, M., & Made, I. (2023). The Role of Using Virtual Reality in Learning in an Education Environment. Advances in Social Science, Education and Humanities Research. *Advances in Social Science, Education and Humanities Research, 1234–1238*, 1234–1238. Advance online publication. DOI: 10.2991/978-2-494069-35-0_148

Florencondia, N. T., Lansangan, M. B., Marcos, E. V., Vincent, J., & Russel, K. (2021). New Normal Set-up on Safety and Health Standards in Government Construction Projects: A case of Covid-19. *International Journal of Engineering and Advanced Technology*, *10*(5), 370–374. DOI: 10.35940/ijeat.E2825.0610521

Forteza, F. J., Carretero-Gómez, J. M., & Sesé, A. (2020). Safety in the construction industry: Accidents and precursors. *Revista de la Construcción*, *19*(2), 271–281. DOI: 10.7764/rdlc.19.2.271-281

Frane, D. (2016) 7 Cool and Unusual Tools from the 2016 STAFDA Show (2016). http://www.toolsofthetrade.net/power-tools/7-cool-and-unusual-tools-from-the-2016-stafdashow_o

Goel, A., & Garg, P. (n.d.). How to Cite. *International Journal of Health Sciences*, *6*(S4), 10806–10823. DOI: 10.53730/ijhs.v6nS4.10900

Haviland, A., Burns, R., Gray, W., Ruder, T., & Mendeloff, J. (2010). What kinds of injuries do OSHA inspections prevent? *Journal of Safety Research*, *41*(4), 339–345. DOI: 10.1016/j.jsr.2010.03.005

. Holtzhausen, D., Fullerton, J. A., Lewis, B. K., & Shipka, D. (2021). Principles of Strategic Communication. DOI: 10.4324/9781003002048

Holtzhausen, D., & Zerfass, A. (2015). *The Routledge handbook of strategic communication*. Routledge., https://www.academia.edu/44638503/THE_ROUTLEDGE_HANDBOOK_OF_STATEGIC_COMMUNICATION_Derina_Holtzhausen_Ansgar_Zerfass_

IJCT Editor. (2016, November 16). VIRTUAL REALITY IN EDUCATION: TRENDS AND ISSUES. Academia.edu. https://www.academia.edu/29888980/VIRTUAL_REALITY_IN_EDUCATION_TRENDS_AND_ISSUES

Khukhlaev, O., Novikova, I., & Chernaya, A. (2022). Interpersonal Mindfulness, Intergroup Anxiety, and Intercultural Communication Effectiveness Among International Students Studying in Russia. *Frontiers in Psychology, 13*, 841361. Advance online publication. DOI: 10.3389/fpsyg.2022.841361

Kotelchuck, D. (1994). Designing an effective osha compliance program by Ilise Levy Feitshans, JD. Volume 1 in Corporate Compliance Series, 1993, Clark, Boardman, Callaghan, Deerfield, IL. *American Journal of Industrial Medicine*, *26*(5), 717–718. DOI: 10.1002/ajim.4700260514

Leeth, J. (2000). *Workplace Safety Policy: Past, Present, and Future*. SSRN Electronic Journal; Elsevier BV. https://www.academia.edu/102794788/Workplace_Safety_Policy_Past_Present_and_Future

Li, R. Y. M., & Ng, P. L. (2017) "Wearable robotics and construction workers safety and health". In: *8th International Conference on Applied Human Factors and Ergonomics*, Los Angeles.

Lindholm, M., Reiman, A., & Väyrynen, S. (2020). On Future Occupational Safety and Health Challenges. *International Journal of Occupational and Environmental Safety*, *4*(1), 108–127. DOI: 10.24840/2184-0954_004.001_0009

Michaels, D., & Barab, J. (2020). The Occupational Safety and Health Administration at 50: Protecting Workers in a Changing Economy. *American Journal of Public Health*, *110*(5), 631–635. DOI: 10.2105/AJPH.2020.305597

Olugbemiga, E. O., Jang, Y., Song, K., & Ahn, J. (2023). Impact of COVID-19 on Social and Psychological Well-Being of Workers in Construction Projects: Comparative Analysis of Managers and Laborers. *Buildings (Basel, Switzerland)*, *13*(8), 1902. DOI: 10.3390/buildings13081902

OSHA. (2023). *Commonly used statistics | Occupational Safety and Health Administration*. Osha.gov; United States Department of Labor. https://www.osha.gov/data/commonstats

Parincu, Z. (2022). Interpersonal Communication: Definition, Examples, & Skills. The Berkeley Well-Being Institute. https://www.berkeleywellbeing.com/interpersonal-communication.html

Patacas, J. Kassem, M., & Dawood, N. (2014, November 10). *Construction health and safety training: the utilisation of 4D enabled serious games*. Academia.edu. https://www.academia.edu/9222629/Construction_health_and_safety_training_the_utilisation_of_4D_enabled_serious_games

Petosa, N. H. & J. (2022, November). *Workplace Injuries and Job Requirements for Construction Laborers: Spotlight on Statistics: U.S. Bureau of Labor Statistics*. Www.bls.gov. https://www.bls.gov/spotlight/2022/workplace-injuries-and-job-requirements-for-construction-laborers/home.htm

. Purushothaman, M. B., Rotimi, F. E., Samarasekara, S., & GhaffarianHoseini, A. (2025). SMART technologies that influence construction health and safety factors risk reduction in the current digital era. Smart and Sustainable Built Environment. DOI: 10.1108/SASBE-09-2024-0400

. Rivas, Y. C. (2020). Virtual reality and 21st-century education. *International Research Journal of Management, IT and Social Sciences*. DOI: 10.21744/irjmis.v7n1.820

Sacks, R., Perlman, A., & Barak, R. (2013). Construction safety training using immersive virtual reality. *Construction Management and Economics*, *31*(9), 1005–1017. DOI: 10.1080/01446193.2013.828844

Saeed, Y. S.SAEED. (2017). SAFETY MANAGEMENT IN CONSTRUCTION PROJECTS. *The Journal of the University of Duhok*, *20*(1), 546–560. DOI: 10.26682/sjuod.2017.20.1.48

Salvi, S. S. (2021). Safety Management and Accident Prevention. *International Journal for Research in Applied Science and Engineering Technology*, *9*(5), 539–543. DOI: 10.22214/ijraset.2021.34163

Seo, H. J., Park, G. M., Son, M., & Hong, A.-J. (2021). Establishment of Virtual-Reality-Based Safety Education and Training System for Safety Engagement. *Education Sciences*, *11*(12), 786. DOI: 10.3390/educsci11120786

Sethi, D., & Seth, M. (2009). Interpersonal communication: Lifeblood of an organization. *The IUP Journal of Soft Skills*, *III*(3&4), 32–40. https://www.researchgate.net/profile/Deepa_Sethi/publication/228271402_Interpersonal_Communication_Lifeblood_of_an_Organization/links/55af387808ae98e661a6fd03/Interpersonal-Communication-Lifeblood-of-an-Organization.pdf

. Shaikh, A. Y., Osei-Kyei, R., & Hardie, M. (2020). A critical analysis of safety performance indicators in construction. *International Journal of Building Pathology and Adaptation, ahead-of-print*(ahead-of-print). DOI: 10.1108/IJBPA-03-2020-0018

. Shankar, A. U., Tewari, V., Rahman, M., Mishra, A., & Bajaj, K. K. (2023). Impact of Virtual Reality (Vr) and Augmented Reality (Ar) in Education. Tuijin Jishu/Journal of Propulsion Technology, 44(4), 1310–1318. DOI: 10.52783/tjjpt.v44.i4.1014

Shringi, A., Arashpour, M., Golafshani, E. M., Rajabifard, A., Dwyer, T., & Li, H. (2022). Efficiency of VR-Based Safety Training for Construction Equipment: Hazard Recognition in Heavy Machinery Operations. *Buildings (Basel, Switzerland), 12*(12), 2084. DOI: 10.3390/buildings12122084

Silbey, S. (1999). Book Reviews: Cultural *Software: A Theory of Ideology*. J. M. Balkin. New Haven, Conn.: Yale University Press, 1998. Pp. xii+335. $35.00. *American Journal of Sociology, 105*(1), 252–254. DOI: 10.1086/210280

Smela, B., Toumi, M., Świerk, K., Francois, C., Biernikiewicz, M., Clay, E., & Boyer, L. (2023). Rapid literature review: Definition and methodology. *Journal of Market Access & Health Policy, 11*(1), 2241234. DOI: 10.1080/20016689.2023.2241234

Sorlini, A., Maxia, L., Patrucco, M., & Pira, E. (2023). Occupational Safety and Health Improvements through Innovative Technologies in Underground Construction Sites: Main Trends and Some Case Histories. *Infrastructures, 8*(6), 104. DOI: 10.3390/infrastructures8060104

Sukhera, J. (2022). Narrative Reviews: Flexible, Rigorous, and Practical. *Journal of Graduate Medical Education, 14*(4), 414–417. DOI: 10.4300/JGME-D-22-00480.1

Tang, P. M., Koopman, J., Elfenbein, H. A., Zhang, J. H., De Cremer, D., Li, C. H., & Chan, E. T. (2022). Using robots at work during the COVID-19 crisis evokes passion decay: Evidence from field and experimental studies. *Applied Psychology, 71*(3), 881–911. DOI: 10.1111/apps.12386

Thach, T. N., Moon, H., Pham, H. D., Kwon, N., & Ahn, Y. (2024). Construction Safety Innovation and Barriers in Different Company Types and Sizes: A Survey in Vietnam. *KSCE Journal of Civil Engineering, 28*(8), 3057–3073. DOI: 10.1007/s12205-024-0779-z

Velev, D., & Zlateva, P. (2017). Virtual Reality Challenges in Education and Training. *International Journal of Learning and Teaching, 3*(1). Advance online publication. DOI: 10.18178/ijlt.3.1.33-37

. Verma, D. S. (2023). OPPORTUNITIES AND CHALLENGES OF USING VR IN EDUCATIONAL SECTOR FOR ENHANCING BETTER LEARNING EXPERIENCE. *Academia.edu.* https://doi.org/DOI: 10.48047/NQ.2022.20.20.NQ109112

Verschueren, F. (2021, December 24). Why and How to Employ Organizational Factors for Foresight in Safety? Academia.edu. https://www.academia.edu/65858104/Why_and_How_to_Employ_Organizational_Factors_for_Foresight_in_Safety

Warren, M. A., & Warren, M. T. (2023). The EThIC Model of Virtue-Based Allyship Development: A New Approach to Equity and Inclusion in Organizations: JBE. *Journal of Business Ethics*, *182*(3), 783–803. DOI: 10.1007/s10551-021-05002-z

Welch, L., Russell, D., Weinstock, D., & Betit, E. (2015). Best Practices for Health and Safety Technology Transfer in Construction. *American Journal of Industrial Medicine*, *58*(8), 849–857. DOI: 10.1002/ajim.22456

Yılmaz, F. (2015). *The Importance of Safety in Construction Sector: Costs of Occupational Accidents in Construction Sites.* Business and Economics Research Journal. https://www.academia.edu/90325943/The_Importance_of_Safety_in_Construction_Sector_Costs_of_Occupational_Accidents_in_Construction_Sites

Zanko, M., & Dawson, P. (2011). Occupational Health and Safety Management in Organizations: A Review. *International Journal of Management Reviews*, *14*(3), 328–344. DOI: 10.1111/j.1468-2370.2011.00319.x

Zhou, N., Ding, L. Y., & Chen, L. Y. (2013). Application of 4D visualization technology for safety management in metro construction. *Automation in Construction*, *34*, 25–36. DOI: 10.1016/j.autcon.2012.10.011

Zhou, Z., Irizarry, J., & Li, Q. (2013). Applying advanced technology to improve safety management in the construction industry: A literature review. *Construction Management and Economics*, *31*(6), 606–622. DOI: 10.1080/01446193.2013.798423

Chapter 12
Artificial Intelligence Applications in Drunk Driving, Public Health, and Safety

Amalisha Sabie Aridi
http://orcid.org/0000-0002-7869-5530
Washington University of Science and Technology, USA

ABSTRACT

Alcohol-impaired driving remains a pervasive public health emergency, causing 10,874 U.S. deaths a year. Traditional countermeasures, sobriety checkpoints, breath testing, and deterrence campaigns often lack scalability and timeliness, necessitating a shift toward artificial intelligence (AI)– enabled prevention. This qualitative focus-group study convened subject-matter experts from public health, law enforcement, crash investigation, AI research, and AI safety. Using structured elicitation and thematic analysis, the study examined how predictive analytics, computer vision, passive in-vehicle sensing, and real-time monitoring can enhance prevention, detection, and enforcement while safeguarding privacy, equity, and accountability. Results articulate mechanisms by which expert deliberation translates technical capability into ethically grounded, operational strategies. The study offers a governance and implementation roadmap for policymakers, technologists, and health administrators seeking scalable AI interventions.

DOI: 10.4018/979-8-2600-1021-1.ch012

INTRODUCTION

Alcohol-impaired driving remains one of the most persistent and devastating public health and safety crises worldwide. Data from the U.S. Department of Transportation's National Highway Traffic Safety Administration (NHTSA) reveal that an alcohol-impaired traffic fatality occurred every forty-eight minutes, resulting in 10,874 deaths; constituting approximately 29 percent of all motor vehicle fatalities in the United States (U.S. Department of Transportation, National Highway Traffic Safety Administration, 2017). These tragic outcomes arise when at least one driver or motorcycle operator possesses a blood alcohol concentration (BAC) of 0.08 grams per deciliter or higher (Fell, 2016). Globally, the toll is even more staggering: nearly 1.2 million individuals die annually in alcohol-related road crashes, and more than one million drivers are arrested for driving under the influence of alcohol in the United States alone (McLester, 2024; McLester & Burrell, 2024). Such figures underscore the scope of a public health problem that is not only preventable but also deeply intertwined with issues of behavioral psychology, enforcement policy, and technology readiness.

Historically, the legal and regulatory frameworks addressing alcohol-impaired driving have evolved unevenly across jurisdictions. For decades, 0.08 g/dL served as the national legal threshold for intoxication until Utah's 2018 decision to reduce its BAC limit to 0.05, establishing a new precedent in state-level public safety policy (McLester, 2024; McLester & Burrell, 2024). Despite such reforms, enforcement remains challenging. Sobriety checkpoints, typically deployed during high-risk periods such as weekend evenings, are constrained by logistical and safety barriers, particularly under adverse weather conditions. Extensive research has long demonstrated that alcohol consumption impairs virtually every dimension of driving competence: judgment, motor coordination, reaction time, and sensory perception all decline measurably as BAC rises (McLester, 2024; McLester & Burrell, 2024). Empirical data show that at 0.08 g/dL, the risk of involvement in a fatal collision increases by as much as 500%, while the probability of nonfatal crashes rises nearly threefold (Blincoe et al., 2015). These physiological and behavioral impairments illuminate why traditional prevention methods, public education campaigns, roadside testing, and legal deterrents, though essential, remain insufficient in isolation.

Recognizing this, the Community Preventive Services Task Force (CPSTF) has emphasized that alcohol-impaired driving represents a major, ongoing public health threat. Adults aged 21–34 reported driving after consuming too much alcohol 112 million times in 2010, and roughly one-third of all motor vehicle fatalities continue to involve intoxicated drivers (CPSTF, 2012). The CPSTF recommends checkpoint-based deterrence programs designed to both heighten the perceived risk of arrest and remove impaired drivers from roadways. Two primary strategies dominate this enforcement paradigm: Selective Breath Testing (SBT), in which officers must first establish reasonable suspicion before administering a test, and Random Breath Testing (RBT), where all stopped drivers are screened for alcohol. While these measures remain the cornerstone of enforcement, they rely heavily on human discretion and physical presence; factors that limit scalability, consistency, and timeliness (McLester, 2024).

ARTIFICIAL INTELLIGENCE AS A TRANSFORMATIVE PUBLIC HEALTH TOOL

Recent advances in artificial intelligence (AI) offer transformative potential for addressing the limitations inherent in traditional approaches to drunk driving prevention. AI-based tools now facilitate predictive prevention, real-time detection, and post-incident accountability, thus extending the reach of both public health interventions and law enforcement systems (Li & Sun, 2024; Iyer et al., 2023; Preethi, 2023; Yang et al., 2024).

From a preventive standpoint, predictive analytics can identify individuals and environments associated with heightened risk of impaired driving (Preethi, 2023; Yang et al., 2024). For example, AI models trained on behavioral and contextual datasets, such as prior DUI offenses, weekend nightlife activity, or ride-share utilization trends, can pinpoint at-risk populations and guide the deployment of targeted educational campaigns. AI-powered chatbots and adaptive prevention platforms can personalize messages based on demographic, psychological, or geographic factors, thereby increasing message retention and behavioral impact. Furthermore, context-aware mobile assistants can utilize calendar data, geolocation, and past travel patterns to provide real-time interventions, such as suggesting a ride-sharing option when a user is leaving a bar late at night. This personalized, anticipatory engagement aligns with the broader public health principle of upstream prevention, wherein interventions occur before risk behaviors manifest (McLester & Burrell, 2024).

Equally compelling are AI-based detection systems embedded in modern vehicles and wearable technologies. Advanced computer vision algorithms, integrated into in-cabin monitoring systems, can assess indicators of intoxication, such as facial pallor, eyelid drooping, or erratic steering, while biosensing technologies track physiological signals, including heart rate variability and micro-saccadic eye movements (McLester & Burrell, 2024). If impairment is detected, these systems can limit engine power, alert emergency contacts, or even prevent ignition. Wearables such as smartwatches or biometric patches capable of estimating BAC from perspiration or pulse rate variability can communicate directly with connected vehicles, initiating immobilization protocols if thresholds are exceeded. In some cases, passive alcohol detection systems embedded in steering wheels or seatbelts can analyze exhaled breath for ethanol molecules, enabling a non-intrusive, continuous safety layer (Li & Sun, 2024; Iyer et al., 2023; Preethi, 2023; Yang et al., 2024).

Artificial intelligence also enhances the precision and efficiency of law enforcement in detecting and deterring drunk driving (McLester, 2024). Machine learning algorithms trained on large-scale datasets of impaired driving behavior can recognize patterns of lane deviation, speed fluctuation, or delayed braking captured by roadside or dash-mounted cameras. These systems can issue automated alerts to nearby patrol units, facilitating faster intervention and reducing the likelihood of human error. In jurisdictions where impaired driving recidivism is high, AI-enabled license plate recognition (ALPR) systems can flag vehicles registered to prior offenders, supporting proactive surveillance. For offenders already under probationary monitoring, AI-driven compliance tools, such as mobile sobriety applications or GPS-linked biosensors, can verify abstinence, detect alcohol use, and report violations instantaneously to supervising officers.

Beyond enforcement, AI can inform policy evaluation and optimization by aggregating and analyzing multimodal data streams, such as crash statistics, enforcement patterns, and behavioral analytics (McLester & Burrell, 2024). For instance, simulations using AI can project how modifying legal BAC thresholds might affect crash rates, or how resource reallocation could optimize checkpoint timing and placement. Such data-driven governance models not only enhance efficiency but also ensure that interventions are both equitable and evidence-based.

Alcohol-impaired driving persists as one of the gravest and most intractable threats to global road safety and public health. However, the integration of artificial intelligence technologies across prevention, detection, and enforcement domains offers a paradigm shift, transforming reactive policing into a proactive public health strategy (McLester & Burrell, 2024). By leveraging AI's analytical precision, adaptive communication, and autonomous sensing capabilities, society stands on the threshold of a future where data-informed systems complement human oversight to reduce alcohol-related morbidity and mortality drastically. As these innovations mature, interdisciplinary collaboration between technologists, public health experts, and policymakers will be essential to ensure that AI-driven interventions are ethical, equitable, and empirically validated in the service of saving lives (McLester, 2024).

PROBLEM STATEMENT

Alcohol-impaired driving continues to represent one of the most enduring and catastrophic public health and safety challenges of the modern era. Despite decades of educational campaigns, legislative reform, and enforcement initiatives, alcohol-related traffic fatalities remain alarmingly prevalent. Data from the U.S. Department of Transportation's National Highway Traffic Safety Administration (NHTSA) reveal that an alcohol-impaired traffic fatality occurred every forty-eight minutes in 2017, culminating in 10,874 deaths and constituting nearly 29 percent of all motor vehicle fatalities in the United States (U.S. Department of Transportation, National Highway Traffic Safety Administration, 2017). The physiological and cognitive deterioration associated with blood alcohol concentrations (BAC) at or above 0.08 grams per deciliter severely compromises driver performance—manifesting as impaired judgment, delayed reaction time, and reduced motor coordination (Fell, 2016; McLester, 2024). Empirical analyses have demonstrated that at this level of intoxication, the likelihood of a fatal crash increases fivefold, and the probability of nonfatal collisions rises almost threefold (Blincoe et al., 2015).

Globally, the toll of alcohol-impaired driving is equally devastating, with approximately 1.2 million fatalities annually and over one million DUI arrests in the United States each year (McLester, 2024; McLester & Burrell, 2024). Despite advancements in legal thresholds, such as Utah's pioneering decision to reduce the BAC limit from 0.08 to 0.05 in 2018, traditional countermeasures, including sobriety checkpoints, breath testing, and deterrence campaigns, remain limited in terms of scalability, operational consistency, and responsiveness (McLester & Burrell, 2024). This persistent gap underscores the need for a paradigm shift that integrates technological innovation, particularly artificial intelligence (AI), into public health and enforcement strategies. The problem, therefore, lies not only in the human and systemic failure to mitigate alcohol-impaired driving but also in the insufficient application of emerging technologies capable of transforming reactive deterrence into proactive prevention.

PURPOSE STATEMENT

The purpose of this qualitative focus group study is to explore and synthesize expert insights on how artificial intelligence (AI) technologies can be effectively leveraged to mitigate alcohol-impaired driving as a major public health and safety issue. This study will draw upon the collective experience, education, and professional expertise of subject matter experts (SMEs), including professionals in public health, data science, transportation safety, and corporate innovation, who possess direct knowledge of how Fortune 500 companies conceptualize, design, and deploy focus groups to inform multimillion-dollar decisions. Through in-depth discussion and thematic analysis, this research aims to elucidate how large-scale organizations operationalize focus groups to derive actionable intelligence and how these best practices can be adapted to advance AI-driven interventions in the domain of impaired driving prevention (Li & Sun, 2024; Iyer et al., 2023; Preethi, 2023; Yang et al., 2024).

The study aims to uncover the underlying mechanisms by which expert-driven deliberation can bridge the gap between technological capabilities and public health applications, thereby generating grounded insights into how AI tools, such as predictive analytics, computer vision, and real-time monitoring systems, can enhance prevention, detection, and enforcement strategies targeting drunk driving. By examining the lived experiences and professional reasoning of experts, this qualitative inquiry aims to provide an interpretive understanding of how organizational decision-making frameworks, similar to those employed by Fortune 500 enterprises, can inform evidence-based approaches to combating alcohol-related roadway fatalities.

SIGNIFICANCE OF THE STUDY

This investigation holds profound significance at the intersection of public health, technology policy, and organizational decision science. Alcohol-impaired driving remains a leading cause of preventable death, exerting immense human, economic, and social costs (U.S. Department of Transportation, National Highway Traffic Safety Administration, 2017). The continuing inadequacy of conventional enforcement and deterrence mechanisms demands innovative approaches rooted in technological adaptation and data-driven prevention. AI's capacity to model behavioral patterns, assess physiological indicators, and automate safety interventions introduces new possibilities for curbing impaired driving before it results in harm (McLester & Burrell, 2024).

Nevertheless, while the technical potential of AI has been widely recognized, translating this potential into scalable, ethically sound public health applications remains underexplored. This study's qualitative design situates the conversation within a framework informed by corporate expertise and strategic foresight, recognizing that Fortune 500 companies have long employed focus groups as critical tools for complex decision-making and innovation investment. These corporations routinely rely on multidisciplinary panels to interpret market signals, evaluate technological feasibility, and anticipate consumer behavior; activities that parallel the collaborative demands of integrating AI within public safety ecosystems. By examining how such decision-making infrastructures function in high-stakes business contexts, this research contributes to the development of a model for interdisciplinary public health problem-solving, where collective expertise guides the responsible implementation of AI systems.

Ultimately, this study advances both scholarly and practical understanding by linking corporate focus group methodologies with public health technology governance, thereby generating actionable insights relevant to policymakers, technologists, and health administrators. Its findings could inform the design of AI-driven interventions that are not only technologically sound but also socially acceptable, transparent, and ethically aligned.

NATURE OF THE STUDY

This inquiry adopts a qualitative focus group design, a methodology particularly suited for eliciting nuanced perspectives from individuals with specialized knowledge and diverse experiential backgrounds. The study will convene subject matter experts (SMEs) from domains including public health administration, AI development, law enforcement policy, and corporate decision-making, particularly individuals who have participated in or facilitated focus groups within Fortune 500 organizations. The qualitative nature of the study enables the exploration of how and why decisions are made, rather than simply what decisions are made, thereby uncovering the underlying thought processes, interpretive frameworks, and organizational cultures that influence technology adoption and the formation of public health strategies.

THE PERSISTENT AND ESCALATING PUBLIC HEALTH CRISIS OF ALCOHOL-IMPAIRED DRIVING

Alcohol-impaired driving remains one of the most intractable public health and safety crises confronting modern societies. Despite decades of public education, legislative reform, and enforcement initiatives, impaired driving continues to exact an intolerable human toll. Among individuals aged 16 to 24 years, vehicular crashes are the leading cause of death, resulting in approximately two million injuries annually across all age groups (McLester, 2024). Of the numerous modifiable risk factors associated with motor vehicle crashes, alcohol use stands as one of the most consequential, both in terms of crash frequency and injury severity. The dual role of alcohol as a socially sanctioned substance and a physiological depressant complicates its regulation, rendering traditional prevention efforts insufficient to curb its devastating impact (McLester, 2024; McLester & Burrell, 2024).

Despite cultural normalization of drinking behavior, the public health ramifications of alcohol misuse are staggering. In a 2015 national survey, 86.4% of U.S. adults reported lifetime consumption of alcohol, with 70.1% consuming within the previous year and 56% within the previous month (Breslow et al., 2017). These statistics reflect widespread social accessibility and deeply embedded consumption patterns that amplify risk exposure across communities. Given that even moderate intoxication impairs reaction time, judgment, and motor coordination, the prevalence of alcohol use across demographic groups signifies a constant threat to roadway safety. Without novel interventions, these statistics portend continued loss of life and public health deterioration.

YOUTH VULNERABILITY AND THE LIFELONG CONSEQUENCES OF EARLY ALCOHOL USE

The prevalence of alcohol consumption among youth and emerging adults compounds the urgency of this issue. Longitudinal analyses reveal persistently high rates of binge drinking, with approximately 32% of college students reporting episodic heavy drinking and 40% reporting frequent alcohol consumption (Schulenberg et al., 2017). The intersection of developmental immaturity, peer influence, and social reinforcement produces an environment where alcohol misuse is both normalized and valorized. Particularly concerning is the rising trend of mixing alcohol with energy drinks, practiced by roughly one-quarter of regular consumers, which masks the subjective perception of intoxication and facilitates reckless behaviors, including impaired driving (Patrick et al., 2013).

The epidemiological data are equally alarming among adolescents. Approximately 72% of high school seniors report lifetime alcohol use, with 43% consuming within the past month and 25% engaging in binge drinking during the preceding two weeks (Grant et al., 2017). These statistics underscore that the initiation of alcohol use occurs during critical phases of neurological maturation. Neuroimaging studies demonstrate that alcohol consumption during adolescence disrupts the development of the prefrontal cortex, the region responsible for executive function, risk assessment, and impulse control, as well as the hippocampus, which governs spatial awareness and memory (Jacobus & Tapert, 2013). The enduring effects of such interference manifest as impaired cognitive function, reduced self-regulation, and increased vulnerability to chronic substance use later in life. Consequently, early alcohol exposure is not merely a behavioral concern but a profound neurodevelopmental hazard with implications for long-term public health.

These findings demand a shift in policy and intervention frameworks. Existing educational programs and punitive deterrents are insufficient to address the biological, psychological, and social mechanisms driving adolescent alcohol misuse. Innovative, technology-enhanced prevention models, including digital behavioral monitoring, AI-based predictive analytics, and interactive educational platforms, are urgently needed to identify risk patterns early and prevent escalation into chronic impairment or tragedy on the road.

MISJUDGMENT OF IMPAIRMENT: THE HIDDEN CATALYST OF TRAGEDY

A critical yet often underestimated driver of alcohol-impaired incidents is the individual's inability to assess their own impairment accurately. Alcohol blunts self-awareness and skews perception, leading to dangerous overconfidence in one's ability to drive (Laude & Fillmore, 2016). Sociocultural and demographic factors also contribute to this misperception. For instance, Kerr and Greenfield (2015) found that individuals from different racial and ethnic groups varied significantly in their self-assessed thresholds for impairment. Black participants estimated they could drink 30% more, and Hispanic participants 26% more, before their fine motor coordination would be affected.

Although public health campaigns have long promoted the concept of the designated driver, real-world adherence often falls short of best practice. Many groups choose a "designated" driver based not on abstinence, but on relative sobriety, a perilous interpretation that leaves safety contingent on subjective judgment rather than objective sobriety (National Highway Traffic Safety Administration, 2017). This behavioral inconsistency underscores a fundamental gap in existing deterrent frameworks: interventions that rely on self-assessment or voluntary abstinence fail precisely where impairment clouds judgment. Innovative, automated, and technology-mediated safeguards, such as in-vehicle alcohol detection systems and smartphone-integrated safety prompts, represent critical next steps toward addressing this structural weakness.

THE EPIDEMIOLOGY OF IMPAIRED DRIVING AND THE NEED FOR SYSTEMIC INNOVATION

The prevalence of alcohol consumption and the frequency of impaired driving reveal a paradox: while approximately 50% of U.S. adults consume alcohol regularly, only a fraction acknowledge engaging in impaired driving. Nevertheless, surveys suggest that 20% of respondents have driven within two hours of drinking, and 6–11% admit to driving in the past year when they believed they were near or above the legal BAC limit (Laude & Fillmore, 2016). Extrapolated nationally, these figures translate into more than 112 million annual drunk driving incidents; a staggering indicator of systemic risk exposure.

Crucially, most alcohol-impaired drivers involved in fatal crashes are not chronic alcoholics or repeat offenders. Over 50% of fatally injured impaired drivers had no documented history of alcohol abuse (Rhoades & Jernigan, 2013), and in 2014, only 7% had prior DUI convictions within the previous three years (Breslow et al., 2017). This data highlights the insufficiency of enforcement mechanisms that target only habitual offenders, revealing instead a broader behavioral epidemic among social and occasional drinkers. The evidence calls for preventive innovations that transcend traditional deterrence; real-time detection systems, predictive behavioral algorithms, and community-based interventions that intervene before impairment results in fatality.

EVOLVING PRODUCT MARKETS AND THE ESCALATION OF RISK

Contemporary shifts in the alcohol marketplace have further exacerbated public health risks. The rising alcohol concentration in beverages, particularly within the craft beer and artisanal spirits sectors, increases both the potency of consumption and the speed of intoxication (Elzinga et al., 2015). Concurrently, the co-consumption of caffeine and alcohol, though prohibited in manufacturing, remains prevalent among younger demographics. Research demonstrates that this combination heightens binge drinking and doubles the likelihood of driving while intoxicated, as the stimulant properties of caffeine obscure physiological cues of intoxication (Babor et al., 2015). Laboratory studies confirm that energy drinks do not mitigate alcohol-induced cognitive decline; rather, they compound misjudgment of impairment (Lalanne et al., 2017; Forward et al., 2017).

Given the increasing potency and affordability of alcoholic beverages, policy efforts aimed solely at taxation or marketing restrictions are inadequate. While Rehm (2016) suggested reducing alcohol content as a harm-reduction measure, conclusive evidence of its efficacy remains elusive. This underscores the necessity for data-driven regulatory innovation, where technology, such as machine learning models analyzing consumption trends, could inform adaptive, evidence-based policies that anticipate rather than react to risk.

ECONOMIC, MARKETING, AND ENVIRONMENTAL DRIVERS

The economic accessibility of alcohol has reached a six-decade low, fueled by reduced excise taxes, intensified competition, and expansive marketing strategies (Kerr et al., 2013). The market's diversification through premixed, high-sugar alcoholic beverages and targeted advertising toward youth has created an ecosystem that sustains and amplifies risky consumption patterns (Babor et al., 2015). Corporate sponsorship of major sports and entertainment events normalizes drinking behavior while embedding it within aspirational cultural narratives (Babor et al., 2015). These commercial strategies not only increase exposure but also undermine public health messaging, contributing indirectly to the persistence of alcohol-impaired driving.

Innovative public health responses must therefore confront the intersection of market forces and behavioral risk, leveraging advanced analytics to identify vulnerable populations and regulate advertising more precisely. Without integrating AI-driven surveillance of marketing exposure, policymakers risk perpetuating conditions that promote early initiation and sustained misuse of alcohol.

TOWARD INNOVATIVE AND INTEGRATED PUBLIC HEALTH INTERVENTIONS

Public health movements such as Mothers Against Drunk Driving (MADD) and Students Against Destructive Decisions (SADD) were instrumental in reframing impaired driving as a moral and social violation rather than a personal indiscretion. Nevertheless, while these grassroots campaigns achieved cultural change, the persistence of alcohol-impaired driving underscores the limitations of awareness alone. The next frontier demands technological, behavioral, and systemic innovation.

Community-based, multicomponent interventions, when coupled with data analytics, AI-enabled prevention systems, and policy integration, offer the most promising path forward. Evidence consistently links increased alcohol availability with greater consumption and higher crash rates (Babor et al., 2010). Therefore, effective prevention must combine restriction of environmental access with intelligent, technology-driven monitoring and education. For instance, predictive algorithms could help municipalities allocate resources for sobriety checkpoints dynamically based on temporal and spatial risk patterns. Likewise, AI-assisted driver monitoring systems could autonomously detect impairment before ignition, preventing tragedies preemptively rather than reactively.

The synthesis of the literature reveals a sobering truth: alcohol-impaired driving is not merely a behavioral lapse but a systemic failure in prevention innovation. Its persistence reflects the lag between technological capacity and policy application.

Only through the convergence of public health science, behavioral research, and artificial intelligence can societies hope to achieve a substantive decline in alcohol-related morbidity and mortality. This convergence represents both a moral imperative and a technological opportunity to reimagine prevention not as punishment but as prediction, protection, and preservation of life.

TECHNOLOGY-DRIVEN STRATEGIES FOR ADDRESSING ALCOHOL-IMPAIRED DRIVING

For decades, alcohol-impaired driving has been addressed primarily through deterrence-oriented public policy, legal reform, and enforcement initiatives. Measures such as blood alcohol concentration (BAC) limits, license suspension, and sobriety checkpoints were designed to create general deterrence, instilling in drivers the fear of detection and punishment. However, misconceptions persist regarding their effectiveness, particularly among occasional and moderate drinkers, who often underestimate their level of impairment or the probability of apprehension. Critics of the 0.08 g/dL BAC limit, implemented nationally in 2000, initially argued that habitual offenders were the true source of the problem. Nevertheless, longitudinal evaluations demonstrated a sustained reduction in alcohol-related crashes across all driver categories following the policy's adoption (Fell, 2016).

Nevertheless, the United States' legal threshold remains relatively lenient when compared to other developed nations, many of which enforce BAC limits between 0.03 and 0.05. For example, Japan's 0.03 g/dL threshold reflects a more precautionary stance on driver impairment. Despite strong empirical support for the 0.08 BAC standard, as well as complementary measures such as minimum legal drinking age laws and sobriety checkpoints, these strategies are inherently reactive. They rely on post-incident enforcement rather than preemptive detection and thus cannot address the root behavioral and contextual factors that precipitate impaired driving (McLester, 2024).

To mitigate this limitation, contemporary public health frameworks increasingly advocate for multicomponent interventions, which integrate programs combining enforcement with education, responsible beverage service, rehabilitation, and access restrictions. Such community-based approaches have demonstrated modest success when executed through coalition-led models, yet their sustainability depends heavily on public engagement, enforcement capacity, and inter-agency coordination. The urgency of the problem demands a paradigm shift toward technologically mediated prevention systems, capable of continuously monitoring, predicting, and deterring impaired driving behavior before it endangers human life.

THE TRANSITION TO INTELLIGENT VEHICLE SYSTEMS

Among the most tangible technological interventions, ignition interlock devices (IIDs) have emerged as a promising mechanism to prevent recidivism among individuals convicted of driving under the influence. These devices measure a driver's breath alcohol concentration and prevent vehicle ignition if the detected BAC exceeds a pre-set limit, typically 0.02–0.04% (Kaufman & Wiebe, 2016). Empirical studies indicate that the installation of interlocks can reduce re-arrest rates by up to 67% during the intervention period, with recidivism rates decreasing by 50% to 90% (Kaufman & Wiebe, 2016; McGinty et al., 2017).

Despite their efficacy, traditional IIDs face several implementation barriers, including enforcement challenges, maintenance requirements, and user compliance issues. Furthermore, their reliance on self-regulation and punitive mandates limits their scalability. Once the device is removed, re-arrest rates often revert to baseline levels, underscoring the necessity for more integrated, adaptive, and intelligent systems.

Recent advances in artificial intelligence (AI) and assistive transport (AT) technologies have begun transforming these static mechanisms into dynamic safety ecosystems (Li & Sun, 2024; Iyer et al., 2023; Preethi, 2023; Yang et al., 2024). For instance, AI-enabled ignition interlocks equipped with machine learning algorithms can analyze not only breath alcohol content but also driver biometrics, steering behavior, and response latency to detect potential impairment in real time. Similarly, sensor fusion technologies, combining facial recognition, eye-tracking, and voice analysis, can identify cognitive and physiological signs of intoxication without requiring direct user input. Such systems enable continuous passive monitoring, significantly expanding the scope of prevention beyond legally mandated offenders to the general driving population.

An example of innovation in this domain is the development of vehicle-integrated AI safety modules, which automatically disable ignition, issue ride-share prompts, or alert emergency contacts when intoxication indicators are detected (McLester, 2024). As these systems evolve, they could be paired with personalized AI assistants that analyze user patterns (e.g., calendar events, geolocation near bars, or recent alcohol purchases) and proactively recommend alternative transportation options. This integration of behavioral prediction and automated control represents a paradigm shift from punitive enforcement toward preventive autonomy, where the vehicle itself becomes an active agent in preserving human life (McLester & Burrell, 2024).

BEYOND ENFORCEMENT TOWARD PREDICTIVE PREVENTION

Traditional deterrence assumes that rational actors will modify their behavior in response to punishment. However, alcohol consumption often impairs rationality itself, rendering punitive deterrence insufficient. Herein lies the transformative potential of AI tools and assistive technologies (AT), their capacity to intervene preemptively by detecting risk patterns before harm occurs. Predictive analytics, for instance, can synthesize large-scale behavioral data, such as time of day, previous DUI records, and geospatial traffic patterns, to identify high-risk scenarios for impaired driving (McLester & Burrell, 2024).

AI-driven behavioral forecasting systems allow law enforcement and public health agencies to allocate resources dynamically. For example, predictive algorithms may determine the optimal deployment of sobriety checkpoints based on real-time data from social events, nightlife districts, and ride-share cancellations. Likewise, smartphone-based AT applications could alert users when patterns of behavior suggest potential impairment. By integrating wearable data, such as heart rate variability, gait instability, or changes in speech cadence, these tools could autonomously suggest calling a ride-share service or temporarily disabling the vehicle ignition.

The advantage of AI-based systems lies in their ability to adapt. Unlike static laws, algorithms continually refine their predictive accuracy through feedback loops, enabling increasingly personalized and contextually sensitive interventions. When linked with connected vehicle infrastructure, these systems can form a national digital safety network, a fusion of personal, vehicular, and environmental intelligence that mitigates risk dynamically. For instance, an AI traffic management platform could identify erratic driving behavior across multiple vehicles in real-time and instantly alert law enforcement units. Such applications demonstrate the convergence of public health surveillance and autonomous mobility technologies, yielding a more agile and responsive prevention ecosystem.

THE CASE FOR TECHNOLOGICAL COUNTERBALANCE

The persistent influence of alcohol marketing undermines prevention efforts by normalizing consumption and promoting risky behaviors, particularly among youth. As Lobstein (2017) demonstrated in a meta-analysis of 25 longitudinal studies, repeated exposure to alcohol advertising is strongly associated with early initiation and increased frequency of use. Similarly, Rhoades and Jernigan (2013) observed that the prevalence of alcohol advertisements rose in direct proportion to the size of the under-21 population in target markets. These campaigns frequently employ highly stimulating or sexualized imagery, designed to associate alcohol with confidence, desirability, and success, narratives that distort risk perception and erode the perceived legitimacy of deterrence campaigns (McLester, 2024).

Emerging AI tools can serve as countermeasures to marketing-driven risk amplification. Through digital surveillance and content recognition algorithms, AI can track the prevalence, placement, and psychological impact of alcohol advertisements on social media, streaming platforms, and gaming environments. Natural language processing and visual sentiment analysis could help policymakers identify deceptive marketing strategies and predict their potential influence on youth consumption trends (Li & Sun, 2024; Iyer et al., 2023; Preethi, 2023; Yang et al., 2024). By coupling these insights with public health messaging platforms, AI systems can deliver targeted, age-appropriate counter-narratives and educational campaigns optimized to reach the same digital spaces where harmful marketing proliferates (Burrell & McLester, 2024).

Such strategies demonstrate how AI's analytic power can rebalance the information ecosystem, counteracting the asymmetric influence of industry advertising and promoting data-informed, culturally adaptive public health messaging.

INTEGRATING PUBLIC HEALTH, TECHNOLOGY, AND BEHAVIORAL INSIGHT

Historically, policy frameworks addressing alcohol-impaired driving have emphasized enforcement and punishment rather than behavioral transformation or systemic adaptation. Nevertheless, evidence increasingly indicates that punitive deterrence, such as license revocation or incarceration, has limited long-term efficacy (Ahlin et al., 2011). In contrast, rehabilitative and educational interventions, when coupled with technology-based monitoring, yield more sustainable outcomes (McKnight & Voas, 1991).

AI technologies now enable the personalization of rehabilitation programs based on cognitive-behavioral profiling. For instance, adaptive learning systems could deliver customized modules to DUI offenders, using gamified behavioral reinforcement to improve risk perception and decision-making. Likewise, telehealth-enabled AT tools could facilitate continuous monitoring of alcohol use during recovery, detecting relapse indicators and providing real-time feedback to both the user and support networks. These innovations transform rehabilitation from a static, punitive process into a dynamic feedback system, one that promotes accountability while supporting behavioral change (Li & Sun, 2024; Iyer et al., 2023; Preethi, 2023; Yang et al., 2024).

The convergence of artificial intelligence, assistive technology, and behavioral health science represents a pivotal inflection point in the fight against alcohol-impaired driving (Li & Sun, 2024; Iyer et al., 2023; Preethi, 2023; Yang et al., 2024). By leveraging predictive analytics, biometric sensing, and intelligent intervention systems, society can transcend the reactive confines of deterrence-based policy and usher in an era of precision prevention (Li & Sun, 2024; Iyer et al., 2023; Preethi, 2023; Yang et al., 2024). In this emerging paradigm, every vehicle, wearable device, and digital platform can act as a node in an integrated safety ecosystem, anticipating risk, adapting to human behavior, and safeguarding lives long before tragedy strikes.

METHODS AND RESEARCH DESIGN

We conducted a multi-stage, qualitative study using a modified Nominal Group Technique (NGT) embedded within homogeneous expert focus groups. The design combined (1) independent elicitation, (2) structured within-group deliberation, (3) cross-group synthesis with duplicate elimination, and (4) cumulative voting/priority setting. This approach was selected to generate actionable recommendations that map AI/AT capabilities to prevention, detection, education, and enforcement needs documented in the impaired-driving literature (U.S. Department of Transportation, National Highway Traffic Safety Administration, 2017; Fell, 2016; McLester & Burrell, 2024; Li & Sun, 2024; Iyer et al., 2023; Preethi, 2023; Yang et al., 2024).

PARTICIPANTS AND SAMPLING

Purposive sampling identified 20 subject-matter experts (SMEs) across five domains (n = 4 per domain):

1. **Law enforcement** (LE): sworn officers or commanders with impaired-driving operations experience;
2. **Automobile crash/forensic investigation** (AIv): collision reconstructionists and traffic safety analysts;
3. **Mothers Against Drunk Driving leadership** (MADD): state or national leaders;
4. **AI research & development** (AIR): ML engineers or HCI researchers focused on mobility/safety;
5. **AI safety & security** (AIS): experts in model risk, privacy, auditability, and human-oversight design.

Inclusion criteria were ≥5 years of relevant experience and current role accountability for policy, technology, or program decisions. Diversity in geography, agency type, and institutional affiliation was targeted to reduce monoculture bias

INSTRUMENTS

A semi-structured protocol posed four prompts (each answered independently before group sessions):

1. *In what ways can AI tools or AI technologies assist in addressing drunk driving?*
2. *What are the ethical considerations and concerns with how these technologies are deployed?*
3. *How can these tools be used to assist in education and awareness about drunk driving?*
4. *How can these tools be used to assist law enforcement?*

RESULTS

Research Question 1: In What Ways Can AI Tools and Technologies Assist in Addressing Drunk Driving?

Theme 1: Integrated In-Vehicle Impairment Detection and Safe-Stop Systems (56 votes)

This theme reflects a consensus that vehicle-integrated AI systems, using computer vision, biosensors, and driver-behavior analytics, represent the most transformative and immediate frontier for preventing alcohol-impaired driving. Participants emphasized that real-time, passive detection paired with automated intervention could shift the paradigm from reactive enforcement to preemptive prevention.

- **[Law Enforcement | LE-3]**: "We've been relying on checkpoints and witness observation for decades. If we had systems that could quietly analyze eye movement, micro-steering corrections, and reaction delays before a vehicle even leaves the parking lot, we'd prevent tragedies before they happen. AI can become the first line of defense rather than the last responder."
- **[AI Research & Development | AIR-1]**: "Our prototypes integrate computer vision with pedal latency and steering-torque deviation. These signals anticipate impairment minutes before a visible error occurs. The AI doesn't have to 'catch' a drunk driver; it predicts one."
- **[MADD Leadership | MADD-2]**: "From families' perspectives, this isn't surveillance; it's protection. A compassionate system that won't let a loved one drive while impaired is an act of prevention, not punishment."

Collectively, participants described this category as "AI seatbelts for cognition," emphasizing its potential to become a universal public-safety feature analogous to airbags.

Theme 2: Predictive Risk Mapping for Prevention and Resource Allocation (48 votes)

This theme captures the belief that predictive analytics can identify temporal and geographic "hotspots" of impaired driving risk. By aggregating contextual data, event schedules, weather patterns, nightlife density, and prior offense histories, AI can inform targeted patrols, public health messaging, and community interventions.

- **[Law Enforcement | LE-4]**: "We could finally move from blanket patrols to precision deterrence. Predictive maps allow us to allocate officers where the data says risk will peak, say, between 11 p.m. and 2 a.m. near a downtown entertainment corridor."
- **[Auto Accident Investigation | AIv-1]**: "Crash reconstruction data already reveal repeating patterns; same locations, same conditions. AI could turn those findings into proactive warnings rather than postmortems."
- **[MADD Leadership | MADD-4]**: "When we know where and when risk concentrates, our volunteers can coordinate community messages and ride-share partnerships right where they matter most."

This theme highlights the shift toward data-informed prevention ecosystems, which reduces enforcement inefficiency while enhancing deterrence visibility.

Theme 3: Context-Aware Mobile Interventions (44 votes)

Participants described AI-enabled mobile assistants that deliver personalized, just-in-time interventions, such as suggesting ride-sharing options, sending reminders, or alerting designated drivers. These tools capitalize on behavioral triggers to dissuade impaired driving before it occurs.

- **[AI Research & Development | AIR-3]**: "A calendar-aware app that recognizes a social outing and proactively pushes a one-tap ride option before the first drink changes the decision point entirely."
- **[MADD Leadership | MADD-1]**: "Behavior change happens in the moment of temptation. A gentle prompt, not a reprimand, helps people make safer choices without embarrassment."

- **[AI Safety & Security | AIS-2]**: "We can geofence nightlife districts so that prompts appear contextually, yet remain anonymous and ephemeral, to maintain privacy integrity."

This theme reflects the potential for AI-driven behavioral nudging to complement regulatory and enforcement strategies.

Theme 4: Standardized Digital Forensics and System Accountability (32 votes)

Participants emphasized the critical need for uniform standards governing the capture, storage, and auditability of AI-derived impairment data. The legitimacy of AI interventions, particularly when vehicles autonomously prevent ignition, depends on transparent, tamper-evident digital records.

- **[Law Enforcement | LE-1]**: "In court, the first question is always, 'What exactly did the system detect?' We need audit trails that are indisputable and human-readable."
- **[Auto Investigation | AIv-4]**: "For crash reconstruction, every manufacturer uses its own format. A standardized schema for sensor data would expedite investigations and ensure fairness."
- **[AI Safety & Security | AIS-3]**: "Cryptographically signed, immutable records protect everyone, from the driver's right to contest to the officer's need for integrity verification."

This theme highlights the intersection of technology, justice, and governance, emphasizing the importance of data integrity as a foundational aspect of deploying ethical AI.

Research Question 2: What Ethical Considerations and Concerns Accompany Deployment?

Theme 1: Privacy and Data Minimization as Design Imperatives (62 votes)

Participants universally agreed that public acceptance of AI in impaired-driving prevention hinges on privacy protection. Systems must analyze data locally, store only essential information, and prevent secondary uses such as insurance profiling or commercial targeting.

- **[AI Safety & Security | AIS-4]**: "Edge computing, process on the device, decide locally, delete immediately, should be non-negotiable. Safety doesn't require surveillance."
- **[MADD Leadership | MADD-4]**: "The moral cost of saving lives cannot be perpetual data retention. People deserve safety without surrendering privacy."
- **[AI Research & Development | AIR-2]**: "Limiting collection to the bare minimum for functionality builds the trust necessary for large-scale adoption."

This theme redefines responsible innovation as privacy-preserving by design rather than as an afterthought.

Theme 2: Equity, Bias, and Performance Parity (54 votes)

Bias and algorithmic fairness emerged as urgent concerns. Participants cautioned that AI systems may misinterpret physiological or behavioral cues in ways that disproportionately affect specific demographic groups.

- **[Auto Investigation | AIv-2]**: "We've seen that fatigue, medications, or neurological differences can mimic impairment. Calibration must include diverse datasets and ongoing bias audits."
- **[Law Enforcement | LE-2]**: "If system alerts cluster in certain neighborhoods or demographics, public trust collapses; and with it, enforcement legitimacy."
- **[AI Safety & Security | AIS-2]**: "We need transparent performance dashboards disaggregated by age, gender, and ethnicity, similar to crash-test safety ratings."

This theme highlights the ethical responsibility to uphold algorithmic equity and ensure continuous validation.

Theme 3: Transparency, Accountability, and Contestability (46 votes)

Participants emphasized that drivers must understand why AI systems act and have avenues for contesting erroneous outcomes.

- **[Law Enforcement | LE-1]**: "If your car won't start, you deserve to know why—and to challenge that decision if it's wrong."
- **[MADD Leadership | MADD-1]**: "Explanations should be clear and human-centered, not buried in technical jargon. Trust begins with understanding."

- **[AI Safety & Security | AIS-3]**: "Blockchain-backed records and independent audit mechanisms ensure the system's word can be trusted even in litigation."

This theme emphasizes procedural justice in technological governance, ensuring that AI decisions remain transparent and reviewable.

Research Question 3: How Can AI Tools Support Education and Awareness?

Theme 1: Personalized Micro-Learning and Risk Awareness (58 votes)

AI's adaptive capabilities enable real-time, individualized education. Participants envisioned systems delivering short, evidence-based prompts tied to user behavior, time, and context.

- **[MADD Leadership | MADD-3]**: "A brief message saying, 'Two drinks in 60 minutes equals triple crash risk,' can do more than a year of school assemblies."
- **[AI Research & Development | AIR-1]**: "When mobile apps contextualize the data—using time, route, and drink history; they become digital conscience assistants."
- **[Law Enforcement | LE-4]**: "Showing how small BAC changes translate to real-world crash probabilities humanizes the statistics."

This theme illustrates how AI-based education can personalize deterrence, bridging awareness and immediate action.

Theme 2: Community Dashboards and Targeted Outreach (52 votes)

Participants endorsed the development of community-level risk dashboards that integrate anonymized data from sensors, ride-sharing services, and police reports to inform public campaigns.

- **[MADD Leadership | MADD-4]**: "Imagine a dashboard showing that Friday nights after local football games carry peak risk; our volunteers could launch awareness drives right there."

- **[Law Enforcement | LE-2]**: "Data-driven outreach aligns enforcement and community messaging so they reinforce each other rather than operate in silos."
- **[Auto Investigation | AIv-3]**: "Transparent, aggregate data builds accountability; citizens can see progress, not just slogans."

This theme highlights AI as a civic engagement tool, democratizing access to risk information.

Theme 3: Simulation-Based and Immersive Education (46 votes)

Participants described virtual reality (VR) and augmented reality (AR) experiences simulating the effects of impairment as potent educational tools.

- **[Law Enforcement | LE-1]**: "When trainees experience delayed reaction time in VR, it changes their empathy for victims and their vigilance on duty."
- **[MADD Leadership | MADD-2]**: "Teenagers internalize consequences when they feel them. VR simulations translate statistics into emotion."
- **[AI Research & Development | AIR-3]**: "We can blend data to simulate how alcohol, fatigue, and distraction interact; realistic multi-factor risk modeling that deepens understanding."

This theme repositions education from passive awareness to embodied learning, where technology fosters behavioral insight.

Research Question 4: How Can These Tools Assist Law Enforcement?

Theme 1: AI-Enhanced Detection and Real-Time Triage (60 votes)

Participants viewed AI as a tactical multiplier for enforcement efficiency. Intelligent analytics could integrate vehicle telematics, roadside cameras, and officer-worn sensors to generate prioritized alerts for high-probability impairment events.

- **[Law Enforcement | LE-3]**: "Fewer but higher-quality alerts mean safer roads and fewer arbitrary stops. The system should help us act, not distract."
- **[Auto Investigation | AIv-1]**: "Multi-signal fusion—combining braking irregularities with head-pose drift—creates a more reliable trigger for intervention."

- **[Law Enforcement | LE-4]**: "A confidence score attached to each alert lets us triage resources responsibly, balancing public safety and fairness."

This theme reflects a shift toward precision enforcement, minimizing both false positives and missed risks.

Theme 2: Digital Evidence Management and Chain-of-Custody (50 votes)

Ensuring evidentiary reliability was a major concern. Participants emphasized the need for verifiable, standardized, and tamper-proof digital records of AI-assisted stops or detections.

- **[Law Enforcement | LE-2]**: "A secure digital chain of custody is non-negotiable. Without verified provenance, evidence collapses in court."
- **[Auto Investigation | AIv-2]**: "Standardized data outputs across manufacturers accelerate investigations and reduce disputes."
- **[AI Safety & Security | AIS-4]**: "Cryptographic time-stamping and immutable logs guarantee authenticity across the data lifecycle."

This theme highlights the importance of technological credibility as a cornerstone of judicial fairness.

Theme 3: Predictive Checkpoint Placement and Patrol Optimization (48 votes)

AI-based spatiotemporal analytics can optimize checkpoint scheduling, reducing inefficiency while maintaining deterrence.

- **[Law Enforcement | LE-1]**: "Predictive deployment means fewer roadblocks but higher yield; targeted, not punitive."
- **[AI Research & Development | AIR-4]**: "Models can learn from historical crash densities, nightlife calendars, and ride-share surge patterns to predict the next high-risk window."
- **[Auto Investigation | AIv-3]**: "Algorithmic randomization retains unpredictability—the psychological core of deterrence; without wasting manpower."

This theme reflects a data-smart enforcement model that harmonizes safety, efficiency, and public trust.

Theme 4: Officer Co-Pilot and Automation Tools (42 votes)

Participants highlighted opportunities for AI to augment officer judgment through real-time decision aids and automated reporting systems.

- **[Law Enforcement | LE-4]**: "AI checklists during field sobriety tests improve consistency and reduce human error under stress."
- **[Law Enforcement | LE-1]**: "Automated narrative drafting tied to objective data points saves hours of paperwork and improves transparency."
- **[AI Safety & Security | AIS-2]**: "Standardized, data-anchored reports prevent disputes over probable cause and reinforce public confidence in enforcement fairness."

This theme portrays AI as an ally to professional discretion, enhancing both procedural accuracy and accountability.

SYNTHESIS

Across all domains, participants converged on a central insight: AI and assistive technologies can transform the fight against alcohol-impaired driving from a reactive enforcement approach to a proactive, ethically grounded prevention strategy. However, this transformation requires rigorous governance, striking a balance between innovation, transparency, privacy, and equity. The collective recommendations constitute an actionable roadmap for public agencies, automakers, and technology developers seeking to harness AI's potential while safeguarding the public trust.

Policy Implications, Practice Implications, and Conclusions

Below are clear, numbered, and practical recommendations distilled from the results you provided, followed by concise Policy Implications, Practice Implications, and Conclusions. The language is intentionally direct for ease of implementation, while remaining aligned with the study's evidence and themes.

Practical Recommendations

A. Preventing Impaired Driving (RQ1)
   1. **Install Passive In-Vehicle Impairment Detection ("AI seatbelts for cognition").** Automakers and Tier-1 suppliers should deploy in-cabin computer

vision, passive ethanol sensing (e.g., steering wheel/seatbelt), and driver-behavior analytics to warn, suggest a ride, and, when thresholds are met, gate ignition or enable a safe stop.

2. **Adopt Fleet-Level Safe-Stop Policies.** Commercial fleets (ride-share, delivery, logistics) should enable automated power-limiting or controlled pull-over when multi-signal impairment is detected, with a human-supervisor override protocol for edge cases.
3. **Use Predictive Risk Mapping for Targeted Deterrence.** Cities and agencies should combine event calendars, weather data, nightlife density, and prior crash/offense records to forecast high-risk windows and geographies, then allocate patrols, outreach, and designated-driver promotions accordingly.
4. **Deploy Context-Aware Mobile Nudges.** With explicit consent, smartphone assistants should surface one-tap safe-ride options, "call your DD" prompts, and parking restrictions when social drinking is inferred (time, location, receipts), before keys are in hand.
5. **Link Voluntary Wearables to Vehicles.** Offer opt-in pairing of wearables (BAC proxies, gait/speech anomalies) to transmit a temporary "not fit to drive" signal; especially useful for teen drivers or high-risk moments (post-games, campus events).

B. Governance, Ethics, and Accountability (RQ2)

6. **Make Privacy Non-Negotiable: Edge First, Minimal Data.** Process impairment inferences on-device; store only what is strictly needed for the safety function; disallow marketing/insurance reuse by default; provide clear, revocable consent.
7. **Mandate Equity Audits and Performance Parity.** Require pre-deployment bias testing and post-market surveillance; publish subgroup error rates (such as age, gender, skin tone, and disability) like crash-test ratings; retrain models when parity drifts.
8. **Standardize Digital Forensics and Contestability.** Adopt a common schema for events, thresholds, and overrides; cryptographically sign logs; deliver human-readable explanations; provide independent appeal pathways when vehicles intervene.

C. Education, Awareness, and Community Engagement (RQ3)

9. **Use Personalized Micro-Learning at the Moment of Choice.** Deliver 15–30 second prompts ("Two drinks in 60 minutes triples crash risk") tied to the current context (bill time, exit from venue, garage entry), with a single-tap ride option.
10. **Publish Community Risk Dashboards.** Share anonymized, neighborhood-level trends so schools, parent groups, bar owners, and MADD chapters can coordinate targeted outreach on peak-risk nights.

11. **Integrate Simulation/VR into Youth & Workplace Programs.** Use brief VR/AR modules to demonstrate reaction-time lag and lane drift at low BAC levels, pairing them with commitment cards and safe-ride codes.

D. Law Enforcement Support and Efficiency (RQ4)

12. **Prioritize High-Confidence, Multi-Signal Alerts.** Provide officers with a small number of high-quality alerts that include confidence scores and top contributing features; fuse road and weather data to reduce false positives.
13. **Harden Digital Evidence and Chain-of-Custody.** Hash records on-device; time-stamp events; standardize export formats across vendors to speed reconstruction and withstand courtroom scrutiny.
14. **Optimize Checkpoints and Patrols with Analytics.** Utilize spatiotemporal models to schedule fewer, better-placed checkpoints and allocate resources to predicted peaks, thereby maximizing deterrence while minimizing the burden on compliant drivers.
15. **Provide Officer Co-Pilot and Report Automation.** Offer guided field-sobriety checklists and auto-drafted narratives anchored to objective signals to improve consistency, save time, and strengthen procedural justice.

Policy Implications

1. Safety Standards: Treat impairment detection as a safety feature (analogous to airbags). Federal regulators can define performance baselines (false-positive/negative targets, explainability) and require edge processing and strict purpose limitation (no marketing/insurance reuse without explicit consent).
2. Parity & Transparency Requirements: Mandate equity reporting (subgroup performance tables) and post-market monitoring; require corrective action when parity thresholds are exceeded.
3. Forensics Interoperability: Establish a national schema for AI safety logs and chain-of-custody (including cryptographic signatures, timestamps, and human-readable summaries) to standardize evidence across vendors and jurisdictions.
4. Data Governance: Enact statutory consent, retention, and redress rules for consumer vs. court-mandated deployments; prohibit secondary use absent explicit, unbundled consent.
5. Public Dashboards: Encourage or fund anonymized community dashboards to align public health messaging, school outreach, and enforcement with real risk patterns.

Practice Implications

1. Automakers & Suppliers: Integrate multi-signal impairment modules; conduct parity audits pre-launch; ship with privacy-preserving defaults; document triggers and overrides in plain language.
2. Law Enforcement Agencies: Shift from saturation patrols to precision deterrence; train officers on confidence-scored alerts; adopt standardized digital evidence workflows; deploy co-pilot checklists and report automation.
3. Public Health & MADD Chapters: Use risk dashboards to time targeted campaigns; deploy micro-learning and VR modules in schools, campuses, and workplaces; partner with ride-share for just-in-time codes.
4. Schools, Bars, and Event Venues: Implement on-premise prompts (closing-time signage, Wi-Fi splash pages) integrated with safe-ride offers; encourage designated-driver programs enhanced by mobile nudges.
5. AI/Tech Teams: Build for edge inference, minimal data, explainability, and contestability; publish model cards with subgroup performance; design appeal pathways into the product, not as an afterthought.

CONCLUSIONS

AI and assistive or automotive technologies have the potential to fundamentally transform impaired-driving prevention, shifting it from reactive enforcement to proactive, ethically grounded safety management. Traditionally, society has addressed impaired driving after harm has occurred, through detection, arrest, and prosecution. This approach, while necessary, treats impairment as an individual failure rather than a systemic risk. By contrast, embedding intelligent sensing, behavioral modeling, and decision-support mechanisms directly into vehicles and transportation networks can move prevention upstream. This allows for early detection and intervention, reducing the likelihood of crashes and injuries before they happen. The shift mirrors a broader evolution in public health: from episodic crisis response to continuous risk management.

A cornerstone of this transformation lies in passive, in-vehicle detection systems equipped with safe-stop or lockout capabilities. Such systems employ unobtrusive sensors, computer vision, and machine learning algorithms to recognize signs of impairment, whether from alcohol, drugs, fatigue, or cognitive decline, without requiring driver participation. By detecting impairment in real time and either preventing vehicle operation or enabling a controlled safe-stop, these systems act as a structural safeguard. They represent a profound step toward reducing systemic risk, much like how automatic braking or lane-keeping assist technologies have redefined baseline safety expectations. In public health terms, they function as early-detection mechanisms; in public safety terms, they constitute a fail-safe for human vulnerability.

Complementing these capabilities, predictive risk mapping can enhance both prevention and enforcement. By analyzing aggregated telematics, mobility data, and contextual information, AI systems can identify spatial and temporal patterns of elevated risk, such as weekends near entertainment districts or rural regions lacking alternative transportation. This information enables targeted outreach, precision resource allocation, and data-informed patrol strategies. When executed within strict ethical and privacy parameters, predictive analytics can optimize safety outcomes while minimizing unnecessary or inequitable enforcement encounters. It transforms policing from generalized deterrence to evidence-based prevention.

In parallel, context-aware nudging technologies can make safe behavior the path of least resistance. By leveraging behavioral science and AI-driven personalization, these systems can anticipate risky contexts and offer real-time interventions, such as suggesting discounted rideshare options, delaying ignition when fatigue is detected, or providing subtle cues at decision points. This human-centered approach aligns incentives, making the safe choice effortless and socially normalized. It reframes safety not as a matter of coercion or compliance, but as a cooperative process between human judgment and machine intelligence. Such systems, when ethically designed, enhance individual autonomy while supporting collective well-being.

Equally vital are standardized, privacy-preserving forensic protocols that maintain legitimacy in both courts and communities. As vehicles and sensors increasingly generate data relevant to legal or insurance proceedings, society must ensure that this information is collected, encrypted, and shared in ways that respect due process and individual rights. Privacy-preserving forensics limit access to verified indicators of impairment, preventing misuse while enabling credible adjudication. By embedding transparency, auditability, and proportionality into these systems, technology can reinforce rather than erode public trust. The legitimacy of safety interventions depends as much on how data are governed as on how effectively risks are reduced.

Underpinning this entire framework are three interdependent principles: privacy by design, equity by measurement, and interoperability by standard. Privacy by design ensures that systems collect only what is necessary and employ encryption and anonymization throughout their data life cycle. Equity by measurement recognizes that fairness cannot be assumed—it must be empirically verified through ongoing monitoring for disparate impact across race, gender, and socioeconomic status. Interoperability by standard guarantees that innovations across manufacturers, agencies, and jurisdictions can integrate seamlessly, avoiding fragmentation and promoting transparency. Together, these principles form the ethical and technical scaffolding for a trustworthy ecosystem of preventive safety.

The public health, safety, and technology management implications of this approach are profound. From a public health perspective, impaired driving remains a leading preventable cause of death and disability; proactive detection and intervention can save lives by addressing the root causes before tragedy occurs. From a public safety perspective, predictive and assistive systems enable finite enforcement resources to be directed where they are most needed, reducing both crashes and inequities in enforcement. From a technology management standpoint, these innovations demand robust governance frameworks, ones that ensure transparency, interoperability, lifecycle accountability, and alignment with democratic norms.

When implemented together, these measures offer a credible and ethically coherent path to fewer crashes, fairer enforcement, and a durable increase in public trust. They represent not only a technological leap but also a moral one: an affirmation that the purpose of automation is not control, but care. Through AI-driven foresight and privacy-conscious design, impaired-driving prevention can evolve from punishment after harm to protection before it. In doing so, it advances a vision of public safety that is intelligent, just, and deeply human.

REFERENCES

Ahlin, E. M., Zador, P. L., Rauch, W. J., Howard, J. M., & Duncan, G. D. (2011). First-time DWI offenders are at risk of recidivating regardless of sanctions imposed. *Journal of Criminal Justice, 39*(2), 137–142. DOI: 10.1016/j.jcrimjus.2011.01.001 PMID: 21603059

Babor, T., Caetano, R., Casswell, S., Edwards, G., Giesbrecht, N., Graham, K., & Homel, R. (2010). Alcohol: no ordinary commodity: research and public policy. *Revista Brasileira de Psiquiatria : Orgão Oficial da Associação Brasileira de Psiquiatria, Asociación Psiqui´trica de la América Latina, 26*(4), 280–283.

Babor, T. F., Robaina, K., & Jernigan, D. (2015). The influence of industry actions on the availability of alcoholic beverages in the African region. *Addiction (Abingdon, England), 110*(4), 561–571. DOI: 10.1111/add.12832 PMID: 25510339

Blincoe, L. J., Miller, T. R., Zaloshnja, E., & Lawrence, B. A. (2015). *The economic and societal impact of motor vehicle crashes, 2010 (revised)* (Report No. DOT HS 812 013). National Highway Traffic Safety Administration.

Breslow, R. A., Castle, I. J. P., Chen, C. M., & Graubard, B. I. (2017). Trends in alcohol consumption among older Americans: National Health Interview Surveys, 1997 to 2014. *Alcohol, Clinical and Experimental Research, 41*(5), 976–986. DOI: 10.1111/acer.13365 PMID: 28340502

Elzinga, K. G., Tremblay, C. H., & Tremblay, V. J. (2015). Craft beer in the United States: History, numbers, and geography. *Journal of Wine Economics, 10*(3), 242–274. DOI: 10.1017/jwe.2015.22

Fell, J. C. (2016). The merits of adopting a 0.05 administrative blood alcohol concentration limit for driving. *American Journal of Public Health, 106*(6), 977–978. DOI: 10.2105/AJPH.2016.303187 PMID: 27153014

Forward, J., Akhurst, J., Bruno, R., Leong, X., VanderNiet, A., Bromfield, H., Erny, J., Bellamy, T., & Peacock, A. (2017). Nature versus intensity of intoxication: Co-ingestion of alcohol and energy drinks and the effect on objective and subjective intoxication. *Drug and Alcohol Dependence, 180*, 292–303. DOI: 10.1016/j.drugalcdep.2017.08.013 PMID: 28942033

Grant, B. F., Chou, S. P., Saha, T. D., Pickering, R. P., Kerridge, B. T., Ruan, W. J., Huang, B., Jung, J., Zhang, H., Fan, A., & Hasin, D. S. (2017). Prevalence of 12-month alcohol use, high-risk drinking, and DSM-IV alcohol use disorder in the United States, 2001-2002 to 2012-2013: Results from the National Epidemiologic Survey on Alcohol and Related Conditions. *JAMA Psychiatry, 74*(9), 911–923. DOI: 10.1001/jamapsychiatry.2017.2161 PMID: 28793133

Iyer, N. G., Arulmozhi, M., Sivakumar, P., Sudharsan, S., & Kavitha, R. (2023, December). AI-Powered Driver Behavior Prediction, Drunk Driving Prevention, Accident Detection, and Insurance Integration. In *the 2023 International Conference on Energy, Materials and Communication Engineering (ICEMCE)* (pp. 1-5). IEEE.

Jacobus, J., & Tapert, S. F. (2013). Neurotoxic effects of alcohol in adolescence. *Annual Review of Clinical Psychology, 9*(1), 703–721. DOI: 10.1146/annurev-clinpsy-050212-185610 PMID: 23245341

Kaufman, E. J., & Wiebe, D. J. (2016). Impact of state ignition interlock laws on alcohol-involved crash deaths in the United States. *American Journal of Public Health, 106*(5), 865–871. DOI: 10.2105/AJPH.2016.303058 PMID: 26985604

Kerr, W. C., & Greenfield, T. K. (2015). Racial/ethnic disparities in the self-reported number of drinks in 2 hours before driving becomes impaired. *American Journal of Public Health, 105*(7), 1409–1414. DOI: 10.2105/AJPH.2014.302276 PMID: 25602892

Kerr, W. C., Patterson, D., Greenfield, T. K., Jones, A. S., McGeary, K. A., Terza, J. V., & Ruhm, C. J. (2013). U.S. alcohol affordability and real tax rates, 1950–2011. *American Journal of Preventive Medicine, 44*(5), 459–464. DOI: 10.1016/j.amepre.2013.01.007 PMID: 23597808

Lalanne, L., Lutz, P. E., & Paille, F. (2017). Acute impact of caffeinated alcoholic beverages on cognition: A systematic review. *Progress in Neuro-Psychopharmacology & Biological Psychiatry, 76*, 188–194. DOI: 10.1016/j.pnpbp.2017.03.007 PMID: 28330787

Laude, J. R., & Fillmore, M. T. (2016). Drivers who self-estimate lower blood alcohol concentrations are riskier drivers after drinking. *Psychopharmacology, 233*(8), 1387–1394. DOI: 10.1007/s00213-016-4233-x PMID: 26861796

Li, A., & Sun, Y. (2024, July). A Data-Driven Driving Under the Influence (DUI) Detection, Notification and Prevention System Using Artificial Intelligence and Internet-Of-Things (IoT). In *World Congress in Computer Science, Computer Engineering & Applied Computing* (pp. 73-87). Cham: Springer Nature Switzerland.

McGinty, E. E., Tung, G., Shulman-Laniel, J., Hardy, R., Rutkow, L., Frattaroli, S., & Vernick, J. S. (2017). Ignition interlock laws: Effects on fatal motor vehicle crashes, 1982–2013. *American Journal of Preventive Medicine, 52*(4), 417–423. DOI: 10.1016/j.amepre.2016.10.043 PMID: 28065516

McKnight, A. J., & Voas, R. B. (1991). The effect of license suspension upon DWI recidivism. *Alcohol, Drugs, and Driving, 7*, 43–54.

McLester, Q. (2024). Impaired Driving as a Public Health Concern and Healthcare Technology Approaches. In Burrell, D. (Ed.), *Innovations, Securities, and Case Studies Across Healthcare, Business, and Technology* (pp. 377–395). IGI Global Scientific Publishing., DOI: 10.4018/979-8-3693-1906-2.ch020

McLester, Q., & Burrell, D. N. (2024). Healthcare Technologies to Address Driving Under the Influence (DUI) of Marijuana. In E. Lewis (Ed.), *Evolution of Cross-Sector Cyber Intelligent Markets* (pp. 158-168). IGI Global Scientific Publishing. DOI: 10.4018/979-8-3693-1970-3.ch008

National Highway Traffic Safety Administration. (2017). Designated Driver Safe Ride Program. Designated Driver/ www.nhtsa.dot.gov/people/injury/alcohol/

Patrick, M. E., Schulenberg, J. E., Martz, M. E., Maggs, J. L., O'Malley, P. M., & Johnston, L. D. (2013). Extreme binge drinking among 12th-grade students in the United States: Prevalence and predictors. *JAMA Pediatrics, 167*(11), 1019–1025. DOI: 10.1001/jamapediatrics.2013.2392 PMID: 24042318

Preethi, K. (2023). An intelligent online drunk driving detection system based on multi-sensor fusion technology. *International Journal of Management Research and Reviews, 13*(2), 7–11.

Rehm, J., Lachenmeier, D. W., Llopis, E. J., Imtiaz, S., & Anderson, P. (2016). Evidence of reducing ethanol content in beverages to reduce harmful use of alcohol. *The Lancet. Gastroenterology & Hepatology, 1*(1), 78–83. DOI: 10.1016/S2468-1253(16)30013-9 PMID: 28404116

Rhoades, E., & Jernigan, D. H. (2013). Risky messages in alcohol advertising, 2003–2007: Results from content analysis. *The Journal of Adolescent Health, 52*(1), 116–121. DOI: 10.1016/j.jadohealth.2012.04.013 PMID: 23260844

Schulenberg, J. E., Johnston, L. D., O'Malley, P. M., Bachman, J. G., Miech, R. A., & Patrick, M. E. (2017). *Monitoring the future: National survey results on drug use, 1975–2016 (Vol. 2, College students and adults ages 19–55).* Institute for Social Research, University of Michigan.

Voas, R. B., Torres, P., Romano, E., & Lacey, J. H. (2012). Alcohol-related risk of driver fatalities: An update using 2007 data. *Journal of Studies on Alcohol and Drugs*, *73*(3), 341–350. DOI: 10.15288/jsad.2012.73.341 PMID: 22456239

Yang, G., Ridgeway, C., Miller, A., & Sarkar, A. (2024). Comprehensive Assessment of Artificial Intelligence Tools for Driver Monitoring and Analyzing Safety Critical Events in Vehicles. *Sensors (Basel)*, *24*(8), 2478. DOI: 10.3390/s24082478 PMID: 38676095

Compilation of References

. A, T. B. (2019). Effectiveness of Construction Safety Hazards Identification in Virtual Reality Learning Environment. *Environment-Behaviour Proceedings Journal, 4*(12). DOI: 10.21834/e-bpj.v4i12.1901

. Demichela M., Baldissone G., & Luzzi, R. (2013). Advances tools for occupational accidents data analysis for prevention purposes. *CRC Press EBooks*, 1595–1600. DOI: 10.1201/b15938-239

. Eze, E., Sofolahan, O., & Siunoje, L. (2020). Health and Safety Management on Construction Projects: The View of Construction Tradespeople. *CSID Journal of Infrastructure Development, 3*(2), 152. researchgate. DOI: 10.32783/csid-jid.v3i2.165

. Holtzhausen, D., Fullerton, J. A., Lewis, B. K., & Shipka, D. (2021). Principles of Strategic Communication. DOI: 10.4324/9781003002048

. Purushothaman, M. B., Rotimi, F. E., Samarasekara, S., & GhaffarianHoseini, A. (2025). SMART technologies that influence construction health and safety factors risk reduction in the current digital era. Smart and Sustainable Built Environment. DOI: 10.1108/SASBE-09-2024-0400

. Rivas, Y. C. (2020). Virtual reality and 21st-century education. *International Research Journal of Management, IT and Social Sciences*. DOI: 10.21744/irjmis.v7n1.820

. Shaikh, A. Y., Osei-Kyei, R., & Hardie, M. (2020). A critical analysis of safety performance indicators in construction. *International Journal of Building Pathology and Adaptation, ahead-of-print*(ahead-of-print). DOI: 10.1108/IJBPA-03-2020-0018

. Shankar, A. U., Tewari, V., Rahman, M., Mishra, A., & Bajaj, K. K. (2023). Impact of Virtual Reality (Vr) and Augmented Reality (Ar) in Education. Tuijin Jishu/Journal of Propulsion Technology, 44(4), 1310–1318. DOI: 10.52783/tjjpt.v44.i4.1014

. Trist, E. L., & Bamforth, K. W. (1951). Some social and psychological consequences of the Longwall Method of coal-getting: An examination of the psychological situation and defences of a work group in relation to the social structure and technological content of the work system. *Human Relations, 4*(1), 3-38. (Original work published 1951)DOI: 10.1177/001872675100400101

. Verma, D. S. (2023). OPPORTUNITIES AND CHALLENGES OF USING VR IN EDUCATIONAL SECTOR FOR ENHANCING BETTER LEARNING EXPERIENCE.*Academia.edu*. https://doi.org/DOI: 10.48047/NQ.2022.20.20.NQ109112

Abdelghani, T. (2019). Implementation of defense in depth strategy to secure industrial control system in critical infrastructures. *American Journal of Artificial Intelligence*, *3*(2), 17. DOI: 10.11648/j.ajai.20190302.11

Abed, L. G., Abed, M. G., & Shackelford, T. K. (2023). Interpersonal communication style and personal and professional growth among saudi arabian employees. *International Journal of Environmental Research and Public Health*, *20*(2), 910. DOI: 10.3390/ijerph20020910

Abeyratne, R. (2020). *Aviation in the digital age: Legal and regulatory aspects*. Springer., DOI: 10.1007/978-3-030-48218-3

Acebes, F., González-Varona, J. M., López-Paredes, A., & Pajares, J. (2024). Beyond probability-impact matrices in project risk management: A quantitative methodology for risk prioritisation. *Humanities & Social Sciences Communications*, *11*(1), 1–13. DOI: 10.1057/s41599-024-03180-5

Addison, A., & Dawood, N. (2025). *THE IMPORTANCE OF ENGAGING ENGINEERING AND CONSTRUCTION LEARNERS IN VIRTUAL WORLDS AND SERIOUS GAMES*. Academia.edu. https://www.academia.edu/7044694/THE_IMPORTANCE_OF_ENGAGING_ENGINEERING_AND_CONSTRUCTION_LEARNERS_IN_VIRTUAL_WORLDS_AND_SERIOUS_GAMES

Adisuria, K. F., & Jayadi, R. (2023). Analysis Of The Implementation GRC Information System in Supporting Performance Optimization. [JOISM]. *Journal of Information System Management*, *4*(2), 97–106. DOI: 10.24076/joism.2023v4i2.975

Adler, S. (2025, June). Aflac Latest Insurer to Suffer Cyberattack and Data Breach. The HIPAA Journal. https://www.hipaajournal.com/aflac-data-breach/

Adler-Milstein, J., & Jha, A. K. (2017). HITECH Act Drove Large Gains In Hospital Electronic Health Record Adoption. *Health Affairs*, *36*(8), 1416–1422. https://www.healthaffairs.org/doi/abs/10.1377/hlthaff.2016.1651. DOI: 10.1377/hlthaff.2016.1651 PMID: 28784734

Administration for Strategic Preparedness and Response. (2023). *Healthcare sector cybersecurity framework implementation guide*. U.S. Department of Health and Human Services. https://aspr.hhs.gov/cip/hph-cybersecurity-framework-implementation-guide/Documents/HPH-Sector-CSF-Implementation-Guide-508.pdf

Agbolosu-Amison, S., & Mondoloni, S. (2012). Modeling system-wide predictability and associated air carrier benefits. *Proceedings of the 11th AIAA Aviation Technology, Integration, and Operations (ATIO) Conference*, AIAA. DOI: 10.2514/6.2011-6810

Agner, J. (2021). Tabletop exercises. In *a guide to healthcare facility dress rehearsal simulation planning: simplifying the complex* (pp. 55-62). Emerald Publishing Limited. DOI: 10.1108/978-1-80117-554-820211006

Ahern, D. (2025). The new anticipatory governance culture for innovation: Regulatory foresight, regulatory experimentation and regulatory learning. *European Business Organization Law Review*, *26*(2), 241–283. Advance online publication. DOI: 10.1007/s40804-025-00348-7

Ahlin, E. M., Zador, P. L., Rauch, W. J., Howard, J. M., & Duncan, G. D. (2011). First-time DWI offenders are at risk of recidivating regardless of sanctions imposed. *Journal of Criminal Justice*, *39*(2), 137–142. DOI: 10.1016/j.jcrimjus.2011.01.001 PMID: 21603059

Akbaş, E. (2023). *The importance of real-time detection and correlation in SIEM/UEBA solutions and criticality for SOAR*. Unpublished. DOI: 10.13140/RG.2.2.12607.69285

Akinlolu, M. T., & Haupt, T. (2019). *Emerging Technologies in Construction Safety and Health Management*. International Conference on Innovation, Technology, Enterprise and Entrepreneurship. https://www.academia.edu/44018807/Emerging_Technologies_in_Construction_Safety_and_Health_Management

Akpa, V. O., Asikhia, O. U., & Nneji, N. E. (2021). Organizational culture and organizational performance: A review of literature. *International Journal of Advances in Engineering and Management*, *3*(1), 361–372. https://www.researchgate.net/profile/Professor-Asikhia/publication/356105838_Organizational_Culture_and_Organizational_Performance_A_Review_of_Literature/links/618bed3907be5f31b762d272/Organizational-Culture-and-Organizational-Performance-A-Review-of-Literature.pdf

Alahmari, S., Renaud, K., & Omoronyia, I. (2023). Moving beyond cyber security awareness and training to engendering security knowledge sharing. *Information Systems and e-Business Management*, *21*(1), 123–158. DOI: 10.1007/s10257-022-00575-2

AlAli, M. S. (2020). Risk velocity and financial markets performance: measuring the early effect of COVID-19 pandemic on major stock markets performance. *International Journal of Economics and Financial Research, 10.*

Albanese, J. (2007). A criminal network approach to understanding & measuring trafficking in human beings. In Savona, E., & Stefanizzi, S. (Eds.), *Measuring human trafficking: Complexities and pitfalls* (pp. 55–71). Springer., DOI: 10.1007/0-387-68044-6_7

Alberts, C. J., Behrens, S. G., Pethia, R. D., & Wilson, W. R. (1999). Operationally critical threat, asset, and vulnerability evaluation (OCTAVE) framework, version 1.0. DOI: 10.21236/ADA367718

Aldemir, T. (2024). Dynamic probabilistic risk assessment (PRA): Theory, tools, and applications for uncertainty quantification. In *Risk-Informed Methods and Applications in Nuclear and Energy Engineering* (pp. 43-54). Academic Press.

Alder, S. (2025). *HIPAA training requirements - updated for 2025. HIPPA Training Requirements.* https://www.hipaajournal.com/hipaa-training-requirements/

Alexander, S. G. (2022). *What is the internet of things (IoT)?* Retrieved from https://www.techtarget.com/iotagenda/definition/Internet-of-Things-IoT

Alhalabi, D., Alawida, M., & Hasan, R. (2025). How secure is CPDLC? A comprehensive review of cyber threats and defense mechanisms in aviation communication. *Journal of Transportation Security*, *18*(1), 23. Advance online publication. DOI: 10.1007/s12198-025-00312-z

Alix, L. (2024). Regulators intensify the pressure on banks: Bank director's 2024 risk survey finds heightened concern among bank leaders around regulation, liquidity management and cybersecurity threats. *Bank Director, 34*(2), 42-46. https://www.bankdirector.com/magazine/2nd-quarter-2024/regulators-intensify-the-pressure-on-banks/

Almansoori, A., AlShamsi, M., Salloum, S. A., & Shaalan, K. (2020). Critical Review of Knowledge Management in Healthcare. *Studies in Systems, Decision and Control*, 99–119. DOI: 10.1007/978-3-030-47411-9_6

Alshammari, B., & Mahinderjit Singh, M. (2025). A systematic literature review on tackling cyber threats for cyber logistic chain and conceptual frameworks for robust detection mechanisms. *IEEE Access : Practical Innovations, Open Solutions, 13,* 67661–67692. DOI: 10.1109/ACCESS.2025.3552689

Alsowaigh, R. E. (2025). CrowdStrike Causes Global Microsoft Outage: A Case Study. *Journal of Information Security and Cybercrimes Research*, *8*(1), 63–76. DOI: 10.26735/QHDD4798

Amazon Web Services. (2025). *Predictive analytics and machine learning in cybersecurity: Enhancing reliability and security.* AWS White Paper. https://aws.amazon.com/whitepapers

American Hospital Association. (2024). *A look at 2024's health care cybersecurity challenges.* https://www.aha.org/news/aha-cyber-intel/2024-10-07-look-2024s-health-care-cybersecurity-challenges

American Hospital Association. (2024). *AHA survey: Change Healthcare cyberattack significantly disrupts patient care, hospitals' finances.* https://www.aha.org/2024-03-15-aha-survey-change-healthcare-cyberattack-significantly-disrupts-patient-care-hospitals-finances

American Hospital Association. (2024). *Change Healthcare Cyberattack: Network Connectivity Issues, Indicators of Compromise.* https://www.connectwise.com/company/trust/security-bulletins/connectwise-screenconnect-23.9.8

Anderson, E. J. (2024). *Business risk management: models and analysis.* John Wiley & Sons.

Anireddy, A. R. (2024). Construction Safety Management: Analyzing the Effectiveness of Safety Training Programs on Job Sites. *INTERANTIONAL JOURNAL of SCIENTIFIC RESEARCH in ENGINEERING and MANAGEMENT*, *08*(11), 1–7. DOI: 10.55041/IJSREM16079

Ansari, M. F., Sharma, P. K., & Dash, B. (2022). Prevention of phishing attacks using AI-based Cybersecurity Awareness Training. *Prevention*, *3*(6), 61–72. DOI: 10.47893/IJSSAN.2022.1221

Arctic Wolf. (2024). Breaking down ransomware-as-a-service. https://arcticwolf.com/resources/blog/breaking-down-ransomware-as-a-service

AuditBoard. (2024). SEC cybersecurity rules update: The complete guide. https://auditboard.com/blog/sec-cybersecurity-rules

Avhad, A. (2007). Certified Organization) Website: www. *International Journal of Innovative Research in Science, Engineering and Technology (an ISO, 3297*. https://doi.org/DOI: 10.15680/IJIRSET.2017.0606276

Awasthi, A. (2025). GRC automation in manufacturing modernizing compliance and risk management. *International Journal of Computer Engineering and Technology, 16*(1), 10–34218.

Babor, T. F., Robaina, K., & Jernigan, D. (2015). The influence of industry actions on the availability of alcoholic beverages in the African region. *Addiction (Abingdon, England), 110*(4), 561–571. DOI: 10.1111/add.12832 PMID: 25510339

Babor, T., Caetano, R., Casswell, S., Edwards, G., Giesbrecht, N., Graham, K., & Homel, R. (2010). Alcohol: no ordinary commodity: research and public policy. *Revista Brasileira de Psiquiatria : Orgão Oficial da Associação Brasileira de Psiquiatria, Asociación Psiqui´trica de la América Latina, 26*(4), 280–283.

Bailey, T., Barriball, E., Dey, A., & Sankur, A. (2019). *A practical approach to supply-chain risk management.* Digital McKinsey and Global Risk Practice. McKinsey & Company

Baldwin, S. B., Eisenman, D. P., Sayles, J. N., Ryan, G., & Chuang, K. S. (2011). Identification of human trafficking victims in health care settings. *Health and Human Rights, 13*, 36–49. https://heinonline-org.ezp.slu.edu/HOL/Page?collection=journals&handle=hein.journals/harhrj13&id=40&men_tab=srchresults PMID: 22772961

Balkin, J. M. (1998). *Cultural Software : A Theory of Ideology.* Yale University Press. Print

Baloglu, G., & Cakali, K. R. (2022). Missing Aspects of the Risk: Speed and Duration. *Journal of Economics Finance and Accounting, 9*(1), 12–21. DOI: 10.17261/Pressacademia.2022.1541

Bandura, A. (2002). Selective moral disengagement in the exercise of moral agency. *Journal of Moral Education, 21*(2), 101–120. DOI: 10.1080/0305724022014322

Bandura, A. (2016). Moral disengagement: How people do harm and live with themselves. *Business Ethics Quarterly, 26*(3), 426–429. DOI: 10.1017/beq.2016.37

Barlow, L., Bendiab, G., Shiaeles, S., & Savage, N. (2020). A novel approach to detect phishing attacks using binary visualisation and machine learning. *2020 IEEE World Congress on Services (SERVICES).* https://ieeexplore.ieee.org/abstract/document/9284172?casa_token=9pQ68r3RPtwAAAAA:hvpoXRjjooVcrnMGfP2qhVZdENYDNDJlY47BijC3tDRCkWuGK0W9Zu9j9bYwFDl-cFQHlRnkFns

Barney, D. (2018). Trafficking technology: A look at different approaches to ending technology-facilitated human trafficking. *Pepperdine Law Review, 45*(4), 747–784. https://heinonline.org/HOL/LandingPage?handle=hein.journals/pepplr45&div=25&id=&page=

Basu, S., Liu, F., & Wang, C. (2019). Hardware supply chain security risks in healthcare systems. *Journal of Cybersecurity*, *5*(3), 1–14. DOI: 10.1093/cybsec/tyz012

Battilana, J., & Casciaro, T. (2021). *Power, for all: How it really works and why it's everyone's business*. Simon & Schuster.

Baugh, B. S., & Stolzer, A. J. (2018). Language-related communications challenges in general aviation operations and pilot training. *International Journal of Aviation, Aeronautics, and Aerospace*, *5*(4). Advance online publication. DOI: 10.15394/ijaaa.2018.1271

Baxter, G., & Sommerville, I. (2011). Socio-technical systems: From design methods to systems engineering. *Interacting with Computers*, *23*(1), 4–17. DOI: 10.1016/j.intcom.2010.07.003

Belea, A. R. (2023, May). Methods for detecting malware using static, dynamic and hybrid analysis. *In Proceedings of the International Conference on Cybersecurity and Cybercrime-2023*, (pp. 258-*265). Asociatia Romana pentru Asigurarea Securitatii Informatiei.*

Ben, S., & Barak, H. (2021). *Security flaws affect hospital pneumatic tube systems*. Retrieved from https://www.armis.com/research/pwnedpiper

Benson, A., & Arksey, H. (2021). Qualitative research using secondary data: A systematic review. *BMC Medical Research Methodology*, *21*(1), 29. PMID: 33568059

Berenson, C. (2023). Identifying a tradition of inquiry: Articulating research assumptions. In *SoTL in Action* (pp. 42–52). Routledge. DOI: 10.4324/9781003447047-7

Bernardez Molina, S., Nespoli, P., & Gómez Mármol, F. (2023). *Tackling cyberattacks through AI-based reactive systems: A holistic review and future vision*. https://arxiv.org/abs/2312.06229

Bertero, C. (2016). Guidelines for writing a commentary. *International Journal of Qualitative Studies on Health and Well-being*, *11*(1), 31390. Advance online publication. DOI: 10.3402/qhw.v11.31390 PMID: 26976608

Bhandari, P. (2024, October 1). Ethical considerations in research: Types & examples. Scribbr. https://www.scribbr.com/methodology/research-ethics/

Bies, R., Tripp, T., & Kramer, R. (1997). At the breaking point: Cognitive and social dynamics of revenge in organizations. In Giacalone, R. A., & Greenberg, J. (Eds.), *Antisocial behavior in organizations* (pp. 18–36). Sage., https://psycnet.apa.org/record/1997-97285-002

Blincoe, L. J., Miller, T. R., Zaloshnja, E., & Lawrence, B. A. (2015). *The economic and societal impact of motor vehicle crashes, 2010 (revised)* (Report No. DOT HS 812 013). National Highway Traffic Safety Administration.

Bloomberg Law. (2024). *Which states have consumer data privacy laws?* https://pro.bloomberglaw.com/insights/privacy/state-privacy-legislation-tracker/#:~:text=Currently%2C%20there%20are%2015%20states,data%20privacy%20laws%20in%20place

Board of Governors of the Federal Reserve System. (2022). *Implications of cyber risk for financial stability*. Federal Reserve Board. Retrieved October 26, 2025, from https://www.federalreserve.gov/econres/notes/feds-notes/implications-of-cyber-risk-for-financial-stability-20220512.html

Board of the International Organization of Securities Commissions. (2016). *Committee on Payments and Market Infrastructures*. Bank for International Settlements. https://www.bis.org/cpmi/publ/d146.pdf?utm_source=chatgpt.com

Boehm, J., Curcio, N., Merrath, P., Shenton, L., & Stähle, T. (2020). *The risk-based approach to cybersecurity*. Digital McKinsey and Global Risk Practice. McKinsey & Company.

Bostrom, R. P., & Heinen, J. S. (1977). MIS problems and failures: A socio-technical perspective, Part I: The causes. *Management Information Systems Quarterly*, *1*(3), 17–32. DOI: 10.2307/248710

Boyce, E. (2024). *Interoperability: Seamless data exchange for government transformation.* Retrieved from https://publicsectornetwork.com/insight/discover-the-knowledge-that-drives-innovation

Boyd, D., & Crawford, K. (2012). Critical questions for Big Data: Provocations for a cultural, technological, and scholarly phenomenon. *Information Communication and Society*, *15*(5), 662–679. DOI: 10.1080/1369118X.2012.678878

Braathe, R. (2021, January 23). *The Schein model of organization culture: Three levels of a robust organization culture*. Robert Braathe's HR & Albany Jobs Blog. https://www.albany.com/hr/2021/01/the-schein-model-of-organization-culture-three-levels-of-a-robust-organization-culture/

Bracken, B. (2023). *11M HCA Healthcare patients impacted by data breach. Dark Reading.* https://www.darkreading.com/cyberattacks-data-breaches/11m-hca-healthcare-patients-impacted-data-breach

Breslow, R. A., Castle, I. J. P., Chen, C. M., & Graubard, B. I. (2017). Trends in alcohol consumption among older Americans: National Health Interview Surveys, 1997 to 2014. *Alcohol, Clinical and Experimental Research*, *41*(5), 976–986. DOI: 10.1111/acer.13365 PMID: 28340502

Brooker, P. (2008). SESAR and NextGen: Investing in new paradigms. *Journal of Navigation*, *61*(2), 195–208. DOI: 10.1017/S0373463307004596

Brown-Jackson, K. L., Burton, S. L., & Burrell, D. N. (2024). Cybersecurity's Shaping of Wearable Healthcare Devices and Digital Marketing: What Leaders Need to Know. In Saeed, S., Azizi, N., Tahir, S., Ahmad, M., & Almuhaideb, A. (Eds.), *Strengthening Industrial Cybersecurity to Protect Business Intelligence* (pp. 294–319). IGI Global Scientific Publishing., DOI: 10.4018/979-8-3693-0839-4.ch013

Bryans, D. (2014). Bitcoin and money laundering: Mining for an effective solution. *Industrial Law Journal*, *89*(1), 441–472. https://heinonline-org.ezp.slu.edu/HOL/Page?handle=hein.journals/indana89&div=16

Burgoon, J. K., Berger, C. R., & Waldron, V. R. (2000). Mindfulness and Interpersonal Communication. *The Journal of Social Issues*, *56*(1), 105–127. DOI: 10.1111/0022-4537.00154

Burrell, D. N. (2023). Cybersecurity in healthcare through the 7-S model strategy. *Scientific Bulletin-Nicolae Balcescu Land Forces Academy, 28*(1), 26-35. https://reference-global.com/download/article/10.2478/bsaft-2023-0003.pdf

Burrell, D. N. (2024). Understanding Cognitive and Behavioral Psychological Factors that Lead to Cybersecurity Breaches in Healthcare. *RAIS Journal for Social Sciences, 8*(2), 43-53. https://ideas.repec.org/a/smo/jornl1/v8y2024i2p43-53.html

Burrell, D. N. (2018). An Exploration of the Critical Need for Formal Training in Leadership for Cybersecurity and Technology Management Professionals. *International Journal of Hyperconnectivity and the Internet of Things*, *2*(1), 52–67. DOI: 10.4018/IJHIoT.2018010105

Burrell, D. N. (2023). *Transformational interventions for business, technology, and healthcare*. IGI Global. DOI: 10.4018/979-8-3693-1634-4

Burrell, D. N., Burton, S. L., Nobles, C., Springs, D., Huff, A. J., Brown-Jackson, K. L., Richardson, K., Wright, J. B., Muller, S. R., & Jones, A. J. (2023). The Managerial Ethical and Operational Challenges of Hospital Cybersecurity. In Burrell, D. (Ed.), *Transformational Interventions for Business, Technology, and Healthcare* (pp. 444–458). IGI Global Scientific Publishing., DOI: 10.4018/979-8-3693-1634-4.ch026

Burrell, D. N., Nobles, C., Cusak, A., Jones, L. A., Wright, J. B., Mingo, H. C., Ferreras-Perez, J., Khanta, K., Shen, P., & Richardson, K. (2023). Cybersecurity and Cyberbiosecurity Insider Threat Risk Management. In Adedoyin, F., & Christiansen, B. (Eds.), *Handbook of Research on Cybersecurity Risk in Contemporary Business Systems* (pp. 121–136). IGI Global Scientific Publishing., DOI: 10.4018/978-1-6684-7207-1.ch006

Burrell, D. N., Sabie-Aridi, A. S., Shufutinsky, A., Wright, J. B., Nobles, C., & Dawson, M. (2022). Exploring Holistic Managerial Thinking to Better Manage Healthcare Cybersecurity. [IJHSTM]. *International Journal of Health Systems and Translational Medicine*, *2*(1), 1–13. DOI: 10.4018/IJHSTM.300337

Burton, S. L. (2024). Securing tomorrow: Synergizing change management and cybersecurity in the digital era. *Holistica, 15*(1), 1. https://reference-global.com/download/article/10.2478/hjbpa-2024-0001.pdf

Burton, S. L., Burrell, D. N., Nobles, C., & Jones, L. A. (2023). Exploring the nexus of cybersecurity leadership, human factors, emotional intelligence, innovative work behavior, and critical leadership traits. *Scientific Bulletin-Nicolae Balcescu Land Forces Academy, 28*(2), 162-175. https://reference-global.com/download/article/10.2478/bsaft-2023-0016.pdf

Burton, S. L. (2021). Cybersecurity leaders: Knowledge driving human capital development. *Science Bulletin, 26*(2), 109–120. https://reference-global.com/download/article/10.2478/bsaft-2021-0013.pdf

Burton, S. L. (2024). Advancements in AI-Driven Education: Transforming Learning and Training with Intelligent Technologies. *World Journal of Business Research, 4*(1), 9.

Burton, S. L., Burrell, D. N., Nobles, C., & Jones, L. A. (2023). Exploring the nexus of cybersecurity leadership, human factors, emotional intelligence, innovative work behavior, and critical leadership traits. *Scientific Bulletin-Nicolae Balcescu Land Forces Academy*, *28*(2), 162–175. DOI: 10.2478/bsaft-2023-0016

Bylund, P. L. (2021). Introduction to the special issue on the centenary of Frank H. Knight's risk, uncertainty, and profit. *Journal of Institutional Economics*, *17*(6), 877–881. DOI: 10.1017/S1744137421000564

Callon, M. (1986). The sociology of an actor-network: The case of the electric vehicle. In Callon, M., Law, J., & Rip, A. (Eds.), *Mapping the dynamics of science and technology* (pp. 19–34). The Macmillan Press., DOI: 10.1007/978-1-349-07408-2_2

Carpenter, G., & Wyman, O. (2022). Realizing New Possibilities. 2022 Annual Report. Marsh & McLennan. https://www.marshmclennan.com/assets/v2/investors/2022/MarshMcLennan 2022AnnualReport.pdf

Carson, R., Pandey, P., Lekhi, A., Keyal, A., Fishman, T., & Chew, B. (2024). *Government's resilience imperative*. Deloitte Center for Government Insights.

Cartwright, A. J. (2023). The elephant in the room: Cybersecurity in healthcare. *Journal of Clinical Monitoring and Computing*, *37*(5), 1123–1132. DOI: 10.1007/s10877-023-01013-5 PMID: 37088852

Chen, C.-K., Zhang, Z.-K., Cho, M. C., Wang, C.-W., Hsu, C.-W., & Shieh, S. (2014). *IOT security: Ongoing challenges and research opportunities. 2014 IEEE 7th International Conference on Service-Oriented Computing and Applications.* DOI: 10.1109/SOCA.2014.58

Chen, H., Wen, Y., Zhu, M., Huang, Y., Xiao, C., Wei, T., & Hahn, A. (2021). From automation system to autonomous system: An architecture perspective. *Journal of Marine Science and Engineering*, *9*(6), 645. DOI: 10.3390/jmse9060645

Cherns, A. (1976). The principles of sociotechnical design. *Human Relations*, *29*(8), 783–792. DOI: 10.1177/001872677602900806

Cherns, A. (1987). Principles of sociotechnical design revisited. *Human Relations*, *40*(3), 153–161. DOI: 10.1177/001872678704000303

Chernyshev, M., Zeadally, S., & Baig, Z. (2018). Healthcare data breaches: Implications for digital forensic readiness. *Journal of Medical Systems*, *43*(1), 7. Advance online publication. DOI: 10.1007/s10916-018-1123-2 PMID: 30488291

Cho, S. Y. (2015a). Human trafficking, a shadow of migration - Evidence from Germany. *The Journal of Development Studies*, *51*(7), 905–921. DOI: 10.1080/00220388.2015.1010158

Cho, S. Y. (2015b). Modelling for determinants of human trafficking. *Social Inclusion (Lisboa)*, *3*(1), 2–21. http://dx.doi.org.ezp.slu.edu/10.17645/si.v3i1.125. DOI: 10.17645/si.v3i1.125

CISA. (n.d.). *Incident response plan (IRP) basics.* Retrieved from https://www.cisa.gov/sites/default/files/publications/Incident-Response-Plan-Basics_508c.pdf

City of Milwaukee. (2020). *Geospatial characteristics of sex trafficking of juveniles and young adults in Milwaukee.* https://www.mcw.edu/-/media/MCW/Departments/Epidemiology/MHRC/2020-Milwaukee-Juveniles-and-Young-Adults-Sex-Trafficking-Report.pdf?la=en

Cockbain, E., & Wallis, A. (2019, April 17). *The social, spatial and temporal systems behind human trafficking.* Delta 8.7. https://delta87.org/2019/04/social-spatial-temporal-systems-human-trafficking/

Cokorilo, O. (2020). Urban air mobility: Safety challenges. *Transportation Research Procedia, 45*, 21–29. DOI: 10.1016/j.trpro.2020.02.058

Cole, J., & Sprang, G. (2015). Sex trafficking of minors in metropolitan, micropolitan, and rural communities. *Child Abuse & Neglect, 40*, 113–123. https://doi-org.ezp.slu.edu/10.1016/j.chiabu.2014.07.015. DOI: 10.1016/j.chiabu.2014.07.015 PMID: 25151302

Comella-Dorda, S., Kaplan, J., Lau, L., & McNamara, N. (2020). Agile, reliable, secure, compliant IT: Fulfilling the promise of DevSecOps. Digital McKinsey and Global Risk Practice. McKinsey & Company.

Committee of Sponsoring Organizations of the Treadway Commission (COSO). (2004). *Enterprise risk management—Integrated framework: Executive summary.* COSO. https://www.coso.org

ConnectWise. (2024). *ConnectWise ScreenConnect 23.9.8 security fix.* ConnectWise Trust Center. Retrieved October 18, 2025, from https://www.connectwise.com/company/trust/security-bulletins/connectwise-screenconnect-23.9.8

Connor, H. (2024). John Graunt FRS (1620-74): The founding father of human demography, epidemiology and vital statistics. *Journal of Medical Biography, 32*(1), 57–69. DOI: 10.1177/09677720221079826 PMID: 35167377

Cook, D., Mayer, R., & Doya, G. (2023). Crises and the resilience of the aviation industry: A literature review. *Transportation Research Interdisciplinary Perspectives, 27*, 101182. Advance online publication. DOI: 10.1016/j.trip.2024.101182

Cooper, R., & Foster, M. (1971). Sociotechnical systems. *The American Psychologist, 26*(5), 467–474. DOI: 10.1037/h0031539

Corporation, I. B. M. (2021). *IBM launches QRadar XDR, a comprehensive open XDR solution.* IBM TechXchange Community. https://community.ibm.com/community/user/discussion/ibm-launches-qradar-xdr-a-comprehensive-open-xdr-solution?hlmlt=VT

Council of Europe. (2022). *Online and technology-facilitated trafficking in human beings.* https://rm.coe.int/online-and-technology-facilitated-trafficking-in-human-beings-summary-/1680a5e10c

Counter Trafficking Data Collaborative. (n.d.). *The Counter Trafficking Data Collaborative.* https://www.ctdatacollaborative.org/

Couretas, J. M. (2022). Cyber Policy, Doctrine, and Tactics, Techniques, and Procedures (TTPs). In *An Introduction to Cyber Analysis and Targeting* (pp. 13–36). Springer International Publishing. DOI: 10.1007/978-3-030-88559-5_2

Coventry, L., Branley-Bell, D., Sillence, E., Magalini, S., Mari, P., Magkanaraki, A., & Anastasopoulou, K. (2020). Cyber-Risk in Healthcare: Exploring Facilitators and Barriers to Secure Behaviour. *HCI for Cybersecurity, Privacy and Trust*, 105–122. DOI: 10.1007/978-3-030-50309-3_8

Coverdale, J. H., Gordon, M. R., & Nguyen, P. T. (Eds.). (2020). *Human trafficking: A treatment guide for mental health professionals*. American Psychiatric Association Publishing. DOI: 10.1176/appi.books.9781615379439

Cracknell, R., Kaplan, J., Richter, W., Shenton, L., & Stewart, C. (2020). *Cybersecurity in a digital era*. Digital McKinsey and Global Risk Practice. McKinsey & Company.

Craig, R., & Corey, D. (2021). Cyber threats in healthcare: A comprehensive review. *Journal of Healthcare Information Management, 35*(2), 112–119.

Crawford, K., Miltner, K., & Gray, M. L. (2014). Critiquing Big Data: Politics, ethics, epistemology. *International Journal of Communication, 8*, 1663–1672. https://ijoc.org/index.php/ijoc/article/view/2167/1164

Creswell, J. W., & Poth, C. N. (2023). *Qualitative inquiry and research design: Choosing among five approaches* (5th ed.). SAGE Publication.

Crothall Healthcare. (2025). *Five building blocks to a resilient healthcare cybersecurity culture.* https://www.crothall.com/blog/five-building-blocks-to-a-resilient-healthcare-cybersecurity-culture/

Crotty, J., & Daniel, E. (2022). Cyber threat: its origins and consequence and the use of qualitative and quantitative methods in cyber risk assessment. *Applied Computing and Informatics*, (ahead-of-print).

Cyber Threat Intelligence, K. E. L. A. (2025). *Third-party risk in healthcare demands immediate attention*. https://www.kelacyber.com/blog/why-third-party-risk-in-healthcare-demands-immediate-attention/

Cybersecurity Help. (2022). *Zero-Day vulnerability statistics.* Retrieved from https://www.zero-day.cz/research/

Cynet. (2022). *Cynet Next-Gen Antivirus (NGAV)*. Retrieved from https://www.cynet.com/platform/next-gen-antivirus/

Dalton, C., & Thatcher, J. (2014). What does a Critical Data Studies look like, and why do we care? Seven points for a critical approach to 'big data.' *Environment and Planning D: Society and Space. Online journal companion.* https://societyandspace.com/material/commentaries/craig-dalton-and-jim-thatcher-what-does-a-critical-data-studies-look-like-and-why-do-we-care-seven-points-for-a-critical-approach-to-big-data/

Daniel-Wrabetz, J., & Penedo, R. (2015). Trafficking in human beings in time and space. A socioecological perspective. In Guia, M. (Ed.), *The illegal business of human trafficking* (pp. 1–19). Springer., DOI: 10.1007/978-3-319-09441-0_1

Dank, M., Khan, B., Downey, P. M., Kotonias, C., Mayer, D., Owens, C., Pacifici, L., & Yu, L. (2014). *Estimating the size and structure of the underground commercial sex economy in eight major US cities.* The Urban Institute (Award No. 2010-IJ-CX-1674, U.S. Department of Justice, Office of Justice Programs, National Institute of Justice). https://www.urban.org/sites/default/files/alfresco/publication-pdfs/413047-Estimating-the-Size-and-Structure-of-the-Underground-Commercial-Sex-Economy-in-Eight-Major-US-Cities.PDF

Dao, N.-N. (2018). Virtual Field Trip for Mobile Construction Safety Education using 360-degree Panoramic Virtual Reality. International Journal of Engineering Education. https://www.academia.edu/37063856/Virtual_Field_Trip_for_Mobile_Construction_Safety_Education_using_360_degree_Panoramic_Virtual_Reality

Darr, S., Ricks, W., & Lemos, A. K. (2008). Safer systems: A NextGen aviation safety strategic goal. In *Proceedings of 2008 IEEE/AIAA 27th Digital Avionics Systems Conference,* (pp. 2.A.1-1 - 2.A.1-8.). IEEE. DOI: 10.1109/DASC.2008.4702772

Dave, K. (2025). Modernizing U.S. air traffic control: The promise and pitfalls of NextGen implementation + comprehensive policy recommendations. *SSRN*. DOI: 10.2139/ssrn.5550998

Davis, M. C., Challenger, R., Jayewardene, D. N. W., & Clegg, C. W. (2014). Advancing socio-technical systems thinking: A call for bravery. *Applied Ergonomics, 45*(2), 171–180. DOI: 10.1016/j.apergo.2013.02.009

Dawodu, S. O., Omotosho, A., Akindote, O. J., Adegbite, A. O., & Ewuga, S. K. (2023). Cybersecurity risk assessment in banking: methodologies and best practices. *Computer Science & IT Research Journal, 4*(3), 220-243. https://fepbl.com/index.php/csitrj/article/view/659

Dawson, C., Julku, H., Pihlajamäki, M., Kaakinen, J. K., Schooler, J. W., & Simola, J. (2024). Evidence-based scientific thinking and decision-making in everyday life. *Cognitive Research: Principles and Implications*, *9*(1), 50. DOI: 10.1186/s41235-024-00578-2 PMID: 39110276

Decker, A., & Galer, D. (2013). *Enterprise risk management straight to the point: An implementation guide function by function*. ERMSTTP, LLC. https://www.amazon.com/Enterprise-Risk-Management-Implementation-Viewpoints/dp/1481287788

Deskin, G. (2025). *Law enforcement pressure is reshaping the global ransomware threat landscape. Security Boulevard.* https://securityboulevard.com/2025/10/law-enforcement-pressure-is-reshaping-the-global-ransomware-threat-landscape/

Dhakal, K. (2022). NVivo. *Journal of the Medical Library Association: JMLA*, *110*(2), 270. DOI: 10.5195/jmla.2022.1271 PMID: 35440911

Dhawan, M., Purohit, L., & Gupta, Dr. N. (2023). A comprehensive study on the latest trends of cyber security in the medical management. *SSRN Electronic Journal*. DOI: 10.2139/ssrn.4361044

Dimas, G. L., Konrad, R. A., Maass, K. L., & Trapp, A. C. (2022). Operations research and analytics to combat human trafficking: A systematic review of academic literature. *PLoS One*, *17*(8), e0273708. Advance online publication. DOI: 10.1371/journal.pone.0273708 PMID: 36037198

Dixon-Woods, M., Agarwal, S., Jones, D., Young, B., & Sutton, A. (2006). Synthesising qualitative and quantitative evidence: A review of possible methods. *Journal of Health Services Research & Policy*, *10*(1), 45–53. DOI: 10.1177/135581960501000110

Dobson, S. (2018). Cybersecurity talent hard to find: Report. *Canadian HR Reporter, 31*(9), *3-18.* https://www.hrreporter.com/focus-areas/recruitment-and-staffing/cybersecurity-talent-hard-to-find-report/299496

Dodla, T. R., & Jones, L. A. (2023). Mitigating knowledge management internal and external risk factors: A literature review of best practices. *Scientific Bulletin-Nicolae Balcescu Land Forces Academy*, *28*(1), 44–54. DOI: 10.2478/bsaft-2023-0005

Dodoo, J. E., Al-Samarraie, H., Alzahrani, A. I., Lonsdale, M., & Alalwan, N. (2024). Digital Innovations for Occupational Safety: Empowering Workers in Hazardous Environments. *Workplace Health & Safety*, *72*(3), 84–95. Advance online publication. DOI: 10.1177/21650799231215811

Dovydaitis, T. (2010). Human trafficking: The role of the health care provider. *Journal of Midwifery & Women's Health*, *55*(5), 462–467. DOI: 10.1016/j.jmwh.2009.12.017 PMID: 20732668

Dude: Fortis Exoskeleton (2014). http://www.dudeiwantthat.com/fitness/equipment/fortisexoskeleton. asp. Accessed 22Mar 2019.

Ebute, M. (2024). CONTINUOUS MONITORING AND ASSESSMENT MECHANISMS IN CYBERSECURITY: BEST PRACTICES FOR SUSTAINED PROTECTION OF CRITICAL ASSETS. *Available at SSRN* 4912624. DOI: 10.2139/ssrn.4912624

Efunniyi, C. P., Abhulimen, A. O., Obiki-Osafiele, A. N., Osundare, O. S., Agu, E. E., & Adeniran, I. A.Christianah Pelumi EfunniyiAngela Omozele AbhulimenAnwuli Nkemchor Obiki-OsafieleOlajide Soji OsundareEdith Ebele AguIbrahim Adedeji Adeniran. (2024). Strengthening corporate governance and financial compliance: Enhancing accountability and transparency. *Finance & Accounting Research Journal, 6*(8), 1597–1616. DOI: 10.51594/farj.v6i8.1509

Eisenbach, T. M., Kovner, A., & Lee, M. J. (2020). Cyber risk and the U.S. financial system: A pre-mortem analysis. SSRN *Electronic Journal.* DOI: 10.2139/ssrn.3522710

Ekbia, H., Mattioli, M., Kouper, I., Arave, G., Ghazinejad, A., Bowman, T., Suri, V.R., Tsou, A., Weingart, S. & Sugimoto, C.R. (2015), Big data, bigger dilemmas: A critical review. *Journal of The Association for Information Science & Technology, 66*(8), 1523-1545. (First published in 2014)DOI: 10.1002/asi.23294

Eleimat, M., & Őszi, A. (2025). Cybersecurity in aviation: Exploring the significance, applications, and challenges of cybersecurity in the aviation sector. *Periodica Polytechnica Transportation Engineering, 53*(2), 169–183. DOI: 10.3311/PPtr.37153

Elzinga, K. G., Tremblay, C. H., & Tremblay, V. J. (2015). Craft beer in the United States: History, numbers, and geography. *Journal of Wine Economics, 10*(3), 242–274. DOI: 10.1017/jwe.2015.22

Engin, Z., Crowcroft, J., Hand, D., & Treleaven, P. (2025). *The Algorithmic State Architecture (ASA): An integrated framework for AI-enabled government.* https://doi.org//arXiv.2503.08725DOI: 10.48550

EUROCONTROL. (2023). *EUROCONTROL Aviation Outlook 2050.* https://www.eurocontrol.int/publication/eurocontrol-aviation-outlook-2050

European Commission. (2017). *European Interoperability Framework: Implementation Strategy.* Retrieved from https://eur-lex.europa.eu/legal-content/EN/TXT/HTML/?uri=CELEX:52017DC0134

Familoni, B. T., & Shoetan, P. O. (2024). Cybersecurity in the financial sector: a comparative analysis of the USA and Nigeria. *Computer Science & IT Research Journal, 5*(4), 850-877. https://www.scirp.org/reference/referencespapers?referenceid=3828230

Farrell, A., & De Vries, I. (2020). Measuring the nature and prevalence of human trafficking. In Winterdyk, J., & Jones, J. (Eds.), *The Palgrave International Handbook of Human Trafficking* (pp. 147–162). Palgrave Macmillan. DOI: 10.1007/978-3-319-63058-8_6

Faruk, M., & Made, I. (2023). The Role of Using Virtual Reality in Learning in an Education Environment. Advances in Social Science, Education and Humanities Research. *Advances in Social Science, Education and Humanities Research, 1234–1238*, 1234–1238. Advance online publication. DOI: 10.2991/978-2-494069-35-0_148

Fauzi, M. A., Yeng, P., Yang, B., & Rachmayani, D. (2021). Examining the Link Between Stress Level and Cybersecurity Practices of Hospital Staff in Indonesia. *The 16th International Conference on Availability, Reliability and Security*. DOI: 10.1145/3465481.3470094

Federal Aviation Administration. (2023). *NextGen annual report, fiscal year 2023.* U.S. Department of Transportation. https://www.faa.gov/nextgen/NextGen-Annual-Report-2023.pdf

Federal Aviation Administration. (2025, November 6). *DOT & FAA announce temporary 10% reduction in flights at 40 airports.* https://www.faa.gov/newsroom/dot-faa-announce-temporary-10-reduction-flights-40-airports

Fell, J. C. (2016). The merits of adopting a 0.05 administrative blood alcohol concentration limit for driving. *American Journal of Public Health, 106*(6), 977–978. DOI: 10.2105/AJPH.2016.303187 PMID: 27153014

Fisher, G. G., Chaffee, D. S., & Petery, G. A. (2024). Research using archival data. In *Advanced research methods for applied psychology* (pp. 87–98). Routledge. DOI: 10.4324/9781003362715-9

Fleury, D. (2019, July 8). *A Rescue Mission: 3 Ways Deep Learning Could Combat Human Tracking*. Towards Data Science. https://towardsdatascience.com/a-rescue-mission-3-ways-deep-learning-could-combat-human-trafficking-85700eb62be5

Florencondia, N. T., Lansangan, M. B., Marcos, E. V., Vincent, J., & Russel, K. (2021). New Normal Set-up on Safety and Health Standards in Government Construction Projects: A case of Covid-19. *International Journal of Engineering and Advanced Technology, 10*(5), 370–374. DOI: 10.35940/ijeat.E2825.0610521

Florido-Benítez, L. (2024). The types of hackers and cyberattacks in the aviation industry. *Journal of Transportation Security, 17*(1), 13. Advance online publication. DOI: 10.1007/s12198-024-00281-9

Foley, S., Karlsen, J. R., & Putniņš, T. J. (2019). Sex, drugs, and bitcoin: How much illegal activity is financed through cryptocurrencies? *Review of Financial Studies, 32*(5), 1798–1853. DOI: 10.1093/rfs/hhz015

Folger, R., & Skarlicki, D. P. (2005). Beyond counterproductive work behavior: Moral emotions and deontic retaliation versus reconciliation. In Fox, S., & Spector, P. E. (Eds.), *Counterproductive work behavior: Investigations of actors and targets* (pp. 83–106). American Psychological Association., DOI: 10.1037/10893-004

Food and Drug Administration. (2025). *Cybersecurity in medical devices: Quality system considerations and content of premarket submissions. Federal Register.* https://www.federalregister.gov/documents/2025/06/27/2025-11669/cybersecurity-in-medical-devices-quality-system-considerations-and-content-of-premarket-submissions

Forrest, A., & Lindemulder, G. (n.d.). *What is a next-generation antivirus (NGAV)? IBM.* Retrieved from https://www.ibm.com/think/topics/next-generation-antivirus/#:~:text=Authors,IBM%20Think

Forteza, F. J., Carretero-Gómez, J. M., & Sesé, A. (2020). Safety in the construction industry: Accidents and precursors. *Revista de la Construcción, 19*(2), 271–281. DOI: 10.7764/rdlc.19.2.271-281

Fortinet (2022). *Brute Force Attack Definition.* Retrieved from https://www.fortinet.com/resources/cyberglossary/brute-force-attack

Forward, J., Akhurst, J., Bruno, R., Leong, X., VanderNiet, A., Bromfield, H., Erny, J., Bellamy, T., & Peacock, A. (2017). Nature versus intensity of intoxication: Co-ingestion of alcohol and energy drinks and the effect on objective and subjective intoxication. *Drug and Alcohol Dependence, 180*, 292–303. DOI: 10.1016/j.drugalcdep.2017.08.013 PMID: 28942033

Frane, D. (2016) 7 Cool and Unusual Tools from the 2016 STAFDA Show (2016). http://www.toolsofthetrade.net/power-tools/7-cool-and-unusual-tools-from-the-2016-stafdashow_o

Fruhlinger, J. (2020, March 9). Top cybersecurity facts, figures, and statistics. *CSO Online.* https://www.csoonline.com/article/3153707/top-cybersecurity-facts-figures-and-statistics.html

Gallagher, A. T. (2010). *The international law of human trafficking*. Cambridge University Press. DOI: 10.1017/CBO9780511761065

Gallagher, A. T. (2017). What's wrong with the Global Slavery Index? *Anti-Trafficking Review*, (8), 90–112. DOI: 10.14197/atr.20121786

Gallagher, A., & Holmes, P. (2008). Developing an effective criminal justice response to human trafficking: Lessons from the front line. *International Criminal Justice Review*, *18*(3), 318–343. DOI: 10.1177/1057567708320746

Gambín, Á. F., Yazidi, A., Vasilakos, A., Haugerud, H., & Djenouri, Y. (2024). Deepfakes: Current and future trends. *Artificial Intelligence Review*, *57*(3), 64. DOI: 10.1007/s10462-023-10679-x

Gardner, W. L., Panaou, T., Watterson, K., Alao, S., & Jacob, B. G. (2017). Predicting potential human trafficking recruiting geolocations using eigendecomposed non-zero spatial autocorrelation coefficients and Poissonian heterogeneous gamma distributed variables. *International Journal of Geographical Information Systems*, *4*(2), 1–23. https://www.researchgate.net/publication/320044978_Predicting_potential_human_trafficking_recruiting_geolocations_using_Eigendecomposed_non-zero_spatial_autocorrelation_coefficients_and_Poissonian_heterogeneous_gamma_distributed_variables

Gartner. (n.d.). *Third-party risk management (TPRM): A complete guide*. Retrieved from https://www.gartner.com/en/legal-compliance/topics/third-party-risk-management-tprm

Gazzan, M., Alobaywi, B., Almutairi, M., & Sheldon, F. T. (2025). A Deep Learning Framework for Enhanced Detection of Polymorphic Ransomware. *Future Internet*, *17*(7), 311. DOI: 10.3390/fi17070311

Gelles, M. (2016). *Insider threat: Prevention, detection, mitigation, and deterrence*. Elsevier., DOI: 10.1016/B978-0-12-802410-2.00015-0

George, A. S. (2024). When trust fails: Examining systemic risk in the digital economy from the 2024 crowdstrike outage. *Partners Universal Multidisciplinary Research Journal*, *1*(2), 134–152.

Gezinski, L. B., & Gonzalez-Pons, K. M. (2022). Sex trafficking and technology: A systematic review of recruitment and exploitation. *Journal of Human Trafficking*, *10*(3), 497–511. DOI: 10.1080/23322705.2022.2034378

Gil-Garcia, J. R., Dawes, S. S., & Pardo, T. A. (2017). Digital government and public management research: Finding the crossroads. *Public Management Review*, *20*(3), 1–14. DOI: 10.1080/14719037.2017.1327181

Goel, A., & Garg, P. (n.d.). How to Cite. *International Journal of Health Sciences, 6*(S4), 10806–10823. DOI: 10.53730/ijhs.v6nS4.10900

Gomes, L., Deshmukh, A., & Anute, N. (2022). Cyber security and internet banking: Issues and preventive measures. *Journal of Information Technology and Sciences, 8*(2), 31–42. https://www.researchgate.net/publication/362013259_Cyber_Security_and_Internet_Banking_Issues_and_Preventive_Measures. DOI: 10.46610/JOITS.2022.v08i02.005

Goraya, M. A. S., Yaqub, M. Z., Khan, M. A., Akram, M. S., & Alofaysan, H. (2024). Transforming performance: How agility, response, resilience and support shape success in digital strategies. *Information Technology & People.*

Grant, B. F., Chou, S. P., Saha, T. D., Pickering, R. P., Kerridge, B. T., Ruan, W. J., Huang, B., Jung, J., Zhang, H., Fan, A., & Hasin, D. S. (2017). Prevalence of 12-month alcohol use, high-risk drinking, and DSM-IV alcohol use disorder in the United States, 2001-2002 to 2012-2013: Results from the National Epidemiologic Survey on Alcohol and Related Conditions. *JAMA Psychiatry, 74*(9), 911–923. DOI: 10.1001/jamapsychiatry.2017.2161 PMID: 28793133

Grojek, A. E., Sikos, L. F., Holmes, D. J., & Guidetti, O. (2024). Incident response drills on cyber ranges. *Psybersecurity: Human Factors of Cyber Defence*, 202.

Guillen, D. (2022). A Simpler Annuity. *undergraduate research journal volume 16*, 102.

Gupta, D., Elluri, L., Jain, A., Moni, S. S., & Aslan, O. (2024). *Blockchain-enhanced framework for secure third-party vendor risk management and vigilant security controls.* arXiv preprint. https://arxiv.org/abs/2411.13447 DOI: 10.1109/BigData62323.2024.10825025

Halkias, D., Neubert, M., Thurman, P. W., & Harkiolakis, N. (2022). *The multiple case study design: Methodology and application for management education.* Routledge. DOI: 10.4324/9781003244936

Halock (2025). Aflac Breach Shows Value Of Rapid Response. https://www.halock.com/aflac-breach-shows-value-of-rapid-response/

Hamir, H., & Sum, R. M. (2021). An analysis of risk management processes and comparison with ISO31000: 2018. *Asian Journal of Research in Business and Management, 3*(4), 16–30.

Hardjomidjojo, H., Pranata, C., & Baigorria, G. (2022, July). Rapid assessment model on risk management based on ISO 31000: 2018. [). IOP Publishing.]. *IOP Conference Series. Earth and Environmental Science, 1063*(1), 012043. DOI: 10.1088/1755-1315/1063/1/012043

Hardy, M. R., & Saunders, D. (2022). *Quantitative enterprise risk management.* Cambridge University Press. DOI: 10.1017/9781009089470

Harris, E., Harris, J., & Beall, M. (2024). Defense in depth: An action plan to increase the safety and security of advanced AI. *Gladstone AI, available upon request at* https://www. gladstone. ai/action-plan

Hart, G. (2025). Conceptual Explorations Of Employee Coaching For Generation Z Sales Professionals. *Land Forces Academy Review, 30*(1), 118-133. https://reference-global.com/download/article/10.2478/raft-2025-0012.pdf

Haruna, A. D., & Taiwo, O. O.Ayegba David HarunaOlugbenga Olayinka Taiwo. (2024). Enhancing aviation maintenance oversight through proactive quality auditing and human factors integration. *World Journal of Advanced Engineering Technology and Sciences, 13*(1), 1180–1199. DOI: 10.30574/wjaets.2024.13.1.0419

Haviland, A., Burns, R., Gray, W., Ruder, T., & Mendeloff, J. (2010). What kinds of injuries do OSHA inspections prevent? *Journal of Safety Research, 41*(4), 339–345. DOI: 10.1016/j.jsr.2010.03.005

Health, I. T. Security. (2021). *Scripps Health ransomware attack disrupts care.* HealthITSecurity.com. https://healthitsecurity.com

Healthcare, H. C. A. (2023). *HCA Healthcare reports data security incident.* https://investor.hcahealthcare.com/news/news-details/2023/HCA-Healthcare-Reports-Data-Security-Incident/default.aspx

Hermes, S., Riasanow, T., Clemons, E. K., Böhm, M., & Krcmar, H. (2020). The digital transformation of the healthcare industry: Exploring the rise of emerging platform ecosystems and their influence on the role of patients. *Business Research, 13*(3), 1033–1069. DOI: 10.1007/s40685-020-00125-x

Hernandez, D., & Rudolph, A. (2015). Modern day slavery: What drives human trafficking in Europe? *European Journal of Political Economy, 38*, 118–139. DOI: 10.1016/j.ejpoleco.2015.02.002

Hillson, D. (Ed.). (2023). *The Risk Management Handbook: A practical guide to managing the multiple dimensions of risk.* Kogan Page Publishers.

Hinings, B., Gegenhuber, T., & Greenwood, R. (2018). Digital innovation and transformation: An institutional perspective. *Information and Organization*, *28*(1), 52–61. DOI: 10.1016/j.infoandorg.2018.02.004

Holomozenko, V., & Stasiuk, Y. (2024). Risk in management decisions of the modern organization and methods of management of this risk. *Challenges and Issues of Modern Science*, *2*, 377–381.

Holtzhausen, D., & Zerfass, A. (2015). *The Routledge handbook of strategic communication*. Routledge., https://www.academia.edu/44638503/THE_ROUTLEDGE_HANDBOOK_OF_STATEGIC_COMMUNICATION_Derina_Holtzhausen_Ansgar_Zerfass_

Hoxhunt. (2025). *Does gamified security training actually work?* https://hoxhunt.com/blog/gamified-cyber-security-training

Hubbard, D. W., & Seiersen, R. (2023). *How to measure anything in cybersecurity risk*. John Wiley & Sons. DOI: 10.1002/9781119892335

Huff, A. J., Burrell, D. N., Nobles, C., Richardson, K., Wright, J. B., Burton, S. L., Jones, A. J., Springs, D., Omar, M., & Brown-Jackson, K. L. (2023). Management practices for mitigating cybersecurity threats to biotechnology companies, laboratories, and healthcare research organizations. In *Applied Research Approaches to Technology, Healthcare, and Business* (pp. 1-12). IGI Global. https://www.igi-global.com/chapter/management-practices-for-mitigating-cybersecurity-threats-to-biotechnology-companies-laboratories-and-healthcare-research-organizations/331637

Hu, Y., Parhizkar, T., & Mosleh, A. (2022). Guided simulation for dynamic probabilistic risk assessment of complex systems: Concept, method, and application. *Reliability Engineering & System Safety*, *217*, 108047. DOI: 10.1016/j.ress.2021.108047

Hyperproof. (2025). NIST 800-53: *Security and privacy controls for information systems and organizations*. https://hyperproof.io/nist-800-53/

Ibanez, M., & Suthers, D. D. (2014). Detection of domestic human trafficking indicators and movement trends using content available on open internet sources. In *2014 47th Hawaii international conference on system sciences* (pp. 1556-1565). IEEE. DOI DOI: 10.1109/HICSS.2014.200

IBM and the Ponemon Institute. (2024). Cost of a data breach 2024: Financial Industry. https://www.ibm.com/think/insights/cost-of-a-data-breach-2024-financial-industry

IBM. (2023). *Cost of a data breach report 2023.* IBM Security. https://www.stickleyonsecurity.com/news.jspx?articlcid=%200F34F898A5586B334B4C8FACC8B02008&v5=1&playerid=407315631#:~:text=Every%20year%2C%20%22IBM's%20Cost%20of%20a%20Data,breaches%20and%20other%20key%20findings%20from%202023

IJCT Editor. (2016, November 16). VIRTUAL REALITY IN EDUCATION: TRENDS AND ISSUES. Academia.edu. https://www.academia.edu/29888980/VIRTUAL_REALITY_IN_EDUCATION_TRENDS_AND_ISSUES

Iliadis, A., & Russo, F. (2016). Critical data studies: An introduction. *Big Data & Society, 3*(2). (Original work published 2016)DOI: 10.1177/2053951716674238

International Civil Aviation Organization. (n.d.). *Global Air Navigation Plan (GANP).* https://www.icao.int/global-air-navigation-plan-ganp

International Labour Office. (2022). *Global estimates of modern slavery: Forced labour and forced marriage.* https://www.ilo.org/publications/major-publications/global-estimates-modern-slavery-forced-labour-and-forced-marriage

International Labour Office. (2024). *Profits and poverty: The economics of forced labour.* DOI: 10.54394/JJJE9035

International Organization for Migration & United Nations Office on Drugs and Crime. (2023). *International classification standard for administrative data on trafficking in persons.* https://www.unodc.org/documents/data-and-analysis/tip/2023/ICS-TIP_2023-v4.pdf

International Organization for Standardization. (2018). *ISO 31000:2018 risk management — Guidelines.* https://www.iso.org/standard/65694.html

Iqbal, M. (2023, January). Probability and Impact Matrix: PMP/CAPM. Monte Carlo Simulation Tool. *Mudassir Iqbal.* https://mudassiriqbal.net/probability-and-impact-matrix/

Ivanov, D., & Dolgui, A. (2022). Stress testing supply chains and creating viable ecosystems. *Operations Management Research : Advancing Practice Through Research, 15*(1), 475–486. DOI: 10.1007/s12063-021-00194-z

Iyer, N. G., Arulmozhi, M., Sivakumar, P., Sudharsan, S., & Kavitha, R. (2023, December). AI-Powered Driver Behavior Prediction, Drunk Driving Prevention, Accident Detection, and Insurance Integration. In *the 2023 International Conference on Energy, Materials and Communication Engineering (ICEMCE)* (pp. 1-5). IEEE.

Jacobus, J., & Tapert, S. F. (2013). Neurotoxic effects of alcohol in adolescence. *Annual Review of Clinical Psychology*, *9*(1), 703–721. DOI: 10.1146/annurev-clinpsy-050212-185610 PMID: 23245341

Jalali, M. S., & Kaiser, J. P. (2018). Cybersecurity in Hospitals: A Systematic, Organizational Perspective. *Journal of Medical Internet Research*, *20*(5), e10059. DOI: 10.2196/10059 PMID: 29807882

Janssen, M., & van der Voort, H. (2020). Agile and adaptive governance in crisis response: Lessons from the COVID-19 pandemic. *International Journal of Information Management*, *55*, 102180. DOI: 10.1016/j.ijinfomgt.2020.102180 PMID: 32836637

Javaid, M., Haleem, A., Singh, R. P., & Suman, R. (2023). Towards insighting cybersecurity for healthcare domains: A comprehensive review of recent practices and trends. *Cyber Security and Applications*, *1*(100016), 100016. DOI: 10.1016/j.csa.2023.100016

Jin, L., Jain, A., Shah, A., & Sykes, R. (2024). Government funding gap impacts on commercial aviation safety: President Carter through Trump (1978-2020). *International Journal of Aviation Research*, *16*(1).

Jones, L. A. (2021). A content analysis review of literature to create a useable framework for reputation risk management. Handbook of Research on Multidisciplinary Perspectives on Managerial and Leadership Psychology, 91-133. DOI: 10.4018/978-1-7998-3811-1.ch006

Jones, L. A. (2024). *Cybersecurity Leadership: Traversing The Interminable Prospective For Cyber Risk Transmogrification.* https://www.researchgate.net/publication/394356399_cybersecurity_ leadership_ traversing_the_interminable_prospective_for_cyber_risk_transmogrification

Jones, L. A., & Burrell, D. N. (2025). Illegal Cybersecurity Threats Created by Organizational Arsonists in Healthcare Organizations. *Law. Economics and Society*, *1*(1), 93–p93. https://j.ideasspread.org/index.php/les/article/view/1427

Kamalanathan, S., Rajan, S. M., & Schell, S. (2025). *Implementing zero trust in healthcare. Cognizant.* https://www.cognizant.com/en_us/industries/documents/cognizant-implementing-zero-trust-in-healthcare.pdf

Kaminski, J. (2022). Editorial. Theory applied to informatics: Socio-Technical Theory. *Canadian Journal of Nursing Informatics*, *17*(3-4). https://cjni.net/journal/?p=10442

Kanter, G. P., Rekowski, J. R., & Kannarkat, J. T. (2024, September). Lessons from the Change Healthcare ransomware attack. [). American Medical Association.]. *JAMA Health Forum*, *5*(9), e242764–e242764. DOI: 10.1001/jamahealthforum.2024.2764 PMID: 39302668

Kapko, M. (2024, March 1). *Change Healthcare cyberattack: What we know, what's next. CSO Online.* https://www.csoonline.com/article/652749/change-healthcare-cyberattack-what-we-know-whats-next.html

Kaplan, J., Richter, W., & Ware, D. (2020). *Cybersecurity: Linchpin of the digital enterprise*. Digital McKinsey and Global Risk Practice. McKinsey & Company

Kaspersky (n.d.). *Malware-as-a-service (MaaS).* Retrieved from https://encyclopedia.kaspersky.com/glossary/

Kaspersky (n.d.). *Malware-as-a-service (MaaS).* Retrieved from https://encyclopedia.kaspersky.com/glossary/malware-as-a-service-maas/

Katta, J. V., Pagadavarapu, U. C., Selvi, G. A., & Subapriya, V. (2025). A comprehensive human trafficking identification and prediction system using machine learning techniques. In *Proceedings of the International Conference On Cognitive Computing And Artificial Intelligence, 3257*(1), Article 020036. DOI: 10.1063/5.0265865

Kaufman, E. J., & Wiebe, D. J. (2016). Impact of state ignition interlock laws on alcohol-involved crash deaths in the United States. *American Journal of Public Health, 106*(5), 865–871. DOI: 10.2105/AJPH.2016.303058 PMID: 26985604

Kazi, M. A., Woodhead, S., & Gan, D. (2022). An investigation to detect banking malware network communication traffic using machine learning techniques. *Journal of Cybersecurity and Privacy, 3*(1), 1–23. https://www.mdpi.com/2624-800X/3/1/1. DOI: 10.3390/jcp3010001

Keller, M. H., & Dance, G. J. X. (2019, September 29). *The internet is overrun with images of child sexual abuse. What went wrong?* The New York Times. https://www.nytimes.com/interactive/2019/09/28/us/child-sex-abuse.html

Kelly, J. T., Campbell, K. L., Gong, E., & Scuffham, P. (2020). The internet of things: Impact and implications for healthcare delivery. *Journal of Medical Internet Research, 22*(11), e20135. Advance online publication. DOI: 10.2196/20135 PMID: 33170132

Kerr, W. C., & Greenfield, T. K. (2015). Racial/ethnic disparities in the self-reported number of drinks in 2 hours before driving becomes impaired. *American Journal of Public Health, 105*(7), 1409–1414. DOI: 10.2105/AJPH.2014.302276 PMID: 25602892

Kerr, W. C., Patterson, D., Greenfield, T. K., Jones, A. S., McGeary, K. A., Terza, J. V., & Ruhm, C. J. (2013). U.S. alcohol affordability and real tax rates, 1950–2011. *American Journal of Preventive Medicine*, *44*(5), 459–464. DOI: 10.1016/j.amepre.2013.01.007 PMID: 23597808

Keshta, I., & Odeh, A. (2021). Security and privacy of electronic health records: Concerns and challenges. *Egyptian Informatics Journal*, *22*(2), 177–183. DOI: 10.1016/j.eij.2020.07.003

Keystride. (2024). *Transforming healthcare through IoMT firmware development. Keystride.* https://www.keystride.com/blog/transforming-healthcare-through-iomt-firmware-development/

Khukhlaev, O., Novikova, I., & Chernaya, A. (2022). Interpersonal Mindfulness, Intergroup Anxiety, and Intercultural Communication Effectiveness Among International Students Studying in Russia. *Frontiers in Psychology*, *13*, 841361. Advance online publication. DOI: 10.3389/fpsyg.2022.841361

Kinyua, J., & Awuah, L. (2021). AI/ML in Security Orchestration, Automation and Response: Future Research Directions. *Intelligent Automation & Soft Computing*, *28*(2), 527–545. DOI: 10.32604/iasc.2021.016240

Kioskli, K., Fotis, T., Nifakos, S., & Mouratidis, H. (2023). The importance of conceptualising the human-centric approach in maintaining and promoting cybersecurity-hygiene in healthcare 4.0. *Applied Sciences (Basel, Switzerland)*, *13*(6), 3410. DOI: 10.3390/app13063410

Klein, M. (2025). NOT OFF-LIMITS: AN EMPIRICAL STUDY OF COVID-19 CYBERSECURITY.

Klimburg-Witjes, N., & Wentland, A. (2021). Hacking humans? Social engineering and the construction of the "deficient user" in cybersecurity discourses. *Science, Technology & Human Values*, *46*(6), 1316–1339. DOI: 10.1177/0162243921992844

Klinghofer, B. (2022). *Introducing Microsoft Defender for Endpoint plan 1*. Retrieved from https://techcommunity.microsoft.com/t5/microsoft-defender-for-endpoint/introducing-microsoft-defender-for-endpoint-plan-1/ba-p/2636641

Kolbasuk, M. (2022). Healthcare data breaches: CaptureRx and MedNetworx case studies. *Healthcare IT Security Journal*, *28*(4), 55–63.

Kotelchuck, D. (1994). Designing an effective osha compliance program by Ilise Levy Feitshans, JD. Volume 1 in Corporate Compliance Series, 1993, Clark, Boardman, Callaghan, Deerfield, IL. *American Journal of Industrial Medicine*, *26*(5), 717–718. DOI: 10.1002/ajim.4700260514

Kotte, D., Venkatesh, R., Satish Kumar, B., Rao, U., & Kshatra, P. (2020). Analysis of data breaches and its impact on organizations. *International Journal of Emerging Trends in Engineering Research*, *8*(10), 6989–6994. DOI: 10.30534/ijeter/2020/588102020

Kotter, J. P. (1996). *Leading Change*. Harvard Business School Press.

KPMG. (2025). *Healthcare – Cybersecurity considerations 2025*. https://kpmg.com/xx/en/our-insights/ai-and-technology/cybersecurity-considerations-2025/healthcare.html

Kuhlmann, S., & Heuberger, M. (2021). Digital transformation going local: Implementation, impacts and constraints from a German perspective. *Public Money & Management*, *43*(3), 1–9. DOI: 10.1080/09540962.2021.1939584

Kummer, T. F., & Mendling, J. (2021). The effect of risk representation using colors and symbols in business process models on operational risk management performance. *Journal of the Association for Information Systems*, *22*(3), 649–694. DOI: 10.17705/1jais.00676

Lalanne, L., Lutz, P. E., & Paille, F. (2017). Acute impact of caffeinated alcoholic beverages on cognition: A systematic review. *Progress in Neuro-Psychopharmacology & Biological Psychiatry*, *76*, 188–194. DOI: 10.1016/j.pnpbp.2017.03.007 PMID: 28330787

Lam, J. (2017). *Implementing Risk Management: From Methods to Application*. Wiley. DOI: 10.1002/9781118922415

Landoll, D. (2021). *The security risk assessment handbook: A complete guide for performing security risk assessments*. CRC press. DOI: 10.1201/9781003090441

Latour, B. (1987). *Science in action: How to follow scientists and engineers through society*. Harvard University Press.

Latour, B. (1996). On actor-network theory: A few clarifications. *Soziale Welt*, *47*(4), 369–381. https://www.jstor.org/stable/40878163

Laude, J. R., & Fillmore, M. T. (2016). Drivers who self-estimate lower blood alcohol concentrations are riskier drivers after drinking. *Psychopharmacology*, *233*(8), 1387–1394. DOI: 10.1007/s00213-016-4233-x PMID: 26861796

Lazarus, S., Chiang, M., & Button, M. (2025). Assessing Human Trafficking and Cybercrime Intersections Through Survivor Narratives. *Deviant Behavior*, •••, 1–18. DOI: 10.1080/01639625.2025.2470402

Lederer, L. J., & Wetzel, C. A. (2014). The health consequences of sex trafficking and their implications for identifying victims in healthcare facilities. *Annals of Health Law, 23*, 61–91. https://heinonline-org.ezp.slu.edu/HOL/Page?collection=journals&handle=hein.journals/anohl23&id=68&men_tab=srchresults

Leeth, J. (2000). *Workplace Safety Policy: Past, Present, and Future*. SSRN Electronic Journal; Elsevier BV. https://www.academia.edu/102794788/Workplace_Safety_Policy_Past_Present_and_Future

Leung, M. (n.d.). The beginning of probability and statistics. University of Texas at El Paso, Department of Mathematical Sciences. https://www.math.utep.edu/faculty/mleung/probabilityandstatistics/beg.html

Li, A., & Sun, Y. (2024, July). A Data-Driven Driving Under the Influence (DUI) Detection, Notification and Prevention System Using Artificial Intelligence and Internet-Of-Things (IoT). In *World Congress in Computer Science, Computer Engineering & Applied Computing* (pp. 73-87). Cham: Springer Nature Switzerland.

Lindgren, I., Madsen, C. Ø., Hofmann, S., & Melin, U. (2019). Close encounters of the digital kind: A research agenda for the digitalization of public services. *Government Information Quarterly, 36*(3), 427–436. DOI: 10.1016/j.giq.2019.03.002

Lindholm, M., Reiman, A., & Väyrynen, S. (2020). On Future Occupational Safety and Health Challenges. *International Journal of Occupational and Environmental Safety, 4*(1), 108–127. DOI: 10.24840/2184-0954_004.001_0009

Linkov, I., Trump, B. D., Poinsatte-Jones, K., & Florin, M.-V. (2019). Governance strategies for a sustainable digital world. *Sustainability, 11*(3), 705. DOI: 10.3390/su11030705

Li, R. Y. M., & Ng, P. L. (2017) "Wearable robotics and construction workers safety and health". In: 8th *International Conference on Applied Human Factors and Ergonomics*, Los Angeles.

Li, S. (2024). Comparative analysis of predicting malware attack trends in cyber supply chain using multiple classification models. *IEEE Access : Practical Innovations, Open Solutions*, •••, 1–1. DOI: 10.1109/ACCESS.2024.3471802

Louisot, J. P. (2024). Managing Risk to Reputation. In *Enterprise Risk Management in Today's World: A Current and Futuristic View of the Complexity, Resilience, Responsibility and Tools in ERM, Part B* (pp. 105-115). Emerald Publishing Limited. DOI: 10.1108/978-1-83608-392-420241009

Low, J., Mansfield, K. E., & Chaturvedi, N. (2022). Secondary analysis of qualitative data. *BMJ (Clinical Research Ed.), 376*, e068270.

Makajić-Nikolić, D. (2023). ISO 31000: Risk Management Guidelines. In *Encyclopedia of Sustainable Management* (pp. 2078–2080). Springer International Publishing. DOI: 10.1007/978-3-031-25984-5_314

Mann, Z. A. (2024, July). Urgency in cybersecurity risk management: toward a solid theory. In *2024 IEEE 37th Computer Security Foundations Symposium (CSF)* (pp. 651-664). IEEE. DOI: 10.1109/CSF61375.2024.00051

Mark & Spark Solutions. (2024). *Medical batteries market to reach USD 3,539M by 2030.* https://marksparksolutions.com/reports/medical-batteries-market-2024-2030

Masud, N., Bassam, A. A., Sobhan, A., & Sourav, M. T. I. (2025). Data-driven solutions for human trafficking: Detection and impact analysis using machine learning. In *2025 International Conference on Electrical, Computer and Communication Engineering (ECCE)* (pp. 1-6). IEEE. DOI: 10.1109/ECCE64574.2025.11014018

Mathieu, P., & Miermont, G. (2023). Blaise Pascal et Pierre de Fermat, géomètres du hasard. *Courrier Blaise Pascal*, *45*, 53–89. DOI: 10.4000/cbp.1058

McGinty, E. E., Tung, G., Shulman-Laniel, J., Hardy, R., Rutkow, L., Frattaroli, S., & Vernick, J. S. (2017). Ignition interlock laws: Effects on fatal motor vehicle crashes, 1982–2013. *American Journal of Preventive Medicine*, *52*(4), 417–423. DOI: 10.1016/j.amepre.2016.10.043 PMID: 28065516

McKnight, A. J., & Voas, R. B. (1991). The effect of license suspension upon DWI recidivism. *Alcohol, Drugs, and Driving*, *7*, 43–54.

McLennan, M. (2022). The global risks report 2022 17th edition. Coligny, Switzerland: World Economic Forum.

McLester, Q., & Burrell, D. N. (2024). Healthcare Technologies to Address Driving Under the Influence (DUI) of Marijuana. In E. Lewis (Ed.), *Evolution of Cross-Sector Cyber Intelligent Markets* (pp. 158-168). IGI Global Scientific Publishing. DOI: 10.4018/979-8-3693-1970-3.ch008

McLester, Q. (2024). Impaired Driving as a Public Health Concern and Healthcare Technology Approaches. In Burrell, D. (Ed.), *Innovations, Securities, and Case Studies Across Healthcare, Business, and Technology* (pp. 377–395). IGI Global Scientific Publishing., DOI: 10.4018/979-8-3693-1906-2.ch020

Menzenski, J., Baumgartner, D. M., Cheng, J., Diffenderfer, P. A., Helleberg, J., Mykityshyn, A., & Wilkins, S. A. (2023). Airspace user–air traffic control information exchange using mobile devices to enhance the future info-centric national airspace system. *Proceedings of the 42nd IEEE/AIAA Digital Avionics Systems Conference (DASC)*. IEEE. DOI: 10.1109/DASC58513.2023.10311312

Mergel, I., Edelmann, N., & Haug, N. (2019). Defining digital transformation: Results from expert interviews. *Government Information Quarterly, 36*(4), 101385. DOI: 10.1016/j.giq.2019.06.002

Meyer, B. H., Prescott, B., & Sheng, X. S. (2022). The impact of the COVID-19 pandemic on business expectations. *International Journal of Forecasting, 38*(2), 529–544. DOI: 10.1016/j.ijforecast.2021.02.009 PMID: 35185229

Michaels, D., & Barab, J. (2020). The Occupational Safety and Health Administration at 50: Protecting Workers in a Changing Economy. *American Journal of Public Health, 110*(5), 631–635. DOI: 10.2105/AJPH.2020.305597

Microsoft Security Response Center. (2021). *Microsoft bug bounty programs year in review: $13.6M in rewards.* Retrieved from https://msrc-blog.microsoft.com/2021/07/08/microsoft-bug-bounty-programs-year-in-review-13-6m-in-rewards/

Microsoft. (n.d.). *US healthcare at risk: Strengthening resiliency against ransomware attacks.* https://www.microsoft.com/en-us/security/security-insider/emerging-threats/us-

Miles, M. B., Huberman, A. M., & Saldaña, J. (2014). *Qualitative data analysis: A methods sourcebook* (3rd ed.). Sage.

Miller, R. (2021). 2021 *Cyberrisk landscape. Risk Management Magazine.* Retrieved from https://www.rmmagazine.com/articles/article/2021/02/01/-2021-Cyberrisk-Landscape-#:~:text=Unfortunately%2C%20this%20appears%20unlikely%20to,data%20exposure%20or%20system%20disruption

Miri, D. H., & Macke, J. (2022). Gamification, motivation, and engagement at work: A qualitative multiple case study. *European Business Review, 34*(2), 263–276. DOI: 10.1108/EBR-04-2020-0106

Mishra, V. (2015). *Combating human trafficking: Gaps in policy and law.* SAGE Publications India. DOI: 10.4135/9789354797965

Mizrak, K. C. (2024). Crisis management and risk mitigation: Strategies for effective response and resilience. *Trends, challenges, and practices in contemporary strategic management*, 254-278.

Mohn, E. (2023). Stuxnet: *A brief history of the cyber weapon.* EBSCO. https://www.ebsco.com/research-starters/computer-science/stuxnet

Möller, D. P. (2023). NIST cybersecurity framework and MITRE cybersecurity criteria. In *Guide to Cybersecurity in Digital Transformation: Trends, Methods, Technologies, Applications and Best Practices* (pp. 231–271). Springer Nature Switzerland. DOI: 10.1007/978-3-031-26845-8_5

Moyo, T. J., Gunes, O., & Jirotka, M. D. (2025). Investigating human trafficking recruitment online: A study of fraudulent job offers on social media platforms. *Proceedings of the ACM on Human-Computer Interaction*, *9*(2), 1–31. DOI: 10.1145/3711016

Muller, S. R., & Burrell, D. N. (2022). Social Cybersecurity and Human Behavior. [IJHIoT]. *International Journal of Hyperconnectivity and the Internet of Things*, *6*(1), 1–13. DOI: 10.4018/IJHIoT.305228

Mumford, E. (2006). The story of socio-technical design: Reflections on its successes, failures and potential. *Information Systems Journal*, *16*(4), 317–342. DOI: 10.1111/j.1365-2575.2006.00221.x

Mustak, M., Salminen, J., Mäntymäki, M., Rahman, A., & Dwivedi, Y. K. (2023). Deepfakes: Deceptions, mitigations, and opportunities. *Journal of Business Research*, *154*, 113368. DOI: 10.1016/j.jbusres.2022.113368

Mwita, K. M. (2022). Strengths and weaknesses of qualitative research in social science studies. *International Journal of Research in Business and Social Science*, *11*(6), 618–625. DOI: 10.20525/ijrbs.v11i6.1920

Naim, A. (2022). Role of artificial intelligence in business risk management. *American Journal of Business Management, Economics, and Banking*, *1*, 55–66.

Narula, R. (2024). From the editor: On writing a perspectives article — what they are, what they are not (and what they should be). *Journal of International Business Policy, 7*(2), 253–259. DOI: 10.1057/s42214-024-00191-6

National Highway Traffic Safety Administration. (2017). Designated Driver Safe Ride Program. Designated Driver/ www.nhtsa.dot.gov/people/injury/alcohol/

National Institute of Standards and Technology. (2020). *Framework for improving critical infrastructure cybersecurity* (Version 1.1). U.S. Department of Commerce. DOI: 10.6028/NIST.CSWP.04162018

National Institute of Standards and Technology. (2024). *Cybersecurity framework version 2.0.* U.S. Department of Commerce. https://www.nist.gov/cyberframework

National Institute of Standards and Technology. (2024). *NVD - CVE-2024-1708 detail.* Retrieved October 18, 2025, from https://nvd.nist.gov/vuln/detail/cve-2024-1708

Neprash, H. T., Dameff, C., & Tully, J. (2024). Cybersecurity lessons from the Change Healthcare attack. *JAMA Internal Medicine, 184*(11), 1283–1284. DOI: 10.1001/jamainternmed.2024.3162 PMID: 39250110

Neprash, H. T., McGlave, C. C., Cross, D. A., Virnig, B. A., Puskarich, M. A., Huling, J. D., Rozenshtein, A. Z., & Nikpay, S. S. (2022). Trends in Ransomware Attacks on US Hospitals, Clinics, and Other Health Care Delivery Organizations, 2016-2021. *JAMA Health Forum, 3*(12), e224873. DOI: 10.1001/jamahealthforum.2022.4873 PMID: 36580326

Nerima, M., & Ralyté, J. (2021). Towards a digital maturity balance model for public organizations. In Cherfi, S., Perini, A., & Nurcan, S. (Eds.), *Research Challenges in Information Science. RCIS 2021. Lecture Notes in Business Information Processing* (Vol. 415). Springer., DOI: 10.1007/978-3-030-75018-3_20

Newton, P. J., Mulcahy, T. M., & Martin, S. E. (2008). *Finding victims of human trafficking.* National Opinion Research Center (NORC) at the University of Chicago (Grant No. 2007VTBX0001, U.S. Department of Justice, Office of Justice Programs, National Institute of Justice). https://citeseerx.ist.psu.edu/viewdoc/download?doi=10.1.1.218.2468&rep=rep1&type=pdf

Ng, K. C., Zhang, X., Thong, J. Y. L., & Tam, K. Y. (2021). Protecting against threats to information security: An attitudinal ambivalence perspective. *Journal of Management Information Systems, 38*(3), 732–764. DOI: 10.1080/07421222.2021.1962601

Niall, K. K. (2023). The Theory of Games of Chance. In *Johannes von Kries: Principles of the Probability Calculus: A Logical Investigation* (pp. 31–46). Springer International Publishing. DOI: 10.1007/978-3-031-36506-5_3

NIST. (2025). *NIST risk management framework.* NIST Computer Security Resource Center | CSRC. Retrieved October 26, 2025, from https://csrc.nist.gov/projects/risk-management?utm_source=chatgpt.com

NIST. (n.d.). *Guide for conducting risk assessments.* [PDF file]. https://nvlpubs.nist.gov/nistpubs/Legacy/SP/nistspecialpublication800-30r1.pdf

Nobles, C. (2018). Botching human factors in cybersecurity in business organizations. *HOLISTICA Journal of Business and Public Administration, 9*(3), 71-88. https://holisticajournal.ro/docs/1589fb80c59c854cabe168f3b7b8c1d7.pdf

Nobles, C. (2022). Stress, burnout, and security fatigue in cybersecurity: A human factors problem. *Holistica Journal of Business and Public Administration, 13*(1), 49-72. https://reference-global.com/download/article/10.2478/hjbpa-2022-0003.pdf

Nobles, C., & Burrell, D. (2024). Exploring the variability of human factors definitions in cybersecurity literature.

Nobles, C., Rangarajan, A., & Burrell, D. N. (2025). Human Factors Engineering-as-a-Service in Cybersecurity. In *New Horizons in Leadership: Inclusive Explorations in Health, Technology, and Education* (pp. 315-342). IGI Global Scientific Publishing. https://www.igi-global.com/chapter/human-factors-engineering-as-a-service-in-cybersecurity/371041

Odetayo, T., & Haruna, A. D. (2024). Assessment of aviation accident datasets in severity prediction through artificial intelligence. *Journal of Air Transport Management, 115*, 102531. Advance online publication. DOI: 10.1016/j.jairtraman.2023.102531

OECD (2019). *Digital government review of Sweden: Towards a data-driven public sector*. OECD Digital Government Studies. OECD Publishing. DOI: 10.1787/4daf932b-en

OECD. (2016). *Digital government strategies for transforming public services in the welfare areas*. OECD Publishing. Retrieved from https://www.oecd.org/gov/digital-government/Digital-Government-Strategies-Welfare-Service.pdf

OECD. (2020). *Digital government index: 2019 Results*. OECD Public Governance Policy Papers, No. 03. OECD Publishing. DOI: 10.1787/14e1c5e8-en-fr

OECD. (2023). *Digital government index*. Retrieved from https://www.oecd.org/en/publications/2023-oecd-digital-government-index_1a89ed5e-en.html

Ogundipe, O., & Aweto, T. (2024). The shaky foundation of global technology: A case study of the 2024 CrowdStrike outage. *International Journal of Multidisciplinary Research and Growth Evaluation, 5*(5), 106–108.

Ohm, M., Plate, H., Sykosch, A., & Meier, M. (2020). Backstabber's knife collection: A review of open source software supply chain attacks. *Lecture Notes in Computer Science, 12223*, 23–43. DOI: 10.1007/978-3-030-52683-2_2

Okafor, C., Kolade, A., Onunka, T., Daraojimba, C., Eyo-Udo, N., & Omotosho, A. (2023). Mitigating Cybersecurity Risks in the U.S. Healthcare Sector [Review of Mitigating Cybersecurity Risks in the U.S. Healthcare Sector]. *International Journal of Innovation and Scientific Research, 10*(9), 177–194. DOI: 10.51244/IJRSI

Olaganathan, R. (2024). Human factors in aviation maintenance: Understanding errors, management, and technological trends. *Global Journal of Engineering and Technology Advances, 18*(2), 92–101. DOI: 10.30574/gjeta.2024.18.2.0021

Olaniyi, O. O., & Omubo, D. S. (2023). The importance of COSO framework compliance in information technology auditing and enterprise resource management. *International Journal of Innovative Research and Development, 12*(4).

Olawoye, S. (2025). *Malware threats and resilience in healthcare IT systems* [Doctoral dissertation, Capitol Technology University]. ProQuest Dissertations Publishing.

Olugbemiga, E. O., Jang, Y., Song, K., & Ahn, J. (2023). Impact of COVID-19 on Social and Psychological Well-Being of Workers in Construction Projects: Comparative Analysis of Managers and Laborers. *Buildings (Basel, Switzerland), 13*(8), 1902. DOI: 10.3390/buildings13081902

Oram, S., Abas, M., Bick, D., Boyle, A., French, R., Jakobowitz, S., Khondoker, M., Stanley, N., Trevillion, K., Howard, L., & Zimmerman, C. (2016). Human trafficking and health: A survey of male and female survivors in England. *American Journal of Public Health, 106*(6), 1073–1078. DOI: 10.2105/AJPH.2016.303095 PMID: 27077341

Orsini, N. F., Hassoon, A., De La Garza, R., Torres, R., Brenner, L. A., Palmisano, J., & Heller, M. (2022). *A systems approach to preparing for cybersecurity incidents in healthcare: A conceptual framework.* https://pmc.ncbi.nlm.nih.gov/articles/PMC9403058/

Osama, O. F., Rahman, M. M., & Kshetri, N. (2025). healthMLsec: Machine learning-based vulnerability assessment in health systems: A framework for enhancing cybersecurity and patient data [Preprint]. *Preprints.org.* DOI: 10.20944/preprints202502.2165.v1

OSHA. (2023). *Commonly used statistics | Occupational Safety and Health Administration.* Osha.gov; United States Department of Labor. https://www.osha.gov/data/commonstats

Ovington, T. (2018, December 16). *How to use Kotter's 8-step model: The key to change success.* The Change Management Blog; Change Management. https://change.walkme.com/kotters-8-step-change-model/

Ozdemir, D., Sharma, M., Dhir, A., & Daim, T. (2022). Supply chain resilience during the COVID-19 pandemic. *Technology in Society, 68,* 101847. DOI: 10.1016/j.techsoc.2021.101847 PMID: 35075312

Ozturk, S., Ayanoğlu, F. B., Parmaksiz, M., Elçin, A. E., & Elçin, Y. M. (2020). Clinical and surgical aspects of medical materials' biocompatibility. *Handbook of Biomaterials Biocompatibility, 219–250.* DOI: 10.1016/B978-0-08-102967-1.00012-8

Palatty, N. J. (2022, December 6). 80+ Healthcare data breach statistics 2023. *Astra Security Blog*. https://www.getastra.com/blog/security-audit/healthcare-data-breach-statistics/

Palo Alto Networks. (2025). *Unit 42 Global Incident Response Report*. https://www.paloaltonetworks.com/resources/research/unit-42-incident-response-report

Parincu, Z. (2022). Interpersonal Communication: Definition, Examples, & Skills. The Berkeley Well-Being Institute. https://www.berkeleywellbeing.com/interpersonal-communication.html

Parker, J. (2023). *80% of ransomware attacks now use artificial intelligence. MIT Sloan School of Management*. https://mitsloan.mit.edu/ideas-made-to-matter/80-ransomware-attacks-now-use-artificial-intelligence

Parkin, R. (2021). What has time to do with risk? A preliminary communication. *New Zealand Journal of Employment Relations*, *46*(2), 26–30. DOI: 10.24135/nzjer.v46i2.61

Pascal, B. (2024). *Blaise Pascal Thoughts*. Lebooks Editora.

Pasmore, W., Winby, S., Mohrman, S. A., & Vanasse, R. (2019). Reflections: Sociotechnical systems design and organization change. *Journal of Change Management*, *19*(2), 67–85. DOI: 10.1080/14697017.2018.1553761

Patacas, J. Kassem, M., & Dawood, N. (2014, November 10). *Construction health and safety training: the utilisation of 4D enabled serious games*. Academia.edu. https://www.academia.edu/9222629/Construction_health_and_safety_training_the_utilisation_of_4D_enabled_serious_games

Patrick, M. E., Schulenberg, J. E., Martz, M. E., Maggs, J. L., O'Malley, P. M., & Johnston, L. D. (2013). Extreme binge drinking among 12th-grade students in the United States: Prevalence and predictors. *JAMA Pediatrics*, *167*(11), 1019–1025. DOI: 10.1001/jamapediatrics.2013.2392 PMID: 24042318

Paul, M. (2021). After-Action Reviews.

Petosa, N. H. & J. (2022, November). *Workplace Injuries and Job Requirements for Construction Laborers: Spotlight on Statistics: U.S. Bureau of Labor Statistics*. Www.bls.gov. https://www.bls.gov/spotlight/2022/workplace-injuries-and-job-requirements-for-construction-laborers/home.htm

Picus Security. (2025). *What is attack path visualization (APV) in cybersecurity? Picus Security*. https://www.picussecurity.com/resource/glossary/what-is-attack-path-visualization

Pinder, C. C. (2008). *Work motivation in organizational behavior*. Psychology Press., DOI: 10.4324/9781315734606

Pollini, A., Callari, T. C., Tedeschi, A., Ruscio, D., Save, L., Chiarugi, F., & Guerri, D. (2022). Leveraging human factors in cybersecurity: An integrated methodological approach. *Cognition Technology and Work*, *24*(2), 371–390. https://link.springer.com/article/10.1007/s10111-021-00683-y. DOI: 10.1007/s10111-021-00683-y PMID: 34149309

Pondurance. (2025, June 25). *Practical strategies for vendor risk management in healthcare. Pondurance.com.* https://www.pondurance.com/blog/practical-strategies-for-vendor-risk-management-in-healthcare

Ponemon Institute. (2022). *Cost of a data breach report.* IBM Security. https://www.ibm.com/reports/data-breach

Prakash, D. S. (2025). Zero-day Vulnerabilities: An In-depth Analysis.

Prasad, G., Gujjar, P., Naveen Kumar, H. N., Anand Kumar, M., & Chandrappa, S. (2023). Advances of cyber security in the healthcare domain for analyzing data. In *Advances in Information Security, Privacy, and Ethics* (pp. 1–14). IGI Global.

Preethi, K. (2023). An intelligent online drunk driving detection system based on multi-sensor fusion technology. *International Journal of Management Research and Reviews*, *13*(2), 7–11.

Priambodo, D. F., Pramadi, Y. R., Briliyant, O. C., Hasbi, M., & Yahya, M. A. (2022). Observe-Orient-Decide-Act (OODA) for cyber security education. *International Journal of Advanced Computer Science and Applications*, *13*(10). Advance online publication. DOI: 10.14569/IJACSA.2022.0131031

Protiviti & North Carolina State University. (2025). *Executive perspectives on top risks for 2025 and 2034: Key issues being discussed in the boardroom and C-suite.* Protiviti. https://www.protiviti.com/sites/default/files/2025-02/nc-state-protiviti-2025-top-risks-survey-global.pdf

Przetacznik, S. (2022). The evolution of risk management. *Zeszyty Naukowe Małopolskiej Wyższej Szkoły Ekonomicznej w Tarnowie*, *53*(1-2), 95–107.

Pujawan, I. N., & Bah, A. U. (2022, January). Supply chains under COVID-19 disruptions: Literature review and research agenda. In *Supply chain forum* [). Taylor & Francis.]. *International Journal (Toronto, Ont.)*, *23*(1), 81–95.

PuppyGraph. (2025). *Visualizing cyber threats: An introduction to attack graphs. PuppyGraph.* https://www.puppygraph.com/blog/attack-graph

Rabb, W. (2025, June). Aflac Hit With Class Action Over Data Breach. Insurance Journal. https://www.insurancejournal.com/news/national/2025/06/25/829012.htm

Radware. (2022). *Supply chain attack trends and mitigation strategies in healthcare*. Radware Security Reports.

Ramadan, R. A., Aboshosha, B. W., Alshudukhi, J. S., Alzahrani, A. J., El-Sayed, A., & Dessouky, M. M. (2021). Cybersecurity and countermeasures at the time of pandemic. *Journal of Advanced Transportation, 2021*, 1–19. DOI: 10.1155/2021/6627264

Ramamoorti, S., Wanserski, J. H., & Stover, R. (2019). The velocity of risk. *Internal Auditor, 76*(2).

Ramamoorti, S., Baskin, D. L.Jr, Epstein, B. J., & Wanserski, J. (2017). Managing risk at the speed of change: A new risk vocabulary and a call to the profession. *The CPA Journal*, *87*(6), 6–9.

Ramluckan, T., Van Niekerk, B., & Martins, I. (n.d.). A change management perspective to implementing a cyber security culture. *In ECCWS 2020 20th European Conference on Cyber Warfare and Security* (, 442-448. https://books.google.com/books?hl=en&lr=&id=lB4EEAAAQBAJ&oi=fnd&pg=PA442&dq=Ramluckan,+T.,+Van+Niekerk,+B.,+%26+Martins,+I.+(n.d.).+A+change+management+perspective+to+implementing+a+cyber+security+culture.+In+ECCWS+2020+20th+European+Conference+on+Cyber+Warfare+and+Security+(,+442-448.&ots=zhgyJUSTzM&sig=QBhDAsQ88v3IeMGZvStJuqI-1eqQ#v=onepage&q&f=false

Rauf, U., Mohsen, F., & Wei, Z. (2023). A Taxonomic Classification of Insider Threats: Existing Techniques, Future Directions & Recommendations. *Journal of Cyber Security and Mobility*, 221-252. https://ieeexplore.ieee.org/abstract/document/10963763

Ravichandran, P., Machireddy, J. R., & Rachakatla, S. K. (2022). AI-Enhanced data analytics for real-time business intelligence: Applications and challenges. *Journal of AI in Healthcare and Medicine*, *2*(2), 168–195.

Rawat, U. Abhishek, Singh, H., & Ur Rehman, A. (2024). Cybersecurity Challenges and Risks in AGI Development and Deployment. In *Artificial General Intelligence (AGI) Security: Smart Applications and Sustainable Technologies* (pp. 291-314). Singapore: Springer Nature Singapore.

Read, G. J., Shorrock, S., Walker, G. H., & Salmon, P. M. (2021). State of science: Evolving perspectives on 'human error'. *Ergonomics*, *64*(9), 1091–1114. https://www.tandfonline.com/action/showCopyRight?scroll=top&doi=10.1080%2F00140139.2021.1953615. DOI: 10.1080/00140139.2021.1953615 PMID: 34243698

Reeves, A., Delfabbro, P., & Calic, D. (2021). Encouraging Employee Engagement With Cybersecurity: How to Tackle Cyber Fatigue. *SAGE Open*, *11*(1), 215824402110000. DOI: 10.1177/21582440211000049

Rehm, J., Lachenmeier, D. W., Llopis, E. J., Imtiaz, S., & Anderson, P. (2016). Evidence of reducing ethanol content in beverages to reduce harmful use of alcohol. *The Lancet. Gastroenterology & Hepatology*, *1*(1), 78–83. DOI: 10.1016/S2468-1253(16)30013-9 PMID: 28404116

Renn, O., Laubichler, M., Lucas, K., Kröger, W., Schanze, J., Scholz, R. W., & Schweizer, P. J. (2022). Systemic risks from different perspectives. *Risk Analysis*, *42*(9), 1902–1920. DOI: 10.1111/risa.13657 PMID: 33331037

Renteria, C., Gil-Garcia, J. R., & Pardo, T. A. (2019). Toward an enabler-based digital government maturity framework: A Preliminary proposal based on theories of change. *In Proceedings of the 12th International Conference on Theory and Practice of Electronic Governanc*e (*ICEGOV2019), Melbourne, VIC, Australia, April 3-5, 2019*, 10 pages. https://doi.org/DOI: 10.1145/3326365.33264190

Resilient, X. (n.d.). *Common third-party risk management challenges and solutions.* Retrieved from https://www.resilientx.com/blog/common-third-party-risk-management-challenges

Reyna, A., Martín, C., Chen, J., Soler, E., & Díaz, M. (2018). On blockchain and its integration with IoT. Challenges and opportunities. *Future Generation Computer Systems*, *88*, 173–190. DOI: 10.1016/j.future.2018.05.046

Rhoades, E., & Jernigan, D. H. (2013). Risky messages in alcohol advertising, 2003–2007: Results from content analysis. *The Journal of Adolescent Health*, *52*(1), 116–121. DOI: 10.1016/j.jadohealth.2012.04.013 PMID: 23260844

Rippling. (2025). *Agentic AI security: A guide to threats, risks & best practices. Rippling Blog.* https://www.rippling.com/blog/agentic-ai-security

Risk Management Association (RMA). (2025). *A playbook for third-party exits.* Retrieved from https://www.rmahq.org/blogs/2025/a-playbook-for-third-party-exits/

Roach, L. (2021, May 11). Embedding speed and agility into strategy execution. *Harvard Business Review.* https://hbr.org/sponsored/2021/05/embedding-speed-and-agility-into-strategy-execution

Rose, S., Borchert, O., Mitchell, S., & Connelly, S. (2020). *Zero trust architecture.* NIST Computer Security Resource Center | CSRC. https://csrc.nist.gov/pubs/sp/800/207/final

RosmarlindaRosl & Almuallimi. (2024). A Theoretical Framework Examining The Impact Of Strategic Agility And Strategic Resilience On Organizational Performance, *Educational Administration. Theory into Practice*, *30*(6), 1835–1845. DOI: 10.53555/kuey.v30i6.5596

Roy, S., & Sridhar, B. (2016). Cyber-threat assessment for the air traffic management system: A network controls approach. *AIAA Aviation and Aeronautics Forum and Exposition.* AIAA. https://ntrs.nasa.gov/citations/20180000393

Rudmark, D., & Andersson, M. (2021). Feedback loops in open data ecosystems. *IEEE Software*, *1*(39), 43–47.

Ryzhakova, G., Reznik, N., Lazebnyk, V., Ivanova, T., Fedorov, V., & Omelianenko, M. (2024, November). Reputation Management in the Age of Information Transparency. In *International Conference on Business and Technology* (pp. 167-177). Cham: Springer Nature Switzerland.

Sacks, R., Perlman, A., & Barak, R. (2013). Construction safety training using immersive virtual reality. *Construction Management and Economics*, *31*(9), 1005–1017. DOI: 10.1080/01446193.2013.828844

Saeed, Y. S.SAEED. (2017). SAFETY MANAGEMENT IN CONSTRUCTION PROJECTS. *The Journal of the University of Duhok*, *20*(1), 546–560. DOI: 10.26682/sjuod.2017.20.1.48

Salihu, A., & Dervishi, R. (2024, October). Evaluating the Impact of Risk Management Frameworks on IT Audits: A Comparative Analysis of COSO, COBIT, ISO/IEC 27001, and NIST CSF. In *2024 International Conference on Electrical, Communication and Computer Engineering (ICECCE)* (pp. 1-8). IEEE. DOI: 10.1109/ICECCE63537.2024.10823548

Salo, A., Tosoni, E., Roponen, J., & Bunn, D. W. (2022). Using cross-impact analysis for probabilistic risk assessment. *Futures & Foresight Science*, *4*(2), e2103. DOI: 10.1002/ffo2.103

Salvi, S. S. (2021). Safety Management and Accident Prevention. *International Journal for Research in Applied Science and Engineering Technology*, *9*(5), 539–543. DOI: 10.22214/ijraset.2021.34163

Sari, I. P., Khairani, L., & Ginting, R. (2023). Enhancing Disaster Resilience: Evaluating the Implementation of an Early Warning System through Table Top Exercises. *PERSPEKTIF*, *12*(4), 1253–1260. DOI: 10.31289/perspektif.v12i4.10341

Schulenberg, J. E., Johnston, L. D., O'Malley, P. M., Bachman, J. G., Miech, R. A., & Patrick, M. E. (2017). *Monitoring the future: National survey results on drug use, 1975–2016 (Vol. 2, College students and adults ages 19–55).* Institute for Social Research, University of Michigan.

SecurityInfoWatch. (2025). *Autonomous and unchecked: The mounting risks of agentic AI. SecurityInfoWatch.* https://www.securityinfowatch.com/ai/article/55316293/autonomous-and-unchecked-the-mounting-risks-of-agentic-ai

Seh, A. H., Zarour, M., Alenezi, M., Sarkar, A. K., Agrawal, A., Kumar, R., & Ahmad Khan, R. (2020). Healthcare data breaches: Insights and implications. *Health Care*, *8*(2), 133. DOI: 10.3390/healthcare8020133 PMID: 32414183

Seo, H. J., Park, G. M., Son, M., & Hong, A.-J. (2021). Establishment of Virtual-Reality-Based Safety Education and Training System for Safety Engagement. *Education Sciences*, *11*(12), 786. DOI: 10.3390/educsci11120786

Servidio, J. S., & Taylor, R. D. (2015). Safe and Sound: Cybersecurity for Community Banks. *Journal of Taxation & Regulation of Financial Institutions*, *28*(4). https://www.civicresearchinstitute.com/online/PDF/Cybersecurity%20for%20Community%20Banks.pdf

Sethi, D., & Seth, M. (2009). Interpersonal communication: Lifeblood of an organization. *The IUP Journal of Soft Skills*, *III*(3&4), 32–40. https://www.researchgate.net/profile/Deepa_Sethi/publication/228271402_Interpersonal_Communication_Lifeblood_of_an_Organization/links/55af387808ae98e661a6fd03/Interpersonal-Communication-Lifeblood-of-an-Organization.pdf

Sève, B., & Wolfe, C. (2024). Playing with Chance. *Figures of Chance I: Chance in Literature and the Arts (16th–21st Centuries).*

Shacklett, M. (2021). *What is an attack vector?* Retrieved from https://www.techtarget.com/searchsecurity/definition/attack-vector

Shields, D., Funk, C., & Bredemeier, B. L. (2015). Predictors of moral disengagement in sport. *Journal of Sport & Exercise Psychology*, *37*(6), 646–658. DOI: 10.1123/jsep.2015-0110 PMID: 26866772

Shringi, A., Arashpour, M., Golafshani, E. M., Rajabifard, A., Dwyer, T., & Li, H. (2022). Efficiency of VR-Based Safety Training for Construction Equipment: Hazard Recognition in Heavy Machinery Operations. *Buildings (Basel, Switzerland), 12*(12), 2084. DOI: 10.3390/buildings12122084

Silbey, S. (1999). Book Reviews: Cultural *Software: A Theory of Ideology*. J. M. Balkin. New Haven, Conn.: Yale University Press, 1998. Pp. xii+335. $35.00. *American Journal of Sociology, 105*(1), 252–254. DOI: 10.1086/210280

Smela, B., Toumi, M., Świerk, K., Francois, C., Biernikiewicz, M., Clay, E., & Boyer, L. (2023). Rapid literature review: Definition and methodology. *Journal of Market Access & Health Policy, 11*(1), 2241234. DOI: 10.1080/20016689.2023.2241234

Smith Law. (2025). *Healthcare cyberattacks are on the rise: Steps to safeguard your organization*. Smith Law. https://www.smithlaw.com/newsroom/publications/healthcare-cyberattacks-are-on-the-rise-steps-to-safeguard-your-organization

Smith, D. (2022). *Fraud and corruption: Cases and materials*. Springer Nature. https://link.springer.com/book/10.1007/978-3-031-10063-5

Smith, M. L. (2024, July 5). *Developing a conceptual framework: A step-by-step guide for researchers*. Blainy. https://blainy.com/conceptual-framework/

Smith, D. P. (2018). Population geography I: Human trafficking. *Progress in Human Geography, 42*(2), 297–308. https://doi-org.ezp.slu.edu/10.1177/0309132516685196. DOI: 10.1177/0309132516685196

Smith, P. J., & Baumann, E. (2020). Human-automation teaming: Unintended consequences of automation on user performance. *Proceedings of the IEEE International Conference on Human-Machine Systems,* 1–9. IEEE. DOI: 10.1109/DASC50938.2020.9256418

Sorlini, A., Maxia, L., Patrucco, M., & Pira, E. (2023). Occupational Safety and Health Improvements through Innovative Technologies in Underground Construction Sites: Main Trends and Some Case Histories. *Infrastructures, 8*(6), 104. DOI: 10.3390/infrastructures8060104

Sowby, R. B., Sela, L., & Salomons, E. (2025). Water System Cybersecurity after the Microsoft–CrowdStrike Disruption of July 2024. *Journal of Water Resources Planning and Management, 151*(3), 02525001. DOI: 10.1061/JWRMD5.WRENG-6828

Spector, P. E., & Fox, S. (2002). An emotion-centered model of voluntary work behavior: Some parallels between counterproductive work behavior and organizational citizenship behavior. *Human Resource Management Review, 12*(2), 269–292. DOI: 10.1016/S1053-4822(02)00049-9

Splunk. (n.d.). *The Internet of Medical Things (IoMT): A brief introduction. Splunk.* Retrieved from https://www.splunk.com/en_us/blog/learn/the-internet-of-medical-things-iomt.html

St. John, M. (2024, August 28). *Cybersecurity stats: facts and figures you should know.* Forbes https://www.forbes.com/sites/chuckbrooks/2024/06/05/alarming-cybersecurity-stats-what-you-need-to-know-in-2024/

Stachowiak, A., & Pawłyszyn, I. (2021). From Fragility through Agility to Resilience: The Role of Sustainable Improvement in Increasing Organizational Maturity. *Sustainability (Basel), 13*(9), 4991. DOI: 10.3390/su13094991

Stevens, R., Votipka, D., Dykstra, J., Tomlinson, F., Quartararo, E., Ahern, C., & Mazurek, M. L. (2022, April). How ready is your ready? assessing the usability of incident response playbook frameworks. In *Proceedings of the 2022 CHI Conference on Human Factors in Computing Systems* (pp. 1-18). DOI: 10.1145/3491102.3517559

Streck, P., & Meyer, M. H. (2025). Ransomware strikes a large healthcare provider. *Journal of Information Technology Case and Application Research, 27*(1), 28–58. DOI: 10.1080/15228053.2025.2477361

Stylianou, A., Xuan, H., Shende, M., Brandt, J., Souvenir, R., & Pless, R. (2019, January 26). *Hotels-50K: A Global Hotel Recognition Dataset.* ArXiv.org https://arxiv.org/abs/1901.11397

Sukhera, J. (2022). Narrative Reviews: Flexible, Rigorous, and Practical. *Journal of Graduate Medical Education, 14*(4), 414–417. DOI: 10.4300/JGME-D-22-00480.1

Sullivan, J. (2022*). Is TLS enough for HIPAA? HIPAA Vault.* https://www.hipaavault.com/resources/is-tls-enough-for-hipaa/

Sun, Y., Zhang, R., & Yu, H. (2018). Software supply chain attacks: Emerging threats and security measures. *ACM Computing Surveys, 50*(6), 1–31. DOI: 10.1145/3106741

Syner-G BioPharma Group. (2025). *Why human factors dictate the safety of medical devices.* https://synergbiopharma.com/human-factors-medical-devices/

Szakonyi, A. (2022). *Trafficking policy analysis using a multidisciplinary approach: Recommendations for US anti-trafficking policies* (29210298). [Doctoral dissertation, Saint Louis University]. ProQuest Dissertations & Theses Global. https://www.proquest.com/pqdtglobal/docview/2681205947

Szakonyi, A., Chellasamy, H., Vassilakos, A., & Dawson, M. (2021). Using technologies to uncover patterns in human trafficking. In S. Latifi (Ed.), *ITNG 2021 18th international conference on information technology - New generations: Advances in intelligent systems and computing, 1346* (pp. 497-502). Springer. DOI: 10.1007/978-3-030-70416-2_64

Tangi, L., Janssen, M., Benedetti, M., & Noci, G. (2020). Barriers and drivers of digital transformation in public organizations: Results from a survey in the Netherlands. *Lecture Notes in Computer Science, 12219*, 42–56. Advance online publication. DOI: 10.1007/978-3-030-57599-1_4

Tang, P. M., Koopman, J., Elfenbein, H. A., Zhang, J. H., De Cremer, D., Li, C. H., & Chan, E. T. (2022). Using robots at work during the COVID-19 crisis evokes passion decay: Evidence from field and experimental studies. *Applied Psychology, 71*(3), 881–911. DOI: 10.1111/apps.12386

Tarasenko, M. Y., Steinmeier, S. K. M., & Zelezinskii, A. L. (2024). MODERN RISK MANAGEMENT TECHNIQUES. *Экономический вектор, 4* (39), 113-120.

Targeted News Service. (2025, October 30). WATCH: Davids discusses impact of government shutdown on aviation safety, workforce. Retrieved from ProQuest database. https://www.proquest.com/wire-feeds/watch-davids-discusses-impact-government-shutdown/docview/3267096786/se-2

Taylor, L., Floridi, L., & van der Sloot, B. (2017). *Group privacy: New challenges of data technologies.* Springer., DOI: 10.1007/978-3-319-46608-8

Thach, T. N., Moon, H., Pham, H. D., Kwon, N., & Ahn, Y. (2024). Construction Safety Innovation and Barriers in Different Company Types and Sizes: A Survey in Vietnam. *KSCE Journal of Civil Engineering, 28*(8), 3057–3073. DOI: 10.1007/s12205-024-0779-z

Thakur, M. (2024). Cyber security threats and countermeasures in digital age. [JASE]. *Journal of Applied Science and Education, 4*(1), 1–20. https://jase.a2zjournals.com/index.php/ase/article/view/42

The HIPAA Guide. (2025). *New HIPAA regulations 2024-2025.* https://www.hipaaguide.net/new-hipaa-regulations/

Thornton, D. (2018). Developing a theory of dynamic risk. In *Dynamic Risk Factors* (pp. 137–149). Routledge.

Tin, D., Hata, R., Granholm, F., Ciottone, R. G., Staynings, R., & Ciottone, G. R. (2023). Cyberthreats: A primer for healthcare professionals. *The American Journal of Emergency Medicine, 68*, 179–185. Advance online publication. DOI: 10.1016/j.ajem.2023.04.001 PMID: 37061434

Tong, E., Zadeh, A., Jones, C., & Morency, L. (2017). Combating Human Trafficking with Deep Multimodal Models. *Proceedings of the 55th Annual Meeting of the Association for Computational Linguistics, 1.*, 1547–1556. DOI: 10.18653/v1/P17-1142

Torrence, R. (2021). *HHS warns of increasing zero-day attacks in healthcare.* Retrieved from https://www.fiercehealthcare.com/tech/hhs-warns-increasing-zero-day-attacks-healthcare

Tripp, T. M., & Bies, R. J. (2009). *Getting even: The truth about workplace revenge—and how to stop it.* John Wiley & Sons.

Truong, Q., Zalog, R., & Chang, B. (2021). Scalable Detection and Drill-down of Cybersecurity Events.

Tsaliki, K. C. Revolutionizing Identity Management with AI: Enhancing Cyber Security and Preventing ATO. *International Research Journal of Modernization in Engineering Technology and Science, 6.*

Turuk, M. (2020). Digital strategy. *International Journal of Contemporary Business and Entrepreneurship, 1*(1), 62–76. DOI: 10.47954/ijcbe.1.1.5

U.S. Department of Homeland Security, Cybersecurity and Infrastructure Security Agency. (2021). *Federal government cybersecurity incident and vulnerability response playbooks.* https://www.cisa.gov/resources-tools/resources/federal-government-cybersecurity-incident-and-vulnerability-response-playbooks

U.S. Department of Homeland Security. (2025). *Homeland Threat Assessment.* Office of Intelligence and Analysis. Washington, DC: DHS.

U.S. Department of Homeland Security. (2025). *What Is Human Trafficking?* https://www.dhs.gov/blue-campaign/what-human-trafficking

U.S. Government Accountability Office. (2020). *Forced labor imports: DHS increased resources and enforcement efforts, but needs to improve workforce planning and monitoring.* https://www.gao.gov/products/gao-21-106

Ubaldi, B., van Ooijen, C., & Welby, B. (2019). *Digital government review of Sweden: Towards a data-driven public sector.* OECD Digital Government Studies. OECD Publishing. DOI: 10.1787/19934351

Uddin, M. H., Ali, M. H., & Hassan, M. K. (2020). Cybersecurity hazards and financial system vulnerability: A synthesis of literature. *Risk Management*, *22*(4), 239–309. https://ideas.repec.org/a/pal/risman/v22y2020i4d10.1057_s41283-020-00063-2.html. DOI: 10.1057/s41283-020-00063-2

United Nations Development Programme (UNDP). (2022). *Digital strategy.* 2022-2025. Retrieved from https://www.undp.org/digital/Digital-Strategy

United Nations General Assembly Resolution 55/25, (2000), Article 3, Protocol to Prevent, Suppress and Punish Trafficking in Persons, Especially Women and Children, Supplementing the United Nations Convention against Transnational Organized Crime (November 15, 2000). https://treaties.un.org/doc/Treaties/2000/11/20001115%20 11-38%20AM/Ch_XVIII_12_ap.pdf

United Nations Office on Drugs and Crime. (2024). *Global report on trafficking in persons 2024*. https://www.unodc.org/documents/data-and-analysis/glotip/2024/GLOTIP2024_BOOK.pdf

United States Digital Services (USDS). (2024). 2024 *Impact report.* Retrieved from https://www.usds.gov/resources/USDS-2024-Impact-Report.pdf

United States Government Accountability Office. (2015). *Air traffic control: FAA needs a more comprehensive approach to address cybersecurity as agency transitions to NextGen.* https://heinonline.org/HOL/Page?handle=hein.gao/gaobaai-ua0001&id=1&collection=gao&index=

United States Government Accountability Office. (2023). *Agencies need to continue addressing critical legacy systems* (GAO-23-106821). Retrieved from https://www.gao.gov/products/gao-23-106821

United States Office of Management and Budget. (2024). *Federal IT dashboard.* Retrieved from https://www.itdashboard.gov/itportfoliodashboard

United States, Department of Health and Human Services, Office for Civil Rights. (2022). *OCR cybersecurity newsletters.* HHS.gov. https://www.hhs.gov/hipaa/for-professionals/security/guidance/cybersecurity-newsletter-october-2022/index.html

van Hoek, R. (2021). Exploring progress with supply chain risk management during the first year of the COVID-19 pandemic. *Logistics (Basel)*, *5*(4), 70. DOI: 10.3390/logistics5040070

Vantage Medtech. (n.d.). *Understanding embedded medical device software.* Retrieved October 19, 2025, from https://vantagemedtech.com/embedded-medical-device-software/

Velev, D., & Zlateva, P. (2017). Virtual Reality Challenges in Education and Training. *International Journal of Learning and Teaching*, *3*(1). Advance online publication. DOI: 10.18178/ijlt.3.1.33-37

Venkata, B. (2025). Unraveling the 2024 CrowdStrike Incident: How a Security Patch Led to Global System Failure and Blue Screen of Death.

Venminder. (n.d.). *4 exit strategies for offboarding a vendor.* Retrieved from https://www.venminder.com/podcast/offboarding-vendor-exit-strategies

Venters, W., Whitley, E. A., & Cornford, T. (2021). The view from the cloud: Organizational design for cloud computing. *Information Systems Journal*, *31*(3), 343–371.

Verizon. (2020). *2020 Data breach investigations report (DBIR).* Verizon Enterprise Solutions. https://www.verizon.com/business/resources/reports/dbir/

Verizon. (2020). *2023 Data breach investigations report (DBIR).* Verizon Enterprise Solutions. https://www.verizon.com/business/resources/reports/dbir/

Verschueren, F. (2021, December 24). Why and How to Employ Organizational Factors for Foresight in Safety? Academia.edu. https://www.academia.edu/65858104/Why_and_How_to_Employ_Organizational_Factors_for_Foresight_in_Safety

Vidals, G. (2025). *Zero trust security for healthcare: Why your HIPAA compliance strategy needs an upgrade. Medium.* https://hipaavault.medium.com/zero-trust-security-for-healthcare-why-your-hipaa-compliance-strategy-needs-an-upgrade-fba4541fbd00

Voas, R. B., Torres, P., Romano, E., & Lacey, J. H. (2012). Alcohol-related risk of driver fatalities: An update using 2007 data. *Journal of Studies on Alcohol and Drugs*, *73*(3), 341–350. DOI: 10.15288/jsad.2012.73.341 PMID: 22456239

Voloshin, D., Derevitskiy, I., Mukhina, K., & Karbovskii, V. (2016). Identifying venues for female commercial sex work using spatial analysis of geocoded advertisements. *Procedia Computer Science*, *80*, 345–355. DOI: 10.1016/j.procs.2016.05.349

Walden, A., & Thomas, J. (2025). Unveiling the narrative around pilot mental health and aviation – A content analysis of FAA and mental-health-related social-media content. *Collegiate Aviation Review International, 43*(1), 19–35. https://ojs.library.okstate.edu/osu/index.php/CARI/article/view/9997/8944

Walsham, G. (1997). Actor-Network Theory and IS research: Current status and future prospects. In A.S. Lee, J. Liebenau, & J.I. DeGross (Eds.), *Information systems and qualitative research: Proceedings of the IFIP (The International Federation for Information Processing) TC8 WG 8.2 International Conference on Information Systems and Qualitative Research* (pp. 466–480). Springer. DOI: 10.1007/978-0-387-35309-8_23

Walsham, G. (1995). Interpretive case studies in IS research: Nature and method. *European Journal of Information Systems*, *4*(2), 74–81. DOI: 10.1057/ejis.1995.9

Walsham, G. (2006). Doing interpretive research. *European Journal of Information Systems*, *15*(3), 320–330. DOI: 10.1057/palgrave.ejis.3000589

Warren, M. A., & Warren, M. T. (2023). The EThIC Model of Virtue-Based Allyship Development: A New Approach to Equity and Inclusion in Organizations: JBE. *Journal of Business Ethics*, *182*(3), 783–803. DOI: 10.1007/s10551-021-05002-z

Wasserman, L., & Wasserman, Y. (2022). Hospital cybersecurity risks and gaps: Review (for the non-cyber professional). *Frontiers in Digital Health*, *4*, 862221. Advance online publication. DOI: 10.3389/fdgth.2022.862221 PMID: 36033634

Welch, L., Russell, D., Weinstock, D., & Betit, E. (2015). Best Practices for Health and Safety Technology Transfer in Construction. *American Journal of Industrial Medicine*, *58*(8), 849–857. DOI: 10.1002/ajim.22456

Welsh, T., & Benkhelifa, E. (2020). On resilience in cloud computing: A survey of techniques across the cloud domain. *ACM Computing Surveys*, *53*(3), 59. Advance online publication. DOI: 10.1145/3388922

Weng, Y., & Wu, J. (2024). Leveraging artificial intelligence to enhance data security and combat cyber attacks. *Journal of Artificial Intelligence General science (JAIGS) ISSN: 3006-4023*, *5*(1), 392-399.

Westin, C., Hilburn, B., Borst, C., van Kampen, E.-J., & Bång, M. (2020). Building transparent and personalized AI support in air traffic control. In *IEEE/AIAA 39th Digital Avionics Systems Conference (DASC)*. DOI: 10.1109/DASC50938.2020.9256708

Wilder, J. (2022, April 27). HHS Warns of Insider Threats in the Healthcare Sector. *Healthcare Innovation*. https://www.hcinnovationgroup.com/cybersecurity/data-breaches/news/21265719/hhs-warns-of-insider-threats-in-the-healthcare-sector

Wilson, J. M., & Dalton, E. (2008). Human trafficking in the heartland: Variation in law enforcement awareness and response. *Journal of Contemporary Criminal Justice*, *24*(3), 296–313. https://heinonline-org.ezp.slu.edu/HOL/Page?collection=journals&handle=hein.journals/jccj24&id=284&men_tab=srchresults. DOI: 10.1177/1043986208318227

Wirth, A., Gates, C., & Smith, J. (2020). *Medical device cybersecurity for engineers and manufacturers.* https://www.goodreads.com/book/show/54494363-medical-device-cybersecurity-for-engineers-and-manufacturers

Wirtz, B. W., Weyerer, J. C., & Geyer, C. (2018). Artificial Intelligence and the public sector: Applications and Challenges. *International Journal of Public Administration, 42*(7), 596–615. DOI: 10.1080/01900692.2018.1498103

WIZ. (2025). *What is a brute force attack? Types and countermeasures. wiz.io.* https://www.wiz.io/academy/brute-force-attacks

Wolford, B. (2024). *What is GDPR, the EU's new data protection law?* Retrieved from https://commission.europa.eu/law/law-topic/data-protection/data-protection-eu_en

Wolfson, R. (2018). *Tracing illegal activity through the Bitcoin blockchain to combat cryptocurrency-related crimes.* Forbes. https://www.forbes.com/sites/rachelwolfson/2018/11/26/tracing-illegal-activity-through-the-bitcoin-blockchain-to-combat-cryptocurrency-related-crimes/?sh=2622b55133a9

Wolniak, R. (2023). *Functioning of real-time analytics in business.* Zeszyty Naukowe. Organizacja i Zarządzanie/Politechnika Śląska. DOI: 10.29119/1641-3466.2023.172.40

World Bank. (2021). *Digital government transformation in Vietnam: Global lessons and policy implications.* Retrieved from https://documents1.worldbank.org/curated/en/099235103032229053/pdf/P16734904490250bd0b6830feee7a77690c.pdf

World Economic Forum. (2024). *Unpacking cyber resilience.* https://www.weforum.org/publications/unpacking-cyber-resilience/

Wright, J., & Burrell, D. N. (2023). Telemedicine cybersecurity protection in reproductive healthcare. *HOLISTICA Journal of Business and Public Administration, 14*(2), 1-14. https://reference-global.com/download/article/10.2478/hjbpa-2023-0012.pdf

Yakovchenko, V., Rogal, S. S., Goodrich, D. E., Lamorte, C., Neely, B., Merante, M., Gibson, S., Scott, D., McCurdy, H., Nobbe, A., Morgan, T. R., & Chinman, M. J. (2023). Getting to implementation: Adaptation of an implementation playbook. *Frontiers in Public Health, 10*, 980958. DOI: 10.3389/fpubh.2022.980958 PMID: 36684876

Yamat, R. (2025, October 15). The government shutdown is putting a renewed spotlight on the cracks in the US aviation system. *The Canadian Press*. https://www.proquest.com/wire-feeds/government-shutdown-is-putting-renewed-spotlight/docview/3262021655/se-2

Yang, G., Ridgeway, C., Miller, A., & Sarkar, A. (2024). Comprehensive Assessment of Artificial Intelligence Tools for Driver Monitoring and Analyzing Safety Critical Events in Vehicles. *Sensors (Basel)*, *24*(8), 2478. DOI: 10.3390/s24082478 PMID: 38676095

Yang, H.-H., Chang, Y.-H., & Chou, Y.-H. (2023). Subjective measures of communication errors between pilots and air traffic controllers. *Journal of Air Transport Management*, *112*, 102461. DOI: 10.1016/j.jairtraman.2023.102461

Yeboah-Ofori, A., & Islam, S. (2019). Cyber security threat modeling for supply chain organizational environments. *Future Internet*, *11*(3), 63. DOI: 10.3390/fi11030063

Yeboah-Ofori, A., Islam, S., Lee, S. W., Shamszaman, Z. U., Muhammad, K., Altaf, M., & Al-Rakhami, M. S. (2021). Cyber threat predictive analytics for improving cyber supply chain security. *IEEE Access : Practical Innovations, Open Solutions*, *9*, 94318–94337. DOI: 10.1109/ACCESS.2021.3087109

Yeoh, W., Liu, M., Shore, M., & Jiang, F. (2023). Zero trust cybersecurity: Critical success factors and A maturity assessment framework. *Computers & Security*, *133*(103412), 103412. DOI: 10.1016/j.cose.2023.103412

Yılmaz, F. (2015). *The Importance of Safety in Construction Sector: Costs of Occupational Accidents in Construction Sites*. Business and Economics Research Journal. https://www.academia.edu/90325943/The_Importance_of_Safety_in_Construction_Sector_Costs_of_Occupational_Accidents_in_Construction_Sites

Yin, R. K. (2017). *Case study research and applications: Design and methods* (6th ed.). SAGE Publications.

Yogev, D., Goldberg, T., Arami, A., Tejman-Yarden, S., Winkler, T. E., & Maoz, B. M. (2023). Current state of the art and future directions for implantable sensors in medical technology: Clinical needs and engineering challenges. *APL Bioengineering*, *7*(3), 031506. Advance online publication. DOI: 10.1063/5.0152290 PMID: 37781727

Yuni, S., Yuniati, A., & Umbing, G. B. (2024). A COSO ERM integrated framework evaluation of it governance risk management. *Journal of Interest: Economics, Business, and Accounting Review*, *1*(1), 38–42.

Zach, C. (2025). *80% of ransomware attacks now use artificial intelligence*. https://mitsloan.mit.edu/ideas-made-to-matter/80-ransomware-attacks-now-use-artificial-intelligence

Zanko, M., & Dawson, P. (2011). Occupational Health and Safety Management in Organizations: A Review. *International Journal of Management Reviews*, *14*(3), 328–344. DOI: 10.1111/j.1468-2370.2011.00319.x

Zhang, Z., Ning, H., Shi, F., Farha, F., Xu, Y., Xu, J., Zhang, F., & Choo, K.-K. R. (2022). Artificial intelligence in cyber security: Research advances, challenges, and opportunities. *Artificial Intelligence Review*, *55*(2), 1029–1053. https://link.springer.com/article/10.1007/S10462-021-09976-0. DOI: 10.1007/s10462-021-09976-0

Zhou, N., Ding, L. Y., & Chen, L. Y. (2013). Application of 4D visualization technology for safety management in metro construction. *Automation in Construction*, *34*, 25–36. DOI: 10.1016/j.autcon.2012.10.011

Zhou, Z., Irizarry, J., & Li, Q. (2013). Applying advanced technology to improve safety management in the construction industry: A literature review. *Construction Management and Economics*, *31*(6), 606–622. DOI: 10.1080/01446193.2013.798423

Zimmerman, C., Hossain, M., & Watts, C. (2011). Human trafficking and health: A conceptual model to inform policy, intervention and research. *Social Science & Medicine*, *73*(2), 327–335. DOI: 10.1016/j.socscimed.2011.05.028 PMID: 21723653

Zwitter, A., & Boisse-Despiaux, M. (2018). Blockchain for humanitarian action and development aid. *Journal of International Humanitarian Action*, *3*(16), 1–7. DOI: 10.1186/s41018-018-0044-5

About the Contributors

Darrell Norman Burrell is a visiting scholar at the Samuel DeWitt Proctor Institute for Leadership, Equity, and Justice at Rutgers University, where he is currently focusing his research on sustainability, health equity, and inclusive leadership. His work as a visiting researcher at the Pellegrino Center for Clinical Bioethics at the Georgetown University Medical Center in Washington, D.C., and as a post-doctoral public health researcher at the University of Maryland School of Pharmacy in Baltimore, MD, has provided him with a unique perspective on issues related to health disparities, health technology access, telehealth, adolescent health, and health literacy. For more than 12 years, he has also served in various roles as a doctoral faculty member, dissertation chair, and research panel participant at Marymount University, the Florida Institute of Technology, Capitol Technology University, the University of Liverpool in the U.K., and The Chicago School of Professional Psychology in Washington D.C. Dr. Burrell is a Certified Diversity Professional and a Certified Executive Coach. Dr. Burrell is an alumnus of the Presidential Management Fellows Program with the U.S. Federal Government and U.S. Nuclear Regulatory Commission, where he managed and developed leadership and diversity programs for professionals in Public Health, Environmental Health, Emergency Response, Technology, and Engineering. Academically, Dr. Burrell has three doctorate degrees and six graduate degrees, including a Master of Research in Artificial Intelligence Biotechnology Applications and Healthcare, along with additional graduate degrees in (H.R. Management, Management, Health Leadership, Sales and Marketing Management, Higher Education Administration, and Interfaith Action and Conflict Management). Dr. Burrell received his first doctoral degree in health education (DHEd), focusing on environmental public health and executive leadership coaching, at A.T. Still University in 2010. Dr. Burrell completed his 2nd doctorate, a Doctor of Philosophy (Ph.D.) in Cybersecurity Leadership at Capitol Technology University. In 2022, Dr. Burrell completed his 3rd Doctor of Business Administration (DBA) in Supply Chain Management at Capitol Technology

University. He has over 20 years of management, teaching, and training experience in academia, government, and private industry. Dr. Burrell has over 200 peer-reviewed publications and more than 1200 Google Scholar citations.

***

Kim L. Brown-Jackson holds a Ph.D.-Cybersecurity Leadership, Doctorate of Business Admin (DBA)-Quality Systems Mgmt. (business process improvement) conc. Health Systems, a Master's-Biomedical Sciences in Pathology & Molecular Oncology with additional Ph.D. course work, an Associates-Biotechnology and Forensic Science, an executive professional MBA certificate, and Bachelors in Biological Sciences with a cluster minor in Business Administration. She is certified in numerous professional areas. Dr. Brown-Jackson has 30 years of experience as a practitioner, academician, quality healthcare leader and performance and learning strategist guiding business process improvement through biomedical services, public health, pandemics, advanced drug development, telemedicine/ telehealth initiatives, and leadership development. Specializes in regulatory compliant industries (pharmaceutical-drugs, therapeutics, biologics, medical devices, financial). She has taught at the collegiate, government, and corporate levels. She has contributed to over 16 book chapters and 30+ peer-reviewed journals, and delivered numerous presentations at conferences and on panels.

Sharon L. Burton leads in product management and development, Organizational Development Change Management, Cyber-Security/Technology, Process Improvement, Telemedicine/Telehealth and Learning & Development. Education includes: Ph.D. in Cybersecurity Leadership, and a DBA in Business Process Improvement; and two MBA degrees - Human Resources Management, and Management. Certifications in the following: AI Prompting Essentials; Project Management Essentials; Master Lean Six Sigma Black Belt; Kaizen Leader; Change Management Professional; Strategic Workforce Planning; Human Capital Strategist; Kirkpatrick Four Levels Evaluation; and Advanced Communicator Gold Toastmaster. As a facilitator and educator of audiences, she has more than 100 academic publications and has presented at over 30 professional conferences. Dr. Burton is available to present at conferences, participate in forums, and other initiatives. She may be reached at sharonlburton2@comcast.net and 302-547-8010.

Kylei Conti is an aspiring forensic interviewer pursuing a M.A. in Legal and Forensic Psychology at Marymount University's Graduate Studies.

Marlena Daryousef holds an MBA and Doctor of Management degree from Colorado Technical University with over ten years of business development and consulting across multiple business verticals. Marlena has a proven track record of helping both startups and established businesses improve their business optimization, stakeholder engagement, quality and risk management processes, and problem-solving. It is important to be apart of social change while assisting businesses to defend their unique place in their community.

Maurice Dawson is an Associate Professor of Information Technology and Management within the College of Computing at Illinois Institute of Technology. Additionally, he serves as Director and Distinguished Member of the IIT Center for Cyber Security and Forensics Education (C2SAFE) and is responsible for working with the faculty who are members of this center. Before joining academia, he was an engineering manager for unmanned air systems and a senior program manager for rotary-wing aircraft. He has a Doctor of Computer Science from Colorado Technical University and a Doctor of Philosophy in Cyber Security from the Intelligent Systems Research Centre at London Metropolitan University. Additionally, he is the co-editor of Developing Next-Generation Countermeasures for Homeland Security Threat Prevention, and New Threats and Countermeasures in Digital Crime and Cyber Terrorism, published by IGI Global in 2017, and 2015 respectively. He has received four Fulbright Scholar Grants.

Hilda Eke is a nonprofit executive, certified Human Resources professional (SHRM-CP), and doctoral candidate at Marymount University. Her scholarly work examines leadership sustainability, psychological safety, and executive attrition in nonprofit organizations. She brings extensive experience in organizational operations, human resources administration, and systems development within mission-driven and community-based contexts. Hilda holds a Master's degree in Healthcare Administration from California State University, Long Beach, and a Bachelor's degree in Linguistics from the University of Benin. Her work integrates theory and practice to advance organizational effectiveness, workforce sustainability, and strategic leadership in nonprofit settings. Her contributions have been recognized through membership in Phi Beta Kappa and the Golden Key International Honour Society, as well as an award for service to nonprofit organizations in Northern Nigeria.

Thomas Cephus Gibbs III is a Construction Scientist at Capitol Technology University. He is currently a Lincoln Vibrant Communities Fellowship Affinity TEAM member at Claremont Lincoln University. He is also an alum of the Lincoln Vibrant Communities Fellowship at Claremont Lincoln University. He is a graduate of the University of the Pacific McGeorge School of Law, where he obtained his master's in public administration. He has an African American Studies research certification from the Bunche Center at the University of California, Los Angeles, UCLA. He is a graduate of the Small Business Academy from the University of Southern California (USC). He is a graduate of the Sacramento Planning Academy. An Alumnus of the Sacramento Transportation Planning Academy. He is an AmeriCorps alumnus, serving three terms. He served one term as an AmeriCorps Volunteer for Hands on Atlanta. He also served two terms as an AmeriCorps Vista for the Sacramento Promise Zone. Additionally, Mr. Gibbs is also an alumnus of Morehouse College, where he graduated with a B.A. in African American Studies. While at Morehouse, he completed his senior practicum and thesis on the prison industrial complex, teaching a cultural diversity class on Hip-Hop at the Atlanta Federal Penitentiary.

Natasha Harris is a doctoral researcher in Business Intelligence at Marymount University. Her interdisciplinary research examines human behavior and systems design across finance, organizational contexts, sustainability, and emerging technologies, with a focus on human-centered, capability-enhancing approaches to institutional decision-making and resilience across complex, evolving systems.

Laura Jones is an award-winning thought leader, educator, strategist, practitioner, and coach with specialties in enterprise governance, information security, risk management, quality assurance, artificial intelligence, and product management. Dr. Jones previously served as an Associate Dean of Student Academic Affairs. She currently serves as adjunct faculty for Carnegie Mellon University's Heinz School of Information Systems and Public Policy, Wake Forest University's School of Professional Studies, and Capitol Technology University's Department of Doctoral Programs. Dr. Jones earned a Ph.D. in Cyber Leadership, a Ph.D. in Product Management, an M.S. in Quality Systems Management, and a B.S. in Management Studies. She has completed executive education programs at Carnegie Mellon University (Chief Risk Officer's Program), Harvard Kennedy School (Leadership Decision Making), UC Berkeley Haas (Business Strategies and Artificial Intelligence), and Wharton Online (Business Strategy and Competitive Advantage). Dr. Jones has several academic publications and writes children's books about Internet safety and cybersecurity. She also speaks domestically and internationally about risk management and cybersecurity.

Eugene J. M. Lewis is a leading International Program Manager with an academic background in Information Systems, having taught in some Business areas such as Marketing, Management, and Information Systems. Dr. Lewis manages a portfolio of over 250 million dollars in the Foreign Military Sales (FMS) industry for the US Army. He is a leading expert in security assistance program management processes and competencies in total package approach (TPA) from hardware, training, case, financials, programmatic, contracting, technical support, logistics, and supply chain management. Currently, Dr. Lewis serves in the Aviation & Defense Industry, working in the Cargo CH-47 Helicopters Foreign Military Sales Program Office. Previously, he served as the Assistant Professor of Marketing at Oakwood University as a full-time and part-time instructor in Marketing, Management (Leadership), and Computer Information Systems. Moreover, lecturing students in areas such as advertising management, consumer behavior, global marketing, marketing management, organizational dynamics, project management, sales management, project management, logistics, and supply chain management integrating marketing methodologies. Dr. Lewis is a Practitioner and Consultant with education and experience in real-world examples of strategic integration within the business field. As an International Program Manager, he gives several briefings to dignitaries and foreign leadership around the world on logistics and supply chain management. Much of his employment experience consists of incorporating new innovative concepts to provide consumers with the requisite knowledge necessary to understand the value of emotional (EQ) and business intelligence (BI) by incorporating technology into the organizational workflow of operational planning. Dr. Lewis enjoys giving back to the community, spending much of his free time assisting young people in underprivileged areas and instructing them in Boxing. Dr. Lewis has been a Boxing Coach and Instructor for over 15 years. He is a registered Coach with the United States Boxing Association for the Southeastern Region. Dr. Lewis believes in the efficacy of developing young people. He is originally from Seattle, Washington. His family still resides in the Pacific Northwest. He enjoys every opportunity available to travel, write poetry, play guitar, and meet inspiring people.

Adina Lundy is the associate director of undergraduate psychology at a small New England Institution. A leading authority on the lasting effects of chattel slavery on poverty and the contemporary structure of the Black family; she brings deep historical insight and interdisciplinary expertise to her work as an expert witness for the Public Defender's Office of the New Jersey Family Court, a professor, and a multiculturalism scholar. A dedicated researcher on racism and systemic inequity, Dr. Lundy's work focuses on how structural barriers—including the lack of social capital, institutional bias, and uneven resource allocation—impact both students of color and faculty of color. Her scholarship illuminates how these inequities limit opportunity, influence academic pathways, and contribute to long-term disparities across disciplines. Through her research, workshops (with institutions such as Duke Medical school and the New Jersey Judiciary) testimony, and community advocacy,

Dr. Lundy provides critical expertise at the intersection of history, policy, and lived experience, advancing efforts to create equitable systems and strengthen outcomes for children, families, and people of color. Dr. Lundy's research program centers the experiences of marginalized populations seeking to improve their socioeconomic status, with a particular focus on the transformative role of social capital and the strategic engagement of white allies committed to meaningful, equity-driven change. Her work interrogates how access to education, resources, and informed accomplices shapes the trajectories of communities striving for liberation and opportunity. Grounded in qualitative inquiry, Dr. Lundy employs phenomenological methods rooted in community building, relational trust, and deep listening. Her approach prioritizes participants' lived experiences as essential sources of knowledge, informing policy recommendations and institutional practices. Dr. Lundy and Dr. Hans Saint-Eloi Cadely are conducting research on a project that investigates the pathways that connect state care to later contact with the criminal justice system, aiming to illuminate systemic vulnerabilities, identify points of intervention, and contribute to long-term institutional change. Dr. Lundy encourages all, who were born with tans: You belong wherever the Black slave labored against their will on land stolen from the indigenous American.

Teresa Manfreda-Foley is an accounting and business management professional with over 25 years of experience across industries, including construction, manufacturing, retail, higher education, and non-profit organizations. Driven by a quest for learning and a deep sense of integrity, she takes immense pride in analyzing situations and providing viable, financially sound options to achieve successful outcomes. Teresa has been with Brookdale Community College since 2013 and has held various management positions throughout her tenure. In 2019, she became the Vice President, Finance & Operations/CFO. Her goals are aligned with the Institution's strategic plan for the future while maintaining the College's financial health and realigning the organization for optimization. She serves on the President's Cabinet, the Executive Leadership Council, and the Information Technology Governance Steering Committee. She holds a BS in business administration/ accounting concentration from Monmouth University, an MBA in accounting from Southern New Hampshire University, and a Doctorate in Business Administration from Marymount University.

Stacey L. Morin is a Chief Financial Officer in the Financial Services industry, serving in the middle-market M&A advisory division of the world's fifth-largest financial institution. She brings over 25 years of experience in the sector, with deep expertise in corporate finance, banking, and capital markets. Dr. Morin holds a Bachelor's degree in Accounting from Eastern Michigan University (1995), an

MBA in Finance from California State University, Northridge (2007), and a Doctor of Business Administration (DBA) from Marymount University (2025). She is currently completing a postdoctoral fellowship at Marymount University, where she continues to advance research in financial strategy and organizational performance. She also has multiple FINRA securities licenses required for her executive role. A dedicated pracademic, Dr. Morin bridges the gap between industry and academia by integrating real-world financial leadership experience with rigorous scholarly research. Her work informs and advances both financial theory and business practice. Throughout her career, she has championed inclusive, resilient, and data-driven organizational strategies. Her research and writing focus on corporate finance, banking, and strategic leadership within the business sector. Dr. Morin's unique blend of academic excellence and executive insight continues to shape her contributions to both professional and academic communities, and she is recognized as a financial data storyteller—translating complex financial information into narrative-driven insights that inform strategic decision-making.

Calvin Nobles is a cybersecurity professional and human factors engineer with more than 25 years of experience spanning military service, industry practice, and higher-education leadership. Dr. Nobles serves as Portfolio Vice President and Dean of the School of Cybersecurity and Information Technology at the University of Maryland Global Campus (UMGC), providing strategic and operational leadership for a large, workforce-aligned academic portfolio that advances cybersecurity education, applied partnerships, and innovation at scale. Dr. Nobles previously served as a Department Chair and Associate Professor at the Illinois Institute of Technology and completed a full career in the United States Navy before transitioning into roles within the financial services sector. Dr. Nobles is the author of a book focused on the integration of technologically advanced aircraft in general aviation and maintains active national service through advisory and professional bodies, including service on the National Cryptologic Foundation Board and the Cybersecurity Association Inc Board. Dr. Nobles is also a former Cybersecurity Fellow at Harvard University.ce and National Security Alliance Cyber Council. He is a Cybersecurity Fellow at Harvard University.

Oladele Stephen Olawoye is an experienced professional in Healthcare Cybersecurity with a Doctor of Philosophy degree. He has over ten years of experience, including malware threat research, asset security management, and secure configuration practices for the DoD Department of the Army and private sector organizations. His academic work focused on three main subjects during his PhD program, which included advanced malware detection, digital forensics, and compliance frameworks. Oladele holds an MBA (General); he also holds a BA in

Logistics and Transportation Management, both from American Military (Public) University. The candidate demonstrates proven leadership abilities that qualify him to handle risk assessment, incident response, and regulatory compliance through NIST, HIPAA, and PCI DSS standards. Oladele utilizes his understanding to connect research findings with operational security needs, enabling him to create effective cyber threat protection systems for modern digital systems.

Jessica Parker is a consultant, researcher, and current DBA student at Marymount University, with a current research focus on cybersecurity and Artificial Intelligence. She has over 25 years of Information Technology experience in executive leadership, financial management, project management, software quality assurance, business analysis, and data visualization. From a global perspective, she has worked with various Fortune 500 companies and multinational teams in countries including Australia, Brazil, China, England, France, Germany, India, Ireland, Italy, the Philippines, Switzerland, and Uruguay.

KerriLaine Prunella is an executive with experience in leadership development, organizational transformation, and human capital strategy across public sector, consulting, and nonprofit entities. As Founder and CEO of VINA79Group, she brings entrepreneurial vision and a deep commitment to leadership excellence, serving as a strategic advisor. As a board member, Ms. Prunella values collaboration and duty of care. She leads risk management and strategic oversight emphasizing opportunities for operational excellence. She is adept at CEO mentorship, guiding organizational transformations, fostering inclusivity, and aligning human capital strategies. She has demonstrated strong governance expertise to maximize stakeholder value through her leadership roles such as Healthcare Access Maryland, where she currently serves as Vice Chair of the Board, former chair of the Nominating Committee, and the Penn State Alumni Association, serving as Chair of Audit and Risk, and former Vice Chair for Governance and Finance Committees. Additionally, she served as a founding Board Member and Executive Secretary of the Management Advisory Council at George Mason University, Costello College of Business. Ms. Prunella formerly served as Chief Human Capital Officer with oversight of strategy and operations for Talent Management, Talent Development, and Executive Compensation across all office locations. As an Acting Assistant Inspector General for Administration, she led six divisions and a $65 million budget. A Big Four Alumni, she led strategies for human capital process re-engineering. Ms. Prunella earned a Bachelor's degree in International Politics from The Pennsylvania State University, a Master's degree in Business Administration from Trinity Washington University, and a Graduate Certificate in Organization Development from Marymount University. She is currently pursuing her Doctorate in Business Intelligence at Marymount.

Philip Reed is a strategic cybersecurity executive with extensive experience leading large, multidisciplinary teams and driving enterprise cyber operations, building and maturing enterprise-wide cybersecurity capabilities, integrating cyber risk into corporate governance, and advising boards and executive leadership. Adjunct faculty teaching cybersecurity.

Amalisha Sabie-Aridi, Ph.D., MBA, CMP-UNGGA, is an esteemed scholar, educator, and executive leader whose career spans over a decade of exceptional contributions to higher education, project management, organizational strategy, and leadership development. As a distinguished graduate professor and doctoral committee chair at multiple institutions, including Marymount University and Washington University of Science & Technology, she has guided countless doctoral candidates and shaped innovative curricula across disciplines such as technology, business, leadership, and project management. Dr. Sabie-Aridi's prolific scholarly output includes over 80 peer-reviewed publications covering diverse fields such as organizational behavior, artificial intelligence strategy, healthcare management, strategic leadership, diversity and inclusion, and cybersecurity. She is renowned for integrating research excellence with practical expertise drawn from her tenure as a senior project manager and executive operations leader, notably in high-stakes environments like NASA Engineering Inc. Internationally recognized, she holds honors including UN Global Goodwill Ambassador.

Gregory K. "GK" Smith is a Senior Principal Operations Research Analyst and Simulation Developer at Raytheon (RTX), leveraging more than thirty years of Department of Defense experience to support complex modernization, modeling, and decision-analysis efforts. A West Point graduate with a Master's in Operations Research and Systems Analysis from the Naval Postgraduate School, he previously served in senior Army analytic and leadership roles across the Pentagon, Joint Staff, and deployed environments, including as the Military Deputy to the Director of the U.S. Army Combat Capabilities Development Command Analysis Center (DAC). He is currently a Doctor of Business Administration (DBA) candidate whose dissertation explores how professionals experience Generative AI pilot programs in capture and bid content management, and he remains active in the Central Arkansas community as President of the Douglas MacArthur Central Arkansas West Point Society and a lifetime member of Alpha Phi Alpha Fraternity, Inc.

Won Song, Ph.D., DBA, MSN, RN, is a multidisciplinary researcher and practitioner specializing in the intersection of healthcare informatics, engineering management, and organizational development. He earned his Ph.D. in Engineering Management from Capitol Technology University (2025) and holds a Doctor of

Business Administration (DBA) from Walden University. With a clinical foundation as a Registered Nurse (MSN, Liberty University; BSN, Rutgers University), Dr. Song has extensive experience in acute care and bedside nursing. His current research focuses on implementing Agentic AI and robotic systems to improve patient adherence and safety in chronic disease management. As the developer of the MADA (Medi-Assist IV System), he integrates reliability engineering with clinical practice to optimize nocturnal therapy. A US citizen and fluent in Korean, Dr. Song is dedicated to fostering cyberliterate organizational cultures that bridge the gap between complex technological adoption and high-quality patient care.

Samantha Thibodeau is a Software Engineering Leader and DBA Candidate at Marymount University. She began her career in medical device design and transitioned to Software Engineering. For the last 10 years, she has held industry roles across Quality Engineering, Software Development, and Engineering Leadership, blending her academic interests within her roles. Academically, Samantha holds a Bachelor of Science in Biomedical Engineering from Florida Gulf Coast University and a Master of Engineering in Engineering Management from Ohio University. She is currently a DBA candidate with Marymount University. She also holds University certifications in Lean Six Sigma and Engineering Leadership, as well as technical certifications including AWS Certified Cloud Practitioner, ICAgile Certified Professional - Foundations of Artificial Intelligence, and the ISTQB Foundation Level Exam (CTFL) with distinction. Her research interests include Engineering Leadership, Leadership Cultural Shifts, Change Management, Cybersecurity, Operational and Business Risk, and Software Quality. Samantha's publications span a breadth of peer-reviewed journals, including those focused on business resiliency and operations, cybersecurity risk management, and engineering leadership.

Index

A

B

C

M

N

O

P

R

S

T

V

W

www.ingramcontent.com/pod-product-compliance
Lightning Source LLC
LaVergne TN
LVHW062324300926
849161LV00007B/1567